# Mastering
## Microsoft Dynamics 365®
## Implementations

# Mastering
## Microsoft Dynamics 365® Implementations

Eric Newell

*To my Stoneridge Software family*

# Acknowledgments

This really was a team effort—I get my name on the title page, but it all came together due to contributions across the Stoneridge Software team. My biggest thanks goes to Jessi Woinarowicz for managing the whole publishing process, reviewing all of the chapters, sending them off to be reviewed by the team, and working through all the back and forth. She's been my partner in this whole project, and I couldn't have done it without her. I also want to thank Paul Kjer for his willingness to serve as the technical editor of the book. Paul has a great perspective, and he is willing to challenge assumptions, which is so valuable on this project. I'd like to recognize Tory Bjorklund and Cody Marshall for their efforts in developing many of the concepts that the Stoneridge Software team has adopted over the years which are represented in this book.

I'd also like to thank a host of folks from Stoneridge Software for reviewing chapters and helping promote the book: Rich Studer, Jayson Read, Sara Jo Larsen, Anne Kaese, Dave Ruelle, Tim Everett, Dustin Pagano, Adele Graser, Heike Peters, Rob Wagner, Craig Conzemius, Mike McCardle, Tammy Plowman, Maggie Foster, Leah Baker, and Sabrina Zimara. I'd like to thank my excellent editing team of Gary Schwartz, Barath Kumar Rajasekaran, Christine O'Connor, and Kenyon Brown for giving me the opportunity to publish this book.

I want to extend a special thanks to my family, my wife Becky and my daughters, Katie and Amelia, for their encouragement and support throughout the entire process and for letting me disappear on weekends to write this book. Thank you.

—Eric Newell

# About the Author

 **Eric Newell** is the CEO and founder of Stoneridge Software, a Microsoft Gold partner specializing in implementation, consulting, and support for Microsoft Dynamics 365 business applications and technologies. In 2012, he co-founded the company with a passion for business excellence and a determination to better serve the market.

Driven by his vision to create an organization with exceptional team members and an outstanding work culture, Eric has led Stoneridge Software through rapid growth, acquisitions, several strategic initiatives, and the consistent successful delivery of ERP and CRM implementations. What started as a three-person organization in 2012 has now scaled to 200 people in the first eight years in business. In 2018, he also co-founded Levridge, a software company focused on delivering modern business applications for the Agriculture industry.

Prior to founding Stoneridge Software, Eric spent 13 years at Microsoft and Great Plains Software where he was instrumental in leading the Premier Field Engineering practice for Dynamics AX across North America to growth rates of 50 percent each year during his time in the role. Throughout his tenure at Microsoft, Eric led strong performing teams across Dynamics support, Global Support and Consulting Operations, and Premier Support.

Eric enjoys the challenge of taking complex business issues and using technology to figure out ways to streamline operations. The combination of solving challenges and assisting clients in tackling obstacles that affect their businesses are two of his biggest passions.

> *"My focus is to ensure our clients achieve their business goals with a straight-forward, yet strategic approach. I take pride in the work our team does every day, and it is a privilege for me to be able to lead that charge."*

—*Eric Newell*

In addition to helping clients achieve their goals, some of the recognition that Eric is most proud of are several "Best Place to Work" awards. Stoneridge Software has achieved a best-place-to-work status every year that it has been eligible, receiving recognition from organizations like *Inc. Magazine, Minneapolis Star-Tribune, Prairie Business Magazine*, and a Gold, top honors, in 2015 for medium-sized businesses from *Minnesota Business Magazine*. Stoneridge Software has also been named to the *Inc. 5000* list of fastest-growing companies in 2020, 2019, 2018, and 2017, and the SPI Research "Best of the Best" Professional Services firms in 2016 and 2017. Eric Newell was also named Entrepreneur of the Year by the Fargo-Moorhead-West Fargo Chamber of Commerce in 2019 and included in *Prairie Business Magazine's* "40 Under 40" in 2017.

Eric's interest in business has also extended to the community, having served many years as chair of the Economic Development Authority. To help encourage businesses to consider moving to the area, Eric worked in partnership with the Economic Development Authority to spearhead a program called the "Barnesville Business Pitch," which awarded cash prizes and a forgivable loan to entrepreneurs.

His community involvement also extends to serving a term on the school board, beginning a kindergarten through second grade basketball initiative for the community education program, coaching youth basketball, and, along with wife Becky, running the Whist tournament every year at the annual Potato Days Festival.

If he's not behind his laptop, you can find Eric attending his daughters' sporting events, visiting his two restaurants—The Purple Goose and The Pitchfork—and cheering on the Minnesota Twins. He is also the author of *Minnesota Whist*.

# About the Technical Editor

**Paul Kjer**, PMP, has played many leadership roles in business software applications since his first ERP implementation in 1991. Paul is currently the Enterprise Practice Director for Stoneridge Software.

# Contents at a Glance

*Introduction* ................................................................. *xxvii*

Chapter 1  • Stages of an Implementation Overview ........................... 1

Chapter 2  • What to Do Before You Begin a Project ........................... 11

Chapter 3  • Four Keys to Consider When Buying an ERP or CRM Solution ....... 31

Chapter 4  • How to Evaluate and Buy Business Application Software ........... 47

Chapter 5  • Organizing Your Team for Success and Project Governance ......... 57

Chapter 6  • Sprints and Tools Needed to Run Your Project .................... 73

Chapter 7  • Change Management Throughout Your Project ..................... 87

Chapter 8  • Organizing Your Business by Processes ........................... 99

Chapter 9  • Independent Software Vendors—Filling Gaps and
             Managing Partnerships ......................................... 109

Chapter 10 • Factors for a Successful Project Kickoff .......................... 121

Chapter 11 • Designing the Software Collaboratively .......................... 133

Chapter 12 • Requirements Gathering and Staying "In the Box" ................. 145

Chapter 13 • Conference Room Pilots ......................................... 157

Chapter 14 • Dealing with Challenges Mid-Project ............................ 171

Chapter 15 • Customizations vs. Configurations and How You Manage Them .... 185

Chapter 16 • Data Migration—Early and Often ............................... 199

Chapter 17 • Environment Management and Deployments ..................... 215

Chapter 18 • Testing ....................................................... 229

Chapter 19 • Training for All ............................................... 245

Chapter 20 • Going Live .................................................... 261

Chapter 21 • Hypercare. . . . . . . . . . . . . . . . . . . . . . . . . . . . . . . . . . . . . . . . . . . 275

Chapter 22 • Support and Enhance Your Project . . . . . . . . . . . . . . . . . . . . . . . . . . . 291

Chapter 23 • Bringing It All Together . . . . . . . . . . . . . . . . . . . . . . . . . . . . . . . . . . . 307

Appendix • The Bottom Line . . . . . . . . . . . . . . . . . . . . . . . . . . . . . . . . . . . . . . . 317

**Glossary** . . . . . . . . . . . . . . . . . . . . . . . . . . . . . . . . . . . . . . . . . . . . . . . . . . . **353**

*Index* . . . . . . . . . . . . . . . . . . . . . . . . . . . . . . . . . . . . . . . . . . . . . . . . . . . . . . . *369*

# Contents

*Introduction* . . . . . . . . . . . . . . . . . . . . . . . . . . . . . . . . . . . . . . . . . . . . . . . . . . . . . . . . . . . . . *xxvii*

**Chapter 1 • Stages of an Implementation Overview** . . . . . . . . . . . . . . . . . . .1
What Is Microsoft Dynamics?. . . . . . . . . . . . . . . . . . . . . . . . . . . . . . . . . . . . . . . . . . . . . 1
The Client Journey . . . . . . . . . . . . . . . . . . . . . . . . . . . . . . . . . . . . . . . . . . . . . . . . . . . 2
Implementation Methodologies. . . . . . . . . . . . . . . . . . . . . . . . . . . . . . . . . . . . . . . . . 5
    Waterfall and Sure Step . . . . . . . . . . . . . . . . . . . . . . . . . . . . . . . . . . . . . . . . . . . 5
    Agile and Scrum . . . . . . . . . . . . . . . . . . . . . . . . . . . . . . . . . . . . . . . . . . . . . . . 7
Triple Constraints. . . . . . . . . . . . . . . . . . . . . . . . . . . . . . . . . . . . . . . . . . . . . . . . . . . 8
The Bottom Line . . . . . . . . . . . . . . . . . . . . . . . . . . . . . . . . . . . . . . . . . . . . . . . . . . . . 9

**Chapter 2 • What to Do Before You Begin a Project** . . . . . . . . . . . . . . . . . . .11
Identify Your Project Team and Stakeholders . . . . . . . . . . . . . . . . . . . . . . . . . . . . . . . 11
    Executive Sponsor. . . . . . . . . . . . . . . . . . . . . . . . . . . . . . . . . . . . . . . . . . . . . . 12
    Project Owner . . . . . . . . . . . . . . . . . . . . . . . . . . . . . . . . . . . . . . . . . . . . . . . . 12
    Business Process Owner(s) . . . . . . . . . . . . . . . . . . . . . . . . . . . . . . . . . . . . . . . 13
    Project Manager. . . . . . . . . . . . . . . . . . . . . . . . . . . . . . . . . . . . . . . . . . . . . . . 13
    Core Team and a Core Team Lead . . . . . . . . . . . . . . . . . . . . . . . . . . . . . . . . . 14
    Subject Matter Experts . . . . . . . . . . . . . . . . . . . . . . . . . . . . . . . . . . . . . . . . . 14
    IT Resources. . . . . . . . . . . . . . . . . . . . . . . . . . . . . . . . . . . . . . . . . . . . . . . . . 15
    Time Commitment by Role . . . . . . . . . . . . . . . . . . . . . . . . . . . . . . . . . . . . . . 17
Identify Your Processes in Scope . . . . . . . . . . . . . . . . . . . . . . . . . . . . . . . . . . . . . . . 18
Clean Up Your Data. . . . . . . . . . . . . . . . . . . . . . . . . . . . . . . . . . . . . . . . . . . . . . . . . 19
    Identify Your "Master" Data . . . . . . . . . . . . . . . . . . . . . . . . . . . . . . . . . . . . 19
    Develop Naming Conventions . . . . . . . . . . . . . . . . . . . . . . . . . . . . . . . . . . . 20
    Identify System Owners. . . . . . . . . . . . . . . . . . . . . . . . . . . . . . . . . . . . . . . . 20
    Find and Resolve Duplicates and Incorrect Data. . . . . . . . . . . . . . . . . . . . . . 20
Define Your Success Metrics. . . . . . . . . . . . . . . . . . . . . . . . . . . . . . . . . . . . . . . . . . 21
Possible Benefits . . . . . . . . . . . . . . . . . . . . . . . . . . . . . . . . . . . . . . . . . . . . . . . . . . . 22
Building Your Business Case and Securing Funding . . . . . . . . . . . . . . . . . . . . . . . . . 23
    How Much Should an ERP Project Cost? . . . . . . . . . . . . . . . . . . . . . . . . . . . 24
    Costs to Include in Your Calculations . . . . . . . . . . . . . . . . . . . . . . . . . . . . . 24
    Capitalizing Costs. . . . . . . . . . . . . . . . . . . . . : . . . . . . . . . . . . . . . . . . . . . . 25
    Contingency. . . . . . . . . . . . . . . . . . . . . . . . . . . . . . . . . . . . . . . . . . . . . . . . . 27
    Return on Investment (ROI) . . . . . . . . . . . . . . . . . . . . . . . . . . . . . . . . . . . . 27
    Gaining Approval . . . . . . . . . . . . . . . . . . . . . . . . . . . . . . . . . . . . . . . . . . . . 28
The Bottom Line . . . . . . . . . . . . . . . . . . . . . . . . . . . . . . . . . . . . . . . . . . . . . . . . . . . 29

**Chapter 3 • Four Keys to Consider When Buying an ERP or CRM Solution** .................................................. **31**

Selection Process.................................................. 31

    Selection Consultant........................................ 32

    Decision Maker ............................................ 33

The Four Keys...................................................... 33

    Fit....................................................... 34

    Platform ................................................. 35

    Implementer.............................................. 39

    Cost .................................................... 41

Building Your Scorecard ........................................... 44

The Bottom Line .................................................. 45

**Chapter 4 • How to Evaluate and Buy Business Application Software** ..... **47**

Buying Process Steps .............................................. 47

    Qualification Stage ........................................ 48

    Discovery and Demonstration Stage .......................... 49

    Selecting Your Vendor ...................................... 51

    Leadership or Board Approval ............................... 54

    Moving Forward ........................................... 54

The Bottom Line .................................................. 54

**Chapter 5 • Organizing Your Team for Success and Project Governance** ................................................... **57**

RACI............................................................. 57

    Your Project Team ......................................... 58

Your Partner's Implementation Team ................................ 59

    Executive Sponsor.......................................... 60

    Engagement Manager ...................................... 60

    Project Manager........................................... 60

    Solution Architect or Solution Delivery Manager ............... 60

    Functional Consultant or Consultants......................... 61

    Technical Consultant ...................................... 61

    Development Lead and Developers............................ 61

    Integration Architect....................................... 61

    Data Migration Specialist................................... 62

Project Governance ................................................ 62

    Project Communication ..................................... 62

    Resource Loading ......................................... 62

    Project Schedule .......................................... 66

    Document Repository....................................... 67

    Budget Tracking .......................................... 68

    Change Requests.......................................... 68

    Project Management Plan ................................... 68

The Bottom Line .................................................. 69

**Chapter 6 • Sprints and Tools Needed to Run Your Project**.............73

Definition of a Sprint......................................73
   Length of a Sprint......................................74
   Start and End of a Sprint................................74
   Delivering Value in a Sprint.............................74
Backlog...................................................75
   Project Backlog........................................75
   Sprint Backlog.........................................76
   Allocating Work to Team Members........................76
   Sprint Success Rate....................................76
Sprint Meetings............................................77
   Sprint Planning........................................77
   Sprint Review..........................................77
   Sprint Retrospective...................................78
   Stand-up Meetings.....................................78
Work Definitions...........................................79
   Epic..................................................79
   Feature...............................................79
   User Story.............................................80
   Requirement...........................................80
   Research Task..........................................80
   Design Task............................................80
   Development Task.......................................81
   Test Task..............................................81
   Other Task.............................................81
   Test Case..............................................81
   Test...................................................81
   Bug (Defect)...........................................81
   Risk..................................................81
   Issue.................................................82
   Change Request........................................82
   Code and Changesets...................................82
Azure DevOps.............................................82
   DevOps Fields.........................................82
   Progress Reporting.....................................83
   Analytical Views.......................................83
The Bottom Line...........................................84

**Chapter 7 • Change Management Throughout Your Project**...........87

Success Criteria...........................................88
Use of Satisfaction Surveys.................................89
Nine Steps to Change Management...........................90
   Leadership Alignment..................................90
   Organization Evaluation................................91
   Outline Your Business Process Change Steps..............92
   Develop a System Vision that Provides Benefits to All Stakeholders............92

Communicate Effectively. . . . . . . . . . . . . . . . . . . . . . . . . . . . . . . . . . . . . 92
Maximize the Team's Time in the New System . . . . . . . . . . . . . . . . . . . . . . 94
Train Effectively. . . . . . . . . . . . . . . . . . . . . . . . . . . . . . . . . . . . . . . . . . . . . 94
Set Realistic Expectations for the System Just After Go-Live. . . . . . . . . . . . . 94
Support Your Team Members After Go-Live . . . . . . . . . . . . . . . . . . . . . . . . 95
Steps to Business Process Change . . . . . . . . . . . . . . . . . . . . . . . . . . . . . . . 95
Importance of Adoption. . . . . . . . . . . . . . . . . . . . . . . . . . . . . . . . . . . . . . 96
The Bottom Line . . . . . . . . . . . . . . . . . . . . . . . . . . . . . . . . . . . . . . . . . . . . . 96

**Chapter 8 • Organizing Your Business by Processes** . . . . . . . . . . . . . . . . . . **99**
Common Language Businesses Speak . . . . . . . . . . . . . . . . . . . . . . . . . . . . . . . 99
Operations . . . . . . . . . . . . . . . . . . . . . . . . . . . . . . . . . . . . . . . . . . . . . . . 100
Sales. . . . . . . . . . . . . . . . . . . . . . . . . . . . . . . . . . . . . . . . . . . . . . . . . . . . 100
Finance and Administration . . . . . . . . . . . . . . . . . . . . . . . . . . . . . . . . . . 100
Standard Processes . . . . . . . . . . . . . . . . . . . . . . . . . . . . . . . . . . . . . . . . . 100
Process Hierarchy. . . . . . . . . . . . . . . . . . . . . . . . . . . . . . . . . . . . . . . . . . . . 102
Process Category. . . . . . . . . . . . . . . . . . . . . . . . . . . . . . . . . . . . . . . . . . . 102
Process Group . . . . . . . . . . . . . . . . . . . . . . . . . . . . . . . . . . . . . . . . . . . . . 103
Process . . . . . . . . . . . . . . . . . . . . . . . . . . . . . . . . . . . . . . . . . . . . . . . . . . 103
Sub-processes, Tasks, Activities, and Requirements . . . . . . . . . . . . . . . . . . 104
Discovering Your Processes . . . . . . . . . . . . . . . . . . . . . . . . . . . . . . . . . . . . . 104
SIPOC . . . . . . . . . . . . . . . . . . . . . . . . . . . . . . . . . . . . . . . . . . . . . . . . . . . 104
Core Team Members. . . . . . . . . . . . . . . . . . . . . . . . . . . . . . . . . . . . . . . . . 106
Rounding Out Your Scope. . . . . . . . . . . . . . . . . . . . . . . . . . . . . . . . . . . . . 106
The Bottom Line . . . . . . . . . . . . . . . . . . . . . . . . . . . . . . . . . . . . . . . . . . . . . 106

**Chapter 9 • Independent Software Vendors—Filling Gaps
and Managing Partnerships** . . . . . . . . . . . . . . . . . . . . . . . . . . . . . . . . . . . . **109**
The Purpose of ISVs. . . . . . . . . . . . . . . . . . . . . . . . . . . . . . . . . . . . . . . . . . . 109
Hosting Providers . . . . . . . . . . . . . . . . . . . . . . . . . . . . . . . . . . . . . . . . . . . . 110
Private Hosting . . . . . . . . . . . . . . . . . . . . . . . . . . . . . . . . . . . . . . . . . . . . 111
SaaS-Style Hosting . . . . . . . . . . . . . . . . . . . . . . . . . . . . . . . . . . . . . . . . . 111
Industry ISVs. . . . . . . . . . . . . . . . . . . . . . . . . . . . . . . . . . . . . . . . . . . . . . 111
Deciding If You Need an Industry ISV . . . . . . . . . . . . . . . . . . . . . . . . . . . . 112
Functional ISVs . . . . . . . . . . . . . . . . . . . . . . . . . . . . . . . . . . . . . . . . . . . . 113
Missing Functionality. . . . . . . . . . . . . . . . . . . . . . . . . . . . . . . . . . . . . . . . 113
Advanced Features. . . . . . . . . . . . . . . . . . . . . . . . . . . . . . . . . . . . . . . . . . 113
Missing Connector . . . . . . . . . . . . . . . . . . . . . . . . . . . . . . . . . . . . . . . . . . 113
Automation . . . . . . . . . . . . . . . . . . . . . . . . . . . . . . . . . . . . . . . . . . . . . . . 114
Reporting Extensions . . . . . . . . . . . . . . . . . . . . . . . . . . . . . . . . . . . . . . . . 114
Deciding If You Need a Functional ISV . . . . . . . . . . . . . . . . . . . . . . . . . . . . 114
Working with ISVs. . . . . . . . . . . . . . . . . . . . . . . . . . . . . . . . . . . . . . . . . . . . 114
Budgeting for ISV Solutions . . . . . . . . . . . . . . . . . . . . . . . . . . . . . . . . . . . 115
Implementation Partner or Customer Managed . . . . . . . . . . . . . . . . . . . . . 115
Buying the ISV License or Subscription. . . . . . . . . . . . . . . . . . . . . . . . . . . . 115
Implementation of ISV Products. . . . . . . . . . . . . . . . . . . . . . . . . . . . . . . . . 116
Manage Your ISV Projects Closely . . . . . . . . . . . . . . . . . . . . . . . . . . . . . . . 116

Microsoft's AppSource Marketplace . . . . . . . . . . . . . . . . . . . . . . . . . . . . . . . . . . . . . . . . . . . . 117
    Product Listing . . . . . . . . . . . . . . . . . . . . . . . . . . . . . . . . . . . . . . . . . . . . . . . . . . . . 118
    Services Listing . . . . . . . . . . . . . . . . . . . . . . . . . . . . . . . . . . . . . . . . . . . . . . . . . . . . 118
The Bottom Line . . . . . . . . . . . . . . . . . . . . . . . . . . . . . . . . . . . . . . . . . . . . . . . . . . . . . . . . . . 119

**Chapter 10 • Factors for a Successful Project Kickoff . . . . . . . . . . . . . . . 121**
Pre-Kickoff Meeting Activities . . . . . . . . . . . . . . . . . . . . . . . . . . . . . . . . . . . . . . . . . . . . . . . 121
    Checklist . . . . . . . . . . . . . . . . . . . . . . . . . . . . . . . . . . . . . . . . . . . . . . . . . . . . . . . . . . 121
    Expectations for the Meeting . . . . . . . . . . . . . . . . . . . . . . . . . . . . . . . . . . . . . . . . . . 124
    Outing . . . . . . . . . . . . . . . . . . . . . . . . . . . . . . . . . . . . . . . . . . . . . . . . . . . . . . . . . . . 124
Kickoff Meeting Content . . . . . . . . . . . . . . . . . . . . . . . . . . . . . . . . . . . . . . . . . . . . . . . . . . . 124
    Executive Overview . . . . . . . . . . . . . . . . . . . . . . . . . . . . . . . . . . . . . . . . . . . . . . . . 125
    Introductions and Role Review . . . . . . . . . . . . . . . . . . . . . . . . . . . . . . . . . . . . . . . 125
    Expectations for Team Members . . . . . . . . . . . . . . . . . . . . . . . . . . . . . . . . . . . . . . 126
    Project Management and Communication Plan . . . . . . . . . . . . . . . . . . . . . . . . . . . 126
    Project Schedule . . . . . . . . . . . . . . . . . . . . . . . . . . . . . . . . . . . . . . . . . . . . . . . . . . 126
    Resources . . . . . . . . . . . . . . . . . . . . . . . . . . . . . . . . . . . . . . . . . . . . . . . . . . . . . . . 126
    Navigation Overview [*Optional*] . . . . . . . . . . . . . . . . . . . . . . . . . . . . . . . . . . . . . 127
    Wrapping Up . . . . . . . . . . . . . . . . . . . . . . . . . . . . . . . . . . . . . . . . . . . . . . . . . . . . 127
Executive Message . . . . . . . . . . . . . . . . . . . . . . . . . . . . . . . . . . . . . . . . . . . . . . . . . . . . . . . 127
Expectations for the Project Team . . . . . . . . . . . . . . . . . . . . . . . . . . . . . . . . . . . . . . . . . . 128
    Time Commitment . . . . . . . . . . . . . . . . . . . . . . . . . . . . . . . . . . . . . . . . . . . . . . . . 128
    Decision-Making . . . . . . . . . . . . . . . . . . . . . . . . . . . . . . . . . . . . . . . . . . . . . . . . . 129
    Power of Positivity . . . . . . . . . . . . . . . . . . . . . . . . . . . . . . . . . . . . . . . . . . . . . . . . 129
The Bottom Line . . . . . . . . . . . . . . . . . . . . . . . . . . . . . . . . . . . . . . . . . . . . . . . . . . . . . . . . . . 130

**Chapter 11 • Designing the Software Collaboratively . . . . . . . . . . . . . . . 133**
Joint Application Design Concept . . . . . . . . . . . . . . . . . . . . . . . . . . . . . . . . . . . . . . . . . . . . 133
Joint Process Design and Other Design-Related Definitions . . . . . . . . . . . . . . . . . . . . . 134
    What Is a Joint Process Design (JPD) Session? . . . . . . . . . . . . . . . . . . . . . . . . . . . 134
    Happy Path . . . . . . . . . . . . . . . . . . . . . . . . . . . . . . . . . . . . . . . . . . . . . . . . . . . . . . 136
    "As-Is" vs. "To Be" . . . . . . . . . . . . . . . . . . . . . . . . . . . . . . . . . . . . . . . . . . . . . . . . 136
Joint Process Design Iterations . . . . . . . . . . . . . . . . . . . . . . . . . . . . . . . . . . . . . . . . . . . . . 137
    JPD1 . . . . . . . . . . . . . . . . . . . . . . . . . . . . . . . . . . . . . . . . . . . . . . . . . . . . . . . . . . . 137
    JPD2 . . . . . . . . . . . . . . . . . . . . . . . . . . . . . . . . . . . . . . . . . . . . . . . . . . . . . . . . . . . 139
    JPD3 . . . . . . . . . . . . . . . . . . . . . . . . . . . . . . . . . . . . . . . . . . . . . . . . . . . . . . . . . . . 140
    JPD4 . . . . . . . . . . . . . . . . . . . . . . . . . . . . . . . . . . . . . . . . . . . . . . . . . . . . . . . . . . . 140
    Keys to Successful JPDs . . . . . . . . . . . . . . . . . . . . . . . . . . . . . . . . . . . . . . . . . . . . 140
    JPD Output . . . . . . . . . . . . . . . . . . . . . . . . . . . . . . . . . . . . . . . . . . . . . . . . . . . . . . 141
SIPOC . . . . . . . . . . . . . . . . . . . . . . . . . . . . . . . . . . . . . . . . . . . . . . . . . . . . . . . . . . . . . . . . . . 142
The Bottom Line . . . . . . . . . . . . . . . . . . . . . . . . . . . . . . . . . . . . . . . . . . . . . . . . . . . . . . . . . . 143

**Chapter 12 • Requirements Gathering and Staying "In the Box" . . . . . . 145**
Staying in the Box . . . . . . . . . . . . . . . . . . . . . . . . . . . . . . . . . . . . . . . . . . . . . . . . . . . . . . . . 145
    Customization vs. In-the-Box Examples . . . . . . . . . . . . . . . . . . . . . . . . . . . . . . . . 146
Requirements . . . . . . . . . . . . . . . . . . . . . . . . . . . . . . . . . . . . . . . . . . . . . . . . . . . . . . . . . . . . 147

Out-of-the-Box Fields as Requirements.................................... 147
Requirements Link to Processes ........................................... 148
Functional vs. Non-functional Requirements............................. 149
Verifying Requirements .................................................... 150
Writing Good Requirements................................................... 150
Requirements Tips ......................................................... 150
Fit/Gap Analysis ............................................................... 151
Fit/Gap Spreadsheet ...................................................... 152
Trade-Offs................................................................. 153
The Cost of Customizations .................................................. 154
Cloud vs. On-Premise Software .......................................... 155
The Bottom Line ............................................................... 155

**Chapter 13 • Conference Room Pilots ........................... 157**
The Purpose of a Conference Room Pilot...................................... 157
How to Organize CRPs ................................................... 158
Common Elements of CRPs............................................... 159
CRP Agenda............................................................... 159
Logistics .................................................................. 160
Issues and Questions .................................................... 160
CRP Roles and Responsibilities .............................................. 161
Session Leader............................................................ 161
Helper/Expert............................................................. 162
Business Process Owner.................................................. 162
Users/Students .......................................................... 162
Who Not to Invite ....................................................... 163
CRP Place in the Overall Schedule .......................................... 163
Can You Do a CRP on One Process Group at the Same Time
That You Do a JPD? ................................................... 164
Entrance Criteria ........................................................ 164
CRP vs. UAT .................................................................. 166
How They Are Similar ................................................... 166
How They Are Different................................................... 166
What to Do Between CRP and the End of the Create Stage.................... 167
CRP Goals .................................................................... 168
The Bottom Line .............................................................. 168

**Chapter 14 • Dealing with Challenges Mid-Project .................. 171**
Managing the Project Status .................................................. 172
Status Report ............................................................. 172
Colors on a Status Report................................................ 173
Managing Your Budget ................................................... 175
Project Pulse.............................................................. 177
Risks and Issues .............................................................. 177
Risk Register ............................................................. 178
Issues vs. Bugs........................................................... 179
Common Project Challenges.................................................. 179
The Bottom Line .............................................................. 183

**Chapter 15 • Customizations vs. Configurations and How You Manage Them** ................................. **185**

Customizations vs. Configurations ............................................... 185

Customization ....................................................... 185

Configuration ....................................................... 186

Integration ......................................................... 186

Master Data ........................................................ 187

Metadata ........................................................... 187

Personalization ..................................................... 187

Reference Data ...................................................... 187

When to Customize vs. Configure .................................... 188

Why Choose to Customize ........................................... 188

Tracking Configurations ................................................. 188

Configuration Tracker ............................................... 189

Gold Environment ................................................... 189

Lifecycle Services ................................................... 189

Functional Design Documents ............................................ 190

Overview ........................................................... 190

Modification ........................................................ 190

Testing ............................................................. 190

Development Quotation .............................................. 191

Revision and Sign-off ............................................... 191

Updates ............................................................ 191

Design Complete .................................................... 191

The Development Process ................................................. 192

Develop the Solution ................................................ 192

Unit Test ........................................................... 192

Code Review ........................................................ 193

Functional Testing (Part 1) .......................................... 193

Finishing Up ....................................................... 194

After Code Complete .................................................... 194

Deploying the Code ................................................. 194

Functional Testing (Part 2) .......................................... 194

Preparing for CRP and UAT .......................................... 195

The Lifecycle of a Customization ........................................ 195

Managing These Tasks .............................................. 195

Wrap-Up ........................................................... 196

The Bottom Line ....................................................... 197

**Chapter 16 • Data Migration—Early and Often** ..................... **199**

Data Migration Plan .................................................... 200

Proactive Cleaning .................................................. 200

Before the Kickoff .................................................. 201

Data Migration Tool ................................................ 202

Iterations .......................................................... 203

Extract .................................................................. 206

Finding the Data . . . . . . . . . . . . . . . . . . . . . . . . . . . . . . . . . . . . . . . . . . . 206
Extraction Tools . . . . . . . . . . . . . . . . . . . . . . . . . . . . . . . . . . . . . . . . . . . . . 206
Transform . . . . . . . . . . . . . . . . . . . . . . . . . . . . . . . . . . . . . . . . . . . . . . . . . . . . . 208
Mapping the Data . . . . . . . . . . . . . . . . . . . . . . . . . . . . . . . . . . . . . . . . . . 208
Mapping Tools . . . . . . . . . . . . . . . . . . . . . . . . . . . . . . . . . . . . . . . . . . . . . . 208
Transforming Mapped Data . . . . . . . . . . . . . . . . . . . . . . . . . . . . . . . . 209
Load . . . . . . . . . . . . . . . . . . . . . . . . . . . . . . . . . . . . . . . . . . . . . . . . . . . . . . . . . 210
Order of Operation . . . . . . . . . . . . . . . . . . . . . . . . . . . . . . . . . . . . . . . . . 210
Load Time . . . . . . . . . . . . . . . . . . . . . . . . . . . . . . . . . . . . . . . . . . . . . . . . . . 210
Validating the Data . . . . . . . . . . . . . . . . . . . . . . . . . . . . . . . . . . . . . . . . . . 210
Technical Validation . . . . . . . . . . . . . . . . . . . . . . . . . . . . . . . . . . . . . . . . . . 211
Business Validation . . . . . . . . . . . . . . . . . . . . . . . . . . . . . . . . . . . . . . . . . 211
Functional Validation . . . . . . . . . . . . . . . . . . . . . . . . . . . . . . . . . . . . . . 212
Go-Live Iteration . . . . . . . . . . . . . . . . . . . . . . . . . . . . . . . . . . . . . . . . . . . . . 212
The Bottom Line . . . . . . . . . . . . . . . . . . . . . . . . . . . . . . . . . . . . . . . . . . . . . . 213

**Chapter 17 • Environment Management and Deployments** . . . . . . . . . . . **215**
Types of Environments . . . . . . . . . . . . . . . . . . . . . . . . . . . . . . . . . . . . . . . . 216
Developer Environments . . . . . . . . . . . . . . . . . . . . . . . . . . . . . . . . . . . . 216
Build . . . . . . . . . . . . . . . . . . . . . . . . . . . . . . . . . . . . . . . . . . . . . . . . . . . . . . . 217
Test . . . . . . . . . . . . . . . . . . . . . . . . . . . . . . . . . . . . . . . . . . . . . . . . . . . . . . . . . 217
Sandbox . . . . . . . . . . . . . . . . . . . . . . . . . . . . . . . . . . . . . . . . . . . . . . . . . . . . 218
Production . . . . . . . . . . . . . . . . . . . . . . . . . . . . . . . . . . . . . . . . . . . . . . . . . 219
Environment Plan . . . . . . . . . . . . . . . . . . . . . . . . . . . . . . . . . . . . . . . . . . . . . 220
Types of Releases . . . . . . . . . . . . . . . . . . . . . . . . . . . . . . . . . . . . . . . . . . . 220
Frequency of Code Moves . . . . . . . . . . . . . . . . . . . . . . . . . . . . . . . . . . . 222
Populating Configurations and Master Data . . . . . . . . . . . . . . . . . . 222
Deploying Code . . . . . . . . . . . . . . . . . . . . . . . . . . . . . . . . . . . . . . . . . . . . . . 223
Application Lifecycle Management . . . . . . . . . . . . . . . . . . . . . . . . . . . . 223
Environment Flow Using DevOps . . . . . . . . . . . . . . . . . . . . . . . . . . . . . 224
Rollback . . . . . . . . . . . . . . . . . . . . . . . . . . . . . . . . . . . . . . . . . . . . . . . . . . . . 224
Security . . . . . . . . . . . . . . . . . . . . . . . . . . . . . . . . . . . . . . . . . . . . . . . . . . . . . . 225
Definitions . . . . . . . . . . . . . . . . . . . . . . . . . . . . . . . . . . . . . . . . . . . . . . . . . 225
How Best to Manage . . . . . . . . . . . . . . . . . . . . . . . . . . . . . . . . . . . . . . . . 226
The Bottom Line . . . . . . . . . . . . . . . . . . . . . . . . . . . . . . . . . . . . . . . . . . . . . . 227

**Chapter 18 • Testing** . . . . . . . . . . . . . . . . . . . . . . . . . . . . . . . . . . . . . . . . **229**
Definitions . . . . . . . . . . . . . . . . . . . . . . . . . . . . . . . . . . . . . . . . . . . . . . . . . . . . 229
Types of Testing . . . . . . . . . . . . . . . . . . . . . . . . . . . . . . . . . . . . . . . . . . . . . 230
Common Testing Terms . . . . . . . . . . . . . . . . . . . . . . . . . . . . . . . . . . . . . . 231
Pre-Deploy Stage Activities . . . . . . . . . . . . . . . . . . . . . . . . . . . . . . . . . . . 232
Testing Strategy . . . . . . . . . . . . . . . . . . . . . . . . . . . . . . . . . . . . . . . . . . . . . 232
Unit Test and Regression Tests . . . . . . . . . . . . . . . . . . . . . . . . . . . . . . . 233
Developing Test Cases . . . . . . . . . . . . . . . . . . . . . . . . . . . . . . . . . . . . . . . 234
UAT Entrance Criteria . . . . . . . . . . . . . . . . . . . . . . . . . . . . . . . . . . . . . . . 235
UAT Exit Criteria . . . . . . . . . . . . . . . . . . . . . . . . . . . . . . . . . . . . . . . . . . . . 236

UAT Sessions . . . . . . . . . . . . . . . . . . . . . . . . . . . . . . . . . . . . . . . . . . . . . . . . . . . . . . . . . . . . . . . 236
    Purpose . . . . . . . . . . . . . . . . . . . . . . . . . . . . . . . . . . . . . . . . . . . . . . . . . . . . . . . . . . . . . . . . . . 236
    Additional Benefits of UAT Sessions . . . . . . . . . . . . . . . . . . . . . . . . . . . . . . . . . . . . . . . 237
    UAT Roles and Responsibilities . . . . . . . . . . . . . . . . . . . . . . . . . . . . . . . . . . . . . . . . . . . . 237
    Executing Your Test Plans . . . . . . . . . . . . . . . . . . . . . . . . . . . . . . . . . . . . . . . . . . . . . . . . . 238
    Tips for the Sessions . . . . . . . . . . . . . . . . . . . . . . . . . . . . . . . . . . . . . . . . . . . . . . . . . . . . . . 239
Post UAT Testing . . . . . . . . . . . . . . . . . . . . . . . . . . . . . . . . . . . . . . . . . . . . . . . . . . . . . . . . . . . . . 240
    Issues List . . . . . . . . . . . . . . . . . . . . . . . . . . . . . . . . . . . . . . . . . . . . . . . . . . . . . . . . . . . . . . . . 241
    Process Sign-Offs . . . . . . . . . . . . . . . . . . . . . . . . . . . . . . . . . . . . . . . . . . . . . . . . . . . . . . . . . 241
    Scenario Recaps . . . . . . . . . . . . . . . . . . . . . . . . . . . . . . . . . . . . . . . . . . . . . . . . . . . . . . . . . . . 241
The Bottom Line . . . . . . . . . . . . . . . . . . . . . . . . . . . . . . . . . . . . . . . . . . . . . . . . . . . . . . . . . . . . . . 242

**Chapter 19  •  Training for All** . . . . . . . . . . . . . . . . . . . . . . . . . . . . . . . . . . **245**
Learning During Interactive Sessions . . . . . . . . . . . . . . . . . . . . . . . . . . . . . . . . . . . . . . . . . . 246
    JPDs . . . . . . . . . . . . . . . . . . . . . . . . . . . . . . . . . . . . . . . . . . . . . . . . . . . . . . . . . . . . . . . . . . . . . . 246
    CRPs . . . . . . . . . . . . . . . . . . . . . . . . . . . . . . . . . . . . . . . . . . . . . . . . . . . . . . . . . . . . . . . . . . . . . . 246
    UAT . . . . . . . . . . . . . . . . . . . . . . . . . . . . . . . . . . . . . . . . . . . . . . . . . . . . . . . . . . . . . . . . . . . . . . . 247
Learning Modalities . . . . . . . . . . . . . . . . . . . . . . . . . . . . . . . . . . . . . . . . . . . . . . . . . . . . . . . . . . . 247
    In-Person, Classroom Style . . . . . . . . . . . . . . . . . . . . . . . . . . . . . . . . . . . . . . . . . . . . . . . . 248
    Remote, Synchronous Training . . . . . . . . . . . . . . . . . . . . . . . . . . . . . . . . . . . . . . . . . . . . . 249
    Asynchronous . . . . . . . . . . . . . . . . . . . . . . . . . . . . . . . . . . . . . . . . . . . . . . . . . . . . . . . . . . . . . 251
    Building Your Training Content . . . . . . . . . . . . . . . . . . . . . . . . . . . . . . . . . . . . . . . . . . . . 251
    End User Training Content . . . . . . . . . . . . . . . . . . . . . . . . . . . . . . . . . . . . . . . . . . . . . . . . . 251
    Product Help Content . . . . . . . . . . . . . . . . . . . . . . . . . . . . . . . . . . . . . . . . . . . . . . . . . . . . . . 252
    Microsoft Learn . . . . . . . . . . . . . . . . . . . . . . . . . . . . . . . . . . . . . . . . . . . . . . . . . . . . . . . . . . . 253
    Recording Sessions . . . . . . . . . . . . . . . . . . . . . . . . . . . . . . . . . . . . . . . . . . . . . . . . . . . . . . . . 253
    Task Recorder . . . . . . . . . . . . . . . . . . . . . . . . . . . . . . . . . . . . . . . . . . . . . . . . . . . . . . . . . . . . . 253
    How Much to Document . . . . . . . . . . . . . . . . . . . . . . . . . . . . . . . . . . . . . . . . . . . . . . . . . . . 254
How to Manage and Distribute Your Content . . . . . . . . . . . . . . . . . . . . . . . . . . . . . . . . . . . 254
    Learning Management Systems . . . . . . . . . . . . . . . . . . . . . . . . . . . . . . . . . . . . . . . . . . . . . 255
Building Your End User Training Schedule . . . . . . . . . . . . . . . . . . . . . . . . . . . . . . . . . . . . . 255
    Pre-Training Learning . . . . . . . . . . . . . . . . . . . . . . . . . . . . . . . . . . . . . . . . . . . . . . . . . . . . . . 256
    Train the Trainer . . . . . . . . . . . . . . . . . . . . . . . . . . . . . . . . . . . . . . . . . . . . . . . . . . . . . . . . . . 256
    Synchronous Sessions . . . . . . . . . . . . . . . . . . . . . . . . . . . . . . . . . . . . . . . . . . . . . . . . . . . . . . 257
    Advanced Concepts . . . . . . . . . . . . . . . . . . . . . . . . . . . . . . . . . . . . . . . . . . . . . . . . . . . . . . . . 257
    Testing Users' Knowledge . . . . . . . . . . . . . . . . . . . . . . . . . . . . . . . . . . . . . . . . . . . . . . . . . . 257
    Office Hours . . . . . . . . . . . . . . . . . . . . . . . . . . . . . . . . . . . . . . . . . . . . . . . . . . . . . . . . . . . . . . . 258
The Bottom Line . . . . . . . . . . . . . . . . . . . . . . . . . . . . . . . . . . . . . . . . . . . . . . . . . . . . . . . . . . . . . . 259

**Chapter 20  •  Going Live** . . . . . . . . . . . . . . . . . . . . . . . . . . . . . . . . . . . . . . . . **261**
Go-Live Criteria . . . . . . . . . . . . . . . . . . . . . . . . . . . . . . . . . . . . . . . . . . . . . . . . . . . . . . . . . . . . . . 261
    Cutover Plan . . . . . . . . . . . . . . . . . . . . . . . . . . . . . . . . . . . . . . . . . . . . . . . . . . . . . . . . . . . . . . . 262
    Bug Criteria . . . . . . . . . . . . . . . . . . . . . . . . . . . . . . . . . . . . . . . . . . . . . . . . . . . . . . . . . . . . . . . 262
    Data Migration and Security Criteria . . . . . . . . . . . . . . . . . . . . . . . . . . . . . . . . . . . . . . . . 263
    Support Readiness . . . . . . . . . . . . . . . . . . . . . . . . . . . . . . . . . . . . . . . . . . . . . . . . . . . . . . . . . . 264
    Training Review . . . . . . . . . . . . . . . . . . . . . . . . . . . . . . . . . . . . . . . . . . . . . . . . . . . . . . . . . . . . 264

Communication Plan . . . . . . . . . . . . . . . . . . . . . . . . 265
Go-Live Scorecard . . . . . . . . . . . . . . . . . . . . . . . . . . 265
Mock Cutover and Final Week Activities . . . . . . . . . . . . . . . . . . . . . . . 266
Disaster Recovery . . . . . . . . . . . . . . . . . . . . . . . . . . 267
System Setup Before Cutover . . . . . . . . . . . . . . . . . 267
Go/No-Go Meetings . . . . . . . . . . . . . . . . . . . . . . . . . . . . . . 268
When to Have It . . . . . . . . . . . . . . . . . . . . . . . . . . . 268
Voting Criteria . . . . . . . . . . . . . . . . . . . . . . . . . . . . 268
Meeting Agenda . . . . . . . . . . . . . . . . . . . . . . . . . . . 269
Order and Outcome of the Votes . . . . . . . . . . . . . . 269
Next Steps . . . . . . . . . . . . . . . . . . . . . . . . . . . . . . . . 270
Live Cutover . . . . . . . . . . . . . . . . . . . . . . . . . . . . . . . . . . 270
Impact of the Cutover Start Timing . . . . . . . . . . . . 271
Completing Cutover Activities . . . . . . . . . . . . . . . . 271
Rollback Plan . . . . . . . . . . . . . . . . . . . . . . . . . . . . . 272
Acknowledge the Team . . . . . . . . . . . . . . . . . . . . . 272
The Bottom Line . . . . . . . . . . . . . . . . . . . . . . . . . . . . . . 272

**Chapter 21 • Hypercare** . . . . . . . . . . . . . . . . . . . . . . . . **275**
Go-Live Support . . . . . . . . . . . . . . . . . . . . . . . . . . . . . . 275
Day 1 . . . . . . . . . . . . . . . . . . . . . . . . . . . . . . . . . . . . . 276
Week 1 . . . . . . . . . . . . . . . . . . . . . . . . . . . . . . . . . . . 276
Project Change Champions . . . . . . . . . . . . . . . . . . 277
Prioritizing Issues . . . . . . . . . . . . . . . . . . . . . . . . . 277
Weeks 2–4 . . . . . . . . . . . . . . . . . . . . . . . . . . . . . . . . 278
First Month End . . . . . . . . . . . . . . . . . . . . . . . . . . . 278
Duration of Hypercare . . . . . . . . . . . . . . . . . . . . . . 279
Role of HelpDesk . . . . . . . . . . . . . . . . . . . . . . . . . . . . . 279
Sample SLA . . . . . . . . . . . . . . . . . . . . . . . . . . . . . . . 280
Project Team Support . . . . . . . . . . . . . . . . . . . . . . . 280
Support Levels . . . . . . . . . . . . . . . . . . . . . . . . . . . . . 281
Refer Users to Training . . . . . . . . . . . . . . . . . . . . . . 283
Making the Transition to HelpDesk Later . . . . . . . 283
Post Go-Live Releases . . . . . . . . . . . . . . . . . . . . . . . . . 284
Planning for Future Releases . . . . . . . . . . . . . . . . . 285
Hotfix Release . . . . . . . . . . . . . . . . . . . . . . . . . . . . . 285
Scheduled Releases . . . . . . . . . . . . . . . . . . . . . . . . . 286
Project Team Transition . . . . . . . . . . . . . . . . . . . . . . . 287
Rolling Off the Project Team . . . . . . . . . . . . . . . . . 287
Documentation . . . . . . . . . . . . . . . . . . . . . . . . . . . . 288
Expectations of Support . . . . . . . . . . . . . . . . . . . . . 288
After the Transition . . . . . . . . . . . . . . . . . . . . . . . . . 289
The Bottom Line . . . . . . . . . . . . . . . . . . . . . . . . . . . . . . 289

**Chapter 22 • Support and Enhance Your Project** . . . . . . . . . . . . . . . **291**
Support After Hypercare . . . . . . . . . . . . . . . . . . . . . . . 291
Extending the Transition from Consulting to Support . . . . . . . . . . . . . . . 292
Engaging Your Partner for Support . . . . . . . . . . . . . . . . . . . . . . . . . . . . . 292

Microsoft and ISV Support Plans . . . . . . . . . . . . . . . . . . . . . . . . . . . . . . . . . . . . 294
After Action Review. . . . . . . . . . . . . . . . . . . . . . . . . . . . . . . . . . . . . . . . . . . . . . . . 295
    Who to Invite . . . . . . . . . . . . . . . . . . . . . . . . . . . . . . . . . . . . . . . . . . . . . . . . . . . 295
    How to Run the Meeting . . . . . . . . . . . . . . . . . . . . . . . . . . . . . . . . . . . . . . . . 296
    What to Do with the Feedback . . . . . . . . . . . . . . . . . . . . . . . . . . . . . . . . . . . 297
Ongoing Releases . . . . . . . . . . . . . . . . . . . . . . . . . . . . . . . . . . . . . . . . . . . . . . . . . 297
    Microsoft Dynamics 365 Release Cadence . . . . . . . . . . . . . . . . . . . . . . . . . 297
    Release Testing. . . . . . . . . . . . . . . . . . . . . . . . . . . . . . . . . . . . . . . . . . . . . . . . . 297
    When to Schedule Your Releases . . . . . . . . . . . . . . . . . . . . . . . . . . . . . . . . . 298
    What to Include in Releases. . . . . . . . . . . . . . . . . . . . . . . . . . . . . . . . . . . . . . 299
Future Enhancements . . . . . . . . . . . . . . . . . . . . . . . . . . . . . . . . . . . . . . . . . . . . . 299
    New Functionality . . . . . . . . . . . . . . . . . . . . . . . . . . . . . . . . . . . . . . . . . . . . . 299
    Usability . . . . . . . . . . . . . . . . . . . . . . . . . . . . . . . . . . . . . . . . . . . . . . . . . . . . . . 300
    Guardrails. . . . . . . . . . . . . . . . . . . . . . . . . . . . . . . . . . . . . . . . . . . . . . . . . . . . . 301
    Business Intelligence. . . . . . . . . . . . . . . . . . . . . . . . . . . . . . . . . . . . . . . . . . . . 301
    Incorporating Dynamics Data into Your Daily Business. . . . . . . . . . . . . . 302
    Integrations . . . . . . . . . . . . . . . . . . . . . . . . . . . . . . . . . . . . . . . . . . . . . . . . . . . 302
    Machine Learning and Artificial Intelligence . . . . . . . . . . . . . . . . . . . . . . 302
Calculating Return on Investment. . . . . . . . . . . . . . . . . . . . . . . . . . . . . . . . . . 303
    ROI Checkpoints . . . . . . . . . . . . . . . . . . . . . . . . . . . . . . . . . . . . . . . . . . . . . . . 304
The Bottom Line . . . . . . . . . . . . . . . . . . . . . . . . . . . . . . . . . . . . . . . . . . . . . . . . . 305

**Chapter 23 • Bringing It All Together** . . . . . . . . . . . . . . . . . . . . . . . . . . . . . **307**
Align Stage . . . . . . . . . . . . . . . . . . . . . . . . . . . . . . . . . . . . . . . . . . . . . . . . . . . . . . 307
Define Stage. . . . . . . . . . . . . . . . . . . . . . . . . . . . . . . . . . . . . . . . . . . . . . . . . . . . . 308
Create Stage. . . . . . . . . . . . . . . . . . . . . . . . . . . . . . . . . . . . . . . . . . . . . . . . . . . . . 311
Deploy Stage . . . . . . . . . . . . . . . . . . . . . . . . . . . . . . . . . . . . . . . . . . . . . . . . . . . . 313
Empower Stage. . . . . . . . . . . . . . . . . . . . . . . . . . . . . . . . . . . . . . . . . . . . . . . . . . 314
Additional Resources. . . . . . . . . . . . . . . . . . . . . . . . . . . . . . . . . . . . . . . . . . . . . 315
The Bottom Line . . . . . . . . . . . . . . . . . . . . . . . . . . . . . . . . . . . . . . . . . . . . . . . . . 315

**Appendix • The Bottom Line** . . . . . . . . . . . . . . . . . . . . . . . . . . . . . . . . . . . . **317**
Chapter 1: Stages of an Implementation Overview . . . . . . . . . . . . . . . . . . . . . 317
Chapter 2: What to Do Before You Begin a Project . . . . . . . . . . . . . . . . . . . . . 318
Chapter 3: Four Keys to Consider When Buying an ERP or CRM Solution . . . . . . . . . 320
Chapter 4: How to Evaluate and Buy Business Application Software. . . . . . . . . . . . . 322
Chapter 5: Organizing Your Team for Success and Project Governance . . . . . . . . . . . 323
Chapter 6: Sprints and Tools Needed to Run Your Project. . . . . . . . . . . . . . . . . . . 325
Chapter 7: Change Management Throughout Your Project. . . . . . . . . . . . . . . . . . . 326
Chapter 8: Organizing Your Business by Processes . . . . . . . . . . . . . . . . . . . . . . . 328
Chapter 9: Independent Software Vendors—Filling Gaps and
  Managing Partnerships. . . . . . . . . . . . . . . . . . . . . . . . . . . . . . . . . . . . . . . . . . 329
Chapter 10: Factors for a Successful Project Kickoff . . . . . . . . . . . . . . . . . . . . . . 331
Chapter 11: Designing the Software Collaboratively . . . . . . . . . . . . . . . . . . . . . . 332
Chapter 12: Requirements Gathering and Staying "In the Box" . . . . . . . . . . . . . . . 334
Chapter 13: Conference Room Pilots. . . . . . . . . . . . . . . . . . . . . . . . . . . . . . . . . . 335

Chapter 14: Dealing with Challenges Mid-Project . . . . . . . . . . . . . . . . . . . . . . . . . . . 337
Chapter 15: Customizations vs. Configurations and How You Manage Them . . . . . . 338
Chapter 16: Data Migration—Early and Often . . . . . . . . . . . . . . . . . . . . . . . . . . . . . 340
Chapter 17: Environment Management and Deployments . . . . . . . . . . . . . . . . . . . . . 341
Chapter 18: Testing. . . . . . . . . . . . . . . . . . . . . . . . . . . . . . . . . . . . . . . . . . . . . . . . . 343
Chapter 19: Training for All . . . . . . . . . . . . . . . . . . . . . . . . . . . . . . . . . . . . . . . . . . 344
Chapter 20: Going Live . . . . . . . . . . . . . . . . . . . . . . . . . . . . . . . . . . . . . . . . . . . . . . 346
Chapter 21: Hypercare. . . . . . . . . . . . . . . . . . . . . . . . . . . . . . . . . . . . . . . . . . . . . . . 347
Chapter 22: Support and Enhance Your Project. . . . . . . . . . . . . . . . . . . . . . . . . . . . 349
Chapter 23: Bringing It All Together . . . . . . . . . . . . . . . . . . . . . . . . . . . . . . . . . . . . 350

**Glossary** . . . . . . . . . . . . . . . . . . . . . . . . . . . . . . . . . . . . . . . . . . . . . . . . . . . . . **353**

*Index*. . . . . . . . . . . . . . . . . . . . . . . . . . . . . . . . . . . . . . . . . . . . . . . . . . . . . . . . . . *369*

# Introduction

I started my career in the world of ERP and CRM back in 1999 when I landed a job as a support engineer for Great Plains Software, supporting Great Plains eEnterprise version 5.5. I had a management and economics degree and a natural affinity for computers, but I certainly didn't know anything about an ERP product or SQL Server. I also hadn't observed project management before, and I didn't understand the impact of it.

My career path at Microsoft (which bought Great Plains Software in April 2001) took several turns as I pivoted to focus on internal applications on which the support team relied, and I became the Support Operations Manager. During that time, my job was to execute projects to make improvements to our incident tracking system, our knowledge base, and the business intelligence needs of our support leadership team. I needed to manage projects and interface with IT project managers. I had not read anything about project management, and I was learning on the fly.

At first, I thought project management was easy—you set up a meeting, invite the right people, take notes, and call it a day. At the time, there weren't good apps like Azure DevOps for tracking every task, and stand-up meetings weren't a thing. Project managers just hoped that team members would get their work done on time. They would ask them about it at the weekly meetings, and that was about it. Some project managers had a good game plan for the order of operation of the activity on the project, but many were just there to make sure that the meetings occurred.

I went through much of the middle of my Microsoft career without a high degree of respect for project managers. I didn't understand what true value they brought to a project. I also saw people who were trying to perform the dual roles of project management and business analyst or subject matter expert. This was my first introduction into how difficult it is to wear both of those hats at the same time.

I switched from an internally focused role back to a client-facing role in 2005, becoming a Technical Account Manager for Microsoft Dynamics GP and CRM. My work gravitated toward CRM, where I worked with some of Microsoft's largest clients. When working with one client, I started to see how valuable project management could be. This project manager ran meetings and took notes like other project managers, but he also knew what needed to be done and when, and he pushed the team to hit the timeline as well as follow up with resources outside of meetings to get their tasks completed. I started to see that a project manager could be a valuable addition to a team.

In my next role, I managed the Premier Field Engineering team focused on the Dynamics ERP products (Dynamics AX, Dynamics NAV, and Dynamics GP—we didn't have any Premier clients on Dynamics SL). In this role, my team performed two primary activities: performance and health check guidance for existing clients and a Dedicated Support Engineer who served as a Microsoft functional or technical resource for clients in all stages of the implementation. We had clients reach out asking if we could run their implementations or support them as they self-implemented. Microsoft's policy was that they should work with a partner; however, they could engage my team for assistance through the implementation. For the most part, my team was an accessory to the implementation, but we ended up getting more deeply involved in a few of them.

This is when my eyes were really opened to the importance of project management and how critical it is to have the right leadership to get you through a complex business application. Every single project suffered from a lack of strong project management, regardless of where it was provided—by the client or the implementation partner—and they were all running over time and over budget. I started talking to my friends on the Customer Relations team at Microsoft to understand the nature of the escalations (when the customer threatens to move off the product or sue the partner or Microsoft due to the lack of progress on the project) they worked on. The Customer Relations team was the first line of defense for any clients who were upset with the success of their implementation project. If someone sent a letter to Bill Gates saying that their implementation was failing, it would come to the Customer Relations team. That team had a lot of data on failing projects and the driving force of the problem. In some of the cases, it was a technical problem—a bug with Microsoft or a missing feature that someone promised them—but the vast majority were project management problems.

The combination of the project problems that my team saw with the problems from the Customer Relations team made me wonder: Does anyone really know how to run a business applications project successfully?

I'm the kind of person who loves to work on the hardest possible projects. I live for challenges. Seeing this huge challenge of how to run implementation projects, I dove in. I learned everything I could about implementation methodologies; I read every book about how to implement Dynamics at the time, and I volunteered to do two things: contribute to Microsoft's Sure Step methodology and teach a class for Microsoft to new consultants about how an implementation works.

Connecting with new consultants about how an implementation works made it abundantly clear that these students had a ton to learn about implementation. This fueled my passion to want to learn even more. This desire was a big reason why I decided to leave Microsoft and start Stoneridge Software. I wanted to put what I had learned into practice and to continue to learn more.

When we started Stoneridge Software, my first consulting job was to serve as a Project Manager for a Dynamics implementation that had been going on for over a year but was stuck. I was able to get it moving and implement quite a bit of it over the next year-and-a-half so the client could earn value out of their system. It wasn't easy, and it made me realize that I had to expand my knowledge every day in that role to keep up with all of the curveballs that I would get from my client.

Managing an implementation is never easy, regardless of how well you know the steps and the "science" behind running an implementation. There's an "art" to working with any different group of humans trying to put this into place. The goal of this book is to teach you the science and to give you some ideas on how to manage through the curveballs that come your way.

## Who Should Read This Book

This book is for anyone who is involved in an ERP or CRM implementation or expects to be involved in one in the near future. The goal of the book is to appeal to all of the players who would be involved in the implementation so that they can learn more about what they should or shouldn't do when they play their part in the project.

The book speaks directly to a project manager on the client side of the implementation. It attempts to teach the project owner and manager each step of the process along the way to help the project be successful. I believe project owners, project managers, executives and executive sponsors, and IT leaders should read the book from start to finish. Subject matter experts or IT resources with a specific function should focus on the content specific to their role.

Some particular roles for whom the book is a fit: Company Leadership (CEO, President, CFO, COO), IT Leadership (CIO, IT Manager), IT roles (Business Analyst, Project Managers, Developers, Business Intelligence resources, IT Operations), and business leaders and members (VP of Manufacturing, VP of Operations, VP of Sales & Marketing, managers in each of these areas, and subject matter experts).

The book speaks more specifically to Microsoft Dynamics 365, but the same concepts can be used for other ERP and CRM systems. There are more specific examples related to Microsoft Dynamics 365, and I reference links to the most up-to-date information there.

## What You'll Learn from This Book

This book will teach you all of the steps that you need to go through to begin and end an implementation of an ERP or CRM system. You will learn about the journey that starts with aligning with the right partner, then define what you want to implement, create the solution that works for you, deploy the solution, and enhance it. The book introduces the Client Journey, which takes you through those five stages, and the chapters are organized into those stages in the journey. The final chapter is focused on the timeline for each event during the project with references back to the detailed steps outlined in previous chapters.

## How This Book Is Organized

This book is made up of 23 chapters. Each chapter walks you through a different key step in the implementation process. The chapters are largely in chronological order, but not the exact order, with several steps spanning different phases in the implementation process. Chapter 23 takes all of the activities and puts them in chronological order so that you can see each of the steps in order.

When I talk about steps, phases, and stages, I am referring to steps as necessary activities that you need to do to get through to completion. Phases are the larger, more chronologically based collections of steps. The way that I define phases in the book follows the typical waterfall approach. I'm using the term "stages" to refer to each of the five stages of the Client Journey, which we'll discuss next.

Let's jump into the steps. We are going to follow what we've determined at Stoneridge Software to be the Client Journey, and we've given it this name as a way of categorizing each of the stages that you need to go through during an implementation. We'll start by talking about the stages of the journey at a high level, and then we'll discuss what each session is associated with.

**Chapter 1: Stages of an Implementation Overview**   This chapter offers a high-level overview and breakdown of the stages of an implementation.

**Chapter 2: What to Do Before You Begin a Project**   This chapter covers all of the preparation one needs to complete before beginning a project, including identifying the project team and stakeholders, building your business case, securing funding, documenting processes, and cleaning up data.

**Chapter 3: Four Keys to Consider When Buying an ERP or CRM Solution**   This chapter covers the four keys to consider when buying an ERP or CRM solution and how favoring one of the dimensions at the expense of the others can greatly reduce your chance of success. A successful selection of an ERP system will incorporate all four dimensions: Fit, Platform, Implementer, and Cost.

**Chapter 4: How to Evaluate and Buy Business Application Software**   This chapter tells you how to go about actually buying the software and where to begin. It includes a breakdown of how to evaluate one's options and what to expect at the final stages of purchase.

**Chapter 5: Organizing Your Team for Success and Project Governance**   This chapter covers the importance of identifying leadership roles, project team roles, and determining how tasks are divided between you and your implementation partner.

**Chapter 6: Sprints and Tools Needed to Run Your Project**   This chapter tells you how to organize your project within a specific duration of time and how to keep you on track with goals and reviews.

**Chapter 7: Change Management Throughout Your Project**   This chapter helps you define change management, its importance in the "people" aspect, and how it affects the pace and project success.

**Chapter 8: Organizing Your Business by Processes**   This chapter outlines the 12 core process categories, including talking through business requirements and comparing "the old way" versus "the new way."

**Chapter 9: Independent Software Vendors—Filling Gaps and Managing Partnerships**   This chapter introduces you to Independent Software Vendors (ISVs) or add-on products and the role they play. Many successful projects include a third-party solution that specializes in a specific area and might fill a valuable niche.

**Chapter 10: Factors for a Successful Project Kickoff**   This chapter uncovers the necessary components you need to have in place to set your project kickoff on the right foot.

**Chapter 11: Designing the Software Collaboratively**   This chapter will demonstrate the powerful process of working collaboratively with your team and your implementing partner to configure the software with the best end results.

**Chapter 12: Requirements Gathering and Staying "In the Box"**   This chapter outlines the important role of requirements gathering and how that plays into taking advantage of processes that come native within the solution you are adopting.

**Chapter 13: Conference Room Pilots**   This chapter will explore conference room pilots for your team and the importance they play in the successful adoption of a new solution.

**Chapter 14: Dealing with Challenges Mid-Project**   This chapter tells you how to explore the inevitable situation of dealing with challenges that occur mid-project. No matter how much planning and preparation goes into a project, there are always unexpected situations that you will need to address.

**Chapter 15: Customizations vs. Configurations and How You Manage Them**   This chapter walks you through the difference between customizations and configurations, why there is a place for both, and how to choose which one is right for your business.

**Chapter 16: Data Migration—Early and Often**   This chapter explains why migrating data early and often is critical to a successful implementation project. You'll learn the steps for data migration, how to clean data, when to start migrating, and working with data migration tools.

**Chapter 17: Environment Management and Deployments**   This chapter covers why preparing the foundation your data and code will be moving to and planning the best way to get there is an integral component of a successful implementation.

**Chapter 18: Testing**   This chapter covers what you need to know about software testing: what is it, how to do it, and why you need it for a successful implementation.

**Chapter 19: Training for All**   This chapter outlines the training tips and guidance for everyone who will be using your system, focusing on the types of interactive sessions before training, the learning matrix, the different learning methods, and the importance of having a Learning Management System.

**Chapter 20: Going Live**   This chapter tells you how to prepare for all of the potential pitfalls of going live with your software system and to put you in a good position for a successful implementation.

**Chapter 21: Hypercare**   This chapter will cover what hypercare is, who the key players are for monitoring your system, and typical issues to look for.

**Chapter 22: Support and Enhance Your Project**   This chapter covers what the transition to support looks like, why you need a plan for it, and what you should expect for system maintenance and enhancements.

**Chapter 23: Bringing It All Together**   This chapter reviews, at a high level, all of the steps we've introduced to get your project live. You'll get an at-a-glance timeline, so you'll know when to do what during your implementation—that's often the hardest part of the overall project.

## How to Use This Book

I suggest that each reader start by reviewing the section "How the Book Is Organized" to get an overview of what's covered in the book. Most readers can start at the beginning and go through each of the chapters to learn the content. If at any time there's a question of when something happens during the implementation, you can jump to Chapter 23, "Bringing It All Together," in order to understand the chronological order of events. If you are a project owner, project manager, or executive, I suggest that you read the book from the beginning. Other roles can jump into the middle of book to find the chapter that best fits what they need to learn.

If you are in the middle of an implementation, you can certainly start the book on the chapter closest to where you are in your project. I suggest that you read backwards to see if there's anything that you should have done already. I also suggest that you read ahead from there to make sure that you stay ahead of the next steps on the implementation.

## How to Contact Wiley or the Author

Sybex strives to keep you supplied with the latest tools and information you need for your work. If you believe you have found an error in this book, and it is not listed on the book's web page, you can report the issue to Wiley customer support team at wileysupport.com.

You can email the author with your comments or questions at eric@stoneridgesoftware.com. You can also visit Eric's website at www.ericnewell.com.

# Chapter 1

# Stages of an Implementation Overview

Welcome to the challenging world of implementing business application software. It's not for the faint of heart, and there aren't many guides that show you how to get there. That's the goal of this book—to provide an actionable guide to implement Microsoft's Dynamics systems successfully.

This book is designed for anyone involved in an Enterprise Resource Planning (ERP) or Customer Relationship Management (CRM) implementation. The content is focused on Microsoft Dynamics, as that is what I have spent my career working on. This book can and should be read by anyone in an executive-level leadership position—the chief executive officer (CEO), chief information officer (CIO), and chief financial officer (CFO)—if you are considering implementing a new business application. Implementing a new business application is something that you will only do a few times during your working career, and there simply is a lack of reputable guides to support you.

**AFTER YOU COMPLETE THIS CHAPTER, YOU WILL BE ABLE TO DO THE FOLLOWING:**

- ◆ Define the Client Journey to complete a Microsoft Dynamics implementation
- ◆ Differentiate between three common implementation methodologies
- ◆ Recognize triple constraints and how they impact an implementation

## What Is Microsoft Dynamics?

*Microsoft Dynamics* is a set of business application software built by Microsoft and focused on Enterprise Resource Planning (ERP) and Customer Relationship Management (CRM). Microsoft sells Dynamics in several different flavors that are ever-changing. The cloud-based solution is called *Microsoft Dynamics 365*, and it includes a very broad set of functionalities across Sales, Customer Service, Human Resources, Finance, Supply Chain, Commerce, Project Service, Marketing, and Customer Data Management. You can see additional information about the product on Microsoft's website at dynamics.microsoft.com.

# The Client Journey

At Stoneridge Software, we developed what we call the *Client Journey*, which provides high-level stages to complete the implementation of Microsoft Dynamics. This takes you all the way from initial internal conversations, to meetings with potential vendors, to the enhancements you want to do after you've gone live on the software (see Figure 1.1).

**FIGURE 1.1**
The Client Journey

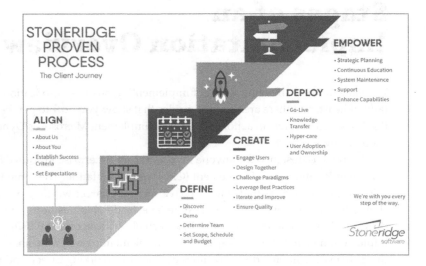

We'll break down the Client Journey in the chapters of this book. It all starts with gaining internal alignment and finding alignment with your chosen implementation partner. If you can do that, you're going to be ahead of most companies out there. The *Align stage* is focused on what you want to accomplish with the project.

Two chapters of the book are focused on the Align stage, starting with what to do before you begin a project and then a session on four keys to consider when buying an ERP or CRM solution. The goal of these two chapters is to get your team internally aligned and then provide you with an idea of what to be looking for in the best product for your company (see Figure 1.2).

**FIGURE 1.2**
The Align stage in the Client Journey

Once you have alignment internally and know the right type of implementation partner for you, you start on the *Define stage*. This is when you answer the (literally) million-dollar questions like what software are we going to buy? Who's going to be on the project? What does our budget look like? The Define stage takes you through the sales process and the pre-kickoff process of the implementation (see Figure 1.3).

**FIGURE 1.3**
The Define stage in the Client Journey

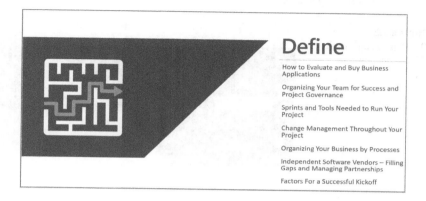

# Define

How to Evaluate and Buy Business Applications

Organizing Your Team for Success and Project Governance

Sprints and Tools Needed to Run Your Project

Change Management Throughout Your Project

Organizing Your Business by Processes

Independent Software Vendors – Filling Gaps and Managing Partnerships

Factors For a Successful Kickoff

Seven chapters in the book focus on the Define stage, starting with the sales process, where we cover discovery, demos, and contract negotiations; then we move into the steps that you need to start the project out right. From there, we dive into the project preparations starting with how you organize your team, to moving to the cadence with which you run the project, and then to change management. We outline how to break down the work by process area, how to evaluate third-party solutions, and finish up with the kickoff meeting.

The *Create stage* is where most of the action happens (see Figure 1.4). This begins after the kickoff meeting, and it takes you through the point where code is complete and you're ready to test and get the software out the door.

**FIGURE 1.4**
The Create stage in the Client Journey

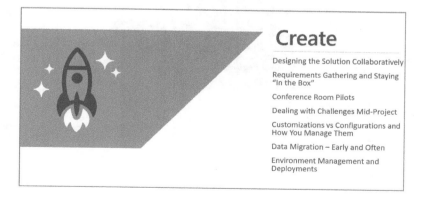

# Create

Designing the Solution Collaboratively

Requirements Gathering and Staying "In the Box"

Conference Room Pilots

Dealing with Challenges Mid-Project

Customizations vs Configurations and How You Manage Them

Data Migration – Early and Often

Environment Management and Deployments

Seven chapters in the book focus on the Create stage. There is a lot to get done during this part of the implementation. I outline how to sort through the processes to generate requirements and how to make those changes to the software while driving toward a cut-off point that allows you to get ready to go live.

The *Deploy stage* is when you take the software and process from the project team and roll it out to everyone (see Figure 1.5). It takes you through the testing, training, and go-live phases. The chapters in the Deploy stage include testing, training, going live, and the post go-live activity we call "hypercare."

**FIGURE 1.5**
The Deploy stage in the Client Journey

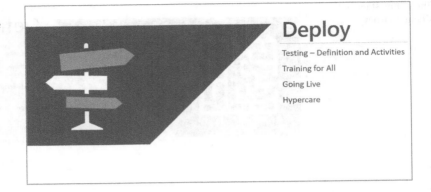

The *Empower stage* is where you find your rhythm for future advances to the solution and look for opportunities to continue receiving additional value from your solution. There is just one chapter in the book on this stage, and we discuss the various paths that companies pursue and the activities with which you want to be consistent after a successful go-live (see Figure 1.6).

**FIGURE 1.6**
The Empower stage in the Client Journey

# Implementation Methodologies

Three common implementation methodologies are used across all different types of IT projects: Waterfall, Agile, and Scrum. Scrum is a variant of Agile, so we'll talk about those two collectively. The methodologies are discussed to provide general knowledge and background information, as they are commonly known in the IT world. What I recommend is a hybrid of these implementation methodologies, which we'll cover as we get further into the book.

## Waterfall and Sure Step

Let's start with the oldest and most common methodology used in business application implementations—the *Waterfall methodology*. Born in the late 1950s, this was the first known implementation methodology and became more commonly known and implemented after 1985. The Waterfall methodology is a step-by-step methodology that tries to keep all of the activities in linear order from start to finish. You start with the Analysis phase, finish all of its elements, and then you move on to the Design phase. You then do all of the Design phase work and then move forward to the Development phase, and so on. In the Waterfall methodology, you are not supposed to work ahead and take on a future task outside of your current phase. The Waterfall methodology is a good fit for an ERP implementation because, in many ways, you do need to work through things in chronological order. You need to define your account structure, customer structure, your products, and other master data that you want to be able to set up early on in a project.

In the decade of the 2000s, Microsoft suggested that all Dynamics implementations follow its *Sure Step Methodology*, which was a Waterfall-based solution (see Figure 1.7).

As you can see, it starts with the Diagnostic phase and then moves to the Analysis phase, the Design phase, the Development phase, the Deployment phase, and finally the Operation phase.

In my days at Microsoft, I learned and used this methodology quite a bit, and it contributed to many of the documents in the Optimization section, as my team was focused on project governance, health checks, and workshops. Partners and Microsoft Consulting Services were directed (but not mandated) to use this methodology, so you saw a lot of adoption, especially in the 2007–2011 time frame.

During that time, a shift started to occur. It began with the Microsoft Consulting organization, as they realized that they needed an implementation that was more flexible than the rigid Waterfall approach. Microsoft started implementing some of the Agile concepts into the classic Waterfall approach, and that is when I realized that there was a better way. Microsoft stopped actively recommending Sure Step and stopped any further development on the methodology. The latest version dates back to 2010, so you can certainly review that information with the knowledge that the content is quite dated.

Customers and partners can find additional resources on Microsoft's CustomerSource site (mbs.microsoft.com/customersource/northamerica). Tons of document templates are available that can prove valuable on projects. You can certainly mine for treasure in the database without following it step-by-step.

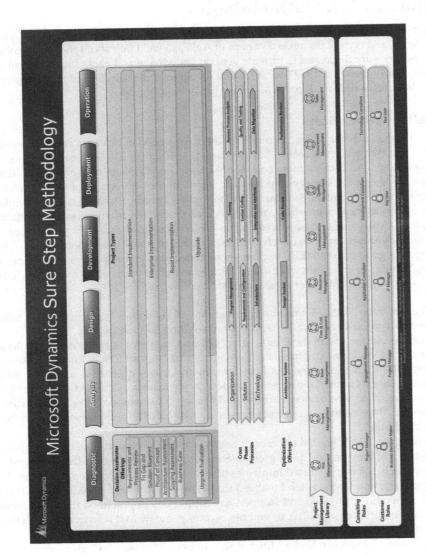

**FIGURE 1.7**
Microsoft Dynamics
Sure Step Methodology

## Agile and Scrum

The *Agile methodology* was born from a meeting in 2001 between 17 IT professionals who felt that there was a better way than the stagnant Waterfall methodology. They wrote the *Agile Manifesto*, which includes 12 principles for developing software efficiently and effectively. The manifesto has four parts (see Figure 1.8):

◆ Individuals and interactions over processes and tools

◆ Working software over comprehensive documentation

◆ Customer collaboration over contract negotiation

◆ Responding to change over following a plan

**FIGURE 1.8**

Four parts of the
Agile Manifesto

| Individuals & Interactions | Working Software | Customer Collaboration | Responding to Change |
|---|---|---|---|
| • Communication is a key reason for project's success<br>• People build software products<br>• Teams self-organize<br>• Motivate individuals and foster interactions among team members, customers, stakeholders. High-context interactions<br>• Focus on people – they are the ultimate source of energy | • Primary goal is to create and deliver value. Satisfy/delight customer<br>• Deliver frequently to give business advantage to the customer<br>• Create documentation that adds value<br>• Customer value/priority focus | • Be flexible and cooperative on customer's Dynamics needs<br>• Work with the customer to deliver the intent of the contract<br>• Closely collaborate & follow customer's product vision<br>• Have flexible contracting models. Maintain relationships | • Change is a reality; reality is the worst enemy of a plan<br>• Changes in customer's business environment impact our plans<br>• Embrace change by adaptive planning. Reflect & improve |

The Agile methodology is the opposite of the Waterfall methodology. It's designed to get software designed, developed, tested, and released quickly. This is great for web development or incremental development on top of a core platform, but it doesn't perfectly fit an ERP or CRM implementation because some components need to be done in a certain order.

The *Scrum methodology* takes the Agile Manifesto and puts it into action. Many great concepts are included in Scrum that help any type of implementation. We'll get into greater detail in Chapter 6, "Sprints and Tools Needed to Run Your Project," but a *sprint* is a Scrum tenet that breaks activity into a two- or four-week cycle that you use to plan out your work. This allows you to manage a product backlog, which is everything you need to do on a project. From this product backlog, you assign activities to each sprint and that becomes your *sprint backlog*. The backlog provides a good idea of how much should be accomplished during a two-week period, and it creates urgency and accountability on a regular interval instead of everyone staying up all night for two weeks straight to get ready for a go-live.

I really like how sprint planning provides the ability to break the project into pieces that can be understood and managed. When you are estimating software development time, you never want someone to say 800 hours because this means that they have no idea how long it will take. If you say "there are several different components of the project, some I estimate at 8 hours, others I estimate at 40 hours, and collectively it comes to 800 hours," I will believe you because you've taken the time to break it into great detail. In an ERP or CRM implementation that is going to take a year, you have to get a better breakdown of the work to know if your projected timeline is anywhere close to being accurate.

## Triple Constraints

One final concept that I want to establish early is this idea of *triple constraints*. To understand this concept, you need to think about a triangle where the three sides are cost, scope, and time. Quality is in the middle, and it is impacted if you shortcut any of the other sides (see Figure 1.9).

**FIGURE 1.9**
Triple con-
straints concept

The way the triple constraints concept works is that you want to find an equal balance between scope, cost, and time. At that equilibrium point, the project quality will be good. If you decide to add to the scope of the project, you have to add cost and time to the project as well to maintain quality. If you decide to decrease time (you want the project done faster), then you have to decrease scope (and cost) to achieve your objective without compromising quality. If one side of the triangle expands, at least one of the other two sides must also expand, but not necessarily both. Another way to look at it is once two sides of the triangle are set, the other side is locked in. Once you have settled on scope and budget, your timeline is something that could be calculated as seen in Figure 1.10.

**FIGURE 1.10**
Triple constraints with
decreased cost

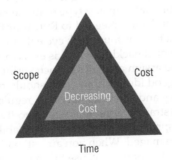

Figure 1.10 shows how the triangle starts in equilibrium. You have a reasonable scope for budget (cost) and time to implement the project. Hopefully, all projects start that way. In Figure 1.10, you decrease cost, and, in that case, you have to decrease time (because consultants will continually bill during the time) and then you're going to sacrifice either scope or quality. If you decrease scope, you can preserve quality, but the amount of benefit you get from the project

is less. If you maintain scope, you are basically saying that you're not going to test the solution thoroughly, or you're not going to train people and you're going to hope for the best once it goes live. You are increasing the odds that the project would result in a disaster.

Figure 1.11 shows a larger triangle. This is the scenario where you increase scope and therefore increase time and cost. Again, if you try to increase scope without increasing time and cost, you're diminishing training and testing and increasing the odds that the go-live could be a disaster.

**FIGURE 1.11**
Triple constraints with increased scope

## The Bottom Line

**Organizing your project in sprints**   One of the key elements of the Agile and Scrum implementation methodologies is the concept of using a sprint to create interim deadlines within a project to make sure that you can deliver the full project on time.

**Master It**   What is the first thing you do during a new sprint?

1. Run a retrospective

2. Do a planning session

3. Do a review session

4. Outline the following sprints

**Waterfall methodology**   The Waterfall methodology is the classic way to execute on an ERP or CRM implementation, but I recommend that you use a hybrid of the Waterfall and Agile methodologies for your project.

**Master It**   What is a part of the Waterfall methodology?

1. The implementation is done in a step-by-step process

2. Sprints are used

3. New requirements are placed in the backlog

4. The Create phase

**Sure Step** Microsoft put together a methodology in the early 2000s called "Sure Step," which was widely adopted for Dynamics implementations during the 2000–2015 period.

**Master It** Microsoft Sure Step follows which methodology?

1. Agile

2. Scrum

3. Client Journey

4. Waterfall

**Challenging projects** ERP and CRM implementations are challenging projects that often go over time and over budget. The goal of this book is to prepare you better for a project so that you can complete it on time and within the budget.

**Master It** What percentage of implementation projects go over budget?

1. 100 percent

2. 60 percent

3. 40 percent

4. 20 percent

**Triple constraints** The triple constraints diagram is a triangle that represents a common concept in project management which shows how a change in one of the sides of the triangle affects the other two sides.

**Master It** Which of the following is not part of the triple constraints of project management?

1. Cost

2. Scope

3. Sprint

4. Time

# Chapter 2

# What to Do Before You Begin a Project

I could use lots of quotes before beginning a project: "Failing to plan means planning to fail" or "You'll never have to recover from a fast start" are two that come immediately to mind. You'll hear me repeat this over and over again throughout this book—the earlier you think about the steps of the project and prepare for them, the better off you will be. This starts way back at the beginning, even before you've committed to do an ERP or CRM implementation. If you can home in on what you want to do and who's going to do it, you can get work done before the project starts, and this can save you a considerable amount of money in the long-term.

This chapter is squarely in the Align stage, as you align your leadership and project team before you seek out an implementation partner. Smart companies take the time to get on the same page before the project begins. I have rarely seen a company execute a pre-implementation project that puts them in a better position to succeed with their implementation . . . but you can be the exception to the rule.

**AFTER YOU COMPLETE THIS CHAPTER, YOU WILL BE ABLE TO DO THE FOLLOWING:**

- Identify your project team and stakeholders
- Identify your processes in scope
- Clean up your data
- Define your success metrics
- Build your business case and secure funding

## Identify Your Project Team and Stakeholders

Let's start by figuring out who from the company is going to lead the project and who will be serving on the team. If you figure this out ahead of time, you can have this team play a big role in the selection of the business application platform. This makes for a more effective transition as you start working on the project. Several roles are outlined, as shown in Figure 2.1; however, not all implementations require each role. Let's discuss each role and figure out which ones fit for your size company and the complexity of your project.

**FIGURE 2.1**
Implementation
core roles

## Executive Sponsor

The *executive sponsor* is the person who takes overall accountability for the project. The executive sponsor reports on the progress of the project to the CEO. As it relates to the project, the executive sponsor spends their time managing project resources and communicating updates to leadership and the company as a whole. The *project owner* reports to the executive sponsor for the purposes of the project. (The owner doesn't have to report to the executive sponsor on the organization chart.) The executive sponsor doesn't work on the project 40 hours a week, or code anything. The executive sponsor's job is to put the right team in place, manage the executive relationship with the implementation partner, and remove blockers for the team.

In a small company, the executive sponsor should be the CEO. The CEO is the one ultimately responsible for the success of the project and needs to answer to the board on its progress. In a large company, the executive sponsor can be someone on the company's leadership team, oftentimes the CIO. My preference would be the Chief Operating Officer (COO) or the VP of sales and marketing—the actual business owner for where the digital transformation is going to take place. You can rely on the CIO to be a business partner on the project, but it's really the COO who is most affected by the process change that comes with the project, so they should be leading it.

## Project Owner

The *project owner* is the most important role to fill on the project, and I find it fascinating that most projects don't have someone in this role. Many projects have a project manager, an executive sponsor, a core team, and IT resources, but they don't have anyone holding it all together and making decisions to keep the project moving. Having one central, authoritative resource running the project is the best way to be successful.

The project owner should have no greater responsibility than the project. This person should be flexible and understand the business, IT, and either has experience on previous implementation projects or has prepared well for this assignment. If you have full-time resources on the core team, those resources should report to the project owner. The project owner should participate in all of the key meetings on the project from the executive meetings to the planning meetings.

It is possible for the project owner and project manager to be the same person; however, I prefer the project owner to be a decision maker, whereas a project manager should be a decision framer. In a small company, you may have to fill the project owner and project manager role with one person.

## Business Process Owner(s)

The purpose of the *business process owner* is to understand and approve any business process changes that affect their area. For example, if you are going from not having purchase orders to mandating purchase orders, the business process owner's responsibility for purchasing should be leading the charge to make that change.

You will need a business process owner for each area of the company that will be affected as part of this project. In large organizations, you may end up with 10 different business process owners if you need to have them weigh in on their area of expertise. If you are implementing an ERP system, you are going to need a business process owner from finance, one or more from operations, and potentially one from sales. For a CRM system, you will need a business process owner from Sales and one from marketing if those are the business areas in the scope of the project.

In small companies, these positions will be filled by your leadership team members who head each division. In large companies, you may have many different business process owners. The fewer owners the better, but each owner has to have knowledge of the details of how things are doing within their division to know if the suggested changes in business process will affect the business in a positive or negative way.

Unfortunately, what happens in most projects is that the business process owners are not involved in the project. They designate a lower-level person to participate in the project and don't weigh in on important decisions on the project. That's a big mistake and a big reason why ERP and CRM projects don't result in the transformation they could achieve. If you are leading an organization going through an implementation, make sure that your department heads are involved in decisions that affect their departments.

## Project Manager

I will describe two different skillsets for a *project manager*. The type of skillset you bring to the project could affect other roles on the project. A *principal project manager* or *senior project manager* is typically a *project management professional (PMP)*-certified resource who has completed ERP or CRM projects before, knows the order of operation, and has the respect of other project team members (pmi.org/certifications/project-management-pmp). A *project coordinator* is a resource who schedules meetings, takes notes, and sends out status reports. The senior project manager needs to do the project coordinator work, too, but the project coordinator typically doesn't lead meetings, report to the executive committee, and update projects schedules as a senior project manager would.

Either on the implementation partner side or on the internal company side, you need to have a senior project manager who can take you through the steps of the implementation in the right order, provide status on the project, manage the budget, manage the risks, and escalate personnel issues. If your implementation partner brings that to the table, the internal project manager needs to serve in the project coordinator role and escalate personnel issues on the company side. Regardless of how good the partner's project manager is, they will not be able to hold company team members accountable, so you will need the project coordinator or project owner to fill that role.

It's very rare to find a senior project manager at a company. If you don't have one, I would recommend either hiring one (full-time or an independent contractor) or appointing a project coordinator and mandating that the implementation partner provide the senior project manager resource.

## Core Team and a Core Team Lead

For the purposes of an ERP or CRM implementation, the *core team* is a set of people assigned to the implementation project from the business areas affected by the project. On a manufacturing implementation, this may be someone from production, someone from purchasing, and someone from distribution. This core team member or lead is going to be heavily involved in the project and will serve as the business analyst for their focus area. They will be invited to every meeting in their area of expertise, collaborate with the functional consultant on the design, test the system, train the users, and serve as the "power user" once the system goes live so that their team members have a colleague to help them.

Core team members should be experienced people within the company, but equally important, they should have interest in process improvement and an understanding of how software can make their lives easier. If they know the business really well but want to keep doing things the way they've always done them, they will be a problem when it comes to the project. If you can find a senior, open-minded, technology-friendly individual, you can teach them what they need to do in the system.

You should have one designated core team member from each area of the business that will experience change. Their involvement could be anywhere from a few hours to full-time depending on the size of the organization and the impact on their business area.

## Subject Matter Experts

A *subject matter expert (SME)*, as it relates to an ERP or CRM project, is a resource who performs a function in the business and knows that function well. Pretty much everyone in your organization is a subject matter expert at something, so you will have many team members to choose from for this particular role. Subject matter experts don't need to attend every meeting on the project, but they should be invited to meetings to talk about business process change in their area of expertise. That's when they should be called on to provide their perspective of the suggested change with the caveat to be open-minded to change. They will also be involved in the conference room pilot, user acceptance testing, and training portion of the project, so they can validate that the system will meet the needs of the business.

Subject matter experts don't need to be full-time on the project; they just need to be brought into meetings when their area is under review and when you get to testing and training with the system.

## IT Resources

IT teams seem to be like snowflakes—no two are alike. Some companies don't have IT teams; others have one jack-of-all-trades resource, some have a handful, and Fortune 500 companies have armies of IT resources. Given that this is a software implementation project, you would think that you need to have IT resources. If you think about this as a cloud/SaaS solution, you might think, "I have no servers, so I don't need IT." The fact of the matter is that you can accomplish the project with zero or 300 people on your IT team. If you have zero IT team members, you'll need to ask for more help from your implementation partner.

### IT Operations

Let's discuss IT Operations team members first. They are the resources who typically work on servers, laptops, and networks. In the pre-cloud days, they would be the ones provisioning servers and installing software on servers and clients. In today's cloud-based world, you don't need to do that anymore; however, you still have multiple environments to manage. Environments are easier to manage, but they still need someone knowledgeable and accountable for them. As we'll talk about in Chapter 17, "Environment Management and Deployments," you need to move code from development to testing to user acceptance testing (UAT) to a production environment, and this is a great place to train your IT Operations team on how that works. You also want to get your IT Operations team engaged in performance and security.

### IT Applications

IT Applications team members could fit into multiple different roles: business analyst (BA), project manager (PM), developer, quality assurance (QA), and business intelligence (BI) specialist. I'll discuss the roles other than project manager in the next sections.

### Business Analyst

A *business analyst (BA)* is a resource whose job it is to translate business requirements into system requirements. The BA should sit in the IT organization but serve as a liaison to one or more divisions within the business. For example, in a manufacturing and distribution business, you may have a BA who focuses on supply chain and one who focuses on finance and sales/marketing. The BA should attend leadership meetings in each of these divisions, so that they understand where the business is going and bring needs back to IT.

For the implementation project, a business analyst can serve as a core team member and help the business resources and implementation consultants translate those business requirements into software design more quickly. They also play a big role in testing, training, and providing user support post going live.

### Developer

If you have experienced developers who are familiar with Microsoft's Visual Studio and .NET programming languages, you may have someone who can help develop customizations for the implementation projects. Each of the Dynamics 365 programming languages will require some ramp-up time before the resource can be proficient at it. If you have developers interested, I'd recommend that you coordinate training with your implementation partner and start assigning work to your developer. Don't set your expectations too high on what they can get done when they are first exposed to the programming languages. Start small, see how comfortable they are with the technology, and then you can set clear expectations for what they can deliver.

## QUALITY ASSURANCE/TESTER

You generally have to have a larger IT organization to have a resource dedicated to *quality assurance (QA)* or testing. A QA resource would be charged with developing test strategies and plans for any custom code that is developed and then executing the tests to make sure that the code that goes out works without major issues.

As there is a lot of testing work that needs to be completed on an ERP or CRM project, this resource is key to help define your testing strategy and coordinate the testing activity of the core team leads, subject matter experts, and anyone else you can get to lend a hand.

## BUSINESS INTELLIGENCE LEAD

Most small IT organizations do not have a team member focused on *business intelligence (BI)*, but given the importance of this role to the executive team, more and more organizations are looking to add one to the team. The *business intelligence lead* is responsible for gathering requirements for and delivering on the key reports that you need to run your business. These may be dashboards, Excel spreadsheets, printed reports, Microsoft Power BI, mobile views, or whatever the best platform is to see this information.

As you go into your implementation project, all of your existing reports will need to be touched. Either you'll need to use or customize the reports from the new system or you'll need to change the data source on your current reports to point to the new system. Engaging this resource early in the project will help put you in a better position to get the value you desire from the new system.

---

### SETTING EXPECTATIONS WITH PROJECT RESOURCES

As you build the team to help you succeed in your implementation project, it is best if you set clear and defined expectations up front, such as how much time they'll need to put into the project, how they will handle ambiguity throughout the project, and the perseverance they'll need to make it through a difficult project.

First, many of these resources will need to work on the project in addition to some portion of their primary responsibilities. When you're on an implementation project, overtime hours are expected. They can be avoided with effective project management, but that's the exception to the rule. In addition to all of the meetings and sessions that consume your project team's day, they will need to take the time to learn and test the new system. It's just not something that most people pick up quickly enough to do during the day.

Ambiguity causes stress, and this falls on leadership to prioritize staffing the project team with folks who can handle stress and roll with a certain level of ambiguity. At some point during the project, you will learn a feature that you need to have is either super difficult or impossible to do. When that happens, you will need to apply creativity and patience to fix the problem. Many team members will want to throw up their hands when the problem arises. Similarly, toward the end of the project, there will be a bug in an important part of the system that will be really difficult to solve (fixing it will take a lot longer than expected), and you will start to think that the system is not going to work for you. You need a project team that is willing to take a punch and get back up and fight for the good of the business.

This project is going to challenge everyone on it. In fact, I would be surprised if your team members do not regret signing up for the project at some point along the way. As I mentioned earlier, perseverance is a job requirement for a business application implementation. In this case, it makes the company considerably better as well.

## Time Commitment by Role

The amount of time commitment by role can vary wildly based on the size of the company and the size of the project, but I've included a time commitment chart in Table 2.1. If the project is for a $500M company, you are likely going to have several resources dedicated full time. If it is a small CRM project that will be used by only five people, you will not need a team member to be dedicated full time. Take this scale and adjust it to the size and complexity of your project. It becomes very evident during the project if you have the wrong project team, so set yourself up for success by building the right team structure and outlining clear expectations for the team on the project.

**TABLE 2.1:**     Time Commitment by Role

| ROLE | REQUIRED | PERCENTAGE OF TIME REQUIRED |
|---|---|---|
| Executive Sponsor | Yes | 10 percent |
| Project Owner | Yes | 50–100 percent |
| Business Process Owners | Yes | 10 percent |
| Project Manager | Yes | 50–100 percent |
| Core Team Lead | Yes | 50–100 percent |
| Subject Matter Experts | Yes | 10–25 percent |
| IT Operations | Yes | 10 percent |
| IT Applications | Yes | 10–50 percent |
| Developers | No | 0 percent |
| Business Intelligence Resources | No | 0 percent |
| Business Analyst | No | 0 percent |
| Quality Assurance | No | 0 percent |

# Identify Your Processes in Scope

As you begin a project, companies often want to reduce the number of systems that they use to as few as possible. They see a new CRM or ERP product and think, "this can do everything for my business." That may be possible; however, you have a couple things to consider. First, you're better off tackling a smaller project first so that you can get through it, figure out how to work effectively on a project, and get a win. Second, no system is the best-of-breed tool at everything that your company does today, so you want to go into a project with an idea of your biggest need. Concentrate on addressing that. For a project to be successful, you need to have a solid idea of the scope as you go into it.

This problem has many solutions, but I'd like to recommend what I find works best. As much as companies say that they are unique and no one does the same thing they do, it's not true. Every company has its nuances, but at the end of the day every company does similar things:

◆ All companies have income statements

◆ All companies collect money from customers

◆ All companies have to send invoices or have a point-of-sale system

◆ All companies have to pay vendors (whether they want to or not)

◆ All companies have something they classify as operations; they may manufacture a product, distribute or resell a product, provide some consulting, or provide hospitality services

◆ All companies pay their employees

◆ All companies have to deliver customer service through some mechanism

These are *core processes* that are consistent across businesses. In fact, there is an organization called the American Process & Quality Center (apqc.org) that has drafted a set of standard processes that can be used by all businesses in all industries. Stoneridge Software has taken those standard processes and built our *Process Catalog*, which contains 13 high-level process areas that we call *Process Categories*, then *Process Groups* a level down, and *Process and Sub-processes* below that.

When narrowing down scope on an implementation, we recommend that you start with these core 12 Process Categories to determine which of these areas are in scope:

◆ Acquire to Retire

◆ Financial Plan to Report

◆ Hire to Retire

◆ Idea to Product

◆ Issue to Resolution

◆ Market to Opportunity

◆ Plan to Inventory

◆ Procure to Pay

- Project to Profit

- Quote to Cash

- Schedule to Produce

- Service Call to Profit

I'll dive into these in greater detail in Chapter 8, "Organizing by Processes." At this stage of the project, you will want to figure out which of these high-level categories are in scope and then start documenting scenarios that occur in your business under these categories.

---

### BUSINESS SCENARIOS

A *business scenario* is a process that occurs in your business today, an example being when you run out of boxes, you order more boxes. This has many more components: How do you know when you're about to run out of boxes, at what threshold should you order more, do you have to issue a purchase order for the additional boxes, who approves the order, who do you order from, what's your lead time, and how do you get them from the arrival location to where you use them on the floor? If you can document all of those steps, it helps to figure out how the new software handles each step in that journey.

The key to useful scenarios is to leave any systems out of the equation. Your implementation partner doesn't need to know how you do it in your current system—they need to know what the steps are, and which actors (roles, people) are involved in the process.

It may be a tall ask to document all of your business scenarios before you even start a project, but my philosophy is that you are going to have to do it anyway, so why not do it right away? If you have these documented before a demo, you can ask the software vendors to walk you through the process to confirm that it will work for your company.

---

## Clean Up Your Data

The biggest, unwelcome surprise that you will get after you go live is a problem that stems from bad data. The concept of "garbage in, garbage out" applies well to data on a business application project. If you build the world's greatest system with duplicate data and no standards for naming conventions, you don't have a good system. No system is smart enough to intelligently clean your data if it's a mess going into the project. Just like the business scenarios described, you're going to have to clean your data at some point during the project. You might as well start early.

I recommend the following steps to get your data in the best shape going into your implementation project.

### Identify Your "Master" Data

*Master data* (as I'll discuss in more detail later) is your system of record for a particular type of data. For example, your HR system is probably your system of record for your employees. If your employee's full name is Robert Johnson, he may be called Bob Johnson in one system and

Bobby Johnson in another. You need to have one system of record that knows that you want him represented as Robert Johnson in your new system.

You will want to identify those systems that you are currently using to manage that master data. Those systems will be the sources that you tap for the data migration activity on a project. You don't have to go through all of your systems that have an employee name in them if you're going to import it from one system.

## Develop Naming Conventions

I live in Minnesota, and when I go to different systems, I have different ways of telling someone I'm from Minnesota. In most systems, I select "Minnesota" from a drop-down box; sometimes I select "MN," or sometimes it's derived from filling in my ZIP code. In some more rudimentary systems, however, I have to type the name of my state. I usually try to figure out what I should type by the size of the text box I use to enter the data—if it's small, I type "MN" and if it's large I type out "Minnesota." With an open text box, users can type whatever they want. Maybe they misspelled it and typed "Minessota."

One little thing that you can do to try to prevent chaos in text boxes is to tell everyone in your company, "When you need to fill in a state, type the two-character abbreviation, such as MN." This won't prevent all data problems, but it might help to reduce the problem.

Naming conventions can be even more important in areas like product or item names. I bet that you work with systems where there are different names for the same thing. Try your best to label these things the same in separate systems in order to reduce confusion and make it easier to tie the systems together.

## Identify System Owners

Find an owner who is knowledgeable about these master data systems and ask them to take on the challenge of cleaning up the data in that system. I had a client who had 70 different names for one customer in their previous system. As you can imagine, that would be a significant problem. There is bound to be someone in your company who knows what the right name should be. That person should be given the authority and access to combine all of those accounts in your current system, so that the data migration flows easily into your new system.

## Find and Resolve Duplicates and Incorrect Data

Once you have the system owner and a good naming convention, you need to start the tedious task of finding and eliminating duplicates and bad data. As mentioned, if you have 70 different names for one customer in your system, you will have a big problem when it comes to data migration. To find all their records, you may need to generate reports to show you a list of customers to review and see if similar names are actually the same customer. Similarly, if you're looking for bad data, the best thing to do is to run a series of reports from different systems and compare the results. If your customer balance in one system is $1,234 and it's $2,134 in another system, you probably have a $900 record that is either missing from the system or unapplied.

Some computer tools are available that might help you find these duplicates or bad data. If you can find something or someone who can help, it's better to do that before the project fully kicks off rather than wait to discover this problem when the project is in full flight.

**DRAFT YOUR SOFTWARE EVALUATION TEAM**

When you're looking to find the right software for your company, you're looking for software that fits your business, a platform that fits your environment and suits your future plans, an implementation partner who will be effective and trustworthy, and a cost that you can swallow without skimping. To figure the best team to evaluate these four criteria you should think about who on your team can best evaluate each area.

With that in mind, you're going to want your business representatives to help you evaluate the fit. If you're about to embark on a CRM project, you'll want sales, marketing, and customer service reps involved in the definition of fit. For the platform, get the perspective of your IT team. For the implementation partner, you may look to an independent party or perhaps your project manager can look at the potential partner's implementation methodology and track record to determine if they are right for you. Regarding cost, focus on your return and the guideline of spending between 3 and 7 percent of your annual revenues on the project. If the project is going to cost 10 percent of your annual revenues, that's too much. If it's going to cost 0.5 percent, you're skimping and not going to get what you're expecting. Your CFO/Finance team should provide suggestions and help you determine if you're getting a price that fits what you can spend.

In addition to these specialists, you'll want to look at your project team and get them involved with the selection process. They are the ones who will work closely with the implementation partner for the next several months, and you want to make sure that the teams will be able to work together effectively.

# Define Your Success Metrics

What does success look like on your project? I'm sure you'd say something like, "We want the project to give us all the features we want" and "We want it done on time and on budget." Those are good goals, no doubt, but those are assumed. Every project team wants to get the functionality they need and get it done within the budget. The success metrics should be deeper and broader than that. They should be as follows:

**Measurable**   Something you can point to in time, dollars, or quantity. For example, "We want to remove all negative inventory and for our inventory to balance every month." You can measure whether you've achieved that.

**Aligned with organizational goals**   Whatever your goals are as a business, your implementation project should support those goals. If you want to grow from $100M to $500M, you need a scalable system. This goal will make the application's performance more important than it was if you were a smaller company.

**Achievable**   More than anything, you want this project to be a victory for the team and proof that your team can create additional value for the business. You want your metrics to be something that you can achieve in a defined period of time.

As you put together these success metrics, you may also want to cite particular pain points—where they are now and where they should be once the project is finished. If your systems are disconnected today and the new system will bring an integration that you don't have today, that's a major plus for the new system. As I mention in Chapter 14, "Dealing with Challenges Mid-Project," the project will have challenges, so it's important to focus on the benefits of the system when things are looking bleak later in the project.

## Possible Benefits

If you're struggling to think about the potential benefits of an ERP or CRM project, I'll give you some ideas. Benefits can be both tangible and intangible, as shown in Figure 2.2.

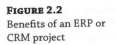

**FIGURE 2.2**

Benefits of an ERP or CRM project

Figure 2.2 outlines several benefits; however, not all implementations will achieve value in each area. Let's discuss them and figure out which ones fit for your size company and the complexity of your project.

**Software costs vs. today's costs**   It could be that you have Oracle or SAP today and you are paying $200,000 a year in maintenance. We've seen several cases where the cost of maintenance of Microsoft Dynamics 365 is significantly less than the annual maintenance cost of some of the most expensive software vendors.

**IT staff or managed service providers required to run the current system**   We've seen several clients who are on old versions of software where they can't receive commercial support any longer, and their IT support team is nearing retirement. One other alternative that can fit into this mix is when you're trying to save money and cut IT or managed services provider spend. It's another option to move to the cloud and reduce the need for your IT staff.

**Reducing inventory and materials cost**   Many companies look to a new ERP system to manage the cost side of their products better. Using a modern ERP system can keep you from over-ordering (because you have a better idea of what you have and what you need) and better visibility to your margins, so that you can potentially substitute materials to lower your product cost.

**Reducing labor costs**   Another big issue for manufacturers is understanding how much time it takes to produce an item. This is often not tracked in the current system.

**Improved production**   In a modern ERP, you can build a work plan that gives you better visibility on when you can be done with production based on the inputs and labor required to make the pieces.

**Reduction in customer service calls**   In a new CRM system, you can evaluate patterns for service calls coming in so that you can create knowledge base articles that deflect future service calls. You could also use the portal functionality to share information to your clients without needing to take a service call.

**Increased efficiency in activities**   With a CRM system, you have visibility to all other activity with your clients. This allows you to view the conversations others have had and share activities with other members of your team. Many clients have asked their sales team to fill out "activity reports" of every visit they made to a client and what happened during the visit.

**Legal and regulatory compliance**   If you are a public company, for example, you need to have Sarbanes-Oxley controls in place, which include segregation of duties security changes that you may not be able to make in your current system.

**Improved accounting controls and month's end**   If you are running a different system for your warehouse than your financial system, you may end up making many general ledger journal entries at the end of each month to represent your financials accurately. This causes many potential problems, one being that your sub-ledger and ledger might not tie out. It's more work for you to do each month.

**Better information to make decisions for the business**   Chances are that your old system doesn't have much in the way of dashboards, and if your data is not in good shape, any reports that you have are unlikely to be accurate. The Microsoft Dynamics 365 system offers a ton of different reports out of the box.

Success metrics are also a very important input for the project in the next section, "Building Your Business Case and Securing Funding."

# Building Your Business Case and Securing Funding

If you've made it this far through the preparation steps, congratulations! You are setting yourself up to be in a good position for the overall project. But all that work is for naught if the project isn't approved to go forward. So, how do you build a business case for this project?

In the previous section, "Defining Your Success Metrics," we talked about the potential project benefits. During this step, you want to try to quantify the value generated from those benefits as best you can. You wouldn't be able to put a dollar amount to an intangible benefit, but you should be able to put a value in dollars to some of your tangible benefits. If you can reduce the cost of your inventory, for example, that would be a project benefit that helps you identify your return on investment from this project.

## How Much Should an ERP Project Cost?

It is amazing to me how little information exists on the Internet about the cost of an ERP or CRM project. What little information does exist comes in some of the annual ERP reports. These reports poll several companies to see how much they have spent over the years on their projects, including all of the internal and external costs that go into a project. It shows that companies typically spend anywhere from 3–7 percent of their annual revenue on a project. The range tends to be closer to 3 percent for larger companies, around 5 percent for most companies, and closer to 7 percent for smaller companies with complex system needs. This means that if you are a company that has annual revenues of $100M, you should be spending about $5M on an ERP implementation.

Most people's reaction to this is: "That's way too much. There is no way it makes sense to spend $5M on a software project." To that I would say, it's not a software project—it's a business transformation. In an ERP project for an enterprise, you will change nearly all of your processes; it will affect nearly everyone in the company, and you will be on this platform for 10+ years. It is a big investment with a big long-term benefit.

## Costs to Include in Your Calculations

Let's talk through each of the major costs associated with an implementation project.

**Software subscription costs**   You will need to acquire a subscription to the software for any of the Microsoft Dynamics 365 solutions. To calculate the costs, you multiply the number of monthly users by the monthly subscription price. If you anticipate more users over time, you will need to budget for additional subscription costs. The positive thing about buying software through a subscription is that you can decrease costs if you have fewer users over time.

**Add-on or ISV licenses**   In Chapter 9, "Independent Software Vendors—Filling Gaps and Managing Partnerships," we'll talk about *Independent Software Vendors (ISVs)* and how they often fill an important gap on an ERP or CRM project. If you require an additional product, you will have to pay a subscription or perpetual license fee for that product, which you'll need to factor into your overall project costs.

**Hardware**   "Wait a minute, I'm implementing cloud software, why do I need to buy hardware?" You might not need to buy hardware, but it's been my experience that you often need to upgrade your network hardware to support more traffic over your routers, switchers, and wireless devices. Depending on the product that you implement, you may also want to buy a server to host virtual machines running instances of the product for your developers. Don't assume that you won't have hardware costs. If you don't have any, that's great.

**Implementation consulting**   This will be your biggest expense on the project—the consulting fees charged by your implementation partner. In Chapter 5, "Organizing Your Team for Success and Project Governance," we'll talk more about the different roles that the implementation partner will fill on the project. You have to have an implementation partner. I've seen a few cases where companies have tried to implement on their own and it does not work. The key is to find a true "partner"—someone who cares about the success of the project, puts capable people on the project, and manages their resources wisely so that you're not spending consulting dollars for no value.

**Internal team costs**   You have several roles to fill on this project, and many roles that should be filled by internal team members. For your internal, salaried team members, you would take someone who makes $80,000 a year and allocate their salary plus benefits to the project at the percentage of time that they are dedicated to the project. You wouldn't assign 3 percent of the CEO's salary to the project if that's the amount of time they spent on the project; you would focus on people specifically allocated to the project.

**Subcontractors**   You may have to bring in outside resources to complement your internal resources on the project. Oftentimes, you may not have a qualified project manager in your organization, so you would want to contract with a firm outside of your implementation partner for that resource.

**Travel and expense costs**   You are going to want face-to-face meetings and training as part of the implementation, so you'll need to allocate costs to bringing people together. Your travel and expense cost for your implementation team can go into the implementation consulting category, but you will have some hard costs in travel for your internal team.

**Learning Management System (LMS)**   You may or may not need this, but often an ERP or CRM implementation brings with it the need to develop an eLearning training platform for your employees. If this is not something you have, but it's something you need, plan to budget for it.

**Selection consultant**   If you decide to use a selection consultant as part of your decision on which software to buy, you should factor this cost into the equation here as well.

## Capitalizing Costs

The following is a summary of the existing guidance around what expenses can be capitalized versus expensed on an ERP or CRM project. By capitalizing the costs of the project, you can depreciate the costs of the project over multiple years rather than having all of the expenses hit the books in the year(s) in which they were incurred.

To sum it up in one sentence: Work done in the implementation phases of the project, with the exception of data conversion, user training, and project management, can be considered capitalized costs.

Table 2.2 outlines the items that can be considered as capitalized costs, which can be depreciated rather than expensed.

**TABLE 2.2:**   Capitalized Cost Items

| ITEM | EXPLANATION |
| --- | --- |
| Analysis | Defining the business requirements, the key business scenarios, defining security requirements, and all non-project management-based analysis work |
| Design | Work on developing the functional, technical, and solution design documents and any prototyping that occurs in the design phase |
| Development | System configuration, moving items between environments, and customization development |
| Test | Any testing of code or environment testing |
| Server Development | Any work related to the cutover of the system including status meetings |
| UAT | All validating work |
| Security | Defining securing requirements and enacting security roles within the system |
| Travel | Required travel costs related to the project |

Table 2.3 outlines the items that cannot be capitalized and must be expensed at the time incurred.

**TABLE 2.3:**   Non-Capitalized Cost Items

| ITEM | EXPLANATION |
| --- | --- |
| Project Management | All project management work incurred throughout the entire project |
| Assessment of the Project | Any costs related to scoping the project or what's considered the solution discovery |
| Project Planning | Meetings to help the project management develop the project plan deliverables |
| Data Conversion | Any time spent writing data conversion requirements, test scripts, and data cleansing, as well as any time developing and testing data conversion |
| User Training | All training team activities (including training development); includes any communications to the field and site readiness reviews |
| Post Go-Live Support | All activities after the system is live, except for any analysis and design work related to the next phase of the project |

Figure 2.3 provides a quick guide to what can and cannot be capitalized on the project. I would recommend talking with your CPA or accountant about the current guidance on this, but it is a way to spread out the net income impact of a costly implementation project.

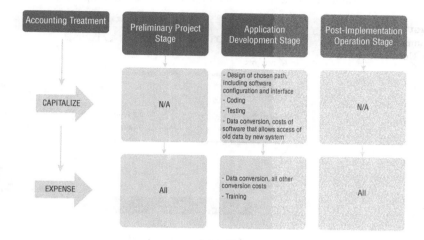

**FIGURE 2.3**
Capitalized and non-capitalized quick guide

## Contingency

There will be costly surprises on an ERP or CRM project—there always are. Certainly, if you follow the guidance in this chapter and really narrow in on the scope, you will not have as many surprises. Nevertheless, there's always something on a project that costs more than it should or some business change that requires new functionality not originally anticipated in the project. You may need to buy an ISV solution that you didn't initially see.

For all of these reasons, you need to leave extra room in your budget for *contingency*. You should take all of the costs that you calculated previously and add 20–30 percent to the costs to prepare for the unknown. You don't want to spend that money, but you certainly will dip into it a little bit. It's better to have budgeted for contingency than to have to go back to the Board of Directors for every change request over your initial budget.

## Return on Investment (ROI)

It's a good idea to develop a *return on investment (ROI)* worksheet for your project. To develop this, you build out the cost of the project over the next 5 to 10 years including the implementation costs and the subscription costs. In the ROI calculation, you would take your tangible benefit dollars, approximate some of the intangible benefits, and then put all of your project costs on the other side of the equation. The resulting calculation will show you when you will recover the cost of the project and receive benefit from there on out. That's your breakeven point, and you want to try to look for a project that is going to pay for itself after 2–3 years. This still provides several years of benefit once the project reaches its breakeven point.

Nucleus Research conducted a study in 2018 on the benefits of implementing Microsoft Dynamics. They found that for every $1 spent on a Microsoft Dynamics project, the company received $16.97 of benefit. This tells a compelling story for the value of product if you can make your money back nearly 17-fold. Figure 2.4 shows a sample ROI calculation by Nucleus Research.

**FIGURE 2.4**
Sample ROI calculation
by Nucleus Research

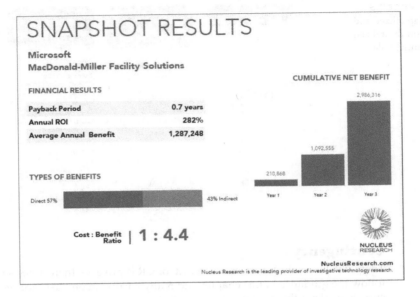

## Gaining Approval

Now that you have everything pulled together, it's time to get approval for the project. Companies certainly have different governance structures, and you better than I can speculate on what your company's approval process would be. If you are spending 5 percent of your revenue on a project, I would have to imagine that you would need approval from your CEO and/or board of directors.

As you go into that meeting to get approval, be sure to give a fair representation of the project. It will take time, cost money, and stretch the team, but it will result in a platform that allows you to grow your business and provides the benefits that you articulated in the success criteria and benefits sections. Most CEOs and boards do not understand the ERP or CRM implementation process, so they often can't provide insight to the leadership team.

At this point of the process, you are asking for the money, the team, and the approval to move forward. Once you've decided on the software and the implementation partner, you'll have to come back to the CEO and/or board to explain the plan.

# The Bottom Line

**Project roles**  Your project team has a number of different roles that play a critical part of the success on the project. It's important to understand and assign people to each of these roles.

**Master It**  Which of the following is not a required role for your implementation project?

**1.** Selection consultant

**2.** Project owner

**3.** Project manager

**4.** Subject matter expert

**Project schedule**  When you are preparing for your project, it's important to understand any seasonality that might impact your schedule.

**Master It**  Which of the following is not something that should impact your proposed go-live date?

**1.** Year-end close of financials

**2.** Seasonality of business

**3.** Everyone is busy all the time

**4.** Expiration of support for existing product

**Process categories**  All businesses have common processes, and when determining your scope, it's helpful to associate your business activities to these common processes.

**Master It**  Which of the following is not one of the core process categories?

**1.** Procure to pay

**2.** Hire to retire

**3.** Quote to cash

**4.** Dollars to cents

**Client journey**  There is a common set of stages that occur on a business application implementation project that we call the Client Journey. This journey has stages that need to go in order, and it's important to understand the order of operation to complete a project successfully.

**Master It**  Determining your project success criteria and ROI should occur in which stage of the ERP/CRM journey?

**1.** Align

**2.** Define

**3.** Create

**4.** Deploy

**Project budget** Implementation projects are expensive, and it's important to set aside adequate budget to make sure that the project is successful. The budget should include internal and external costs.

**Master It** An ERP project should cost between which percent of your annual revenues?

**1.** 0 and 0.5 percent

**2.** 1 and 2 percent

**3.** 3 and 7 percent

**4.** 10 and 20 percent

# Chapter 3

# Four Keys to Consider When Buying an ERP or CRM Solution

As you can tell already if you've made it this far in the book, buying an ERP or CRM solution is difficult and expensive, but it's potentially a company-changing endeavor. Throughout my years of experience, I haven't witnessed anyone go about it in the best possible way. Some companies make decisions without much forethought, and others overdo the selection process so much that it takes six months to arrive at the answer they should have chosen from the start. The answer, as always, lies in between those extremes.

The goal of this chapter is to give you a framework for making this important decision. We'll cover the four areas that you should examine and use as your criteria for making the purchasing decision:

- Fit

- Implementer

- Platform

- Cost

Most companies only look at fit, but different companies fall prey to biases in the other areas as well. The goal is to look at all of these areas and then make the best decision for your business.

Before discussing these four key areas, we'll talk about the selection team and process and then dive into an explanation of each area.

After you complete this chapter, you will be able to do the following:

- Understand the selection process

- Identify the four keys to consider

- Build your scorecard

## Selection Process

In the previous chapter, we discussed the different roles that you'll need throughout an implementation to deliver the project successfully. I mentioned how you generally want that same team to be responsible for the selection of the software. The software selection process should be led by your project owner, who is ultimately responsible for the success of the project. This person would work in tandem with the executive sponsor, the CIO, and would ultimately have some involvement from the CEO.

You will want to include subject matter experts, IT members, and representation from finance on the overall committee that makes the decision. Plan to develop a scorecard that allows each member to rate the vendors in the participant's area of expertise. I frequently see every participant rating vendors on all of the criteria during the selection process. If you're a manager in the manufacturing division, you are likely not an expert on the platform and methodology, so you should focus your rating on the fit instead of the platform. Similarly, the IT team needs to be focused on the platform and not as much on the fit.

Before you jump into it, narrow down the selection to six or so vendors, so that you don't give the team whiplash by showing them 30 different kinds of software. You can start with a questionnaire with more than six options, but you don't want to receive a demo from more than six software vendors, or your team will start suffering from analysis paralysis. Once you have narrowed the field, organize a meeting with the team before the selection process starts to outline the process and the expectations for each person on the project. In the next chapter, we'll dive into what happens during the sales cycle.

## Selection Consultant

I honestly didn't know selection consultants existed until I left Microsoft to start a partner organization and had to sell software. At first, I thought it was crazy to pay someone to help you pick the software, but as I grew to understand the complexities more, I see why it makes sense. If your collective leadership team has no experience selecting ERP or CRM software, I think you should take a hard look at bringing in an outside consultant. Many firms will guide you through the process and provide their methodology on making the best selection. My general guidance is, if you are inexperienced in this process, seek to employ a selection consultant.

With that said, I've never been thoroughly impressed by the selection consultants that I've seen in action. They often have their favorite software (they may actually be resellers for one of the vendors that's part of the selection process); they may not understand cloud technology and how the industry has changed recently; or they may just be biased toward one of the four key areas without factoring all of them in. It is hard for a selection consultant (no matter how good they are) to come in, learn your business, understand your leadership team, and prepare you for the process successfully in a short period of time.

I see a good amount of value from a selection consultant when it comes to the contract negotiations portion of the sales process. If your leadership team has not negotiated professional services agreements and doesn't have a pulse on what these consultants cost, it's a good idea to have a selection consultant work through that process for you. One of the most compelling ways that a selection consultant can structure their fees is to say, "I will negotiate a discount on the implementation consultant's fees and that's how you pay me." If they can negotiate a 10 percent reduction in fees on a $1M project, you now have $100,000 available to put toward their cost.

Selection consultants will provide you with a quote for their services, and you can make a decision from there if it's the best thing for your business. You may be surprised by the overall cost, and that's why we have it factored into your budget.

### Decision Maker

Chapter 2, "What to Do Before You Begin a Project," discussed building your team to review the different software packages and work on the implementation. As part of that team building exercise, you should also determine how and who is going to make the decision on what software you select. If that person is the CEO, they need to understand the criteria on which you are making the decision. One of the things we often see is the case where a team reviews all of the different software options, makes a recommendation, and presents it to the CEO—who hasn't been involved in the process—to make the decision. That CEO, who knows nothing about the process and who is presented with several options, inevitably makes a decision on one thing—cost. This is not a criticism of the CEO. If you asked me if I want a sedan that cost $30,000 or a sedan that cost $50,000 that both do the same thing, I might choose the cheaper car, too.

You would rarely ever make a decision about a car based solely on cost alone. You would want to know about its features: What color is the car? Who is the manufacturer of the car? What kind of gas mileage does it get? How many people does it hold? What type of warranty comes with the car? Where can I get the car serviced? and many more questions. In the same way, you wouldn't come home to your partner and say that we are buying a sedan, and it's either $30,000 or $50,000 without additional information. Similarly, you shouldn't expect to present a limited number of facts to your CEO.

If the decision is ultimately going to be made by the CEO, the CEO has to sit in on some of the sessions or, at a minimum, have the team explain the four keys in order to understand that the decision will be made across multiple factors and not just on price. If you are a CEO who is being presented such limited information, push back on the team and say that they must present you with a ranking based on these four key areas before making a decision.

## The Four Keys

Now that you understand more about how to make the decision, let's talk about the criteria that you should use to make this decision. I stress it throughout this section, but you should not make the decision based on only one of these criteria. If you do, you are making a mistake. In each section, I will talk about the problems that occur if you only focus on one particular criterion. I suggest these four factors because they cover the areas that are most important to the successful implementation of a project.

The four factors are as follows:

- **Fit:** Is this product a good fit for your industry and your requirements?

- **Platform:** What is the technology involved, and does it fit your business needs?

- **Implementer:** Does your implementer have the right plan and the right team to work with you to make this project a success?

- **Cost:** The cost should fit the job. Not too high and not too low.

I've seen it time and time again where the decision comes down to one factor and not four. In almost every case, the one factor is either fit or cost. Companies almost always under weigh the importance of the platform and the implementation partner. At the end of each section, we will talk about the perils of making a decision based on just one factor.

## Fit

As an example, let's say that you run a dental clinic. If you run a dental clinic that is looking for a new patient management system and the system does not have access to information about teeth or HIPAA protections, it's not going to be a good solution for you. Similarly, you couldn't run a manufacturing company on an ERP that doesn't have a production module. Some key features must be a fit for your particular industry.

The best way to assess *fit* is by conducting a high-level *fit/gap analysis*. It's high level because you will conduct two fit/gap analyses during this journey. The first will occur during the sales cycle, as you try to identify the major areas of functionality that you want covered. The second occurs during the implementation process, in the Create stage, where you break down each gap and provide estimates to make decisions on which customizations to complete and which ones are not worth the cost. In the sales cycle, you are trying to focus on the critical requirements that you need to have in the new system.

When you are determining your system needs, I highly recommend that you think not only about what you need today, but also about where you want to go as a business and make sure that you have those critical items identified.

As you go through the demonstrations of the various software options, you're going to want to score those products based on their ability to meet the requirements that you identified in your fit/gap preparation work. I often see people using scoring sheets to determine the degree of fit— and that's great. The problem is it's the only thing they score throughout the entire selection process.

Once you see the software, you will be able to compare each requirement to the software to determine if it is a fit. If you don't see that functionality in the software, ask a question during the demo on how your requirements would be handled. It could be that the vendor hasn't configured that portion of the software, so it may be handled without a customization. It could be that the functionality doesn't exist, and it requires a customization. If that's the case, mark it on your sheet as a gap to indicate that it will cost additional consulting dollars. There will be gaps on every project; don't be alarmed if you see a few of them. Be alarmed if over half of the product ends up being a gap.

Once you identify it's a gap, you will want to get a sense of the complexity required to make the system work for you. There are small gaps, like a report that is missing a column that you need, and there are large gaps, such as you don't have any way of integrating a core system. You will want to guesstimate the effort for those gaps to put into your overall calculation of the cost of this system.

During the fit/gap analysis, you will score the software based on the percentage of requirements that are met (fits) and the requirements that are missed (gaps). Typically, you're going to want a solution in the 70–80 percent or higher rate of fit. If it's lower than 50 percent, it isn't the right solution for you and your needs.

### PROS OF SELECTING ON FIT

Choosing ERP software based on best fit is absolutely a key factor to making a decision. You need to be able to assess the "degree of fit" of the product to know you don't have to add a huge amount of functionality to get it to work. If you disregard the product and industry fit in your evaluation, you will end up spending a lot of extra time and money customizing the solution to your business and carrying the ongoing burden of managing those customizations.

## PROBLEMS IF YOU ONLY CONSIDER FIT

The most common mistake companies make is to value the industry/product fit and nothing else. To make the selection, you bring in all of your subject matter experts, leave out the IT and finance people, and bring in team members only concerned with the fit of the product. Fit is important, but it's not the only criterion, as you'll see in the upcoming sections.

If you neglect the platform, you end up with a vertically specific product that has an outdated user interface running on a server under someone's desk, supported by a three-person company that originally wrote the software back in 1990. If you neglect the implementer, you will spend far more money than you should and increase your risk of failure dramatically. If you neglect cost, you will end up implementing something much more expensive, such as SAP or Oracle, when it might not be needed. If this were the case, it would also take two to three times longer to get up and running in your environment.

Companies make this mistake most often when the ERP selection process is run by business division leaders.

## Platform

When we started Stoneridge Software, I knew nothing about selling software. I had spent my career at Microsoft on the service side, focused on consulting and support, and with my only exposure to sales coming from sitting in the back of the room for a few sales demos. One interesting example came our way in the early days at Stoneridge. It was a manufacturer who needed a new ERP system, but all of their servers were running on Linux and all sorts of different open source Office solutions. They didn't have a single Windows Server in their company. As a Microsoft partner trying to sell them a system built on Windows and SQL Server, we decided to spend time and energy demoing software to them. That was a complete waste of time (which anyone with more sense would've known), as we had a complete mismatch on the platform. You don't want to make the same mistake we did and put a bunch of time and money into a project on a platform totally inconsistent with what you have today.

I use the term *platform* in a broader sense. It's not about if you like Microsoft or not. I include the following items in the platform category:

- Cloud or on-premise

- Technology platform

- Upgrade

- Supportability of the product

- Performance at scale

## CLOUD OR ON-PREMISE

Let's first define the terms *cloud*, *hosted*, and *on-premise*. By cloud, I mean any software that is hosted directly by the vendor and accessible via a browser. This could be a *Software-as-Service (SaaS)* solution like Business Central or Customer Engagement or *Infrastructure-as-a-Service (IaaS)* like Finance and Operations. Hosted software is really on-premise or Windows client software hosted by the provider or a third party; for example, if you were running Dynamics GP hosted on Azure, on-premise software is Windows client software that you host. You may host it on a centralized server at your headquarters office, but in this scenario you are responsible for the uptime of that server. This would be how most Dynamics GP customers are hosting their environments today.

If I were writing this book in 2010 and I suggested that you go to the cloud, that would a risky proposition because there weren't many solutions available, and those that were didn't offer much in terms of functionality. As of 2021, however, that has all changed. Every top-tier vendor has either moved their solution to the cloud or are working on it. There's a reason why this shift has occurred: Most small companies don't have the IT staff to manage Windows and SQL Servers, backups, and all that comes with keeping software up and performing. Hosting software in the cloud aggregates the need to support the system across all of the customers and puts that burden on the software provider. The software provider allocates sufficient hardware resources in their data center to give you the performance that you need. They worry about uptime, backups and recovery, and performance, so that you don't have to think about it.

When the cloud was in its infancy, there were security concerns about putting your customer's private information on some server that you can't touch and see. The concerns were well founded then, but now that paradigm has shifted, and you are actually safer to have your data in the cloud. I'm sure that everyone has heard about data breaches over the past few years, so you are better off trusting your data to a vendor who employs the resources whose job it is to keep hackers out. You likely cannot afford those people at your small business.

Again, in the infancy of the cloud, it was really expensive per user. Even today, if you take the on-premise license costs against the cloud, it will likely be that the on-premise license cost is cheaper. However, you must add the expenses related to the labor to keep those servers up, the cost of backups, and the risk of data breaches or crashes. By the time you add all that up, your costs are likely to be more expensive than a cloud-based option.

In today's world, you should be looking for a cloud solution. If you choose a hosted or on-premise solution, you have to go into it with eyes wide open to the resources and costs that you'll need to put into it.

## TECHNOLOGY PLATFORM

This is what I referred to in the introduction—it is certainly easier for users if you use tools that are designed to work together. The operating systems and productivity tools of most companies fall into these groups:

- Microsoft Windows and Microsoft 365 (most companies)
- Microsoft Windows and Google/Slack
- Apple OS with Google/Slack
- Linux OS with Open Source tools

If you are running Linux or another open source platform with open source productivity tools, you probably shouldn't be buying Microsoft Dynamics. The login and user experience will be different from what your users are familiar with, which increases the complexity of the implementation. If you are in that first category where you use Windows as your OS and you use Microsoft 365, then Dynamics 365 will fit very well in your organization.

This may seem obvious—and it probably is obvious to the IT leader—but if the decision is made by the business with no IT involvement, you could end up choosing a platform that looks nothing like what you have internally at this point and that would be a mistake.

## UPGRADE

Software is not static—it is always changing with new enhancements, major features, and bug fixes. You may or may not want to be able to take advantage of new functionality when it comes out, but you want to deploy necessary updates or bug fixes if you have a problem. Many on-premise customers are on older versions of the product on which they couldn't accept a hotfix if they needed one because their version of the software is no longer being supported for such fixes. That's a precarious position to be in if your system is unable to ship product due to a bug that can't be fixed. The business could lose significant money and customer credibility.

In many cases, the cost of upgrading on-premise software to the latest version can be 2/3 to 3/4 of the original implementation depending on how much customization you need to bring forward. If you decide to buy on-premise software today and you spend $1M on the implementation, you are looking at a future bill of $500–750k for the upgrade to the latest platform in 5–10 years. As you calculate your costs, you have to think about what a future upgrade will cost in your 10-year total cost of ownership model.

The *Microsoft Dynamics 365* platform and other cloud-based platforms have a big advantage here as you will never need an upgrade event in the future. You will have to apply updates on a regular basis, and there is some cost associated with those, but they are typically small incremental costs.

## SUPPORTABILITY OF THE PRODUCT

This is an overlooked component of the platform evaluation criteria. During the evaluation process, you want to understand what support will look like for your product once you go live. If you decide to implement a COBOL solution built on an AS/400, you are going to struggle to find anyone under the age of 50 who can support the solution. The lack of supportability of the product is the event that triggers most companies to choose a new ERP system.

This is really just a measure of risk. If you buy a brand-new add-on product from three guys in Denmark that fits your business, it might work out great for you. You must consider the possibility that they all quit someday, and then you would have no one who can support your business. When working with software providers from overseas, you also must take into account their support hours and whether you can get an immediate turnaround to a system down problem.

## PERFORMANCE AT SCALE

The value of the performance of your application differs among organizations. If you are retailer who is flowing 100 people through your *point-of-sale (PoS) systems* every hour, performance is critical. Consumers expect that you will be able to check them out at your PoS within seconds. If it takes minutes, those consumers won't likely be coming back. If you are creating an ERP system for a real estate holding company that records two transaction a year, you don't have to think about performance.

This may go without saying, but you wouldn't choose to run General Motors on QuickBooks. ERPs are typically grouped into three tiers, which have to do with the scale of those applications and also how prevalent the applications are. These three tiers are outlined in Table 3.1.

**TABLE 3.1:**    Performance at Scale Tiers

| TIER 1 | TIER 2 | TIER 3 |
| --- | --- | --- |
| ◆ Oracle | ◆ Acumatica | ◆ Appian |
| ◆ SAP | ◆ Deltek | ◆ Ascentis |
| ◆ Microsoft | ◆ Epicor | ◆ JustFoodERP |
| Dynamics 365 F&O | ◆ IFS | ◆ Lots of solutions specific to |
| ◆ Infor | ◆ Microsoft Dynamics 365 | an industry |
| | Business Central | |
| | ◆ Oracle NetSuite | |
| | ◆ Sage Inacct / X3 | |
| | ◆ Syspro | |
| | ◆ Workday | |

You generally want to pick from the Tier 1 list if you are a Fortune 500 company or a billion dollar plus company. For small to mid-size companies, you would generally choose from Tier 2 and Tier 3 providers. I would not recommend Tier 3 providers, because they likely won't have the supportability that you would get from a Tier 2 provider due to their being niche solutions.

Performance should generally be a criterion in your evaluation process, but you aren't going to know how a system performs for you specifically until your customized solution is in the deployment phase. Look for whitepapers where the vendor has performed simulations to determine how many transactions and users the system will support. I also suggest that you ask references about their experience with the performance of the system.

With cloud software, you will have to look at the Internet speeds available in all of your office locations. You want to be able to get 100 ms or less response time on the application you use, and if the response time is greater than that, look to increase your bandwidth at your locations in order to make sure that those users aren't frustrated by the lag time.

## SELECTING AN ERP BASED ON PLATFORM

When you select an ERP based on a platform, you are looking at the technology stack and user interface of the solution and determining if this platform is going to receive the right amount of investment to stay on the product long-term. In this case, you're selecting a Tier 1 or Tier 2 solution that you believe is going to be a great long-term investment. Consider the five elements I discussed earlier: cloud vs. on-premise, technology platform, upgrade, supportability, and performance as key criteria within the Platform section of your analysis of the products.

When selecting a product based on platform, you want to have knowledge of the current technology to understand if it fits within your existing infrastructure. You also want a grasp of the upgrade plans for the product so that you know if it will be a long-term technology fit for your initiatives. Remember, you wouldn't buy QuickBooks to run General Motors, so find a solution that fits the scale of your business.

## PROS OF SELECTION BASED ON PLATFORM

Prioritizing selection based on platform will make your IT team happy. It ensures that the solution fits well in your current infrastructure, is supportable by your current IT team, and doesn't have a big, hidden price tag waiting for you in the future. Selecting an ERP based on platform will present the users with an interface that is current and easy to use. You are likely to have less downtime in this scenario, as your team will understand the underlying technology well.

## PROBLEMS IF YOU ONLY CONSIDER THE PLATFORM

This scenario occurs when the ERP or CRM selection process is led and completely managed by the IT team. If only IT is involved, they may pick the most cloud-friendly, technology-forward platform without thinking about how well it fits your business. When this happens, a lot of functionality is given up and the implementation approach is typically not understood at all. The upfront cost is generally less, but a 5- or 10-year *total cost of ownership (TCO)* study will show the costs to be greater than a solution that fits the business's needs.

## Implementer

Whether the project succeeds or fails is going to come down to how well your organization can work with your implementation partner. If you choose the wrong product, you can still make it work with the right *implementer*. If you choose a bad platform, it might lead to significant costs down the road, but you can get the original implementation done with the right implementer. Most of the time when I've seen projects outright fail, it's due to a combination of a poorly organized customer project team with a mediocre implementer. There aren't too many horrible implementers out there, but I have witnessed where a middle-of-the-road ready organization partners with a poor implementer and it goes south. By reading this book and organizing your team for success, you should become a highly functioning organization that will be successful—as long as you don't partner with a poor implementer. Table 3.2 provides an example of how prepared a customer is for an implementation alongside the quality of an implementation team.

Selections based solely on the implementer are uncommon. The only time I recall that happening is when a company didn't evaluate multiple vendors and relied on a connection between the CEO and some implementer that the CEO knew to come in and do the work. A few occasions exist where people have weighted the implementation team's experience greater than the other factors. When they do, it's typically because they have been burned in the past by a failed implementation, or they're in the middle of a problem right now and looking for the right team to get them out of their spiral. ERP implementations fail anywhere between 10 and 15 percent of the time. They are delivered on time and on budget about 40–50 percent of the time. If you want your project to be successful and on budget, you must consider the implementer's ability to get this project done. ERP implementations are very hard to do right, and just because the implementer can demo the product well doesn't necessarily have any bearing on their team's ability to deliver the full solution.

**TABLE 3.2:** Customer Readiness and Implementation Team Quality Levels

| IMPLEMENTATION TEAM QUALITY | CUSTOMER READINESS FOR IMPLEMENTATION | | |
|---|---|---|---|
| | High | Medium | Low |
| High | Implementation successful<br>On time<br>On budget<br>Most objectives met | Implementation successful<br>Likely slightly over time<br>On budget<br>A good number of objectives met | Implementation will likely be completed but will take much longer than expected due to lack of decision-making on the customer side<br>Scope will need to be scaled back dramatically |
| Medium | Project will likely be completed<br>Over time<br>Over budget<br>Many success criteria items will be completed later | Project will likely be completed<br>Over time<br>Over budget<br>Scope will need to be scaled back dramatically | Project will most likely fail. It may get done over twice as long as originally anticipated and over-budget. Both parties will leave upset. |
| Low | Project will likely be completed with customer doing all of the heavy lifting or replacing the partner mid-project | Project will likely fail unless implementer changes mid-stream<br>Guaranteed to be over-budget and over time | No chance of success |

### PROS OF SELECTION BASED ON IMPLEMENTER

If you are convinced that you have the right implementer for your project who can work successfully with your team, this gives you the best chance of success on the project. Your project will get done, and potentially even on time and on budget. At the end of the day, it's more important to have a working system than a perfect system, so if you selected based on an implementer, you will probably have a happy leadership team because they've got a system up and working.

### PROBLEMS IF YOU ONLY CONSIDER THE IMPLEMENTER

You can end up spending more money than you need to if you consider only the implementer. Some bigger accounting and consulting firms have strong track records of implementation success but demand a much higher rate for their services. You can also end up spending more money on customizations during the project if you didn't consider the product fit. The business team could also be lacking some of the company-specific functionality that they sought going into the project.

## Cost

While more people look at industry and product fit than anything else when selecting an ERP solution, selections based on cost as the key driver are going to lead to problems more than any other factor. With that said, cost is definitely important. ERP implementations are quite expensive, so anything that you can do to make it more affordable will impact your bottom line. Most companies spend around 5 percent of their annual revenue on the implementation of an ERP system, so it's a sizable cost. The higher the cost, the more functionality a product will likely have. Likewise, the higher the cost of an implementer, the more experience they likely have.

Let's examine a few traps that people fall into on the cost side, and a few things that you can do to save money on an implementation.

### IMPLEMENTATION TRAPS

#### 1. THE TIER 1 TRAP

There is a perception if you are a billion-dollar-a-year or more revenue company, you need to implement one of the two "big dog" Tier 1 products—SAP or Oracle. Those products have been the de facto standard in the Fortune 500 world for many years, so some CIOs feel that they have to implement one of these products to look like they belong in the enterprise. They may be the right product for you, but you can end up spending a lot more money on these solutions rather than on other ones that might get the job done. Rather than being biased toward one of the two big dogs, go into the selection process with an open mind.

#### 2. OUR ERP OR CRM SYSTEM DOESN'T MATTER

This is at the very opposite end of the spectrum where you buy a QuickBooks or a free CRM tool to accomplish your goals. In your effort to save money, you buy a solution too cheap for the current state of your business. As you try to grow your business, you end up with a solution that is a hindrance rather than a benefit to your business. If you buy one of these solutions, you may not have accurate inventory information by site, or the ability to send essential email marketing to clients because the system doesn't allow it at the price point at which you purchased that software.

### 3. THE CEO IS NOT INVOLVED

This is the most common trap, and the one that leads to poor outcomes more than anything else I've described in this entire chapter. Here's the scenario: You have a 10-person project team and a CIO who is new to the role. They spend two months going through the evaluation process, but the CEO wants to be involved with the final decision. The project team does its due diligence and comes back with three possible candidates. Let's say the candidates look like this:

### PRODUCT A

The team liked the product, but it's not the recommended solution as it's missing some functionality and it will require a big upgrade in three years because it is not currently a cloud-based solution. The total implementation cost is $500,000.

### PRODUCT B

This is the selection team's favorite solution. It's a good fit with the requirements, and the project team likes the implementer. It's a cloud-based solution that should grow as the company grows. The total implementation cost is $550,000.

### PRODUCT C

The selection team believes that this product will work, but the implementation appears as though it will be delivered remotely by offshore resources. The implementer says that they've done it before and had success, but the selection team has not been able to meet with the implementation team. The total implementation cost is $300,000.

As the CEO of this fictional enterprise, you have the selection team's preferred choice at $550,000, but a cheaper option at $300,000. This means you could choose Product C and save $250,000. Just think how good you would look to the board if you saved that much money! If you haven't been involved in the selection, you don't have the understanding that Product B is better than Product C because you haven't met any of the parties. Nine out of 10 times, the CEO will look at these options and choose Product C, thereby throwing out all of the selection committee's work.

### 4. I JUST WANT CHEAP RATES

When you first hear the rates that you'll be charged by implementation consultants, you can be surprised. You will see rates as high as $400/hr. for these consultants. That's a lot to swallow if you look at it compared to rates that you might pay for a developer or your IT-managed services provider. Implementing ERP and CRM is a much more difficult job than that, but it's human nature to do the math and figure out how much more you'd save if you had a resource at $200/hr. instead of $400/hr.

In the early days of our company, we had a client who was using us and an offshore vendor to get work done. They had negotiated a rate of $100/hr. with their offshore vendor, and we were doing the work for $170/hr. They had a project that they decided to send to the offshore vendor because the rate was lower. That vendor spent 48 hours on the problem and couldn't achieve a resolution. We got involved and solved it within three hours. You must consider the quality of the resource in light of the rates you are being charged. A Cadillac and a Chevy Spark are both cars, but you wouldn't necessarily buy the Chevy Spark just because it's one-fourth the cost; you'd consider the quality as part of the equation as well.

The scenario I mentioned in Trap 3, "The CEO Is Not Involved," actually happened to us a few years ago, but it looked a bit different. In our case, there were six different ERPs vying for the work and five of those ERPs came in with implementation costs of around $550,000. One came in with an implementation cost of $175,000. You would that think alarm bells would go off if you saw five people selling something for one price and one person selling the same thing for less than half that price. But skepticism wasn't part of the equation on this decision, and the client went forward with the lowest cost implementer. They spent nine months working on that implementation before they had to return the product and quit the project. They called us back, being the originally preferred choice, and we implemented Microsoft Dynamics ERP and CRM solutions for them.

## TRAVEL COSTS

One of the biggest costs of an implementation is for travel by the implementation consultants onsite at your location. This can often end up costing 15–20 percent of the entire implementation budget to cover the cost of flights, hotels, meals, travel time, and rideshares to get the consultants to your locations. You could lessen the cost of travel on the project in a few ways, which will lessen your overall cost of the project.

**Request local implementation resources**   If you live in a major metropolitan area, there is likely a good implementer of your solution within your metro area. Look for implementation partners who have local resources. Those resources will be able to be onsite more frequently with much less cost, as you would only need to pay for mileage and lunches.

**Conduct more sessions remotely**   It is important to have a great working relationship between your consultants and your project team, and it's harder to build that relationship when you never meet in person. I suggest travel during the initial part of the implementation to build comradery and trust. Also, several sessions during the implementation are better done onsite like white-boarding sessions, warehouse tours, and so forth. That said, a lot of the implementation can be done remotely; your consultants should write designs remotely, update project plans remotely, and do all of the work that requires focus-time remotely. As a rule of thumb, I believe that the implementation should be done with 20–30 percent of the time delivered onsite. If you cut your travel down from 100 percent to 25 percent, that's going to save a lot of money and save wear and tear on the consultants involved in the project.

**Negotiate bulk discounts with hotels or taxi companies**   If you are going to have resources onsite all throughout the project, take the time to call a nearby hotel and see if you can negotiate a lower rate for all of the business that you will bring to them over the upcoming months. Work with your implementation partner to get agreement that they are willing to have their team stay at that hotel. Just doing this could save you 10–15 percent on your hotel costs, which adds up over a long project.

**Set a maximum per diem**   Some consultants out there love to travel and spend money when they are on the road, and they choose to travel that much because they like to go to fancy restaurants and take in the city. That's great, but you have a budget to maintain, so set a reasonable limit on the amount that they can spend on breakfast, lunch, and dinner in a given day. $75 is usually more than reasonable. If they are going out for a Wagyu beef filet every night on your dime, that will impact your overall project costs.

When it comes to cost, you just need to consider if you are getting good value for your money. Like every other purchase you make, you need to understand the quality and the cost and choose the best option from there. Then you can start saving a few bucks on travel costs to keep your expenses down.

### PROS OF SELECTION BASED ON COST

It seems obvious, but you'll save money on the product if you choose the lowest-cost product. Just remember to balance the cost with the platform and industry/fit dimension. Ask yourself the reason why the product is cheaper. In most cases, the inexpensive product likely either has less functionality or a limited investment in the future platform. If you select your implementer based on the lowest cost per hour, it may not save you money in the long run. If you can adequately compare value and experience, you can certainly save money by selecting based on price. Just be very sure that you are comparing apples to apples, or it could end up taking more time and adding cost in the end.

### PROBLEMS IF YOU ONLY CONSIDER COST

As just mentioned, if you look for the lowest-cost product, you are probably selecting a product that will have inferior functionality and fit, and more likely than not, it will be on an older platform without a strong future roadmap. If the product doesn't have a strong future outlook, you have a product that can get you by for a few years, but you'll end up having to do this process all over again, as your ERP will likely not keep up with user demand and technology.

If you look for the lowest-cost implementer, you'll often be using offshore resources who are not going to understand your business. Your risk related to the implementation success goes up dramatically when you eschew implementation experience for lower-cost resources. When you get a low-cost implementation resource, there's a reason why: they are less experienced or offshore.

## Building Your Scorecard

Now that you understand the four major components that make up your decision criteria for the ERP or CRM system you want to select, you should build a scorecard where you can tabulate the results. I am of the belief that selecting an ERP or CRM system is not a completely democratic process; you want to get opinions from across your organization, but it's ultimately the leadership team's decision. Going against the consensus of your team is a dangerous idea, but it may be the best decision in your particular scenario. The key is to get good information and make the best decision from there.

**Fit** For the Fit criterion, seek feedback from your operations or sales team. You want feedback from the people who will be using the software every day to make sure that it is usable and fits the needs of the people in that division. Set up a scorecard that shows the fits and gaps, and make sure that it has a section on usability, as that will be key to overall adoption of the product.

**Platform** For the Platform criterion, you will be looking to your IT team to evaluate if this is a good, long-term platform and what hidden costs there may be in the future. No offense to this person, but you do not want a mid-level manager in your manufacturing division evaluating the platform—this is the domain of IT. You should ask IT to rank the platforms and give the pros and cons for each of them.

**Implementer**   For the Implementer, you want to seek feedback from your project manager and anyone who's gone through an ERP or CRM project before. You may want to involve your HR team as well to see if that group will gel well with your team. Identify a lead evaluator of the implementer and give them criteria based on what we discussed earlier in the chapter.

**Cost**   For the Cost, this primarily comes down to the Finance and Leadership teams. You should take all of the other areas into consideration and take a hard look at the ROI calculations for each of the solutions that you're reviewing. It may be that you spend more money on a solution that provides more value. This is the line of thinking that you want to take when making this decision.

Best of luck putting this all together. If you do a great job preparing for the implementation and pick the right solution and partner, you'll be in a very good position to succeed on this project.

## The Bottom Line

**Selection criteria**   In this chapter, we reviewed the four keys to make the right software selection. Review the summary to understand which is the most important—if there is one that is most important.

**Master It**   Which of the following is the most important factor to consider when buying an ERP or CRM system?

1. Product fit

2. Cost

3. Implementation partner

4. You need all the above plus the platform

**Degree of fit**   The degree of fit is the percentage of features in the software that meet your particular requirements. You are very unlikely to have a 100 percent degree of fit, so you should compare the results from the different products you reviewed and rate the products based on the one closest to 100 percent.

**Master It**   How do you best determine the degree of fit?

1. Run a fit/gap analysis

2. Ask your ERP evaluator to determine

3. Look at industry benchmarks

4. Estimate it based on your team's gut reaction

**Platform criteria** Several elements go into the decision about the right platform for your ERP or CRM solution. Review the section of the chapter that covers this to familiarize yourself with the various elements.

**Master It** Which is a reason why the platform matters when choosing an ERP or CRM system?

1. It keeps costs down

2. Your upgrade costs could be minimal for your industry

3. It makes sure that your product is a good fit for your industry

4. You can keep track of your project plan on that platform

**Implementation partner experience** Your implementation partner will help guide you to a successful project with experience from similar projects in the past. You should rate this criterion based on your perception of their ability to lead you to a successful project.

**Master It** Your implementation partner should have experience with all of the following except:

1. The specific version of the product

2. Active Directory and Exchange

3. Yours or a similar industry

4. Your agreed-upon implementation methodology

**Project costs** One of the four keys to consider when deciding on the right software and partner is the cost of the project. Business application implementations are expensive, and it's important to understand all of the costs so that you are not surprised in the end.

**Master It** Which of the following is not one of the costs to consider during an implementation?

1. The implementation partner's consulting fees

2. The cost of subscription fees of the software

3. Board member compensation

4. Internal resources and contractors

# How to Evaluate and Buy Business Application Software

Now that you have your team ready and your criteria selected, let's talk through the steps to buy software. Quite a few steps are involved, so it's not like going to Best Buy to grab some software off the shelf. We're talking about buying software that is going to help you run most of your business operations for decades. So, let's take it seriously and make the best decision.

In Chapter 3, "Four Keys to Consider When Buying an ERP or CRM Solution," we talked about the criteria that you would use to select the right ERP or CRM solution and partner. Now we want to explore the steps of the buying process so that you know what opportunities you will have to evaluate your vendors.

**AFTER YOU COMPLETE THIS CHAPTER, YOU WILL BE ABLE TO DO THE FOLLOWING:**

- ◆ Identify the steps of the buying process
- ◆ Select your vendor
- ◆ Get leadership or board approval

## Buying Process Steps

Let's talk about the steps for buying business application software. At a high level, first you need to figure out what your selection process is going to be to decide who's going to be involved and who's going to lead the process. What will your criteria be? How much detail are you going to be asking for, and how many vendors are you going to select? There's quite a bit to figure out in the initial selection process. Once you've decided on your selection process, you move into your initial meeting.

The initial meeting is a *discovery session*, where you share with the vendor what you want to see during the software demonstration. After the software demonstration, you will work on the contracts. At the very end of this phase, you can actually buy the software.

## Qualification Stage

As you assemble your team to evaluate the software and vendors, put together your game plan. You have several options to consider as you go through the process. Let's start by examining those options and make sure that you are qualifying the right vendors for your project needs.

### How Many Vendors?

You should decide early on how many vendors you want to bring into the process. If you're not going to consider a vendor seriously, then it's not worth including them. If your company makes $10 million a year in revenue, you shouldn't add SAP and Oracle to your selection list. On the flip side, if you are General Motors, you should not be considering QuickBooks.

Focus on the vendors that are relevant to you. Keep the platform in mind. If you are on an open source platform, maybe you'll want to look at an open source ERP solution. If you're on the Microsoft platform, you want to look at products that are going to play nice with your Microsoft infrastructure.

I would suggest a thorough review of somewhere between two and six vendors. In our first sales process, we were one of 14 vendors, but after a brief survey, they cut the group down to six vendors very early on in the process. The ERP selection consultant sent around a one-page questionnaire that focused on the solution and platform fit, and that approach made a lot of sense. You are just torturing the vendors and your team if you decide to put 14 vendors through the full evaluation process.

If you select six vendors to evaluate more fully, you still want to reduce further the number of vendors who will be involved in demonstrations or demos. You will give your team whiplash if they see six demos. It is way too much of a time commitment, and it becomes hard to distinguish between them when you look at that many. Many of the demos will take a whole day or maybe even two days, so you want to be mindful of your team's time. Determine your criteria for whittling down your vendors from six to three, with demos provided on your top two or three systems.

### To RFP or Not to RFP

Let's start with the *selection process*. Within the selection process there are a few decisions that you'll want to discuss and decide how you want to move forward. One common initial question is, "Do you want to do a *request for proposal (RFP)*?" Within an RFP, you put out a questionnaire and ask the vendors to fill it out.

Your ultimate goal with an RFP is to determine what products have a high degree of fit for your solution within your industry. You can do an RFP and use that to gather most of the information, or you can prepare information for that discovery session and then have your team evaluate the vendors based on how they demonstrate the software you asked for in the session.

My guidance would depend on the size of the organization. Smaller organizations don't necessarily have to do an RFP; however, you still should be prepared to have all of the critical and nice-to-have features outlined so that you can compare how the vendors did against them along with what the timing is going to be for your evaluation process. If you want to formalize the process, you can prepare a *request for information (RFI)* so that you can collect information about potential vendors without it being a formal or binding process.

### QUALIFICATION MEETING

If you did an RFP, you would look at the results of that before deciding which vendors you'd like to bring in for an initial meeting—the so-called *qualification meeting*. At that meeting, you will be trying to understand if the vendor is mature, is established, and has experience in your industry. You should know that your vendor will be analyzing you for "BANT" to make sure that you're ready for this project. *BANT* stands for the following:

**Budget**: "Do you have enough budget set aside to do this project?"

**Authority**: "Do you have leadership approval to do this project?"

**Need**: "Do you have a defined need or pain driving you to do this project?"

**Timeline**: "Do you expect to do this project in the next 12 months?"

If you prepared properly for the project, you should have no problem answering those questions. If you haven't prepared appropriately, you may have good vendors walk away from the project thinking that there's too much risk that the project won't go forward or won't work well.

Be upfront about your answers to the BANT questions and be upfront about what you want in a partner. It's going to save you and the vendor a lot of time if you both can be honest about the quality of the fit from the beginning. A recent study from CSO Insight's Annual Sales Enablement Study (copyright ©2019, Miller Heiman Group) indicated customers spend 44 percent of the total time spent evaluating a vendor doing research online and checking with connections. Most of the time, all of the work is done before they initially meet with the vendors. I think it's great to spend that kind of time. If you've done your homework already, focus the qualification meeting on validating if the company looks as good in reality as it does online.

Use that qualification meeting to ask the important questions that you've researched, such as the following:

*Is this a fully cloud-based solution?*

*IaaS or SaaS?*

*What's the upgrade cycle?*

*What is your implementation methodology?*

*What does the sales process look like?*

This is a good time to ask questions related to the four keys to making your selection spelled out in Chapter 3 in order to see if this vendor might be a fit for you.

After the Qualification stage, you should review the vendors and pare the list down to three (or two) to move on to the next stage. Once you've settled on those vendors with whom you would like to move forward, you'll next move into the Discovery and Demonstration stage of the buying process.

## Discovery and Demonstration Stage

When I first got involved in sales, I honestly didn't understand why prospective buyers would set aside time for vendors to do the act—what we call *discovery*. A discovery session is when a vendor gets a chance to visit the buyer's site and ask questions to prepare for their demo. The reason why a buyer wants to do a discovery session is to make sure that the demos hit the mark. If you just say that you manufacture widgets and tell the vendor to come and give you a demo, they might totally miss the fact you use substitute products or that you need travelers to move between workstations. The better the answers you give during discovery, the better the demo you'll get, and if you get a good demo, you'll have a really good idea if the product is a fit for you.

If you've done an RFP, you may indicate on your requirements list those items that you want to see during the demo. This will give your vendors a good idea of what you're expecting. If you haven't done an RFP, you should proactively share details about your business processes in advance of the discovery so that the vendors understand better what's in scope. If you make them come in completely blind, you will have to give them more time to do discovery, and they'll likely end up missing major areas of focus in the demo because you didn't tell them, and they didn't think to ask about them. If a mobile app is vital to your business but you don't tell that to the vendors, don't be surprised if one of them completely misses it in the demo. They might have that functionality, but they may have decided not to show it in the demo just because they didn't have time to get to it.

**TIP**    *Rule of Thumb*: If it's important to you, make sure to bring it to the vendor's attention.

To plan for the discovery session, propose a high-level agenda to the vendor to give them time to cover each process that's particularly important to you. A good idea is to make time for a site tour to give the vendor the "lay of the land." They may think of ways to improve your setup if they have a chance to see it with their own eyes. By having an agenda, you'll also be able to get the right people from your team to attend the session so that you can answer the questions well for the vendors.

During the discovery session, be open with them about your top priorities. You want to share the "pain points" in the current system so that they are aware of what's important to you. Expect the vendor to understand the core of your business, but since every business is unique, share what's unique about your business and what challenges you collectively may face as you try to implement the new system. For example, you may have manufacturing as part of your requirements, but you're really struggling with warranties and repairs. Bring that up so that the vendor can help provide solutions to that problem. You may even get free advice from a vendor that you don't end up selecting.

## DEMONSTRATION

Moving on to the actual software demonstration, this is the big day and what you're building up to. You've been researching these vendors and their software for a while, and now is your time to see it in action. The purpose of this demo is a "day in the life" of your business. You want to see how the software is going to work for you. You've seen generalities, but now you want to see the feature functionality you'll need to run your business. The focus is going to be on the areas that are most important to you.

For the demo, you should expect the vendor to prepare the agenda and send it to you in advance so that you can see if it will fit with what you want to see. You will also need to bring in your subject matter experts for each of the areas relevant to them so that they can help evaluate the software. Depending on how much you want to do with your new system, you could have demos take anywhere from an hour to two days. If you're implementing a combo ERP and CRM session that affects your whole company, you'll want to do two days' worth of demos.

During the demo, plan to ask questions if there's anything that you don't understand or if something isn't clear. This is your opportunity to make sure that you achieve complete understanding.

You'll also want to make sure that the vendors include a technology or technical section where they explain the technology platform. This is the opportunity for your IT team to ask questions related to the platform so that you can help determine the fit.

Make sure that after the demo, you have a complete understanding of those key processes and pain points and how the vendor plans to address them. You're going to want to rate these presentations to see which is the best fit from a feature functionality standpoint and which is the best platform for you.

### ANALYZING THE FIT

During the demo, each of your subject matter experts should have a worksheet that they complete to help analyze the fit of the software to your requirements. You want to gather their general feedback on usability and how easily they think their departments could adopt the software. Collect those worksheets and review their perspectives to analyze the overall fit of the software for your business. Also, plan to poll the IT team members on their assessment of the platform after having seen the demo.

Coming out of the demo, your three candidates should be ranked first, second, and third. You still have work to do:

1. Discuss implementation strategy.

2. Review their implementation approach.

3. Estimate and go through the contracting process.

You don't want to tell the #2 and #3 vendors that they are out and just focus on the #1 ranked vendor at this point; you need to keep them engaged to make sure you make the best selection that evaluates the implementer and cost factors.

## Selecting Your Vendor

Now that you have a good idea of the vendor's fit and platform capability, assess the implementation strategy, the team, and the implementation estimate. Once that is completed, you can negotiate with your preferred vendor and make your selection. Don't assume that this process can happen quickly. It takes time to go back and forth on the costs, and you'll need to do a legal review of the contracts, which never goes as quickly as you would like.

### IMPLEMENTATION REVIEW

The *Implementation Review* could be included in the demo section, but the implementation discussion is not always done during the demo. Sometimes it happens at the same time, while at other times it does not. During the implementation discussion, you want to understand if this implementer will be the right fit for your team. You'll ask about their implementation methodology:

*Do they use a waterfall approach? Agile? Scrum? Or some kind of hybrid?*

*What does their project team look like, and how will it partner up with your project team?*

You'd like to get an idea of the project team and what experience the resources who would be dedicated to your project have.

Make sure that they present you with their high-level project schedule to give you an idea of when the project will be completed. You'll want to see if the steps and the staffing make it possible to complete the project within that amount of time.

I recommend that your key project team members sit in on the discussion of the implementation team and methodology. Your company's leadership team should be represented as well. Your CEO, CIO, and CFO could all lose their jobs if this implementation goes horribly wrong, so they should at least take the time to meet the people who will be doing this work that can change the course of the enterprise. You will work extremely closely with your implementation team over the next three months to five years. More than anything, you need a partner that you can trust.

## PROJECT ESTIMATE

During the implementation discussion, talk to your vendor about their overall estimate of costs including the software costs, the ISV costs, and the implementation costs. They should prepare an overall budget for you based on the requirements that you have given to them. This will likely not be a detailed estimate, but you'll have an idea of what you will be expecting to spend for each of these ultimate solutions.

Many consulting organizations are now offering a "paid discovery" or "enterprise process review," which is a short consulting engagement allowing them to get a deeper understanding of your business while helping you to prepare for the kickoff of your project. I'll talk about this in the next few chapters, but that's an option where you can "try before you buy" with some of these vendors. If you're considering a $3M project with a vendor, it's worth it to spend $50,000 to see if this vendor will be a good fit for you while still getting value from that initial engagement.

## MAKING YOUR DECISION

As you've seen in this chapter and the previous one, many factors contribute to the decision of which vendor to select (see Figure 4.1).

One common mistake is to make a decision solely on the degree of fit from a requirements perspective; say this vendor is an 85 percent fit and another is an 82 percent fit. That's just one-fourth of the criteria. Don't make a decision on who has the best fit because the difference between 85 percent and 82 percent is not that much.

Evaluate the four criteria collectively:

◆ Fit

◆ Platform

◆ Implementer

◆ Cost

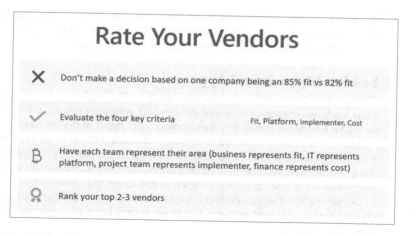

Make sure that they are equally weighted as part of your decision.

I suggest that you get all of the parties together for this decision with the final decision-maker. Ask your business owner to rank the fit of the vendors—rank them #1, #2, and #3, and share if they are close. Then ask your IT leader to rank the vendors #1, #2, and #3 across the platform. Next ask your project owner to rank the vendors #1, #2, and #3 on who would be the best fit as an implementer. Then ask your project owner and finance representative to review the ROI calculations across each of the vendors to assess cost. Rank those vendors #1, #2, and #3 and see where it all comes out. If one vendor is #1 across the board, then you have an easy decision. However, it usually doesn't work out that way. If it's close, I'd suggest that you break the tie by choosing the implementer for whom you have a clear preference.

## CONTRACTS

Once you've settled on your first choice, ask them to send you their contracts. The vendor will send you at least two contracts—one called a *Master Services Agreement (MSA)* or *Professional Services Agreement (PSA)* and one called a *Statement of Work (SoW)*. The MSA is the overarching contract that stipulates who owns the intellectual property to the works created, the limits on liability for each party, the billing terms, and the process for any potential conflict. Signing the MSA doesn't commit you to any dollar spending—it contains the terms under which future SoWs will be governed. The SoW is where the scope and dollars are outlined. This is the one that you want to examine closely to ensure that it's correct. It is essentially the contract that stipulates what you get and how much you are paying.

I also suggest that you have your legal representative (whether internal or external) review these contracts. It may add more time in the process, but it's an opportunity to negotiate the terms of the contract if you see something that could cause risk for your business.

## VERBAL COMMITMENT

At the point where you have seen the contracts and believe them to be fair, it's a good idea to make a verbal commitment to the vendor to let them know they are your top choice. Why would you show your hand like that? The reason is that you want them to organize their team to be ready to start on your project as quickly as possible. If you wait until the last drop of ink is dry on the contract to inform the top vendor of the selection, you may be waiting two to six weeks for them to get the project team in place to get the project moving. If time is of the essence, you will want to communicate the decision and move forward.

### Leadership or Board Approval

The last hurdle you'll face to move forward on the implementation is to get final approval from your leadership team or board of directors. If you need approval from the board, you may have to wait a few weeks until their next board meeting; if that's the case, plan accordingly.

I've never heard of a board reversing a decision related to an ERP or CRM decision, so I would not expect you to have a board member suggest that you change course completely, but the possibility exists. You may have a board member mention previous experience with a vendor, and if that's the case, it would've been better to get that feedback early on. In Chapter 2, "What to Do Before You Begin a Project," we talk about how to prepare for an implementation, and you should poll your board at that point to see if they have any perspective on the process or on potential vendors.

When you present to the leadership team or the board, walk them through the selection process and mention how you gathered feedback from the team across the four key areas to make your selection. Most leadership teams (who weren't involved in the process) and boards have no experience with ERP or CRM projects and implementations, so you will want to use this opportunity to educate them on the process and make sure that they understand the gravity of what they are approving. Also share with them that these projects present a high degree of risk, so there is always the possibility you'll be back in front of them talking about project challenges and asking for more money in the future. That shouldn't happen, but you should set the expectations that it might if the project isn't moving as it should.

### Moving Forward

Once you have board approval, you can sign the contracts and move forward with the project. In the past, you would jump into a kickoff meeting to start the project, but we suggest that you take several steps in advance to make sure that your project will run successfully. The next several chapters give you the background and preparation steps that you'll need to go through to make sure that you can kick this off successfully.

## The Bottom Line

**Steps in the Sales Process**   It's important to understand each of the steps in the sales process so that you know what to expect as you go on this journey and so that you can set proper expectations on the amount of time it will take to make the selection.

**Master It**   Which of the following is not a step in the purchase of enterprise software?

1. Discovery

2. Demo

3. Deployment

4. Contract negotiations

**Matching the Software to Your Key Requirements**   As you review software solutions for your business, you should first understand and prioritize the requirements that you have for this software. The more time you take to define your requirements upfront, the better fit you'll be able to achieve for your needs.

**Master It**   What is the purpose of a request for proposal (RFP)?

1. Compile a list of vendors

2. Assess the vendor's degree of fit based on your requirements

3. Gather high-level information about the vendor

4. Overload the vendor with work to see how badly they want the business

**Steps in the Sales Process**   Each step in the sales process accomplishes a particular goal that's important to the overall decision to purchase the right software for your business.

**Master It**   What is the purpose of a discovery session?

1. To demonstrate the product

2. To determine the implementation timeline

3. To finalize contracts

4. To provide the vendors with your requirements and pain points

**Four Key Criteria**   There are four key criteria to use to make the best decision on which software to buy and which implementation partner will help guide you through the process.

**Master It**   What are the four key criteria for evaluating a vendor for a business application implementation?

1. Fit, platform, implementer, cost

2. Budget, authority, need, timeline

3. Cost, cost, cost, cost

4. Industry fit, industry experience of implementer, degree of fit, industry references

**Understanding Contracts**   As you get ready to move forward on the project, you will need to sign several contracts that govern software and consulting terms.

**Master It**   Which of the following is not a contract you'll need to sign before starting the project?

1. Master services agreement

2. Statement of work

3. Software subscription or end user license agreement

4. Change request

# Chapter 5

# Organizing Your Team for Success and Project Governance

You have made the decisions to start an implementation project. You've chosen the right software and the right implementation partner, and now it's time to get the project rolling.

In this chapter, we will focus on how you and your partner can put together the optimal team to get this project done on time and on budget while achieving your success criteria. In addition to that, we'll tackle this thing called "project governance," which in practice is the hierarchy of the project team and the set of meetings you need to have in place in order to make sure that the project stays on course.

**AFTER YOU COMPLETE THIS CHAPTER, YOU WILL BE ABLE TO DO THE FOLLOWING:**

- ◆ Understand how RACI fits into your project team
- ◆ Map out your implementation partner roles and accountabilities
- ◆ Recognize how project governance contributes to a successful implementation

## RACI

Before we jump into the main content theme of this chapter, I want to take a minute to explain an acronym that you may hear on projects quite a bit. The acronym is *RACI*, and it stands for Responsible, Accountable, Consulted, and Informed. To do project governance successfully, you will want to map out responsibilities and accountabilities with your project team early in the project. Before I refer to these terms over the rest of the chapter, let's explain them first in Table 5.1.

**TABLE 5.1:**     RACI

|   | TERM | # | MEANING | EXAMPLE |
|---|------|---|---------|---------|
| R | Responsible | 1* | The party who does the work/task | Liam, the functional consultant, writes the design for the finance customization. |
| A | Accountable | 1 | The party who reviews and approves the work/task | Olivia, the solution architect, reviews the design for the customization and signs off on it. Is ultimately accountable for the design to work. |

**TABLE 5.1:** RACI *(CONTINUED)*

| | TERM | # | MEANING | EXAMPLE |
|---|---|---|---|---|
| C | Consulted | N | Parties for whom feedback is requested on the work/task | Noah, the supply chain consultant, reviews the design for the finance customization to know how it works and how it might impact his work. |
| I | Informed | N | Parties who are updated on progress | Emma, the project manager, is informed on the progress of the design of the customization. |

Table 5.1 highlights each letter and its corresponding term, the number of potential people in that role, the definition of the role, and an example to help illustrate the point. You'll see in the # column that there can only be one accountable party for each task. If two people are accountable for something, it just causes confusion and conflict between those parties. If no one is accountable for something, then it won't get done. I put an asterisk next to one responsible party to indicate that there is generally only one responsible party, but it can be more than one person if necessary. For example, you may have two developers responsible for all of the development work, and you may not want to delineate in this chart which one is working on each specific customization. In that case, you have two responsible parties for the purposes of the chart, knowing that each one will be assigned the specific work later.

## Your Project Team

Chapter 2, "What to Do Before You Begin a Project," covered a lot of the roles on the project; as a reminder, Figure 5.1 outlines the core roles previously discussed.

**FIGURE 5.1**
Implementation
core roles

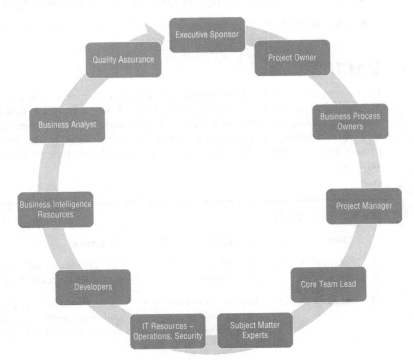

I won't reiterate the points I made in Chapter 2, other than to remind you that if you didn't appoint people into the roles that you need before the selection process, you need to do it now. If you can't find a good project manager, I'd suggest you look to outside resources or staffing firms that may be able to provide you with someone.

To build on the RACI definition discussed previously, let's take a look at each role and what they are accountable for.

**Executive Sponsor**   The *executive sponsor* has overall accountability for the success of the project. This role shouldn't be involved in every decision, though. It's more a matter of putting the right people and processes in place to be successful while providing sufficient budget and executive air cover.

**Project Owner**   The *project owner* role has the day-to-day accountability for the project and is the person who will be judged on the outcome of the project. The project owner needs to work with the executive sponsor at times for budget, resources, and executive air cover, but ultimately needs to deliver on the project.

**Business Process Owners**   These individuals are accountable for the process changes and adoption in their business units. *Business process owners* must be willing to make changes to their process and to champion it within their business units.

**Project Manager**   The *project manager* is accountable for the project schedule and making sure that the information they bring to meetings is accurate and accessible. In many cases, they queue up project decisions for the project owner and business process owners.

The other roles have more responsibilities than accountabilities, but it's critical that each of these leadership roles understand that they are ultimately accountable for their areas of the project.

## Your Partner's Implementation Team

Your partner's team should be set up to mimic your team so that natural working relationships can be built between the two. In this section, we'll talk about what those roles are and the work they do on the project. Figure 5.2 is an example of the levels and hierarchy that are established by the implementation partner. Implementation partners may have slightly different names for each of the roles. I don't show a branch for the "Executive Sponsor," but that's another role that's part of the project, although that person is not actively involved in the project.

**FIGURE 5.2**
Implementation team example

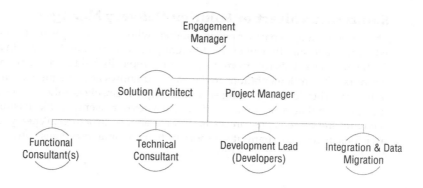

Let's break down these roles in greater detail, covering how involved they are on the project and what their accountabilities and responsibilities are from the partner side.

## Executive Sponsor

Implementation projects may or may not have a designated executive sponsor on the partner side. If they don't, you will want to learn who the leadership team members are at the partner organization and ask who your resource would be if you have concerns about the project that aren't being addressed by the engagement manager. The executive sponsor at your organization should be connected to the executive sponsor at the implementation partner organization.

## Engagement Manager

The *engagement manager* is the leader of the implementation project from the partner side. Depending on the size of the project, they are typically not a full-time resource. They are account-able for putting the right people on the project and should participate in steering committee meetings to make sure that the project is moving the right direction. They will be the resource to connect to the ISVs and other parties involved in the project.

Engagement managers are the business partners of the project owners on the client side. It's important to the health of the project that those resources have a trusting relationship and can work well together. If that relationship is tense and untrustworthy, the teams will be unlikely to work well together.

## Project Manager

The implementation partner project manager is accountable for the overall schedule and resourc-ing for the project. This person should be an expert in CRM and ERP implementation projects and someone who can lead the project through the steps that need to be taken to get through the project successfully. The partner and client project managers work together to build out the many artifacts that need to be managed throughout the project. These include the *Project Management Plan*, the *Project Schedule*, the *Risk/Issues Registers*, and the *Budget* file; as well as providing ongoing leadership and development of communications, status updates, and timely events like *go/no-go meetings* and *cutover plans*.

It's important to get agreement between the partner and client project manager about who is responsible for each of these artifacts. Usually, the partner project manager takes on a bigger role since they are experienced in these areas, but clients need to understand that they need to pay for that time and make sure that they have the budget to accommodate an active project manager.

## Solution Architect or Solution Delivery Manager

The implementation partner needs someone who is accountable for the entire solution—someone who can make sure that all of the different pieces are coming together in a way that makes sense for the business. This role from the partner is typically held by a very experienced resource who has done 10+ implementations in the past and knows how the pieces come together. The person in this role should not be doing specific designs themselves—they are responsible for outlining the approach that you will take with key master data elements like customers, vendors, chart of accounts and dimensions, products, and warehouse structures. When you have multiple divisions in your company, it's important that common processes between divisions work the same way in your system (or you'll be paying extra to customize them), so this role helps bring all that together in the most efficient way possible.

The project leadership team from the partner side is made up of the engagement manager, project manager, and *solution architect*. These are the people who should be joining project leadership meetings.

## Functional Consultant or Consultants

A *functional consultant* is a person who is an expert in functionality in a certain area of the product. On the ERP side, you may have a financial functional consultant and a supply chain functional consultant. On a CRM project, you may have a sales consultant and customer service consultant. Their job is to work with the core team, subject matter experts, and business owner to understand the processes in scope in that area and configure and design the system to meet your needs. They will be actively involved and usually full-time for the duration of the project, so it's important to build a trusting bond with them throughout your time together.

Overall, they are responsible for all of the customization design, all of the configuration, the training of your project team, and testing the functionality in their designated area of the product.

## Technical Consultant

A *technical consultant* is responsible for environments, security, performance, and releases that are part of the implementation process. They are typically not dedicated to a project, but they have several key areas of responsibility to make sure that it all comes together. They are also the ones who do some after-hours work trying to get releases pushed out.

They will be coordinating with your IT team to understand the system environment and layout. They will also train your IT Operations team on how to move code and configurations between environments, how to set up users and security, and how to handle any system outages.

## Development Lead and Developers

On a large project, you will have multiple developers from your implementation partner, but there is usually one *development lead* who will be the resource tasked with understanding the customizations, estimating them, and updating the project team on progress. The development lead will join the stand-up meetings, provide updates, and take on any changes that might be necessary as they relate to development activities.

The developers are largely behind the scenes on the project from the client perspective. Developers take functional designs once they are approved, work on those customizations, and then review them with the functional consultant. Once they are approved by the functional consultant, the functional consultant interacts with the client team on further testing and any changes to the customization.

## Integration Architect

If your project has integrations to other systems, you will typically have a resource tasked with the design of the integration. This is typically an *integration architect*. The job of the integration architect is to understand the data structure and application programming interfaces (APIs) of each of the systems involved so that a solution can be modeled to connect the data between the systems. For this work to be done quickly and efficiently, I recommend having your system diagrams available and contact information for people at the integrating party, so the integration architect can get the information needed to connect the dots.

This is often the only job of this role. They are typically specialized in developing integrations.

### Data Migration Specialist

Every project is going to have some amount of *data migration*, as long as you have data somewhere when you start the project. Chapter 16, "Data Migration—Early and Often," is a full chapter on data migration, so rather than spoil that surprise, I will let you know that the implementation partner typically designates a resource to serve as the data migration specialist. This person is tasked with understanding the existing data and building the Extract, Transform, and Load (ETL) plan to move the data from the existing system to the new Dynamics 365 system.

This resource will work with your IT applications resource dedicated to the data migration effort to get the data and move it over to the new system.

## Project Governance

*Project governance* is the management framework in which project decisions are made. It's important to spell this out as the first thing you do once the project is officially started so that everyone knows how you'll make decisions and who makes what decisions. In the first half of the chapter, we talked about the *who*; now we'll talk about the *how* this gets done.

### Project Communication

No one loves meetings, but meetings with a purpose, an agenda, and outcomes are very important to the success of the project. Use your time in meetings wisely to get the team in sync and get decisions made.

Table 5.2 identifies our recommended meeting cadence for projects with information on how often they should occur, who should be in those meetings, who should lead them, and their overall purpose. These are the meetings that both the client and partner should attend. It's a good idea for you to organize a meeting with your project team internally weekly, as the partner will be doing the same thing.

In addition to these sessions, there will always be ad hoc meetings that come up to discuss designs, to build your game plan for UAT and training, and more. The project manager should try to stay 2–4 weeks ahead, scheduling meetings ahead of time to work around any schedule conflicts.

### Resource Loading

The project manager has many tasks in this part of the project, and one of their biggest tasks is to build a project schedule. Before building the schedule, the project manager needs to *resource load* the project by taking the amount of work and dividing it up into each of the resources available on the project. The implementation partner should have created a detailed project estimate so that the project manager can review and allocate the hours to each resource.

**TABLE 5.2:** Project Meeting Recommendations

| COMMUNICATION | FREQUENCY | AUDIENCE | OWNER | PURPOSE |
|---|---|---|---|---|
| Project Management Status & Planning | Weekly | ◆ Project managers (partner and client)<br>◆ Solution architect and client business owners<br>◆ Engagement manager<br>◆ Client project owner | Project manager | The purpose of this meeting is for the project leaders from both the partner and the client to remain aligned on the activities and status of the project. |
| Work Stream Stand-up | Variable (Daily, 2 times/week, 3 times/ week, or weekly) | The stand-up meeting can be introduced for individual work streams, where needed. Examples of useful stand-up meetings:<br>◆ Weekly: All work stream leaders<br>◆ Weekly: Functional Team<br>◆ Broken out by functional area, when warranted<br>◆ Development—during Create phase, based on volume<br>◆ Data Migration—during Create phase, based on volume<br>◆ Bi-weekly Leading Change/OCM<br>◆ Testing/Quality—during test case creation and test execution | Project manager and workstream leader | The purpose of this meeting is to ensure that the entire team is aware of current tasks and potential impediments to delivering on time and to provide an opportunity to reassign or plan for assistance where needed. Project management will identify and document risks based on input from work stream team members. |

**TABLE 5.2:** Project Meeting Recommendations *(CONTINUED)*

| COMMUNICATION | FREQUENCY | AUDIENCE | OWNER | PURPOSE |
|---|---|---|---|---|
| Steering Committee | Monthly (Can be bi-weekly in some cases; ad-hoc if triggered by "Key Decisions") | Steering Committee | Project manager | The purpose of this meeting is to enable the executive sponsor and other leadership stakeholders to monitor the quality of the project, provide advice, make key decisions, and provide oversight and support. |
| Project Sponsor Sync | Weekly or every 2 weeks | ◆ Engagement manager ◆ Client project owner | Engagement manager | The purpose of this meeting is to keep project leaders informed on progress of the project and to seek input, feedback, and support. |
| Sprint Planning Meeting | 1 per sprint (Depends on sprint cadence— every 2 or 4 weeks) | ◆ Project managers ◆ Solution architect ◆ Core team leaders | Project manager | The purpose of this meeting is to agree on what is to be achieved in the next sprint, document those targeted outcomes, and determine how those outcomes will be achieved. |

**TABLE 5.2:** Project Meeting Recommendations *(CONTINUED)*

| COMMUNICATION | FREQUENCY | AUDIENCE | OWNER | PURPOSE |
|---|---|---|---|---|
| Sprint Review and Retrospective | 1 per sprint (Depends on sprint cadence— every 2, 3, or 4 weeks) | ◆ Project managers<br>◆ Solution architect<br>◆ Core team leaders | Project manager | The purpose of this meeting is to review progress against stated objectives and to discuss what is working and what is not, making adjustments where valuable. If necessary, team members may be asked to show/display progress (demo/show and tell). |
| Bug Triage | Weekly (More if bug volume is high)* | ◆ Project managers<br>◆ Functional consultants<br>◆ Development lead<br>◆ Core team leaders | Project manager | The goal is to stay aligned on open issues during testing. Review active bugs:<br>◆ Status check in<br>◆ Identify risks/ issues and plan mitigation<br>◆ Review test cases<br>◆ Progress and status<br>◆ Identify risks/ issues and plan mitigation |

* Only during testing cycles.

During the sales cycle, the implementation partner may use a technique of *T-shirt sizing* to determine how much work is needed for each task, as shown in Table 5.3. The idea behind T-shirt sizing is to guesstimate the number of hours required to get a task done. That amount of work gives you a guide to estimate the work, and it serves as a good starting point, but you'll see by the range in these estimates that it certainly requires more definition. There is no standard range of hours for T-shirt sizes, but I will share the most common ranges I've seen.

**TABLE 5.3:** T-Shirt Sizing Scale

| SIZE | RANGE OF HOURS |
| --- | --- |
| Small | A day or less |
| Medium | More than a day, less than a week |
| Large | One to two weeks |
| X-Large | Three to five weeks |
| XX-Large | Six weeks or more |

The project manager attempts to schedule the work into your 2- or 4-week sprints. If you are using 2-week sprints, this means that you have a maximum of 80 hours of work that can be done during those weeks. (Typically, you would assume less than that due to meetings and any other obligations the project resources might have.) In order to build out your sprints, you need to break tasks into chunks of 40 hours or less. Why 40 hours? Any estimate for work that's over 40 hours is a bit of a guess, meaning that you shouldn't be very confident in that estimate. You want to ask the resource to break down the work that needs to be done into its parts so that you can divide it up into the sprints and so that you can refine the estimate to be something that's more accurate.

Next, you need to understand any long vacations or seasonality constraints. If you see that someone will be gone for two weeks, you can't assign them any work in that 2-week sprint. The project manager should poll everyone on the project to understand what vacations they have planned, so the schedule will not put tasks on them during that time.

## Project Schedule

Now that you have information about the tasks and the resources, you want to build out your *project schedule* (sometimes called a *project plan*). This is your *Microsoft Project* file, which shows the key activities on the project and when they should be occurring. You don't have to put every task into Microsoft Project, but you should put the key activities and milestones in there. I always prefer a 200-line project schedule to a 1,200-line schedule. No one wants to read a 1,200-line project schedule. If you create a 200-line project schedule, you will need to put all of the tasks into a tool like *Azure DevOps*, as not everything will be in your project schedule. You can think of Microsoft Project as a project planning tool and Azure DevOps as a project control tool. Microsoft Project is good at modeling—it's easy to change a date and see the impact on the rest of the project. Azure DevOps is not designed for that, so it should be used once you have a high-level project schedule.

We recommend that you use the auto-scheduling tool in Microsoft Project because you can adjust timelines quickly. If you have to move a task back two weeks, you can see the impact that has on the rest of the tasks on the project.

Microsoft Project is the best tool for the job, but because most people don't have a license to Microsoft Project, I suggest project managers upload the schedule to SharePoint. On SharePoint, you can see the whole project schedule without having to have a license to Microsoft Project.

## Document Repository

Every project needs a *document repository*, or a centralized site to store all of the documents and artifacts from the project. We recommend using a *SharePoint* or *Microsoft Teams* site, which you can use to build custom lists for information like your risk register or issues list, as well as storing the Functional Design Documents and other artifacts.

Figure 5.3 is an example of a Microsoft SharePoint repository. On this SharePoint site, we track the following information:

◆ Project Schedule

◆ Project Roles and Contact Information

◆ Processes

◆ Deliverables

◆ Background Documents

◆ Risk Register

◆ Issue List

**FIGURE 5.3**
Microsoft SharePoint
repository site example

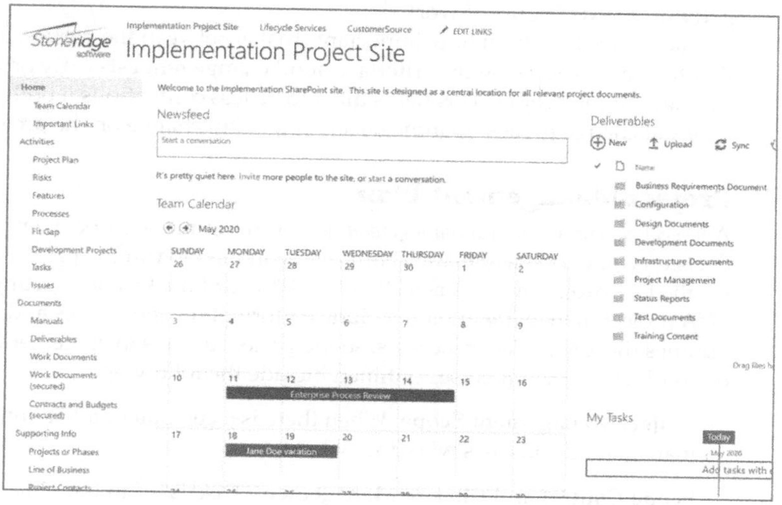

Having all of these documents in one place allows the project team members to access information quickly, creating efficiencies on the project.

## Budget Tracking

The project manager is tasked with managing and updating the budget file. The budget file is a Microsoft Excel document that shows the estimated number of hours to be spent each week against the actual number of hours billed by your implementation partner. The estimated number of hours that should be worked is based on your resource-loaded sprint schedule. If you have a resource who is working far fewer hours than expected, this could impact your schedule if their work isn't getting done. On the other side, you may have budgeted 40 hours of work for someone who is working 60 hours a week. That's chewing into your budget, so you need to account for that as part of your budget tracking.

In construction, there's a term called *earned value*, and that process attempts to put a value on the amount of work that has been completed. Earned value is the best way to measure activity on a project because you may have a resource who put in 24 hours on a task that took only 8 hours. It's hard to calculate earned value, but if you can assign an amount of time to an outcome, you can at least look back to see if they stayed close to their estimates on the work that's been done.

In Azure DevOps, you can use the Burndown charts to show what work has been done, so it makes it much easier to track earned value than it used to be.

## Change Requests

A *change request* is a formal document that should be signed by both parties anytime there is a change in the project that impacts scope, schedule, or budget. You may sign a change request to take something out of scope that you expected to complete—those are easier. It gets difficult when your implementation partner tells you what they thought would take 80 hours is now going to take 200 hours due to scope that has been added. Now you must add 120 hours' worth of time to your budget, along with figuring out how to maintain your existing timeline while getting 120 extra hours of work done.

I talked earlier about how important trust is between the parties, and that's why I recommend that the parties agree on the criteria around change requests early on and use them liberally throughout the project. This helps them to be less contentious if both parties know that you'll use a formal change request to indicate any impactful change on the project.

## Project Management Plan

A *project charter* or *project management plan* is the summary document that pulls together all of the decisions that you have made about how you plan to run the project. This is the key deliverable for the two project managers as they work toward the kickoff meeting.

A project management plan includes information about roles and responsibilities, and it outlines the key project processes, so the project team is in agreement about how the project will be conducted. The processes outlined include the following:

**Project Management Scope**: When there is a customer and an implementation partner project manager, this outlines who does what.

**Scope Control and Change Management**: Discussed in the "Change Requests" section earlier.

**Communication Management**: This process has three main parts:

1. The first component is what meetings you will have, which was discussed in the "Project Communication" section.

2. The second component is the strategy around the status report component, which is covered in Chapter 14, "Dealing with Challenges Mid-Project."

3. The third component is your plan for communicating updates to the broader organization, which is covered in Chapter 7, "Change Management Throughout Your Project."

**Quality Management**: This outlines the approval process for deliverables from the project.

**Budget Management**: As discussed in the "Budget Tracking" section.

**Risk Management**: This is how you manage potential issues that could have a major impact on the project. This covered in Chapter 14.

**Issue Management**: This is how you manage real issues that are impacting your project. This is covered in Chapter 14.

**Release Management**: This is the cadence with which you do lower environment releases and how you plan for your go-live and future enhancement releases. Environment management and release management are introduced in Chapter 17, "Environment Management and Deployments." Chapter 20, "Going Live," and Chapter 21, "Hypercare," discuss the go-live and post go-live release cadence.

**Conflict Management**: This outlines how you will resolve conflicts among the customer and implementation partner's project teams.

**Entrance and Exit Criteria**: These are the criteria that determine when you should move between milestones. This is covered in the upcoming chapters related to those milestones.

**Project Closure**: This sets the criteria for when the project is to be deemed complete and how responsibility for activities changes once that occurs.

The project management plan should be reviewed and signed off by the customer and implementation partner's executive sponsor before the official project kickoff meeting. By agreeing to how the project will be run upfront, the project team will save many future arguments and have a roadmap for how the teams can work together effectively to complete the implementation on time and on budget.

## The Bottom Line

**Project Governance**   Before you formally kick off the project, you should prepare several documents that outline how you want to run the project. There is one central document that captures the key elements of how the project should be run.

**Master It**   What is the document that encompasses all areas of project preparation, which is required in advance of the kickoff meeting?

1. Plan of record

2. Project management plan

3. Budget file

4. Success criteria

**Project Roles**   In this chapter, we reviewed the roles on the project, looking at both your team and the partner's implementation team. Review these roles to make sure that you have people in the most important roles.

   **Master It**   Which of these internal roles is optional on a project?

1. Executive sponsor

2. Project manager

3. Subject matter expert

4. Business intelligence designer

**Responsibilities for Project Roles**   Each different role on the project brings with it a certain set of responsibilities. Reporting on the budget activity is a key responsibility fulfilled by one of the project team members.

   **Master It**   Who updates and manages the budget file weekly on the project?

1. Executive sponsor

2. Project owner

3. Project manager

4. Core team

**Project Estimates**   To complete your project on time, you will need to estimate how much time it takes to complete the full project. Once you get into the project, you'll need to update the estimates continuously in order to know if you're still able to complete the project within the original timelines.

   **Master It**   What is T-shirt sizing?

1. Estimating the project work at a high level

2. Getting swag for the project team

3. Creating a project schedule

4. Another name for the daily stand-up meeting

**Project Meetings**   As explained in this chapter, key meetings should be held on projects with different purposes. Review the list of meetings and make sure that your project team is following them.

**Master It**   At which meeting do you report progress to the executive team?

1. Weekly internal team meeting

2. Daily stand-up

3. Sprint planning

4. Steering committee

# Chapter 6

# Sprints and Tools Needed to Run Your Project

In previous chapters, we talked a bit about sprints, but we haven't yet explained them in depth. This chapter focuses on defining sprints and what tools you should use to track the work that needs to get done on the project.

We are still in the phase of trying to make sure that your project is going to be successful. In the Define phase, we outlined the purchase process, organizing your team, and project governance.

This chapter emphasizes how you manage your project. The concept of sprints is part of the Agile and Scrum methodologies, so we'll be taking a step away from the Waterfall methodology and concentrating on the tools to manage concurrent workstreams with sprints. We prefer to use a hybrid of Waterfall and Agile, and the way I explain it is that we primarily use an Agile approach, but we organize some of the events in a more typical Waterfall way.

**AFTER YOU COMPLETE THIS CHAPTER, YOU WILL BE ABLE TO DO THE FOLLOWING:**

- ◆ Set up the appropriate sprint duration
- ◆ Place work in the right backlog
- ◆ Run the various sprint meetings
- ◆ Define the work on a project
- ◆ Track your work with Azure DevOps
- ◆ Report on progress

## Definition of a Sprint

My wife worked for Microsoft Development back in the mid-2000s, before they adopted sprints. Her workload then was the normal 40 hours a week until they were about three months from product release. Once they got close to releasing software, she would work 60 hours a week because they were behind and needed to catch up. When it came to the last few weeks, that number grew to 80 hours a week. There were several reasons why this happened:

◆ They didn't prepare detailed estimates of what they committed to put into a release, so they didn't know how much work they had to do.

◆ They didn't coordinate activities between the people on the team, so if you had a dependency on another person's task, you might not get it until shortly before go-live.

◆ They didn't spread out the work. They could've been more effective in the early part of the project, and that would've kept them from working late for three months straight at the end.

Sprints were designed to fix these three problems.

## Length of a Sprint

You can choose whichever sprint length best suits your project and business. You want to find a happy medium between a sprint that is short enough to course-correct if needed, but not so short that you are spending all of your time in planning meetings. The length of the sprint doesn't really matter—what matters most is that once you set your sprint duration, you need to stick to it. I prefer a two-week sprint because it holds people more accountable to get their work done in a shorter period, and it allows you to see if you are off-track quickly. We recommend two-week sprints on our projects, and that's what we use with our product development team internally. We use a four-week sprint with our IT group because we have a small number of people there and we do mini-releases every four weeks, so it corresponds well with our activity level. Each situation can be different, but I recommend two-week sprints on ERP or CRM projects.

## Start and End of a Sprint

We have spent more time than I'd like to admit debating what day of the week is the best day to start a sprint. Often, I see sprints starting on a Monday and ending on a Friday. That works, but it has the downside of having to start your week off with your planning meetings and keeping you late on Fridays to do your review meetings. It also doesn't provide people the weekend to catch up if they are running behind on a project. On our product development team, we switched to running our sprints from Wednesdays to Tuesdays, and that has worked well. On the last weekend, if you are behind on your task, you can put in a few hours to get it done (in the purest sense of agile, you should have the work so well planned out that you don't have to have anyone work on a weekend, but the reality is often different). Then the sprint meetings are in the middle of the week when there is less vacation time, so attendance is typically higher.

Another consideration is the timing of your releases. As in the previous example with our IT team, we do a release each month, so we build our sprint to be two weeks of development, one week of testing, and one week of release prep and preparation for the next sprint. We do a release on the weekends every four weeks, so it works to have a Monday through Friday sprint cycle.

## Delivering Value in a Sprint

Sprints allow you to deliver value in short amounts of time, so everyone has visibility to progress, but they also provide an opportunity to adjust if needed. Operating in sprints allows you to shorten the feedback loop and quickly identify if a task is going to greatly exceed the allocated time. It also allows you to pull in new requirements quickly if you need to move the dates of your delivery around. In the world before sprints, resources could go into a cave and work, and work, and work on one single delivery and never have to report on progress to another member of the project team. This led to some bad surprises when it was finally time to check in. If they did something wrong or took a poor approach, it was too late to change it. Shortening the feedback loop encourages not only accountability, but transparency and visibility to the team and other stakeholders.

At the end of Chapter 5, "Organizing Your Team for Success and Project Governance," I mentioned this concept of the *earned value curve*, which shows the value of the work done versus the time spent on the work. Without sprints, you wouldn't have the yardsticks to show you how much was done and how much value was created from that work.

# Backlog

In the Agile and Scrum framework, the backlog is the known and ordered list of work that has been requested. It doesn't mean that it has to get done, and it doesn't typically specify when it will be completed. It's a list of work that has been requested and then refined from there. When you hear "We put this on the backlog," this typically means that the work has been logged and we don't yet know when it will be done. Any stakeholder should be able to add something to the backlog, but the project manager and project owner should be the ones prioritizing and ordering the work in this database of tasks.

You have two different ways of narrowing the timeline of the backlog: setting up a project backlog and a sprint backlog.

## Project Backlog

The *project backlog* is the list of all work that has been requested to be completed on this project. This includes work that you would classify as "must have," as well as work best considered as "nice to have." All of the work that anyone can dream up should be in the project backlog, but those "nice to have" items would be prioritized down to the bottom of the list. For this ERP or CRM project, the scope of activities required to deliver on your success criteria should be logged in the project backlog. As nice as it would be, the project backlog is not a static list; it will evolve over the project, and you should budget for unexpected items as you lay out your schedule. For example, you can never accurately predict how many bugs you'll have and when they need to be fixed. As a rule, we typically budget 35 percent of the customization effort for bugs and rework on design. If you have 100 hours of development on the project, you should build in 35 hours for rework and bugs. When planning your schedule, you can allocate time for this in one of two ways:

- ◆ You can put placeholders for design, development, testing, training, and bugs/rework into your project backlog.

- ◆ You can decrease the available time for other tasks to reserve time for bugs.

As you learn more about the project, you can remove the placeholders or expand the available time when you have a more accurate prediction.

## Sprint Backlog

The *sprint backlog* is the amount of work to be done within this sprint. Let's use a two-week sprint for this illustration. You will assign backlog items to be done within that sprint and assign it to one person who can see what tasks need to be accomplished during that two-week period.

The project manager who is assigning the work will try to allocate the right amount of work to the resources during that sprint so that it can be accomplished. This provides a measure of accountability to the resource if the work is appropriately allocated. During the sprint planning meeting, you want to ask each resource if they can get their work done during that sprint. Sometimes, you have to push certain team members, while others you have to stop from over-committing.

When you have a task that needs to be completed during that sprint, you adjust the sprint or iteration value on the task so that it's clear when it is scheduled to be done.

At the end of each sprint, you will undoubtedly have something that didn't get done as scheduled. When that happens, you ask the person to update the remaining hours on the task so that you can allocate that work to the forthcoming sprint or determine if someone else has the capacity to pick up the remaining work. On each task, you will have an original estimate and a remaining work value. If the task was slated to take 40 hours and the resource has 4 hours left, you allocate 4 hours of work to the subsequent sprint so the resource can get that done.

## Allocating Work to Team Members

How many hours of work should you allocate to each resource during a sprint? If we assume a two-week sprint, that gives you 80 hours to assign. You can navigate this in two ways: either you can pad the estimates to allow for email time, bathroom breaks, random questions from neighbors, and so on, or you can assign them a smaller number of hours to allocate for those realities. If you both pad estimates and give them less than 80 hours of work, you may be not be getting as much done as you need. I recommend having accurate estimates and assigning 35 hours a week (7 hours a day) of work to give some time for other distractions. I wouldn't recommend allocating 80 hours of work unless you expect them to work overtime.

Your team members will take vacations and sometimes be out of the office (or pulled away) unexpectedly. First, you want to ask them to put their vacation days into the DevOps calendar so that you can reduce their task load to reflect that time off. If someone is off for a week, you can only assign them 35 hours of work for that sprint if you expect to be accurate. Emergencies happen, and sometimes a resource will be pulled off scheduled work to handle one. If that happens and it's project-related, add that task or event to the schedule so that you know it happened. You'll ultimately have to move their scheduled task to the next sprint. For a non-project-related task, you will need to reduce their availability to reflect that time away.

## Sprint Success Rate

I'd love to say you should hit 100 percent of what you schedule each sprint, but that doesn't typically happen, and it becomes an unrealistic goal. Often a task from another sprint or something that wasn't scheduled ends up getting completed in the sprint, so there is the potential for bonus work to be completed. Overall, a good target is 95 percent of the work to be completed in a given sprint. Since you're not expecting 100 percent to be completed within any particular sprint, you shouldn't build your project schedule assuming 100 percent of your sprint work is done when you expect. I would plan for 85–90 percent of what you need to get done in each sprint if I'm laying out the initial schedule.

# Sprint Meetings

Sprints have defined meetings used for planning and checkpoints during each sprint cycle. These meetings are critical to the overall success of the project; you have to have these checkpoints and planning sessions to hold people accountable and to adjust during a project. If you don't have these meetings, you should forego using sprints.

## Sprint Planning

The *sprint planning meeting* is held either right before the start of the sprint or on the morning of the start of the new sprint. This meeting is led by the project manager, and the purpose of the meeting is to allocate work for the upcoming sprint. The project manager will first look at the resource allocation during that sprint—are any people taking vacation when they had been expected to do lots of work?

When it comes to work planning, the meeting begins by reviewing what work didn't get completed from the previous sprint and allocating the remaining hours into the new sprint, assuming that it still needs to get done. Next, the project manager will move to the items expected to be scheduled during this sprint to affirm that they still make sense and that they should still be scheduled. Then the project manager will look at new requests that are timely and find room to get them done during that sprint if they need to be done. Lastly, the project manager will look at how much work has been allocated to each person and try to validate with them if it's reasonable for it to be completed in the next two weeks.

The project owner needs to be at this meeting to advocate for key work that needs to be done during this sprint. The project owner may have to push the team to work extra hours during a given sprint if something is particularly time-dependent; but they also know that they can't do that every sprint without negatively affecting the morale of their project resources.

This doesn't necessarily need to be a 60-minute meeting. One way that I've seen work well is for the project manager to reach out to each resource on the team to work with them on their upcoming work. Often, the resources know what they need to work on next, and they can do most of the sprint planning work on their own.

After each sprint planning session, the project manager should send out a message to the project team indicating the key project goals to be accomplished during the upcoming sprint.

## Sprint Review

The *sprint review meeting* should happen at the end of each sprint. My preference is to have it occur just before the sprint planning session so that you understand how much work was completed in the previous sprint before you allocate work into the next sprint. I've seen situations where teams skip the sprint review meeting altogether, and the project manager does the sprint review and follows up with people directly if there were tasks that didn't get done when expected.

Ultimately you want to be able to measure your success during that two-week period and identify if any resources consistently can't complete their tasks during their sprints. You should generate a report showing the work output expected versus the work output achieved.

After each sprint review session, the project manager should send out a message to the project team indicating what was and wasn't completed during the previous sprint. It works best to send the sprint planning and review content out at the same time.

## Sprint Retrospective

I never liked the term "post-mortem" for a meeting to review how well a project went. That sounds like a funeral. I much prefer the term "retrospective" as a way to look back and evaluate the success and failures of a project. That's the purpose of the sprint retrospective—to provide some analysis on what went well and what could go better after each sprint.

You can choose whether or not you want to invite everyone to this meeting every two weeks—it can indeed get repetitive if you have the same person underperforming each week. I think it's a good time for the project owner, engagement manager, and two project managers to reflect on what went well and what could go better. Sending a brief survey to the team members to collect any feedback is a quick way of getting reactions that can be useful to the trajectory of the project.

## Stand-up Meetings

*Stand-up meetings* (also known as a daily scrum or huddle) are among the most valuable meetings that you can have on a project. They are often meetings that start out being run correctly but ultimately devolve into mini status reports. It's important to run these meetings correctly and stick to the formula that has proven effective here.

They are called stand-up meetings because the goal is to get everyone in a room and have them provide an update while they are, literally, standing up. They shouldn't bring their laptops to the meeting—they should come prepared to listen, focus, and then head back to their desks. In a more virtual world, they often can't be done in person, but the spirit of everyone standing up and paying attention should be honored.

The meeting should last no longer than 15 minutes and should include no more than 10 participants. The project manager should keep the meeting moving with the goal of trying to wrap up early.

Each person in the meeting answers three questions in less than one minute:

1. What have I completed since we last met?

2. What do I plan on completing by our next meeting, or what am I working on?

3. What's preventing me from reaching my goal, or what do I need help with?

A typical response should be, "Yesterday I finished up task 2345, the button for the customer portal, and today I'm working on task 2346, which allows people to update their contact information on the portal. I could use help from Bob because I don't know where to connect to the contact information in the CRM system." That response hit on all of the high points and was delivered quickly. From there, the project manager would ask Bob, "Do you have time to help?" If so, you and Bob should set up a separate session to work through whatever information you need. You do *not* try to solve the technical problem in the meeting.

The project manager needs to listen closely to the updates, and if a resource is running behind on a deliverable, the project manager should specifically ask that person if they need help. If a resource was supposed to be done with their task on Tuesday, and it's now Thursday and it's not done, they either missed on the estimate of the work or they need help. As a project manager, it's your job to listen for that and help remove any barriers or roadblocks that person might have.

At the end of the meeting, the project manager can give a quick update on any meetings that are happening that day and any prep work that the team should be working on. The project manager also then asks if any blockers/dependencies are holding anyone up, so there's a chance to share that information before the meeting ends.

The stand-up meeting should happen every day on a big project. It's important to check in on project status and hold everyone accountable in order to make continuous progress. For smaller projects or projects in the Empower phase, you can move to a two- or three-day-a-week cycle. If they are run efficiently, it doesn't represent a big time commitment, and it gives everyone a chance to connect on a daily basis.

If you have more than 10 people on your project, I suggest that you break up your stand-up meetings into two or more groups. Perhaps you have all of the finance resources together in one meeting and all of the technical and development resources in another. Then the project owner and project managers can do a quick meeting afterwards to share any notes and raise any concerns for that day.

## Work Definitions

There is a lot of work to be done on an ERP or CRM implementation project, so let's dig into what type of work there is and how best to classify it. Figure 6.1 gives you a sense of the hierarchy of items and the goal for each level of the hierarchy. Following is a paragraph on each of the project activities to give you a sense of the definitions and how to use them on a project.

**FIGURE 6.1**
Hierarchy of work
definitions

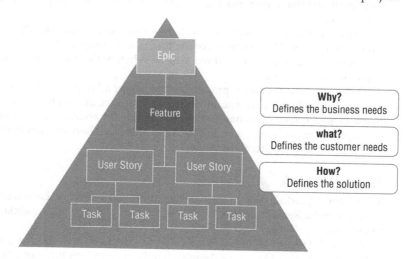

### Epic

An *epic* is defined as a large user story that incorporates many user stories, features, and requirements. We typically associate an epic with a Process Category, such as Project to Profit. An epic essentially serves as the top of the hierarchy for a collection of work within a Process Category.

### Feature

A *feature* is a business function or an attribute of a system. Features typically comprise multiple requirements and typically include many user stories. Features can be functional or non-functional, but they typically sit in the middle of the hierarchy with epics above them and user stories and requirements below them. We equate a feature to a Process Group and a Process, so we typically have two levels of features in the system: one at the Process Group level (for example, Managing Vendors) and one at the Process level (for instance, Creating a Vendor).

## User Story

I often equate a *user story* to a business scenario. It outlines the physical activities that the company resource must perform in order to complete a process. User stories may contain multiple requirements and may span multiple features, but they generally sit in the hierarchy below the feature that best relates to the work being performed.

User stories typically consist of a description of the activity (in business terms and not in the way it was done in the previous software), an estimation of effort, and an acceptance test. User stories are very important for testing purposes as functional tests should relate to these business scenarios.

## Requirement

A *requirement* is defined as a condition or capability needed by a user to solve a problem or achieve an objective. Requirements can be functional (I need to show this field on a report) or non-functional (the report must generate in less than 5 seconds) and typically come with an associated task.

Requirements can sit under a feature or a user story on the DevOps hierarchy and are important to track. When you're conducting your fit/gap analysis, you will be looking at custom requirements and the associated work to see whether this requirement will be included in the implementation project.

There is often a debate on projects as to whether all requirements should be tracked or just requirements related to a customization. For example, do you track the requirement that the create vendor screen must have a field for the vendor address? This exists in all ERP solutions, so it is typically considered a standard feature. This is a determination that should be made early in the project to avoid potential confusion.

## Research Task

The following tasks make up the common place to store work. Each work item has an Original Estimate and a Remaining Work hour area, which allows you to associate the work effort to the task.

A *research task* is a set of hours allocated to a resource to research a potential solution. This is not the time it takes to create a design—it's the time to look into potential options for a larger problem. For example, if you need to research the different potential software vendors, you will need to set up calls with the vendors, and that would be a case where you'd want to assign a research task.

## Design Task

A *design task* provides the necessary hours to create a functional design document or another form of a design for a customization. This customization would need to be designed and approved within this time frame, so be sure to build in a little additional time for the review with the developer, the review with the core team, and the approval by the business process owner.

## Development Task

Once a design is approved, it's passed over to the developer, and the *development task* is where the developer allocates their time. During the development task time, the developer needs to review the design, develop the game plan, write the custom code, develop a unit test, write up how it was done, and show the customization to the functional consultant. We typically set a 4-hour time frame on the easiest of customizations because of all of the effort it takes to get it moving and reviewed.

## Test Task

A *test task* is not to be confused with a test case or a test. A test task is typically the time required to write up a test case and do the initial testing of a customization.

## Other Task

You may create other tasks for any reason you would like. Assign hours and a resource to it and do your best to describe its purpose.

## Test Case

A *test case* is the outline of the steps required to accomplish a scenario in the software. Test cases are typically associated with user stories. If you outline the steps there to complete a task, you should create a test case to reflect those steps once you have it working in the software.

## Test

A *test* is the act of a running a test case. A test should be run by multiple resources to validate that it is working. Ideally, you would run the test case with an automated test, and you would record the result of each run as the test activity.

## Bug (Defect)

In software, a *bug* is a defect. If you wanted the software to show an alert saying, "Hello World" and it says, "Hello Moon," you have a bug. Bugs are common in software development, and they should be prioritized for completion according to the priority scale outlined in the next section regarding DevOps fields.

There is a difference between a bug and a design change, but this is often not articulated on a project. Going back to my basic example, if the requirement were to give an alert that says, "Hello Moon" and the core team now wants it to say, "Hello World," that's a design change, not a bug. A design change should generate a change request to approve the change in direction.

## Risk

A *risk* is a potential issue—it is something the project team is worried about occurring. When you define a risk, you provide a description, your plan to avoid this risk, note any potential triggers, and your contingency plan in case it occurs. Risks should be defined at the beginning of the project and updated throughout.

## Issue

An *issue* is something that has occurred that requires some kind of mitigation plan. An issue is not the same as a bug—it's bigger than a bug. An example of an issue may be a resource leaving the project. You now have to develop a plan to bring in a replacement resource, which may affect multiple tasks and delay the project.

## Change Request

A *change request* activity type in DevOps is an indication that one of the tasks is a design change or outside of the original scope of the project. Change requests should be approved before you proceed with work on them as they affect the scope, schedule, and/or budget of the project.

## Code and Changesets

When you make a customization in a Dynamics product, you can tie that customization back to a DevOps task and check it into the code repository. Collections of code become a *changeset*, and those are what make up the changes that you see when you release the latest code.

# Azure DevOps

The term "DevOps" may be foreign to most people. *DevOps* is a set of practices that combines software development (Dev) and IT Operations (Ops). The Azure DevOps product from Microsoft is designed as a database that you can use to track all activity on a project, including development and how you release the code or configurations to production IT systems.

## DevOps Fields

The following are the core fields that you'll find on a DevOps task and how each field should be used. Depending on the template you use, there may be many more fields. Table 6.1 outlines the core fields that you should be using.

**TABLE 6.1:**     DevOps Core Fields

| CORE FIELD | CORE FIELD DESCRIPTION |
| --- | --- |
| Owner | The user who currently owns the effort. This should only be one person. |
| State | **Proposed**: Not yet started<br>**Active**: In progress<br>**Resolved**: Completed, not verified<br>**Closed**: Done |
| Iteration | The sprint in which the work will occur. Iteration is another name for a sprint. |
| Estimate | **Original Estimate**: The expected amount of time to complete the task.<br>**Remaining Work**: The remaining hours left to get done. |

| **TABLE 6.1:** | DevOps Core Fields *(CONTINUED)* |
| --- | --- |
| **CORE FIELD** | **CORE FIELD DESCRIPTION** |
| Priority | **Priority 1**: A critical business function or application is not working correctly or is not available to a majority of users.<br>**Priority 2**: A high-priority business function is not working correctly; functionality is limited or is not available for some users. A workaround or manual process is available.<br>**Priority 3**: A non-critical business function is not functioning correctly, or an individual or small group of people is unable to perform functionality that is not an everyday occurrence.<br>**Priority 4**: The issue does not affect core functionality or data. It is typically an "inconvenience" or minor user impact. |

## Progress Reporting

You can report on data in DevOps in many ways, just like many ways exist to report on information in Microsoft Dynamics. Some of the more common solutions are as follows:

**Kanban Boards**   These create a list of tiles within DevOps where you can see the activities in the given sprint.

**Queries**   You can use this to build whatever views or grids you want to see within DevOps. You can also easily export this data to Excel. This is typically where you see views built to show Priority 1 (P1) and Priority (P2) bugs and what tasks are assigned to a given resource.

**Dashboards**   You can create a dashboard to summarize the most important information at a glance inside DevOps. You can pull in charts as well as summarize query values.

## Analytical Views

These are *entity definitions* that you can use to create reports in Power BI. This allows you to indicate which columns you want to expose so that you can connect to them in Power BI and build the visuals there that you want to see. Figure 6.2 is a mock-up of the Kanban board functionality.

**FIGURE 6.2**
Kanban board
functionality mock-up

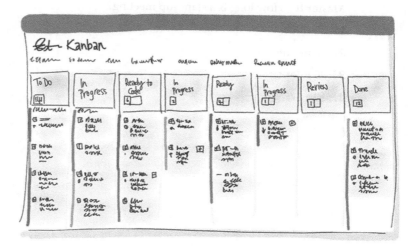

# The Bottom Line

**Setting up the Appropriate Sprint Duration**   Sprints allow you to deliver value in short amounts of time, so everyone has visibility to progress but also as an opportunity to adjust if needed. When choosing your sprint length, you want to find a happy medium between a sprint that is short enough to course-correct if needed, but not so short that you are spending all of your time in planning meetings. It's important that once you set your sprint duration, you stick with it.

**Master It**   All sprints must be the following length:

1. 2 weeks

2. 4 weeks

3. 30 days

4. Whatever the project team agrees to

**Coordinating the Necessary Sprint Meetings**   Sprints have defined meetings used for planning and checkpoints during each sprint cycle. These meetings are critical to the overall success of the project. You need to have these checkpoints and planning sessions to hold people accountable and to adjust during a project.

**Master It**   Which is not one of the core sprint meetings?

1. Sprint retrospective

2. Sprint planning

3. Steering Committee meeting

4. Stand-up meeting

**Organizing the Stand-up Meeting**   Stand-up meetings are among the most valuable meetings that you can have on a project. They are often meetings where they start out being run correctly but ultimately devolve into mini status reports. It's important to run these meetings correctly and stick to the formula that has proven effective here.

**Master It**   How long is a stand-up meeting?

1. 2 minutes

2. 15 minutes

3. 30 minutes

4. 1 hour

**Tracking Work with Azure DevOps**   DevOps is a set of practices that combines software development (Dev) and IT Operations (Ops). The Azure DevOps product from Microsoft is designed as a database that you can use to track all activity on a project, including development and how you release the code or configurations to production IT systems.

> **Master It**   What field on a DevOps item do you use to show how much work is ahead of you?
>
> 1. State
>
> 2. Remaining Work
>
> 3. Original Estimate
>
> 4. Completed Hours

**Reporting on Progress**   An issue is something that has occurred that requires some kind of mitigation plan. An issue is not the same as a bug—it's bigger than a bug. An example of an issue may be a resource leaving the project. You now have to develop a plan to bring in a replacement resource, which may affect multiple tasks and delay the project. These then become Priority issues.

> **Master It**   Which of the following definitions is considered Priority 1?
>
> 1. The issue does not affect core functionality or data—it is an inconvenience.
>
> 2. A non-critical business function is not performing correctly, or an individual or small group of people is unable to perform something that's not an everyday occurrence.
>
> 3. A high-priority business function is not working correctly, or functionality is limited but still achievable with a workaround.
>
> 4. A critical business function is not working or is unavailable to the majority of users.

# Chapter 7

# Change Management Throughout Your Project

Change management has recently entered the mainstream conversations on ERP and CRM projects—and that's a good thing. In this chapter, we'll talk about what change management is, what it isn't, and what steps you want to put into place to make it real for your organization.

*Change management* is a set of approaches that you need to prepare your team and support them through the process of organizational change. To reiterate, change management is a series of different approaches—it isn't one thing. You can't say, "I did this one thing. I talked about change management. Therefore, change management is done for my project." Several different steps are involved in change management, and I'll talk about them as we go through the chapter.

John Kotter, a Harvard Professor of Leadership, wrote a landmark book in 1996 called *Leading Change*, and the concept has been slowly building momentum since then. Many books are now available on the topic, and I encourage you to read one to get a more in-depth look at change management if you will be leading a project in your organization.

**AFTER YOU COMPLETE THIS CHAPTER, YOU WILL BE ABLE TO DO THE FOLLOWING:**

- ◆ Define the success criteria for a project
- ◆ Identify the nine steps of change management
- ◆ Outline the key steps to business process change

---

### WHY DO YOU NEED CHANGE MANAGEMENT?

Change is hard. Did you know that there is actually a part of your physical brain that combats change? It takes overcoming your nature to adapt to change. Certainly, some people are better at it than others, but in an organization full of different personalities and experiences, you'll need to adopt your approaches for the various parties.

For those leaders who haven't considered change management, they tend to have some of these attitudes toward the project:

◆ We change all the time. We don't need a plan.

◆ The new software is supposed to be user friendly; the team will pick it up quickly.

◆ Leadership can be "hands off" and let the project team run with it.

◆ People will do what they are told. If we tell them to adopt the new system, they will.

◆ We have a training plan—that's all we need.

These statements are common and all short-sighted. Change is hard, and you need a plan to achieve adoption of the new system.

Change management doesn't guarantee success; however, it does elevate your chance for success. It defines what success is so that you can measure your progress toward it, and it also tends to increase your employees' engagement in the process and improve their adoption of the new tool.

## Success Criteria

We talked about *success criteria* in Chapter 2, "What to Do Before You Begin a Project," but it's a key element of a good *change management* plan. Many businesses go into an ERP or CRM project with their main goal being "Get it done." While getting it done is important and harder than getting most other projects done, you want to aim higher on your goals for the project.

As shown in Figure 7.1, the difference can come down to thinking about the project as an *implementation* instead of an *installation*.

**FIGURE 7.1**
Project success
definition

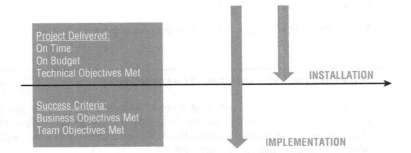

I'm sure that you are all familiar with a software implementation project that falls flat. You've seen someone roll out new software without telling anyone about it and hoping everyone just figures it out. This happens all the time. I've been guilty of it myself many times.

So how do we turn an installation into an implementation? We start by identifying the criteria that separates the two—the success criteria.

Success should be agreed upon by the leadership team and should meet the following criteria:

**Measurable**   Something you can point to in time, dollars, or quantity. For example, we want to remove all negative inventory and for our inventory to balance every month. You can measure whether you've achieved that.

**Aligned with Organizational Goals**   Whatever your goals are as a business, your implementation project should support those goals. If you want to grow from $100M to $500M, you need a scalable system. This goal will make the application's performance more important than it was if you were a smaller company.

**Achievable**   More than anything, you want this project to be a victory for the team and proof that your team can create additional value for the business. You want your metrics to be something that you can achieve in a defined period of time.

As you lay out your success criteria, you'll want to determine when to measure the success of the metrics. It's a good idea to measure them after being live on the system for six months, one year, and two years. If you focus on achieving those metrics, you should be able to recoup your cost by the two-year mark.

Many of the success criteria are related to reporting and business intelligence; and, unfortunately, that can be one of the first things to get cut in an effort to make your go-live date. If you define business intelligence as key to your success, you may have to take something else out of scope to preserve the business intelligence requirements. The difference can come down to thinking about the project as an implementation instead of an installation.

# Use of Satisfaction Surveys

I hear many leaders state that they want their project to increase customer and employee satisfaction, or they will say something like they want their employees to feel more empowered with more data at their fingertips. Those are great goals to have, but if you are going to choose them as a goal, you want to make sure that you have a mechanism in place to measure success against those goals.

For measuring customer satisfaction, you would want to have customer satisfaction surveys in place and compare the results before the new system was implemented to the results after the new system is in place. It can take a long time to get a good measurement because you probably won't see a measurable difference in satisfaction for three to six months after the new system is in place, and even at that time, the results may be affected by some other variable.

One common step to take during an implementation is to send out a "pulse" type survey of the members of the implementation team. This survey gathers feedback from the team on how they are feeling about the progress of the implementation thus far and asks for suggestions. I strongly recommend that you do a survey like this throughout the project; it will help you see risks before they become full-fledged issues and allow you to understand and address concerns early. In addition to the core project team, it's important to survey subject matter experts. They may not see everything that's happening on the project, but you can get their perspective on their area to understand if they see the change as a positive one. Don't be discouraged if the numbers aren't great (people are naturally resistant to change). The goal is to digest that feedback and see what you can do to make it a more positive change for them.

# Nine Steps to Change Management

We recommend that you take the following nine steps to make change management real within your organization:

1. Leadership Alignment

2. Organization Evaluation

3. Outline Your Business Process Change Steps

4. Develop a System Vision that Provides Benefit to All Stakeholders

5. Communicate Effectively

6. Maximize the Team's Time in the New System

7. Train Effectively

8. Set Realistic Expectations for the System Just After Go-Live

9. Support Your Team Members After Go-Live

Experienced consultants might look at this list and say that it's standard to do a lot of these steps on a project, and that's true. It is more important to do each step thoughtfully and purposefully. Let's dig into each of these steps.

## Leadership Alignment

If you can do just one thing right on the entire project, focus on this: Make sure that everyone on the leadership team is actively supporting the project. I rarely ever see this on a project. Almost every project I've seen features a few executives saying that they support the project, but they act as silent objectors; that is, they don't actively support it. As a CEO or leader, you must make sure that your team is fully aligned on the value of the project. If they aren't yet, you need to talk to each of them to make sure that you understand their objections and help them work through them. This is the step that I do not see happen which must occur on every project.

In practice, an aligned leadership means the leaders not only support the project in executive meetings, but actively support their team members throughout the project. I typically see support for the team members as they often work extra hours and carry additional stress to try to get the project completed. The area I don't see is the willingness to take accountability for problems in their domain. Time after time I see leaders attempt to blame another department or their implementation partner for problems in their domain. For the project to be successful, they have to be willing to admit mistakes and try to work through them for the best interest of the company.

In addition to leaders taking accountability for their domain, the four factors that need to be in place in the organization are as follows:

**A culture of accountability in the organization**. People throughout the organization need to stand up and admit their problems and take ownership to resolve these problems.

**CEO visibility**. The CEO or department leader needs to know and care about what's happening on the project. He or she should attend sessions from time to time to see how the project is going and be willing to push the mantra that this is a digital transformation and not just "getting new software."

**The leadership team needs to discuss the project**. Again, on many projects, the leadership team only talks about the project when it's over budget or over time and they have to face the music with the board. If they had been talking about progress all along, they could have prevented an unpleasant board meeting.

**Leadership must make itself available to make business process change decisions**. This may require diving into the details a bit if it's a really important change or an impactful change. Business leaders have to be willing to engage and make difficult calls that may make them unpopular with their team in the short-term. Most leaders don't seem to want to make those calls.

With an aligned leadership, your project stands a chance of a much higher degree of success. Challenges can be overcome if everyone is trying to overcome those challenges; decisions can be made with trust that the team has the best interest of the company in mind; and the leadership team can make business process changes knowing that it was part of the strategy all along.

## Organization Evaluation

In this evaluation of the organization, you want to understand two things about this change:

◆ The size of the change

◆ The team's attitude toward advancement

**NOTE**   Sending surveys to your team is a great way to gather how they view the change across the company and their attitude surrounding it.

For the size of change, ask them to give their impression on how big of a change the new system will be for them from their perspective. You will want to compare that to how big of a change you feel there will be in their department. If they respond by saying "It's a small change," and the project team believes it's a small change, that's good because you are in alignment. If you are out of alignment, you will have to talk to that individual, so that he or she better understands what change is about to happen.

For the attitude toward advancement, ask the team how they feel about the change. Do they feel that the change will be positive for their department, and if so, why? Do they feel that the change will be negative, and if so, why? You then want to compare their answers to your perception of their willingness to change. Some people try to sound good on surveys but aren't truly open to change, so leaders need to assess the answers to see how well they reflect reality.

By conducting this exercise, you are seeking to understand a few things. First, if most people surveyed admit that the proposed change will be negative for their department, you need to go back and better understand the value that they will be getting and reiterate it to the team and their leader. If you have a few objectors, you should understand how much influence they have within the organization. Influential objectors will make the project much harder than it needs to be. You will need to convince those people that the project is good for the organization.

Leaders have to be willing to sell the project one-on-one if necessary. It's crucial that everyone is aligned and understands the value of the project.

## Outline Your Business Process Change Steps

In the next section, I'll talk through this in more detail, but as a leadership team you should agree to a framework for your business process changes. You may go into the project knowing that you will make some business process changes, but soon find out that you will need to make more changes. Go into the project knowing how you're going to make those decisions, how you'll communicate those decisions to the team, and how you will address non-compliance with the new process changes.

## Develop a System Vision that Provides Benefits to All Stakeholders

When we recently applied change management to one of our internal projects, we took the time to list out each of the different user groups who will use the new system. For us, the four groups were those interested in financial statements, the accounting team, project managers, and time entry users. For each group, we took the time to document the difference between the current experience and the new experience. From there we tried to identify what was better or worse about the new experience. Once we had that information, we communicated to them the change and highlighted the benefits of the new system. We then customized a training plan to each of those groups.

Situations exist where a user's job actually gets harder or more time consuming as a result of the new system. You have to be really thoughtful with these users to outline a change in the design of their job to help accommodate the extra activity they now need to take on. Change management is hard enough already, but when you add extra tasks onto the role with the new system, it becomes even more challenging.

I'll cover the communication and training plans in more detail in the next sections, but the big takeaway is that you need to identify each of the stakeholder groups and provide a customized approach to each group.

A high-level way to look at this is to examine the three levels of the organization affected: the leadership, the managers, and the end users, as shown in Figure 7.2.

You can see what might be important to each group. Keep these in mind as you articulate the vision to these groups.

## Communicate Effectively

You may look at this heading and say, "Of course we should communicate effectively." Communication has so many layers that it's hard to give this section an adequate title. In the previous section, we talked about breaking down the team into different groups. Once you do that, you should build a communication plan for each stakeholder group.

At a general level, you want to provide regular communications to the broader company on the progress of the project, and you certainly want to provide updates coming up to the go-live and after the system is live. One of my clients did a weekly video with various members of the leadership and project team highlighting the progress and what benefits the new system would provide. I thought that was a great communication vehicle.

**FIGURE 7.2**
Three levels of organiza-
tion affected

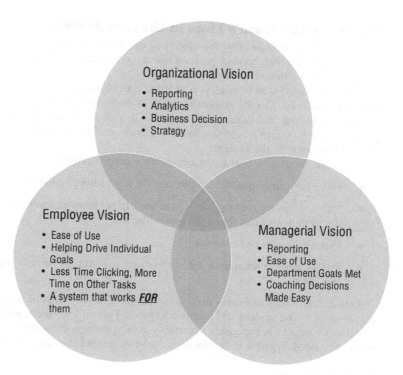

You can never communicate too much when you are doing an ERP or CRM implementation. In fact, it's good to keep in mind the *Rule of 7* for marketing, which states that it takes seven interactions with your brand before a purchase will take place. If you translate this to the business application implementation, it takes seven times to hear about the benefits of this system before users are willing to "buy-in" that the system is a good thing for them. Keep communicating the value so that it becomes ingrained in the company. Doing so will help keep everyone focused on making the project a success.

You should also remember that diverse parties contribute to the success of the project, including:

◆ Suppliers

◆ Independent software vendors

◆ Contractors who work on a small part of the project

◆ Your network technician

All of these stakeholders should receive regular updates on the project. In addition, they must also be given clear tasks and deadlines so that they know what they need to do and when. You would hate to miss your deadline due to the lack of communication on a small piece of the overall puzzle.

## Maximize the Team's Time in the New System

I have long had the belief that the more you use a system, the more you like it. As a new system becomes more familiar to you, you can use it more quickly and effectively; and everyone loves to do things more efficiently.

If you believe this to be true, you should be thinking about how you can get the project team and all of your users in the system as much as possible. You do have to be careful here; if you put people in a system that doesn't work, they will walk away with the belief that the system is no good, they will communicate this to their friends, and pretty soon you will have a major confidence problem with the system.

Let's talk about how best to maximize time in the system:

◆ Have your implementation partner show you the product early and often.

◆ Run conference room pilots where the project team and subject matter experts can get into the system and run through certain steps.

◆ Have the users test extensively.

◆ Put the project team in charge of training so that they have to prepare to train the rest of the users.

One gotcha I see customers do that causes more trouble than it provides in value is to give users access to the system and let them explore. This almost never works well. ERP and CRM systems are complex, and users invariably go somewhere they aren't supposed to go and get stuck. You need to guide them through the system until they are comfortable with each area.

## Train Effectively

The title of this section is rather generic, but there's a lot to explore here. So much so, that Chapter 19, "Training for All," is dedicated to this. Rather than explore this in great detail here, I'll set the expectation that you should have a training plan that is customized for the stakeholder groups and teaches people bite-sized content at any given time.

## Set Realistic Expectations for the System Just After Go-Live

If your users have been following all of the communications and going through all of the training, they are probably thinking that the new system will be the greatest thing since sliced bread. Unfortunately, the first few days after go-live are often marked by confusion, panic, and frustration. If you had a realistic training plan that went through the day-to-day life of each stakeholder group, you may be in a place where users feel good about the system on day one. Most of the time, the training provides a cursory overview of the system and now that users have to work with it for real, they don't remember how or know what to do. Then they do something wrong, and it takes a long time to unwind the problem.

Another issue is that reports may not be terribly effective early on if you didn't import transactional history from the old system. The report they used to run now shows only a handful of recent transactions, so they suspect that it's not working correctly.

The big takeaway here is to set expectations during the training session that it will take your users some time to get comfortable in the new system. They will experience several clumsy days in the system, and that's completely normal. The key is to preach patience and reiterate that the new system will provide the promised benefits once they get used to it.

## Support Your Team Members After Go-Live

This whole chapter has been about change and how hard it is. If you force change upon a group and don't support them after the change has been made, you're asking for trouble. We'll cover this more in Chapter 20, "Going Live," but it's critical from a change management standpoint to have a great Help Desk experience right after go-live. It's also critical to have business process owners ready and available to reiterate the new process as you evolve into this new system.

## Steps to Business Process Change

This is one of the nine steps to change management, but I wanted to pull this one out more specifically to talk about the steps along the way in more depth.

You don't have to follow this system with every little process change you make, but you should absolutely follow it for big changes and have it in mind as you consider those small changes. Let's go through the 11 steps and provide color for each of them:

1.  **Gather feedback from current users during process reviews.** Before you make a change, garner feedback from the team. Is everyone in favor? Are the majority of team members opposed? Do they believe that the change makes their life easier or harder? That last question may impact any potential labor cost or savings from the change.

2.  **Analyze the options with experts.** Before you make the change, make sure that your process owners and your system experts agree on the best course of action. If the best way to do it is super-expensive from a system perspective, seek the best alternative that doesn't cause you to rewrite the system.

3.  **The business process owner makes the process change decision.** It's good to gather perspective, but you can't wait forever to make a decision. It's better to make good decisions quickly than great decisions slowly.

4.  **The functional consultant writes up the system design.** You want to make sure that the design matches the spirit of the change you want to see.

5.  **The project team approves the design.** You want to get feedback from the core team, the business process owner, and the subject matter expert that the proposed design will work well.

6.  **The development team makes the customization.** Once approved, the customization is made. Once it's complete, the functional consultant and core team lead tests the customization to make sure that it satisfies the new process.

7.  **Document and build training for the new process.** Since this is new to the users, you need to make sure to write up solid documentation and build training material for the process change. This documentation and training must explain the why as well as the what.

8.  **Determine the adoption plan.** As part of this, you want to make sure that the team has what it needs to adopt the new process successfully. You also need to consider what happens if people don't follow the new process. Generally, you want to use the carrot and the stick here; at first you help and incent them to follow the new process, but if they don't pick it up over time, you may have to discipline them for not following the process.

9. **Train the team**. Make sure that you take ample time to show them the new process and collect feedback from the training.

10. **Monitor the adoption**. After you have provided training and they start using the process, review your adoption plan to see if it's being followed. If not, tweak the process to make it easier for users, or you may have to reiterate the importance of the new process.

11. **Seek feedback and adjust**. Not all plans are perfect, and you may need to adjust over time. Be open-minded and adjust as needed.

## Importance of Adoption

You may think steps 8 and 10 are harsh, but I see those as important to the process change. If users don't follow the process, the process change has lost all of its potential effectiveness. Adopting new software is hard, and it's common for it not to be followed well right away. Have a support plan in place to get the best adoption you can.

CRM systems, in particular, suffer from lack of frequent adoption. Because they are not transactional systems, you often don't *have* to use them to run your business. If a salesperson meets with a client and doesn't record the conversation in the central CRM system, what's the harm anyway? There may be real harm if other account team members rely on that information. If that's the case, you need to impress upon the team member the importance of teamwork and their role in making the whole account team more effective.

If you walk away with any lesson from this chapter on change management, try to remember that having a plan, even an imperfect one, is better than having no plan.

# The Bottom Line

**Understanding Change Management**   Many project stakeholders don't understand the definition of change management and therefore aren't in a good position to implement it on the project.

**Master It**   What is change management?

1. A series of sessions that talk about how change impacts a project

2. The approaches that you need to prepare your team for and support them through the process or organizational change

3. Trainings before go-live

4. A leadership seminar to prepare the leadership team to be aligned

**Components of Change Management**   Implementing change management successfully requires nine steps. It's important to understand each of these steps and make sure that you have a game plan for each one.

**Master It**   Which one of these is not a step in the change management process?

1. Leadership alignment

2. Organization evaluation

**3.** Communicate effectively

**4.** Hypercare

**Organization Assessment**    One of the steps in change management is to assess your organization to understand how willing and able they are to accept the change that is about to come.

**Master It**    Your organizational assessment should include which step?

**1.** Attitude toward advancement

**2.** Joint process design

**3.** Enterprise process review

**4.** Training plan

**Project Motivation**    When the leadership team agrees to go forward with a business application implementation project, it's important for all team members to understand the success criteria and the motivation for the project.

**Master It**    Which benefit is most commonly sought by the leadership team on a project?

**1.** Limited clicks

**2.** Ease of use

**3.** Reporting and analytics

**4.** Uncluttered screens

**Setting Expectations**    A core component of change management is setting proper expectations for the end users. If they expect the system to be perfect and easy, they will be disappointed when they discover reality.

**Master It**    Just after go-live, which of the following situations is most likely to occur?

**1.** The system is bug free.

**2.** Users can find all of the reports they need.

**3.** Security is set up perfectly.

**4.** It will take longer to get through processes.

# Chapter 8

# Organizing Your Business by Processes

You will get a lot of different answers when you ask businesspeople how different their business is from others—what makes their business unique is what drives people to be in business. The more specifics that you know about a business, the more you can say that businesses are very different at the detail level. A venture capitalist would say all businesses are the same in the abstract or summary. In reality, you are both right. Businesses are both similar and different, and that's what makes them so interesting.

The goal of this chapter is to find the common language that all businesses speak. By using this common language, focusing on the common denominators that businesses have at their core operating level, we can bring many advantages to the implementation. We can take advantage of the out-of-the-box functionality within the systems to help us implement them more quickly, more easily, and with fewer customizations and future spend to maintain that system. We're still in the Define stage of the journey, which means that we're setting the stage for the work to be completed once the full implementation effort starts. We're still trying to set ourselves up for a successful project. The goal is to identify this common language in order to make sure that you are comfortable with where your scope is before you hit the kickoff meeting.

**AFTER YOU COMPLETE THIS CHAPTER, YOU WILL BE ABLE TO DO THE FOLLOWING:**

- ◆ Identify the common language that all businesses speak
- ◆ Understand high-level process categories
- ◆ Uncover key business processes

## Common Language Businesses Speak

I've had the opportunity to provide guidance to entrepreneurs as they look to start or grow their businesses. Entrepreneurs are highly intelligent, motivated, and passionate people who can't wait to change the world with their product or idea. Oftentimes, however, the realities of what it takes to run a business are not understood and lead to the downfall of the idea or product. What I tell entrepreneurs is that there are three common core areas of their business where they need a strong foundation or capability to be successful in the long-term. It doesn't matter what the business is—all businesses need to have these capabilities.

## Operations

First, you need the product. Whatever you're intending to sell, you need to know how to make it or perform the service. You need to have people or resources for the business to work. If you make widgets, you need to know how to make them, and you need the raw material to put into them. If you run a taco truck, you need to buy the ingredients and know how to make a great taco. If you own real estate, you need to know where best to buy that real estate and how to maintain it for tenants. That's what I consider the operations side of the business.

## Sales

You have to be able to sell whatever it is you have or are building. You need to have a resource or platform that can convince someone to buy it, or you need to look to match a solution to a problem. If you make widgets, you need to sell your widgets to another manufacturer or to an end user. If you run a taco truck, you need a sign, prices, and someone out front taking the orders. If you own real estate, you need to commission a realtor to find a buyer for your land. Sales can be very different across these different businesses, but they all need an approach for sales and marketing.

## Finance and Administration

Entrepreneurs know that they need a product or service, and they need to sell that product or service. Most entrepreneurs do not care about anything in the (what some say unexciting) finance and administration category: "Let's go make money first, and we'll hire a CPA firm to sort it out later" is often the strategy. Creating processes, creating procedures, developing efficiency in your operations, and knowing your numbers helps you make good decisions about your business, so this is not an area to ignore. To continue with my divergent examples from the previous two sections, if you make widgets, you need to know the cost of each part and for how much you can sell them, know how many you sold during the last period, and perhaps own a system to track your formula and build instructions, as well as to identify the vendor who supplied the raw materials. If you run a taco truck, you need a point-of-sale system to take credit cards, and you need to report if your revenue was greater than your labor plus food costs. If you own real estate, you need to look at your leases to see if you are making enough to afford your loan payments. Every business needs a balance sheet, a profit/loss statement, and a cash flow statement no matter what you sell.

## Standard Processes

There is a non-profit organization called APQC, or the American Productivity & Quality Center, that seeks to be the world's foremost authority on process improvement and knowledge management. APQC started in 1977 with the mission to improve American competitiveness in the growing global market. The founder, Jack Grayson, saw that productivity growth was failing and businesses needed a common language of processes to improve their productivity.

Over the years since its start, APQC has developed and continuously iterated its cross-industry *process classification framework (PCF)*. The framework lays out a hierarchy of processes that can apply to businesses across different industries. Not every one of their processes will apply to your business, but if it's a common core process, it's in there.

At the highest level, APQC identified *process categories,* and there are 13 core categories under which all the other processes exist. The core categories are as follows:

- Develop Vision and Strategy

- Develop and Manage Products and Services

- Market and Sell Products and Services

- Deliver Physical Products

- Deliver Services

- Manage Customer Service

- Develop and Manage Human Capital

- Manage Information Technology

- Manage Financial Resources

- Acquire, Construct, and Manage Assets

- Manage Enterprise Risk, Compliance, Remediation, and Resiliency

- Manage External Relationships

- Develop and Manage Business Capabilities

Underneath that category level, the process framework lays out subsidiary levels, as explained in the following sections. As shown in Figure 8.1, these levels build out a hierarchy of process flow content from the category or title level all the way down to a single task or transaction.

**FIGURE 8.1**

Process classifica-
tion framework

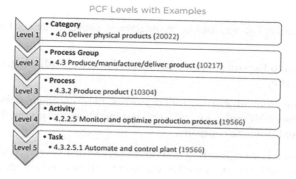

PCF Levels with Examples

- **Category**
- Level 1 • 4.0 Deliver physical products (20022)

- **Process Group**
- Level 2 • 4.3 Produce/manufacture/deliver product (10217)

- **Process**
- Level 3 • 4.3.2 Produce product (10304)

- **Activity**
- Level 4 • 4.2.2.5 Monitor and optimize production process (19566)

- **Task**
- Level 5 • 4.3.2.5.1 Automate and control plant (19566)

At Stoneridge Software, we used this framework as a guide for developing a framework that was a better fit for ERP and CRM implementations. Our framework uses terms more commonly heard during those implementations like Quote to Cash and Procure to Pay, and it has grown out of the APQC highly regarded standards and approach, though modified to support software implementations in a business.

To learn more about the APQC, you can check out its website and sign up to get access to its content for free at apqc.org.

# Process Hierarchy

Building our queues or process flows from the APQC, we have organized a standard Process Catalog that we believe works well for ERP and CRM implementations. We kept most of the concepts from the APQC work in terms of naming our hierarchy Process Category, then Process Group, then Process, and from there we diverge a little bit as sometimes you may have a sub-process, an activity, a task, or a requirement that fits under that process label. We wanted to provide more flexibility at that detail level.

To give you a sense of this common framework, I'll provide definitions for the high-level process categories and some examples of what might fit in the process groups and processes so that you have a better sense of how this classification process works.

## Process Category

We envision a *Process Category* as an end-to-end business process where you take a transaction from start to finish through a series of logically connected processes. One of the core categories is *Quote to Cash*. This process takes you from initiating a discussion about a product or service with a customer or prospect all the way to collecting cash from that customer upon the successful conclusion of the sale. In the restaurant business, this may be a very brief transaction: a person walks up to a counter, sees the menu, and orders a burger for $5. The customer hands the cashier $5, receives the burger, and walks away. Many system requirements are still happening inside that seemingly easy process, but I wanted to illustrate the fact that some transactions may be pretty straightforward. A large sale for an engineered and manufactured piece of equipment may have quotes that become a sales order, which when production is complete, allows the item to be crated, shipped, and invoiced. But at its heart, there is a demand, a sale, a handover of goods at an agreed-upon price, and a payment.

We introduced our 12 process categories in Chapter 2, "What to Do Before You Begin a Project," but we didn't spend much time talking about them in depth. The 12 categories are as follows:

**Acquire to Retire:** The acquisition, management, preventive maintenance, and retirement of assets.

**Financial Plan to Report:** All processes around finance, budgeting, cash management, and financial reporting.

**Hire to Retire:** From advertising for employees, to hiring them, onboarding them, managing them while they are employed, including paying them and giving them benefits all the way to their retirement from the company.

**Idea to Product:** The engineering and development of a new or modified product offering, the build structure or formula, as well as the resource times and equipment needed to produce the item.

**Issue to Resolution:** The customer service process of identifying an issue to the point where you resolve it to the customer's satisfaction.

**Market to Opportunity:** The development of marketing plans to the point where a customer wants to speak to you about buying your product or using your services.

**Plan to Inventory:** The forecasting, production, and distribution planning of demand and supply or the management of your site, warehouses, and bins for inventory.

**Procure to Pay:** The process of acquiring a part, product, or service at negotiated prices; receiving the product and paying your vendor for that part, product, or service.

**Project to Profit:** Everything related to tracking projects whether they be for external services that you provide to customers, internal resources, or capital project tracking.

**Quote to Cash:** The process of generating a quote or selling something with shipments to the point where you collect the cash for the product or service.

**Schedule to Produce:** Taking the production and distribution plans to drive production orders per the schedule to meet demand and create inventory for distribution or consumption in other items.

**Service Call to Profit:** Field service processes like dispatching, service contracts, and collections.

It's important to understand which of your processes fit into these 12 high-level groups. Plan to organize your processes in these groups before starting your ERP or CRM evaluation, and then work with your partner to dig deeper throughout the implementation, starting with the core processes and then adding edge processes.

## Process Group

A Process Group is a set of three to seven processes that fit a particular function within the business. One example that would apply to either ERP or CRM is "Configure Product Sales Information." This is a process group that sits inside the Quote to Cash process category. It's a fancy way of saying price your product. Many customers struggle with knowing the right price to set for a product, so you have many considerations inside this process group, such as determining margin, discounts (by customer, by quantity, and so on), writing your description of the product for your website, adding in taxes, and ultimately configuring the price. Anything that you do within your company that relates to pricing should fit into this process group.

The important thing to remember about all of these process groups is that you want to be consistent across all lines of business. If you have three distinct lines of business, you would consider all of their pricing needs at one time; this allows you to gain consistency and reduce the amount of customization that might be needed for a standard process in your organization.

## Process

A *process* is a basic set of steps that you complete to perform a function inside of your business. It's harder to explain than it is to show examples. One example in the Idea to Product process category and the "Develop Products" process group is "Create or Maintain a Product Bill of Material." This means that any steps, activities, or requirements needed to manage your bill of materials would be part of this process. When a new product is produced that has a bill of materials, you would need to complete the steps for this process to put it into the system. You would also need to consider the steps taken when an engineering change order is required or when an item is obsoleted and will no longer be produced. Once again, you want to consider every department or area of the business that would use this information as you put together your consistent process here.

Another example of a basic process that applies to both ERP and CRM systems is "Create and Maintain a Customer." This process falls into the Manage Customers process group of the Quote to Cash process category, and it controls what information you need to collect at the time you create a customer. You will want their company name for sure, but maybe you will also want their legal name (in other words, Contoso is the company name, but Contoso Ltd. is the legal name). This is an example of a requirement that relates to the Create/Maintain Customer process.

### Sub-processes, Tasks, Activities, and Requirements

The standard hierarchy that we bring to a project includes the process categories, groups, and processes, and underneath the process layer, we like to leave that open for each business to identify the process components to suit their specific needs. For example, to extend the Create/ Maintain Customer process, maybe you have a different process that you follow if the customer is a government agency. Perhaps for that you need to track two or three different fields, and you require government approval before recognizing them as a customer. That would be a sub-process underneath the standard process that you would want to track. I referenced previously how we track legal names as a separate field in our system when we create a customer, which is a custom requirement for our system. You may require a form to be completed to create this customer in your system, and you may also require the completion of a W-9 form. These would be examples of tasks associated to that process.

As you can see, the further you break down the steps that you take to do these core elements of your business, the easier it is to build a system around it.

## Discovering Your Processes

Now that you know about standard processes, you may be thinking, "That's great, but how do I know what processes we use?" As a way to start, I would recommend that you try to document as many business scenarios as you can and organize them into those 12 high-level process categories. This is a big task and not something that someone can do in a couple of hours. This takes a coordinated effort across multiple people and multiple departments in the business to come up with a good set of documentation for your processes.

You may say, "We don't have time to do this." You need to make the time. You need to ascertain the priorities or focus areas within the business. If you don't do it up front, you will have to do it as part of the implementation, and once that starts, you'll be busier than you want to be. Also, you'll end up having to create test cases for every area of the business, so if you take the time to document those scenarios, you can provide them to your implementer so that the implementer knows what the system needs to do. Those scenarios make great test cases when you enter the Deploy stage of the project.

### SIPOC

One great tool to use to help identify what your processes are is a tool called *SIPOC*. What it stands for basically tells you how it works:

*Suppliers*: Who provides you with inputs?

*Inputs*: What are the inputs that you need to create your output?

*Processes*: What do you do with the inputs to create your output?

*Output*: What do you generate from these inputs?

*Consumers*: Who consumes your output?

This is a great whiteboarding exercise that you can use to discern and discover what your processes are. Figure 8.2 outlines the process.

**FIGURE 8.2**
SIPOC diagram

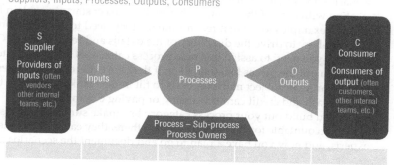

Pick a process category (like Quote to Cash) and ask subject matter experts to tell you all about the quoting process. You can start at either end of the diagram. Perhaps you will start with the consumer side and ask questions like the following:

"Who do we give quotes to?"

Let's say that you are a home builder, and you give quotes to families who want to buy a new house.

"What do you give them?"

You give them a written quote breaking out the key areas and costs for those areas.

"What are the inputs that you need to give a good quote?"

You need to know what type of siding they want and how big the house is and what type of floor covering they want.

"Who gives you that information?"

First, you get the basic requirements from your families looking for a new home and then you reach out to suppliers to find out how much things will cost. Now you're starting to figure out the process just by talking through what happens.

The processes are as follows:

1. Get requirements from the family (or better yet, blueprints from an architect).

2. Divide the house into all of the different suppliers you would need to complete the project.

3. Seek a quote from each of those vendors based on the requirements and specifications that you were given.

4. Produce a nice-looking quote for the family that shows each of those areas and a description of how their requirements will be met.

This didn't require an expensive business analyst to help you figure out your processes; you just broke down the inputs, outputs, supplies, and consumers, and you pieced together the steps necessary to get them what they need.

## Core Team Members

To come up with a broad view of your business processes, you need to engage your project's core team members so that they can understand the process hierarchy and how to break down the scenarios and organize them into common processes. The best practice would be to organize a meeting with each of the members before the project starts to explain the theory and walk through examples to make it real for them—they need to own their process hierarchy and have a vision of how to drive the discovery of the details and requirements. Once you've done that training, you need to assign business process categories to your core team members so that they can try to put the pieces together. Even if they are experts in your sales operations, they may still need to bring in subject matter experts to fill in the blanks of some of the more detailed processes, such as cash and credit card processing or paying commissions.

As you build out your process category list, make sure that you also list the core team member who is accountable for that category. From there, they can add the relevant subject matter experts, and now you have a plan to go and document the scenarios and processes.

## Rounding Out Your Scope

Setting an accurate, achievable scope is instrumental in completing your project on time and within budget. By reviewing your processes and scenarios early in the project, you can have a really good idea where you are going with this implementation so that you can make sure you get there.

The more time you take to document these processes and scenarios ahead of time, the better positioned you will be throughout the implementation. If a new scenario pops up in the middle of the implementation, it's easy to document it, but it's hard to make it work in the system while the rest of the implementation is going on. The recommendation to take the time to be well prepared as you go into your implementation and be thorough in your process discovery is hard work, but it is vital. You can always choose to postpone work on a scenario if you need to prioritize other, more important areas during an implementation, but the impact of that decision is visible and can be planned around.

# The Bottom Line

**Associating Activities to Process Categories**   It's important to identify the common activities you do in your system today and associate them back to the top-level categories so that you can start to see all of the activities across your different departments that are really the same.

**Master It**   In what process category would creating a vendor belong?

1. Quote to Cash

2. Procure to Pay

3. Acquire to Retire

4. Financial Record to Report

**Understanding the Process Hierarchy**   You will want to understand the process hierarchy so that you can quickly classify activities into the correct level on the hierarchy.

**Master It**   Which of these process levels is the top level (broadest)?

**1.** Process Category

**2.** Process Group

**3.** Process

**4.** Sub-Process

**Setting Up the Proper Hierarchy in Azure DevOps**   Azure DevOps is a valuable tool to use on your project. You want to set up a hierarchy in that system that maps to the hierarchy of Process Categories, Process Groups, and Processes.

**Master It**   A process category most closely aligns to what type of record in DevOps or Agile methodology?

**1.** Requirement

**2.** User story

**3.** Feature

**4.** Epic

**Adding Work Impacts Your Timeline**   Anytime a new process becomes part of the project scope, this adds work to the project. That work will need to be managed, and resources will need to be assigned to complete it. You will need to notify the project stakeholders about this change.

**Master It**   If you add a major requirement or scope item after the beginning of the project, you will need to complete which of the following?

**1.** A Master Services Agreement

**2.** A Process Category

**3.** An Earned Value Curve

**4.** A Change Request

**Understanding Terms**   It's important to create a common language on your project—some team members may not be familiar with implementation project terms, so you will need to educate the team involved on the project.

**Master It**   Which of these constitutes a software requirement on a project?

**1.** A user story

**2.** A function or piece of information needed to run your business

**3.** Everything you do in the business

**4.** Showing up to work

# Chapter 9

# Independent Software Vendors— Filling Gaps and Managing Partnerships

*Independent Software Vendors (ISVs)* are software companies that provide extensions to the Microsoft Dynamics platform to fill a particular gap in the software. Some ISVs write their code on top of the Dynamics platform, and others write solutions independently and integrate them into Dynamics.

Microsoft's Chief Technical Officer (CTO) has shared with me the philosophy that Microsoft Dynamics is really designed to incorporate about 80 percent of what you're going to need to run your business. The bulk of the capability is going to be provided by Microsoft, but certain things are best suited to be filled by different types of ISVs. This chapter will include examples of the different types of ISVs so that you can learn more about what common gaps are and how they are filled.

## AFTER YOU COMPLETE THIS CHAPTER, YOU WILL BE ABLE TO DO THE FOLLOWING:

- ◆ Understand the purpose of ISVs and how to work with them
- ◆ Recognize hosting providers
- ◆ Identify the value of industry ISVs
- ◆ Fill gaps with functional ISVs
- ◆ Find solutions on Microsoft's AppSource Marketplace

## The Purpose of ISVs

Microsoft Dynamics was designed with a broad set of features across the core functions that a business could perform. As of this writing, Microsoft Dynamics provides functionality across the following business areas:

- ◆ Sales
- ◆ Marketing

◆ Customer Service

◆ Field Service

◆ Project Management

◆ Human Resources

◆ Finance

◆ Supply Chain Management

◆ Commerce

You may look at this list and think that it covers everything you need. At a high level, it probably does. The potential gaps usually sit at a much more granular level.

I classify ISVs into one of three types:

◆ **Hosting Providers**: Partners who focus on providing hosting services for the environments needed to run Microsoft Dynamics

◆ **Industry ISVs**: Solutions designed to fill gaps in a particular industry

◆ **Functional ISVs**: Solutions designed to fill a gap that could affect any particular industry

# Hosting Providers

Microsoft Dynamics 365 has been designed to be hosted in the cloud by Microsoft. The major platforms of Microsoft Dynamics 365 Customer Engagement, Finance & Supply Chain Management, and Business Central are all built on top of Microsoft's Azure hosting platform, and when you buy a license for the software, the hosting is included as part of the price.

This section wouldn't apply to a company using the latest version of Microsoft Dynamics 365—you wouldn't need a hosting provider. If you are using an older version of Microsoft Dynamics, you may need a hosting provider. The following Microsoft Dynamics solutions are not cloud-hosted and could require a hosting provider:

◆ Microsoft Dynamics AX

◆ Microsoft Dynamics NAV

◆ Microsoft Dynamics GP

◆ Microsoft Dynamics SL

◆ Microsoft Dynamics CRM On-premises

If you are using one of these older versions of Microsoft Dynamics, you have three different options for hosting your software. You can host the software yourself (the most common); you can work directly with Microsoft to host your solution on its Azure cloud, or use a hosting provider or hosting ISV.

## Private Hosting

Private hosting is where you buy the licenses, and you look for a provider to host the software for you. You may look to Microsoft's Azure platform for this, or you can work with many different hosting providers. In this case, you own the software licenses, and you pay a monthly fee to your hosting provider to host the servers and provide the network and uptime to make sure that your software is running when you need it.

## SaaS-Style Hosting

A slightly different option that's become popular on the Microsoft Dynamics GP product is to have a hosting provider combine the software and the hosting as part of a package. In this case, you pay one monthly fee that includes everything you need to run the software. The provider will often include functional ISVs as part of this package as well. You have greater flexibility with this model, and you only have to worry about one provider.

## Industry ISVs

Microsoft has built Dynamics as a platform, and it's intended to appeal to a wide variety of businesses everywhere from companies in healthcare to agriculture to manufacturing to distribution to construction and to government. While all of these businesses have core functions that they must perform, they certainly have differences as well. If you are a "make to stock" manufacturer, you may have over 90 percent of your needs met by the core solution. If you make custom apparel that you sell online to any configuration anywhere around the world, you will likely need to extend Dynamics in several ways to accomplish your solution goals.

Depending on your industry, you may need or want to have an industry-focused ISV to fill the gaps in your solution. One easy example is the healthcare industry. A hospital calls its customers "patients," so if you went live with a system that called everyone who comes in to get treated a customer, you would confuse many people. Microsoft has built some healthcare accelerators (which are similar to ISVs) that will convert the word "customer" to "patient" across the application to make it more suitable to that industry. In the construction industry, contractors are generally asked to produce "AIA-compatible documents" for contracts. This is a standard industry form mandated by the American Institute of Architects, and if the core software doesn't have contracts in the AIA-approved form, you will look to an industry ISV to fill in that gap.

That example helps paint the picture, but an *industry ISV* is just an ISV who is focused on extending the functionality of the product for a particular industry. Depending on how important customizations are to that industry, this may make the ISV solution required for that industry.

Typically, the need for an industry ISV is determined early in the sales process. Because customers are referred to as patients in healthcare, you need a solution to bridge that gap. There is a Dynamics 365 Healthcare Accelerator that treats customers as patients and provides HIPAA and HITRUST compliance as well as entities and forms that integrate well with other Electronic Medical Record systems.

Levridge (levridge.com) is an ISV solution dedicated to the agriculture industry. If you are thinking of using Dynamics and you're in the agriculture industry, it is likely that you will need the features that Levridge has built for that industry. Agriculture has several unique requirements that don't exist in most core ERP and CRM solutions, such as:

**Farms, fields, and zones:** Growers keep track of their farms and which fields make up those farms. They often associate transactions with a particular field, so the ERP or CRM system needs to be able to associate activity with a field, and that construct doesn't exist in these systems by default.

**Split transactions:** In agriculture, growers often need to split the purchase of agronomy products, or the sale of grain products among family members, or landowners, so this requires you to split transactions at the point of sale, and that's not in standard ERP systems.

**Bid/offer system:** When buying grain, you can place a "bid" to sell your grain at a future date based on the market price at that time, or you could put in an "offer" to indicate that you are willing to sell grain at a specific market price. These are not concepts found in core ERP systems.

**Advanced settlements:** All ERP systems have the ability to settle a payment against an outstanding balance, but many, many more options exist for settling deliveries of grain. You can settle it against an existing contract, put the grain in storage, sell it at the current market price, or any combination thereof.

**Scale tickets:** A scale ticket is like the receipt at a restaurant or department store; it's the record of how much grain was taken in at the elevator. This value starts the whole settlements process.

The Levridge ISV solution has many more agriculture-specific features, but this gives you an idea of how many critical features are included in that package, which makes it a required part of the Dynamics solution if you're in that industry.

Critical industry ISVs should be a core part of the selection process and should be demonstrated during the sales cycle. You want to make sure that this solution will work in harmony with the rest of your Dynamics solution.

## Deciding If You Need an Industry ISV

There may be certain industry ISVs that aren't critical, but that provide functionality that you need even though it's not obvious during the sales cycle. For example, you may use the Project Operations or Job Cost functionality inside Dynamics for construction projects, but you may be lacking an AIA-approved contract or procedures to close out the project. Those features may be included in a construction or project-based industry ISV that you can purchase.

You should be running a *fit/gap analysis* during the sales cycle to expose the major gaps in your system. You run another fit/gap analysis in the Design phase of the implementation, and you will look at what degree of fit exists in the solution at that time. If it's a high degree of fit, you are likely best off with filling in the gaps with customizations. If you find that you are missing several features in an area, that's when you should look to an industry ISV to fill that gap. You may need a project-based ISV to provide additional functionality there. The decision comes down to weighing the cost of the ISV compared to the cost of developing those features as customizations. You should weigh each option, review the relevant ISVs, and make your decision from there.

## Functional ISVs

Functional ISVs are solutions that provide functionality or an extension in an area where the core Dynamics solution either doesn't have an answer or the answer doesn't meet your business needs. The following are five scenarios where you may look to bring in an extension from a functional ISV:

1. Dynamics lacks specific functionality (missing functionality)

2. Dynamics has a base level of functionality, but you need more advanced functionality in that area (advanced features)

3. A built-in integration to an outside product that you need is unavailable (missing connector)

4. Dynamics has the functionality, but this software automates the function (automation)

5. Reporting aggregation solutions (reporting)

## Missing Functionality

One example of missing functionality that I like to use is a *Learning Management System (LMS)*. Many times during an implementation, you need a place to store links to Microsoft's learning content, documentation, and the eLearning that you've developed about your system that you need end users to study. Dynamics doesn't have an LMS out of the box, so if you want that functionality to exist within your Dynamics system, you will need to look to an ISV to provide it. It isn't an industry ISV, because it isn't industry-specific. This need could apply to any industry.

## Advanced Features

All of the Dynamics platforms have the means to add sales tax to an invoice and track the collection of the tax. No Dynamics platform has functionality that will take the tax paid by the customer and automatically send it to the jurisdictions in question. If you operate in multiple states, I recommend that you invest in one of the three major ISVs that provide a more advanced sales tax solution: Avalara (`avalara.com`), Wolters Kluwer (`salestax.com`), or Vertex (`vertexinc.com`). With these more advanced solutions, they will automatically update the sales tax rates for you in all of your jurisdictions, track the collections of that tax, file it with the proper local, state, or federal governments, and often take on the liability if there's a sales tax error. If you compare the cost of managing those rates and filings compared to the cost of the ISV solution, you may find that paying for this functional ISV is well worth the investment.

Another common advanced feature depends on the number of banks you use. If you use five or more banks, you may want to invest in an eBanking solution that allows you to do ACH transactions with all of those different banks.

## Missing Connector

Microsoft does not typically build connectors with defined integrations between Dynamics and other common software solutions. With the *Power Platform*, Microsoft has created many connectors that give you the chance to make the connection. Tools like *Power Apps*, *Power Automate*, and *Power BI* may allow you to interact with them in certain ways, but you're not going to find a complete two-way integration provided by Microsoft to other software solutions.

An example of this would be an eCommerce connector. Let's say that you use Magento to run your website, and you want to make sure that Microsoft Dynamics 365 Business Central connects to this eCommerce site. Microsoft is not going to provide a complete connector there, so you would have the option of building your own or buying a solution that exists on the ISV marketplace today.

## Automation

You can certainly pay invoices out of your Dynamics ERP system, but if you want a solution that provides automation of your accounts payable, you will need to look to an ISV to provide that capability; many are available on the marketplace today. Typically, they allow you to take an existing vendor invoice and map the fields back to Dynamics so that the next time you receive one of those invoices, you can scan the invoice and automatically create the payable transaction from it. You only want to buy an AP automation tool if you have sufficient payables volume. If you do, however, you can save money in the long run by buying an ISV solution to create greater automation.

## Reporting Extensions

Depending on what type of reporting you want to do with the system, you may look to bring in an ISV to help build your data structure. If you build a data warehouse, for example, ISVs are available that have pre-built cubes that make it easier to create visualizations from that data, rather than having to put the data together before building the report.

### Deciding If You Need a Functional ISV

You may (and certainly should if you can) uncover the need for a functional ISV in the sales cycle. If you do, make the decision then so it doesn't potentially impact your project timeline.

If you didn't make a selection in the initial purchase, you should look at the situation after you run your fit/gap analysis in the Design phase of the implementation. During that analysis, you will look at what degree of fit exists in the solution. If it's a high degree of fit, you are likely best off with filling in the gaps with customizations. If you find that you are missing several features that a functional ISV could fulfill, that's when you should look to an ISV to fill that gap. You should weigh each option, review the relevant ISVs, and make your decision from there.

## Working with ISVs

When you bring ISVs into your implementation, you are introducing another variable that needs to be managed. Many times, managing the ISV can be a big challenge and risk to the project, so you have to make sure that you have a good plan to get what you need from that provider when you need it.

Typically, when you buy an ISV product, some amount of implementation expertise is required to install, configure, and train on the product. This introduces additional consulting time to your project. Hopefully, you planned for this in the sales cycle; if you didn't, you will need to execute a change request to add the hours needed to get this ISV working for you.

## Budgeting for ISV Solutions

If you outlined your needs while thoroughly preparing for the sales cycle, you should have identified all of the areas where you would need solutions. Your partner should be up front with you on what the product can and cannot do, so you would know whether you need an ISV to fill a gap. In the vast majority of cases, you should identify the need for the ISV in the sales cycle, thus allowing you to budget for the license and implementation costs associated with it. You build the costs into the budget that's approved by your leadership team or board, and you go on with your project.

If you discover the need for an ISV solution after the initial budget has been ratified, you will need to tap into your contingency budget for the ongoing software fees and the implementation. If the implementation will be managed through the partner, you will need to create a change request to indicate the expected cost of the implementation and the impact on your budget. Remember, anytime you change your budget and add more work, you will need to assess the impact on your timeline. If you don't bring on additional resources, you will likely need to extend the timeline for your project.

For the implementation of the ISV solution, plan to add hours to your consulting budget to cover the project management time, technical consultant time, and functional expertise. Oftentimes, the project management and technical consultant work will be done by the implementation partner and the functional resource may come from the ISV.

## Implementation Partner or Customer Managed

One of the first decisions you have to make when you bring in an ISV is whether you should contract with and manage the ISV, or if you want your implementation partner to manage them. Customers have different philosophies on this, so determine what is most important to you. If as the customer you want to contract with the ISV directly, you may have more leverage in your negotiations, which may save money on the project. If you do that, however, you are likely taking on the burden of managing that part of the implementation. If you are managing the ISV implementation, and the implementation partner is managing the rest of the project, those two parties may not be aligned.

I strongly recommend working through your implementation partner to find and negotiate with the ISV. If the partner is responsible for selecting and working with the ISV, they are then responsible for the delivery of that portion of the project. The implementation partner may not choose the cheapest ISV solution, but that's probably because they have experience working with a variety of ISVs. It's in their best interest to find the solution that will be the easiest to implement in your environment. At the end of the day, the most important thing is to get the project done successfully, so if you pay a little extra for an ISV solution, it won't matter in the end.

## Buying the ISV License or Subscription

Once you determine that an ISV solution is necessary, you will need to work to be granted access to their software. In cloud implementations, this likely means buying a subscription to access the software in the cloud. In the on-premise world, this would mean buying a license to the software. Either way, you need to work with the ISV to negotiate for the software. Most ISVs prefer to work with the partner on the negotiation for the software, so you will likely end up having to work across three parties to complete the deal. You can leave the selection process up to the implementation partner and give them a budget to work with to find the right solution.

When you acquire the software, you will likely be required to sign a separate license or subscription agreement that governs the terms of the use of that product.

Implementation partners typically make a margin on the sale of ISV products, and this sometimes impacts a customer's willingness to allow the partner to negotiate directly with the ISV because they are incented to have the price be higher. If you have trust built with your partner, count on them to do what's in the best interest of the project.

## Implementation of ISV Products

Most ISVs want to have their partner implement their software for them. Many times, the partner is not experienced enough with that software to implement it. In those cases, the partner needs to pull in consultants from the ISV organization to complete the install, configuration, and training. The best-case scenario is if your partner has consultants who know the software well enough to implement it. You are then able to work with your partner's resources to complete that portion of the project.

Adding another ISV brings another variable to the project that has to be managed. I suggest giving your implementation partner the accountability to make sure that the solution is delivered with the same methodology and within the same structure as the rest of the project.

The first step to get the ISV product working is to install their solution into your development or test environment. From there you will likely need to give permissions to the solution components so that you can begin to see the capability in your system. Once you've installed the solution and provided access to it, you can begin configuring it to meet your particular requirements. Your team will need to learn how to configure and use the software to get the most out of this capability.

## Manage Your ISV Projects Closely

The ISV implementation can be a very big risk to your project. One company that ended up being a customer of ours implemented NetSuite with a field service ISV that wasn't compatible with the version of NetSuite they were forced to use and ended up having to abandon the project because they couldn't adequately use NetSuite without that field service solution. You have to mitigate quite a few potential problems here:

**Understand your partner's experience with the solution**. Regardless if you or the partner will be managing the ISV portion of the implementation, the project will go much smoother if the ISV and implementation partner can work well together. If the partner has worked extensively with the ISV in the past, they may be able to implement it on their own, which lowers the risk of the implementation. If they say that they know it but don't, it can be risky to the project because it will take them a long time to learn and then implement that solution. Get a true answer from your partner on their experience, and make sure that you budget for potential issues due to lack of knowledge of the solution.

**Validate the compatibility of the ISV with Microsoft Dynamics**. You not only need to validate that it works with your current version of Dynamics, but you have to make sure that the ISV has an ongoing plan to remain compatible with the upcoming releases of the product. If it's compatible now, but they won't promise compatibility on later versions, you are taking a big risk that the solution won't work in the future. If it's not compatible with the current version, you should pass on this solution, as it's too big of a risk that they don't prioritize remaining compatible.

**Identify who is making any customizations to the ISV software.** Most ISVs will want to "own" any customizations that are made to their system so that they can incorporate it into their product long-term. This can slow down the process of getting your implementation done, so it's often better to have your partner make the ISV customizations.

**Identify an escalation point with the ISV organization.** You may want your partner to own the relationship with the ISV organization, but you need to be able to work with the ISV directly if problems arise.

**TIP** Working with an ISV solution introduces risk to the project. It's certainly worth it if you need that solution, just make sure that you have a good plan to mitigate any issues that arise.

## Microsoft's AppSource Marketplace

Now that you've learned more about ISVs, you are probably wondering, "Where do I find these ISVs?" You can certainly use your standard search engine to find a particular solution to fit your needs, but Microsoft has a specific search engine that you can use called *AppSource*.

Microsoft's AppSource (`appsource.microsoft.com`) was officially launched in July 2016, and it serves as the one-stop shop to find approved Microsoft ISVs across all of the Microsoft business applications including Microsoft Dynamics and the Power Platform. AppSource also includes Consulting Services so that you can look for consulting packages from Microsoft implementation partners as well.

To be listed on AppSource, the solutions have to pass through a validation process with Microsoft. Each Dynamics product has a bit of a different validation process, but Microsoft partners need to work through Microsoft to get their products or services listed on AppSource.

As you can see by the search options shown in Figure 9.1, you can refine your search by category, industry, or product. If you are a government organization looking for a Human Resources solution on Dynamics 365, you can refine your search to the few solutions that meet these criteria.

**FIGURE 9.1**
Microsoft AppSource Marketplace search functionality

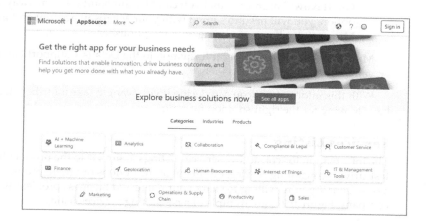

## Product Listing

When you find an ISV solution that might meet your needs, you can click into the detail where you can see more information about the product. Within that screen, you can see many different options:

**Product Title**: This is the marketed name for the product.

**Publisher**: This is the company that created the app.

**Rating**: Here you can see the rating from users of the software. As of this writing, there are very few ratings in AppSource, so I recommend that you take these ratings with a grain of salt until you have many more ratings out there.

**Preferred Solution**: Under the rating, there's an optional designation that will indicate if this is a preferred solution. Microsoft defines this as a cloud application selected for its quality, performance, and ability to address customer needs in a certain industry vertical or solution area.

**Overview**: This is the general text showing a description of the software along with its features.

**Reviews**: This tab will show you the results from anyone who has reviewed the software.

**Screenshots and Videos**: Publishers are required to provide screenshots of their solution, which will appear on the right of the screen. Publishers may also provide videos.

**Contact Options**: In the header, you will see some different options, such as:

**Contact Me**: This means that you will need contact the publisher in order to try and/or buy the software.

**Save for Later**: When you click this option, AppSource will remember this app as something in which you are interested.

**Test Drive**: This allows you to start using a trial version of the software. A preconfigured environment that demonstrates the application's key features and benefits will be created for you to try.

**Get It Now**: This means that you can buy this solution right away. If you choose this option, you will need to sign in with your Microsoft account and give permission to allow Microsoft to share your name with the publisher.

**Metadata**: You will see other information in the Details + support tab, like the categories, version, and supported products.

With this information, you can decide if you want to take a further step to contact the ISV or keep looking for the right solution for you.

## Services Listing

The information for consulting services listings is similar to the product listing. You can't test-drive a consulting service, but many of the options out there provide you with a free assessment if you're willing to share your name and business problem with a consulting company. Figure 9.2 is an example of a consulting services listing.

**FIGURE 9.2**
Services listing example

The consulting services listings don't include the rating or review options at the time of this writing, so you will have to contact the service provider to see if they are the right fit for you.

## The Bottom Line

**Common Terminology**    It's important for project stakeholders to understand commonly used terms in the industry.

   **Master It**    What does the abbreviation ISV stand for as it relates to Microsoft Dynamics?

   1. Integrated Solution Vendors

   2. Independent Software Vendors

   3. Isolated Solution Vehicles

   4. Third Parties

**Different Focuses of ISVs**    There are three types of ISVs, and each focuses on providing different functionality to augment Microsoft Dynamics.

   **Master It**    Functional ISVs are used to provide which of the following?

   1. An add-on solution specific to an industry

   2. A solution for gaps in one functional area

   3. Core Microsoft Dynamics capability

   4. Hosting for the software

**ISV Examples**   Many different ISVs could be useful in your project. It's important to understand if the ISV is focused on an industry or a functional gap.

**Master It**   A sales tax filing software extension would be an example of what type of ISV?

1. Industry ISV

2. Functional ISV

3. Integrated ISV

4. Hosting ISV

**Role of Industry ISV**   Industry ISVs can be a mandatory part of the solution depending on the industry you are in.

**Master It**   An Industry ISV provides which of the following?

1. Core Microsoft Dynamics capability

2. An add-on solution specific to an industry

3. Hosting for the software

4. A solution for gaps in one functional area

**AppSource Marketplace**   Microsoft introduced a marketplace for customers or prospects to look for approved products and services.

**Master It**   What is AppSource?

1. Microsoft's app store where you can download apps for your Microsoft Surface computer

2. Microsoft's business application marketplace for extensions and consulting services

3. An independent site with community information about ISVs

4. Microsoft's partner portal

# Chapter 10

# Factors for a Successful Project Kickoff

The *kickoff meeting* is your chance to explain to the whole company how important your business applications project is and how you are going to deliver it successfully. You can use this opportunity to set the tone for the project and get everyone excited about what it will mean for the future of your company. The kickoff meeting is the gate between the Define stage and the Create stage. This is where you transition from planning for the project to delivering on the project. It's also a key opportunity to set the tone for how you operate the project going forward.

The kickoff meeting is the most important communications activity that you do on the project. As we talked about in Chapter 7, "Change Management Throughout Your Project," communication is key to helping your organization understand the changes that are coming on the project.

The first step to change management is executive alignment, and this is your chance to show leadership solidarity and engagement in this critical project. It's both a validation activity and a momentum-building activity—this is the first experience with the project for many team members, so it's critical to set a positive tone and provide them with the knowledge base to help them navigate this foreign world of business application implementation.

After you complete this chapter, you will be able to do the following:

◆ Prepare for your kickoff meeting

◆ Structure the kickoff meeting content

◆ Land the executive message

◆ Set expectations for the project team

## Pre-Kickoff Meeting Activities

The key to success with the kickoff meeting is what you do to prepare for it. If you execute on the elements of the Define stage, as laid out in this book, you'll be in a great position to deliver a successful kickoff meeting.

### Checklist

Following is the checklist of items that should be validated before the kickoff meeting. If you have all of these items completed and agreed-upon between you and your implementation partner, you are way ahead of most implementations. If you follow only one thing in the book, please try to have all of these completed before your kickoff meeting:

◆ Success criteria

◆ Project roles and responsibilities defined

◆ Project charter/project management plan

◆ Project schedule

◆ Project communication plan

◆ Project budget maintenance

◆ Change request process

◆ Risk and issue management

◆ Project collaboration site

◆ Task management system

◆ Change management plan

◆ Processes in scope

◆ ISVs

◆ Data migration plan

◆ Environment management plan

◆ Testing plan

◆ Entrance criteria/exit criteria

These are all items that we've either touched on already, or will be touching on in future chapters, so let's take each item individually and reference where to learn more about them.

**Success Criteria**   *Success criteria* is the process of setting out the goals for the project so that you can validate you've achieved them. Refer to Chapter 2, "What to Do Before You Begin a Project," and Chapter 5, "Organizing Your Team for Success and Project Governance."

**Project Roles and Responsibilities**   *Project roles and responsibilities* is your roster of who's doing what, your list of accountabilities, and who has the ultimate authority for each area of the project. Refer to Chapter 2 and Chapter 5.

**Project Management Plan**   The *project management plan* includes everything on this checklist. Refer to Chapter 5.

**Project Schedule**   The *project schedule* is the artifact that is typically called a *project plan*, as it's often a Microsoft Project file laying out the key activities and timelines for the project. You need to show the project schedule to the team at the kickoff meeting. If you are using sprints as part of your project, this is a good opportunity to explain the sprint concept and how it works to the broader team. Refer to Chapter 5.

**Project Communication Plan**    The *project communication plan* is the list of meetings that you will be having and who's invited to which meetings, along with what broader communications will go out to support the project. Refer to Chapter 5.

**Project Budget Maintenance**    Generally, you don't share this with the broader team during the kickoff meeting (though sometimes I've seen it done, especially when the company is the Employee Stock Ownership Plan [ESOP] variety), but you need to have your file ready to go and ready to be maintained each week. Refer to Chapter 5.

**Change Request Process**    The *change request process* is the one that you will use to approve any changes to scope or resources that might affect the project budget or timeline. Refer to Chapter 5.

**Risk and Issues Management**    *Risk and issues management* are the actual and potential problems you can face on a project and your game plan for how to address them. Refer to Chapter 5 and Chapter 14, "Dealing with Challenges Mid-Project."

**Project Collaboration Site**    The *project collaboration site* is the SharePoint site, Teams site, or Slack channel that you use to share documents and updates on the project. Refer to Chapter 6, "Sprints and Tools Needed to Run Your Project."

**Task Management System**    The *task management system* is the tool you are using to keep track of all the tasks on the project and your progress on each of them, such as SharePoint list or Azure DevOps. During the kickoff meeting you should tell the team that you will train them on how to use this tool as part of the implementation project. Refer to Chapter 6.

**Change Management Plan**    The *change management plan* is your agreed-upon plan for making the transition as seamless as possible by creating an environment where change is seen as a benefit to the organization and supported by the entire organization. Refer to Chapter 7, "Change Management Throughout Your Project."

**Processes in Scope**    *Processes in scope* is where you lay out what you will and won't do on the project. This is also something that you want to make sure to cover during the meeting, so you need to have this clearly outlined. Refer to Chapter 8, "Organizing Your Business by Processes."

**ISVs**    If applicable, you will lay out to your team during the kickoff meeting what third-party software will be involved in the implementation and where that fits in to the overall project schedule and project management plan. Refer to Chapter 9, "Independent Software Vendors—Filling Gaps and Managing Partnerships."

**Data Migration Plan**    The *data migration plan* is your game plan for moving your data from your existing system to Microsoft Dynamics and all the steps required to make that migration successful. Refer to Chapter 16, "Data Migration—Early and Often."

**Environment Management Plan**    The *environment management plan* is a list of all of the environments you need to run your project (test and production) and how you will manage your deployments. Refer to Chapter 17, "Environment Management and Deployments."

**Testing Plan**    The *testing plan* outlines what type of testing you will do and how you will do it. This is almost never addressed before the kickoff meeting, but it should be. Refer to Chapter 18, "Testing."

**Entrance Criteria/Exit Criteria for Milestones**   Going live is the process of establishing agreed-upon criteria that must be met before you can move to the next step in the project. In order to begin CRP, you will need to have received approval on the process design through the Joint Process Design (JPD) process, for example. Refer to Chapter 13, "Conference Room Pilots," Chapter 18, "Testing," and Chapter 20, "Going Live."

On masteringmicrosoftdynamics.com, you can take an assessment to make sure that you have completed these checklist items before you are ready to kick off the project.

## Expectations for the Meeting

When the leadership team announces the product that you selected for your business application implementation, one key message in that communique should be that there will be a kickoff meeting where the project plan and schedule will be explained. Expect the kickoff meeting to occur somewhere between one and six weeks after the selection is made. The only way it would happen one week after the selection is made is if it's a Quick Start–style project with very narrow scope. For most major implementations, you will need three or more weeks to go through the content that we outlined in the preceding checklist.

When you have your project preparation meetings on the calendar, you can figure out the best date for the kickoff meeting. You want to make sure you that have your executive team at the meeting, and having representation from your partner is key, too. Make sure that you put your best foot forward at that meeting. You want to set this up at least two weeks in advance and send the calendar invitations out to all of the key project participants. Once the date is set, make sure that your executives still plan to attend—if they travel frequently, their plans may change with little notice. Their presence at the meeting is critical to showing solidarity for the project.

You will not always get 100 percent attendance at the meeting, so if a key business process owner can't make it, ask another member of their team to attend the meeting and represent them.

## Outing

One idea that you may want to consider before the kickoff meeting is to have some kind of outing with your key project team members. This could be something as simple as going bowling together; the idea is to get some non–work time together to build camaraderie among the team members. If you can get your team and the implementation partner team together for a fun event, it can help develop positive relationships that will be key to success on the project. If you can afford some kind of retreat where you get out of the office, you could spend some time working on the project management plan and some time on team building. It may sound like an unnecessary expense, but it's important to build trust in the team, and if this can help, it's well worth the cost.

# Kickoff Meeting Content

Now that we've made it to this long-awaited kickoff meeting, we are ready to outline the content that should be included. I like to see six components in all kickoff meetings, with an optional seventh component. Let's dive into each of these.

## Executive Overview

I'll discuss this a little more in the "Introductions and Role Review" section, but the beginning of the meeting should commence with the most senior executive available (preferably the CEO) addressing the team on why you're doing this project and what the success criteria are. This should be a 2- to 4-minute speech that inspires everyone to do their best to make sure that you achieve the success criteria.

## Introductions and Role Review

There is a tendency to start a meeting with introductions, but the introductions in a kickoff meeting take several minutes and include each person's role on the project, and because of that, I prefer to start with a message from the executive. Once everyone is excited about what the project will do for the business, it's time to introduce the team members and their roles.

The best way to go about this is to put up a slide outlining everyone on your company's team and what role each person plays on the project. The slide should show the hierarchy of the project team, starting with the executive sponsor and project owner. Each business process owner should be identified as well as the decision-makers for their business area. The project manager should be the one leading this process, so he or she can introduce their role as well. Core team members are next, and then you can introduce the IT team members and subject matter experts. I like to see everyone prepared to speak a little bit about their role, so when you get to each person, ask them to say the following:

- Their name
- Their title or day job
- Their role on the project
- A short description of what that role does for the project
- What they are looking most forward to about the project

This will take a good 10–15 minutes to get through, but it's important for everyone to know what roles others in the company play on the project.

Next, you hand it off to the engagement manager or executive sponsor from the implementation partner to have them introduce their team. First, they will share a slide that outlines the positions the partner has on the project and what they are accountable for. They will cite how those roles correspond to similar roles on your project. When the partner is introducing their team, you might ask them to share the following information:

- Their name
- Their title
- Their role on the project
- How long they've worked with Microsoft Dynamics/ERP or CRM systems
- Where they are located

With the introductions complete, you are now ready to move on to expectations.

### Expectations for Team Members

I'll give this more time in the "Expectations for the Project Team" section, but I will introduce it enough here to say that this is an extension of the introduction section where you talk about the dedication level of the team members and what that means for their "day jobs." You also discuss how frequently the implementation partner's team will be onsite.

### Project Management and Communication Plan

The project management plan is an extensive document that you won't be able to cover in its entirety during the kickoff meeting. Thus, plan to focus your content for the kickoff meeting on the meeting schedule, project scope, and risk management. You'll cover the project schedule next, so for the meeting schedule, outline what types of meetings you will have on the project and who's expected to attend them. This is covered in depth in Chapter 5, so you can share that information with the greater team.

Next, you'll outline what's in scope and what's out of scope. I typically suggest that you focus on the Process Group level with your scope definition and highlight notable processes that you want to make sure the team knows are either in or out. This is an important step as you need everyone focused on what's in scope; specifically, ask them to stay away from out-of-scope items so that they don't become a distraction to the project.

For the risk section, explain what a risk and an issue is, and explain how they are different but related. Identify some of the key risks going into a project, and let the team know that the project leadership team will be watching for them and reacting to them quickly to make sure that the project continues forward on schedule.

### Project Schedule

Everyone in the room is dying to get the answer to one question: "When will we go live?" You won't be able to walk out of the room without answering that question, so it's important to be able to share the project schedule with the broader team so that everyone knows what needs to happen to get you to go-live.

Most people who are new to implementing ERP or CRM software will be surprised by how long it takes to get the system live. Because of that, make sure that you are taking the time to talk through each of the steps in the process as you outline the project schedule. Reiterate how important it is to test the system and have a broad set of test cases, so that you make sure all of the keys areas get tested.

### Resources

Shortly before you close the meeting, plan to introduce the key terms and tools used on the project. Chances are good that the team hasn't heard the term JPD before, and they may not know what UAT is. I recommend that you put up a slide of the common acronyms and terms you plan to use on the project and then share that list to your SharePoint site.

Speaking of SharePoint sites, this is a great time to give the entire project team a quick tour of the site that you will be using to exchange information on the project. If you are using SharePoint, you will want to show everyone where they can find the information covered in this meeting. If you are using Azure DevOps for task management, briefly touch on that as well and indicate that there will be further training based on their role coming soon.

### Navigation Overview [*Optional*]

This last step is optional, and it's typically built on as an extension to the kickoff meeting. You can append 30 minutes onto the regularly scheduled meeting to show an overview of the navigation of the product. It is often helpful to know basic terms used in the project and to get a sense of the navigation. It's good to do this when everyone is present and paying attention and to share this with the broader team.

### Wrapping Up

You can keep the wrap-up short and sweet; take one last chance to remind the team of the success criteria and your expectations for them and let them know who they can contact with questions. This will be a challenging project, so set the expectation that it won't be easy, but you'll get through it together as a collective team.

## Executive Message

As mentioned previously, the kickoff meeting should start with a 2- to 4-minute introduction by the highest ranking executive possible talking about the "why" behind the project. As discussed in Chapter 7, to get buy-in on the project, you need your leadership team on the same page consistently throughout the project. This is a great way to start that show of solidarity by having your CEO set the tone for the project. If the CEO cannot attend, confirm the attendance of a divisional vice president if you are in a larger organization.

As an aside, it's always a huge surprise to me (and a warning sign for the sake of the project) if the CEO isn't interested in attending the kickoff meeting. If they aren't interested in talking about a project that's going to cost 3–7 percent of the annual revenue of the company, they better be out closing a huge deal. ERP or CRM projects are significant investments in the future of the company, so you need to convince the CEO that this is worth their time.

In the message, the CEO should highlight the reason why the company decided to embark on this project. The CEO should also outline the future direction of the company and how this technology platform plays a big role in the company's ability to achieve that success.

We talked about the success criteria in Chapter 2 and in Chapter 5, and this is a great time to explain each criterion and why they are important to the future direction the CEO just discussed. Each success criterion should be discussed in terms of how it makes the company better. Whether it's greater visibility to data or more accurate customer statements, it's important to the business and it's important to share with the team who will make this happen.

Another key message to get across is the commitment the company is expecting on the project. Acknowledge that there will be long hours and that there will be juggling between each team member's day job and their time on the project. It is not easy, and there will be challenges. This is why you are putting the best and brightest on this project. You need the best your company has to offer to make the project successful.

The final message to share (and this is certainly up to your CEO, but I would suggest it) is to empower the team to make decisions. Many decisions need to be made on the project, and if all of them come back to the CEO, the project won't get done on time. If your CEO is comfortable delegating authority on business process decisions, this is the time to make that clear. It's better to make good decisions quickly than great decisions after considerable time. Make a point to understand that the team may not always make the optimal decision, but they need to make good decisions quickly for the project to move forward.

If your executive is not comfortable writing this message, you can ask your implementation partner to help. I have written these messages several times, and I am happy to help, but I would refuse if asked to be the one sharing that message with the group. The reason is that if it appears to be the implementation partner's project, the company's project team is not excited about it. They need to understand that it's important to the CEO of the company; it's the new direction for the business, and no outsider can share that message no matter how eloquently they say it.

## Expectations for the Project Team

We talked in Chapter 2 about the project roles and time commitment necessary to complete the project. Before and at the time of the kickoff meeting, it's important to make sure that you get the commitment necessary from the team members on the project. After you read that sentence, you may think "they said they'd do it, what is there to worry about?" Many times, people on projects haven't had to deal with the amount of pressure from all areas of the business before, so it's good to lay that out for them.

### Time Commitment

Larger organizations will sometimes dedicate 100 percent of a person's time to the project. If that's the case, make sure that person can shed their previous responsibilities so that they can be fully dedicated to the project. Having a fully dedicated resource is a luxury on projects that most companies choose not to afford. If you have a dedicated team, it's much easier to focus.

That is generally not the case, however. In most cases, people are participating on the project in addition to doing some part of their "day job." Hopefully, they have some help with their day job so that they don't have to work 40 hours a week on their core role and 10–40 hours a week on the implementation project. If you are asking anyone to do that, you should incent them to give up that much personal time. I don't recommend asking people to work over 50 hours a week for a long period of time due to the risk of burnout. If you are going to ask them to do that, you should pay them a bonus regularly throughout the project to compensate them for the additional workload.

If you want to dedicate a significant portion of your team member's time to the project, consider backfilling their role with another resource. If you have a controller who's about to retire, hire your new controller and put them on the project so they can learn the job while helping to shape the way of the future. For subject matter expert roles, consider hiring temporary workers who could give them the time to focus on the project.

In most cases, core team members and project managers are able to shed some of their day job responsibilities in an effort to focus on the project. It's usually a good thing for them to delegate some of their responsibilities, as it's a chance for their team members to grow while they are still around to help. For these people, you should be very clear on what meetings and sessions they should attend and what the turnaround time should be for deliverables. A finance core team member, for example, should be expected to attend the core team meetings and go to all of the JPD, CRP, and UAT sessions related to finance. They will likely also have individual sessions going over the chart of accounts and learning how to build financial statements in the new software. This person will also be responsible for reviewing and approving any design changes in finance, reviewing any finance-related ISVs, developing the test cases and training documentation for finance, and then leading end-user training on the finance portions of the project. That is a lot to do—between 10 and 20 hours most weeks, and in certain weeks it will represent 40 hours of work. The project manager should try to set expectations with the team member about what's expected from them. This should be shared with their manager as well so that they know how much to cut back from their day job. As you can see, it takes many conversations to come up with the right plan for each of the key members on the project.

I'm assuming everyone reading this far into this book would want to see the project meet the success criteria on time and on budget. If you are raising your hand right now, I would like you to consider providing a bonus to your project team upon successful completion of the project. This offers two benefits: first, you are rewarding them for the extra time they have put into the project, and second, you are incenting them to get the project done. If they know there's a good incentive waiting for them at the end of the project, they will be more driven to make it happen. You may think that giving a team member a $5,000 or $10,000 bonus is too much, but in the grand scheme of what you're paying to get this project done, it's a very worthwhile investment.

## Decision-Making

I mentioned in the "Executive Message" section that many, many decisions will need to be made on this project. Do you stick with your current chart of accounts? Do you come up with different customer groupings? Nearly every day, your core team members and business process owners will have to make a decision that affects how you operate your business. They need to be prepared and empowered to make these decisions.

The business process owner especially must know that they have to make decisions and make them quickly. At the end of Chapter 7, I went through the 11 steps it takes to change a business process during an ERP or CRM project, so it's not a trivial decision. I have seen it too many times; the business process owner doesn't want to make a difficult decision, and the project suffers because of it. Every core member of the project team needs to know the scope of their decision-making power and be ready to exercise it for the good of the project.

## Power of Positivity

Throughout the book I've talked about how difficult the project is, and I am not kidding. It's a grind. Your project team is likely to be disillusioned at some point (maybe at many points) during the project. The team will be seeing a lot of software that doesn't work the way the current software does, and they will discover many bugs along the way. If they are not prepared for this, they will be frustrated.

Your goal as a project leader is to set expectations about the issues that your team will encounter. Be real with them. Then you have to ask them an important question: Can you deal with these challenges and still have a positive outlook on the project? If they can't, they may not be the right people for the project. You should set the expectation that it's not enough to show up to do the work; each resource needs to approach the work with a positive attitude so that everyone else in the organization will be positive about the project. More projects go down because of general negativity than you would imagine. Often, it's not a technical problem, it's a perception problem. If the people on the project have endured too many issues such that they can't be positive about it anymore, the project will find a way to be unsuccessful.

Anyone can fake positivity for a short time, but you are asking the team to remain positive consistently. That's why it's important to set expectations and keep them thinking about the big picture value that will be driven by this project.

# The Bottom Line

**Kickoff Meeting Timing**   It is often assumed that the kickoff meeting starts while the ink is still wet on the contract. It's important to set expectations about when it occurs and what needs to be done to be ready for it.

**Master It**   When should the kickoff meeting happen?

1. As soon as the contracts are signed and the software is purchased

2. At the end of the Define phase before the Create phase begins

3. As you are ready to begin testing the software

4. Before you start evaluating vendors

**Order of Operation**   Throughout a project, it's critical to understand the order in which events need to occur. The kickoff meeting ends up being the culmination of a lot of preliminary work.

**Master It**   Which of the following does not have to be done before your kickoff meeting?

1. Define your success criteria

2. Outline your project schedule

3. Define your change management plan

4. Develop your go-live checklist

**Kickoff Meeting Agenda**   In this chapter, I outline the suggested agenda for the kickoff meeting. Many people start with introductions, but I suggest a different approach that has proven to be more successful.

**Master It**   Who should speak first at the kickoff meeting?

1. The project manager

2. The project owner

3. The executive sponsor

4. The implementation partner

**Success Criteria**   We defined success criteria in Chapter 2 and talked about them again in Chapter 5. They are a critical part of the kickoff meeting, as it's your executive's chance to explain them and get everyone on the same page with the direction the company is heading and why this project is important.

**Master It**   What are the success criteria?

1. Top, measurable goals of the project

2. Top reports that need to be created

**3.** The process categories in scope

**4.** The project manager's communication plan

**Project Artifacts**    A project manager should be knowledgeable about the core artifacts or deliverables needed on the project. The project manager also needs to communicate the definition of these terms to the rest of the participants on the project team.

   **Master It**    What is a project schedule?

**1.** Your DevOps sprint cycles

**2.** Your Microsoft Project plan, which lays out the events on the project

**3.** The plan for the first two weeks of the project

**4.** The change management plan activities

# Chapter 11

# Designing the Software Collaboratively

As much as we wish it weren't true, ERP or CRM software is never going to work 100 percent out of the box. I had a client tell me that her implementation partner said that there would be no modifications in her new system. I told her, "I'm sorry that's not true." She argued with me for a few minutes, and I walked away saying, "We'll have to agree to disagree." That implementation ended up with many customizations, so I'm not sure why the original partner told them they wouldn't have any.

You will absolutely have some amount of customization in your system. Hopefully, it's not much, but you'll have a good sense of how much customization will be necessary based on the results of the "degree of fit" or "fit/gap" high-level exercise you did during the sales cycle. Chances are good that you will have a few integrations or larger customizations that will take time to sort through. You are also likely to have some business process decisions that you'll want to spend a good amount of time debating the best way to approach.

The goal of this chapter is to outline the best way to design software. I recommend that you use a collaborative approach to give you the best results. We'll walk through the approach we use at Stoneridge Software and why I think it's the best way to design business application software.

**AFTER YOU COMPLETE THIS CHAPTER, YOU WILL BE ABLE TO DO THE FOLLOWING:**

- ◆ Explain the Joint Application Design concept
- ◆ Understand Joint Process Design and other design-related definitions
- ◆ Recognize the Joint Design Process iterations
- ◆ Learn the SIPOC approach

## Joint Application Design Concept

The idea of designing software collaboratively is not new. The concept originated at IBM, and it was called a *Joint Application Design (JAD)*. The idea was first pioneered by Chuck Morris and Tony Crawford of IBM in 1977, and it evolved over time with IBM publishing the JAD overview in 1984. A Joint Application Design is a process of involving the client in the design of an application through a succession of collaborative workshops known as JAD sessions. With a JAD session, you bring all of the relevant parties together at one time to deliberate on what should be done in a structured and organized manner.

The JAD process replaced the siloed method of software design and development. In the earliest days, software was often designed by having someone type up a bunch of requirements and send those off to someone else, and then a different somebody coded in the background, and finally, when delivered, you would see if it worked or not.

The JAD session was something inherited at Stoneridge when we brought on several consultants who had been implementing Dynamics NAV. They had used JAD sessions in the past and found them to be great ways to go through the complex designs in the software. Once we saw that in action, we thought it was great for designing extensions or add-ons to the product, but we found that there was a gap in working with the core part of the application we just needed to configure. We also felt that it wasn't focused as much on the end-to-end process, so we decided to create a variant of it that filled those gaps.

## Joint Process Design and Other Design-Related Definitions

A *Joint Process Design (JPD)*, pronounced J-Pod, is the result of our tweaks to the original JAD concept. We really liked the idea of working together with the client to design the process collaboratively. We think this is the best way to implement an ERP or CRM system because we're not necessarily designing software from scratch. We're trying to work within the box, staying with out-of-the-box software as much as possible.

As discussed elsewhere in this book, all businesses are comprised of similar processes at their core. All businesses need to acquire a customer, sell something, deliver it, invoice it, and then receive payment. That is an end-to-end business process. Instead of workshops being designed to dream up what you want, the workshops in a JPD world are focused on the design of those processes. What are those business processes? The question we're really trying to answer is how we optimize those business processes for the desired flow and then translate it into how it works within the application. That's the big distinction between JPD and JAD and why we call it something different.

### What Is a Joint Process Design (JPD) Session?

First, we should start off by explaining that JPDs are iterative, which means that you will take each process group and run it through two to four JPD sessions. This means that each iteration of the session will be different. JPD Iteration 1 is notably different from JPD Iteration 4. During each iteration, we dive deeper into those areas that require more attention as our list of resolved processes gets longer. Once we find a design that works, we try to move on to the next part of the process until we've worked through all elements of that process.

I say this a lot, but it's certainly proven to be true over time—people like the systems they know. It could be a terrible system, but if you know it really well, you probably like it. One problem in many CRM systems in particular is a lack of adoption once you go live. Why is there a problem getting people to adopt the system? Because they don't like it. Why don't they like it?

Because they don't know it. That was a long way of reinforcing the point, but the more you get people comfortable with the system, the more they're going to like it.

That's a critical reason why we suggest this model—users of the system need to see and touch the system to get comfortable with it. One key item you use during the implementation is "knowledge transfer" between the consultants and the eventual users of the system. We recommend using JPDs and CRPs as a means to transfer the knowledge of the system because the team is seeing and using the software frequently, working within the software, and designing the processes that are important to them. SMEs and BPOs are actively learning to use the software in a targeted and outcome-oriented manner before they get to the testing cycle.

Figure 11.1 is a high-level visual describing all of the things that occur as part of the JPD cycle.

**FIGURE 11.1**

Joint Process Design

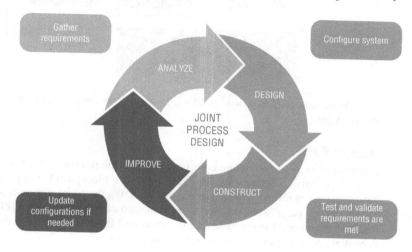

Each session is broken down into process categories and process groups. Let's take Procure to Pay as an example. You would do your JPD sessions related to Procure to Pay over a three-day period (as an example) and then break down those three days into five sessions focused on the six core process groups inside Procure to Pay:

◆ Manage Vendors

◆ Manage Vendor Invoices

◆ Manage Purchase Pricing

◆ Manage Purchase Orders

◆ Configure Procurement

◆ Pay Vendors

Each of these sessions would be led by a functional consultant who has expertise in Purchasing and Accounts Payable functionality in the system and someone who has worked with many other companies on their Procure to Pay workflow.

Figure 11.2 is another example of the process groups associated with the Quote to Cash process category.

**FIGURE 11.2**
Quote to Cash
process flow

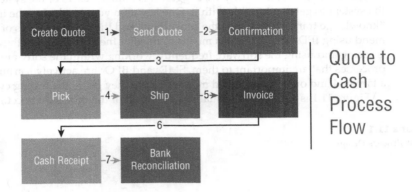

Quote to
Cash
Process
Flow

In this example, you would hold a JPD session on the process groups outlined in the boxes in the diagram.

## Happy Path

One term that I want to define before we get into the iterations is a concept called *Happy Path*. There is probably a better term for it, but it is the typical path that a process should take—the path most users follow within a process stream. It's the most common scenario with no complicating factors, edge cases, or alternates. When you first go through a JPD, focus on the Happy Path. After you get through the first iteration and this "clean" path is defined, then add all of the potential complications, variations, and edge cases.

## "As-Is" vs. "To Be"

One of the major issues that occurs in ERP and CRM implementations is the leadership team who wants the new software to focus on the future, or "to-be" process, versus the subject matter experts who have to work in the software are only concerned about the current, or "as-is" process. This is an issue that I like to see companies address head-on as the project gets started. The goal of the software implementation is to create a system for the future, not for the past. This is an opportunity to review and start with a clean slate to serve your business better for the future. You want to be focused on the "to-be" processes.

In defense of the subject matter experts that I mentioned, they may very well not know what the to-be process is going to be. They may have asked their leader for their thoughts on the to-be process, but they may not have heard them. If the business process owner isn't communicating their future vision for the process to the team on the ground, it's unlikely to be captured in the requirements for the new system. To make the new system effective, either (1) the leader needs to communicate the to-be process or process goals in advance or (2) the leader needs to sit in on these sessions and communicate the vision and business needs, and the why behind it, so that the software can be set up to accommodate the new process.

Not every process needs to have a different to-be process. You probably shouldn't come up with new, exciting ways to write checks to vendors, but maybe you want to consider an Accounts

Payable Automation system that automatically pays your vendors. It's an option to add on to your Microsoft Dynamics system, so if you want to explore it, indicate that you want the investigation of it to be part of the overall project scope. Consultants may have good ideas to offer that enrich the process and use of technology based on their knowledge and experiences. So collaboratively, with both parties offering expertise, the goal to create an improved process can be achieved.

# Joint Process Design Iterations

Each Process Group may go through between two and four iterations of JPDs. The more straightforward the process, the quicker you should be able to go through the JPD iterations. The complex processes will require more time, and I suggest that you start on those as soon as you can so that they don't slow down the entire project schedule.

Let's work through what typically happens in each iteration, as outlined in Table 11.1.

**TABLE 11.1:**    Iterative Sequence

| JPD1 | JPD2 | JPDN | CRP |
|---|---|---|---|
| Process Group Overview | Demonstrate the Process Happy Path | Demonstrate Alternate Process Paths | Demonstrate Entire Process Category |
| Identify All Processes to be Implemented in Process Group | Use "Demo Data" | Use a Subset of Data | Use Mostly Migrated Data |
| Identify and Document Gaps | Obtain Approval for Demonstrated Processes | Obtain Approval for Demonstrated Processes | Obtain Approval for Entire Process Category |
| Identify and Assign Follow-up Tasks | Identify Alternate Paths and New Requirements | Identify New Paths and New Requirements | |
| | Identify and Document Gaps | Identify and Document Gaps | |
| | Identify and Assign Follow-up Tasks | Identify and Assign Follow-up Tasks | |

## JPD1

In the first iteration of a JPD, *JPD1*, the goal is to show the standard process flow in the out-of-the-box functionality. Your hope is that the business process resembles the best practice standard and that the out-of-the-box functionality covers the process effectively. If that's the case, you will have limited design and customizations to do here.

In the first iteration, the functional consultant explains the JPD flow and the goals of the session and encourages the core team lead, subject matter experts, and business process owner to speak up if they have any questions. This dialogue is critical if the flow presented is not the flow used in the business. The session needs to be interactive or you will end up with a system with just the standard functionality, which probably won't meet your needs.

After starting the session, ideally the functional consultant is able to show two screens, but often there is just one screen to share and one screen to track the process. We want to show the functionality of the software in this area and overlay that with the standard business process.

As the team sees something that isn't consistent with their to-be process (note how I didn't say as-is process), the participant should raise their hand and indicate the requirement that is being missed. A requirement is a piece of data or a process that you need the system to track. For example, in our CRM system, we wanted to track our client's legal name in addition to their friendly name. We wanted to track both Contoso and Contoso Ltd., because when we send a contract to them, we want Contoso Ltd. to be the legal name on the contract. The need to track that "legal name" field is a requirement. As you sit through a JPD session, if you see that there is not a place to store information you need, raise your hand and indicate that you have a new requirement.

In the older Waterfall or Sure Step model, customers would write down all of their requirements and send them to the partner, and then the partner would have to sort through these requirements to indicate if they are met by the software or not. In the JPD model, the customer and partner walk through the process collaboratively, allowing the customer mentally to check off the requirements as they see the standard functionality in action. The original way of doing things left many, many requirements undiscovered until it was too late in the process. It was too easy for a customer to forget to mention a requirement, and then, when they finally got to see the system during user acceptance testing, they would see that a field they needed was missing, and it would be too late in the project to get it added back in. The beauty of the JPD is that the customer has multiple opportunities to see the software in use and call out requirements. If the first time that they get their hands on the software is in a conference room pilot, they still have time to see if the system does what it needs to do before you are code complete on changing the system.

As you go through JPD1, don't be surprised if you have to bring up many requirements. As I mentioned at the start of the chapter, you will find gaps in the software and you need to document them so that they can be addressed.

During JPD1, you will not have had a chance to pull data into the Microsoft Dynamics system from your existing system because you won't know the definition of your new table structure. It can be difficult to imagine your business process when you are seeing data about bicycle or computer parts in your system. The best way to approach the first JPD is by entering some sample "real" data into your system so that the users can understand better what they are looking at.

At the end of JPD1, as you look over the feedback from the session, you will see that you have requirements that fall into three buckets:

◆ **Obvious Fits**: This means that the out-of-the-box system has what you need, and you can just use the system as it was intended. For example, as a place to store a vendor address.

◆ **Obvious Gaps**: You identify a process or sub-process that you do today that the software doesn't have, and you know that you will need to design a solution to handle that gap. For example, perhaps when you add a vendor you look at their Better Business Bureau profile before you validate that they should become a vendor to you. You could handle that with process documentation or some automation.

◆ **Notes Requiring More Investigation**: Not everything is black and white coming out of the session, so you'll often find a handful of items where a subject matter expert needs to go back and validate the process, or the consultant didn't understand the requirement that was brought up, or you touched on something but didn't have time to determine if it was a fit or a gap.

For those items that are obvious fits, plan to note them and validate that they are fits in the next iteration of the JPD. For those obvious gaps, the consultant will think through a potential design for that gap and plan to come back to JPD2 with a suggested path forward. For the ones requiring more investigation, the best option is to have discussions with the subject matter expert to get to the bottom of the requirement and then decide if it should be presented as a fit or a gap in the next JPD.

There is typically a three-week gap between JPDs in the same Process Category to allow for time to do this investigation and preliminary design work and to prepare for iteration 2. ERP and CRM systems require a good amount of configuration as well, so setting up sample master data, configurations, and parameter settings takes a good amount of time to complete.

## JPD2

For the second iteration of the JPD of a given Process Group, *JPD2*, the setup is similar—you have a functional consultant in front walking through the process as they understand it in the software. This time the software may be more configured, and the process flow will likely be a little more customized to your business process, but there is more work to be done to get it right. We want the same resources in the room—the core team lead for that area, the subject matter experts, and the business process owner.

In this session, you will go through each of the processes again with the updated configurations mostly focused on the Happy Path. You will want to do a few different things as part of this walkthrough:

**Try to validate processes that fit out-of-the-box**   If the process shown meets your needs, then validate it and consider it design complete. Once that's done, you can check it off your list and focus on the more complicated areas.

**Explore Unhappy Paths**   If the standard path is working well in the system, now is the time to bring up the exceptions. Let's focus on the exceptions that you want to handle in the software. You'll always find examples of something that happens so rarely that it's not worth building a system around.

**Validate designs for slightly customized areas**   If you have some requirements that lend themselves to minor customizations, this is a good time to validate those so that the consultant can write up the functional design document for those minor customizations.

**Develop a game plan for the highly customized areas**   At this point, you'll have a pretty good idea for those areas where the process is different than the out-of-the-box software. You want to explore that during the JPD2 session and try to come up with design approaches that would work to utilize as much of the out-of-the-box solution as possible. If you can, great; if not, the consultant should test a few options and come back with recommendations including one suggested path. This will likely lead to a meeting outside of the JPD schedule to go over the suggested path to handle this new customization.

During JPD2, you will still not have migrated data in your testing system. The best way to approach the second JPD is to enter another layer of "real" data into your system so that the users can see familiar data in the system as you run through the examples.

There is typically another three-week gap between JPDs in the same Process Category to allow for further investigation, design work, and configuration. A larger task will be the data setup for iteration 3. It is possible that this will be the last iteration of a particular process group. If you manage to wrap up that process group, that's great. You can now focus your work on the more complex areas.

## JPD3

For the third iteration of the JPD of a given process group, *JPD3*, it's another round of the similar concept—you have a functional consultant in front walking through the process as they understand it in the software, or better, the core team lead is leading the demonstrations. This time the software should either be ready or close to ready. The software should be more configured, and the process flow should be customized to your business process. Again, you'll want the same resources in the room—the core team lead for that area, the subject matter experts, and the business process owner.

As this is a continuation of the work in JPD2, the goals are similar:

◆ Validate the Happy Path

◆ Validate the Unhappy Path

◆ Finalize designs

◆ Identify areas that need further work

During JPD3, you certainly won't have all of your real data in the system. At that point, you should have completed your first real test of your data migration, so that will likely leave you with some data that is useful and some data that is incorrect. Take what you can from the data migration process and use that data as part of the third round of JPDs.

Generally, at the end of JPD3, you should have the process nailed down and the design right for any changes needed to the system. If you do, you can wrap up that process group and start to focus on the next step, which is the conference room pilot. If you are not finished at this point, you will need to do another iteration of a JPD just on the particular areas that you have yet to validate.

## JPD4

If you have made it to the fourth iteration of the JPD, or *JPD4*, you are likely dealing with a complicated, multistep process. If you need extra time to figure out a complex problem, you should set up additional sessions in between JPD events to get into the details. The goal here is to walk through the custom process one last time to make sure that you have validated that the designed flow will work for this process area. You can always say it doesn't work—just remember that time is getting tight, so you'll want to have another session to address that problem as quickly as you can so that you don't fall behind.

Once you've finalized the iterations, your next step is to move on to the conference room pilot phase, which we'll discuss in Chapter 13, "Conference Room Pilots."

### Keys to Successful JPDs

Here are a few keys to remember as you go through these interactive sessions to make them successful:

**Make sure that you have decision makers in the JPD sessions** If your session only has subject matter experts, you won't be able to get decisions made on possible changes to the process. You are going to need to change your processes somewhat during this process, so you need someone accountable for that process to be there to make those decisions.

**Raise alternate paths**   I defined the Happy Path in the previous section, and you should certainly start by walking through the Happy Path. It's not often that problems after you go live emanate from the Happy Path—they often come from a path you hadn't considered that happens in real life. If you don't talk about them during the JPDs, they won't be in the software, and you'll be scrambling to address them when they come up in your live system.

**Identify roles involved in the process**   As you see the processes and explain how your process works, be sure to identify who does these processes in your business. Specifically, the consultant needs to know which roles perform these processes so that security can be set up for them.

**Provide real-world examples relevant to these processes**   If you have an invoice, customer statement, or report related to this process, bring that to the JPD session and share it with the consultant. If the consultant knows what the output of the process should be, it's much easier to design the system to create that output.

**Give feedback and approve the proposed processes**   This collaborative process only works if it is indeed collaborative. It's the consultant's job to drive the process, but they can't set up the system perfectly for you if you don't contribute feedback and identify requirements. It's also important to say "that's good" when the process displayed will work for you. If you keep asking to see changes, you won't be able to get your project done on time.

**Task list for next steps**   Everyone will have work to do between iterations of the JPD—the consultant will be configuring the system and designing customizations, and the core team should be preparing artifacts and talking through potential requirement changes, reviewing the Happy Path in the software, and considering edge cases as well as documenting processes.

It takes everyone working together with the goal of creating the best software experience to make this successful.

## JPD Output

At the end of the JPD iterations, you will have the following artifacts:

- Complete list of processes in each process category to be implemented.

  - You will know what's in scope and out of scope for this phase.

- Complete list of process requirements.

  - Your requirements will refer back to the process, process group, and process category, so you know how they fit into the end-to-end process flow.

- SIPOC for each process.

  - This is an optional but helpful way to walk through the process, especially if it's not a common business process.

◆ List of identified fits and gaps.

    ◆ All of the requirements classified as a fit will be identified.

    ◆ All of the requirements classified as a gap will be identified, and you will have, at least, preliminary estimates on the work required to fill these gaps.

To sum it up, you should walk out of the JPD iteration cycle with a detailed list of what's going to be done that's tied back to your core processes.

# SIPOC

Many processes will be standard in the software, and you won't have trouble talking through what happens in those scenarios. In the process catalog, we've identified a standard set of processes that sit under the process groups and process categories. If this classification matches your reality, you should be good walking down those paths.

What happens if the standard processes just don't match what you do? That happens from time to time, and there's a great tool that can help you get a good picture of what components make up this process flow.

I like to start this at an end-to-end scenario level. If there's a scenario that doesn't have a match within the standard process catalog, it's time to use the SIPOC tool, shown in Figure 11.3 and outlined in Table 11.2. Let's explain what this tool is.

**FIGURE 11.3**
SIPOC process flow

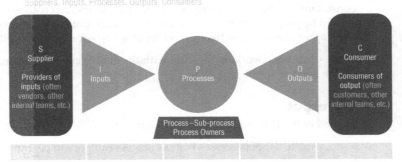

**TABLE 11.2:** SIPOC Acronym

| ABBREVIATION | STANDS FOR | EXPLANATION |
| --- | --- | --- |
| S | Supplies | The companies or people providing the input to the process. This is often your list of vendors. If you are talking about how you manufacture something, this would be your list of material providers. |
| I | Inputs | The list of what is provided by these various suppliers. For example, if you are manufacturing cabinets, this would be the oak and pine boards that you need to do the manufacturing. |

| ABBREVIATION | STANDS FOR | EXPLANATION |
|---|---|---|
| P | Processes | The process or the processes that you perform on these inputs. To continue our example, this would be the cutting of the boards to get them to the right shapes. This would also be the assembly of and the staining of the cabinets. In this example, there are several processes that need to occur to generate the output. |
| O | Outputs | This is what is created by the process. In our example, this would be the cabinets themselves. You may have 100 varieties of cabinets that you produce, and if that's the case, you should list the common varieties here. |
| C | Consumers or Customers | The processes or the customers who will consume this output. In our cabinet example, this may be end customers, or it could be a distributor who turns around and sells your cabinets. If you sell both direct and indirect, you need to tell the consultant this because it impacts the sales process flow. |

I find it easy to deconstruct any process by asking questions related to this SIPOC process flow. I usually start by asking about what inputs are needed by the process. Then I ask, "Who supplies these inputs?" Then I go to the question of what the outputs are from the process. Next, we talk through the consumers of the outputs. At the very end, we come back and talk in more detail about what you do to those inputs to create the outputs. It seems to be easier for non-software people to talk through what they want to do to get a job or process done in this format.

# The Bottom Line

**JPD Definition**   This chapter is focused on how to design software collaboratively using a concept called a Joint Process Design. To design the software, you end up going through several JPD sessions.

> **Master It**   Which of these features is part of a Joint Application Design or Joint Process Design approach?
>
> 1. Identifying requirements in a spreadsheet
> 2. Iterative workshops to develop the approach and software together
> 3. Questionnaires that need to be returned with answers to requirements questions
> 4. Tracking system for all requirements

**JPD Elements**   The cycle of going through each iteration of JPD sessions leads to a variety of outputs that are needed to move forward on the project.

> **Master It**   Which one of these steps is not a part of the Joint Process Design flow?
>
> 1. Analyze
> 2. Design

3. Construct

4. Hypercare

**Incorporating Data into the JPDs**  We'll discuss this in greater depth in Chapter 16, "Data Migration—Early and Often," but you want to coordinate your data migration efforts with your JPD sessions. The more relevant data that you have while you go through examples, the easier it is for the team to understand the processes.

> **Master It**  In which JPD session would you start using a subset of your actual data in the system?

1. JPD1

2. JPD2

3. JPD3

4. None

**Order of Operations**  Throughout an implementation, it's important to understand the logical order of operations throughout the project. As you go through iterative design sessions, there is an order of operation to be followed to get the best output.

> **Master It**  Which comes last in the iterative sequence of events through a project?

1. JPD1

2. JPD2

3. JPD3

4. CRP

**JPD Goals**  The ultimate goal of the Joint Process Design iterative design session is to develop the best software to meet the company's needs. Within that flow are other benefits as well, like the one in the question that follows.

> **Master It**  Which of the following is one of the goals of a JPD session?

1. Demonstrate Dynamics functionality for selected processes

2. Design the entire application

3. Training the end users

4. Teach change management concepts

# Chapter 12

# Requirements Gathering and Staying "In the Box"

We've talked a few times in the book about how it's important to limit the number of customizations that you have in your software. Customizations require the work of designing the customization, writing the code, developing the test plan, testing it, writing documentation for it, training it, and maintaining it. Some amount of customization is unavoidable, but, in this chapter, we want to talk about some of the ways that you can minimize it by using the "out-of-the-box" software. We also talk about how you can minimize the cost of customizations by writing clear requirements.

**AFTER YOU COMPLETE THIS CHAPTER, YOU WILL BE ABLE TO DO THE FOLLOWING:**

- ◆ Understand the meaning of staying in the box
- ◆ Define requirements and the specific types of requirements
- ◆ Complete a fit/gap analysis
- ◆ Write good requirements
- ◆ Understand the cost of customizations

## Staying in the Box

I will admit that this terminology is confusing. I sometimes confuse my own team with the phrases "out-of-the-box" and "in-the-box," because they sound like opposites when I'm really trying to have them mean the same thing.

When you use commercial software, you want to use as much of it as possible without having to create customizations. Using the software as it was designed can be called "using the system out of the box." The intent is to assume that you pull the software out of an imaginary box and start using it. In a similar way, we sometimes refer to the fact that you want to use the software (that comes in this imaginary box) as-is, so you want to stay "in the box." When I use either of those terms, I will be talking about using the software from Microsoft without any customizations.

Why do you want to stay in the box? You want to minimize the amount of customizations on your project because customizations cost money and they take time to complete. Everyone wants to spend the least amount of money possible on their project, and they want to get it done on time. Given that, staying in the box should be a goal for everyone on the project.

Everyone "says" that they want to stay in the box, but in reality, many people don't. Many, many people want the new system to work exactly like the old system. If the old system generated a report with a certain six columns, this software had better generate a report that looks exactly the same. If the report puts those columns in a different order out of the box, then it needs to be fixed.

This is a change management problem. As we discussed in Chapter 7, "Change Management Throughout Your Project," change is going to happen, so everyone is going to need to embrace it, or at least tolerate it. As a project owner or business process owner, you will find yourself repeatedly talking about the difference between the "as-is" and "to-be" process that I discussed in the previous chapter. The new software is the "to-be" process, and the reality is that you need to be thinking about the system you want for the next 20 years, not the system that you used to have.

## Customization vs. In-the-Box Examples

What are examples of customizations that get you outside of the imaginary box? Let's talk about what is "out of the box" and what is a customization.

### Out-of-the-Box Examples

◆ Using the Microsoft Dynamics functionality provided as part of the core package or original source code

◆ Configurations, security (if done through the user interface), or settings changes

◆ Personalization of the software (where you set up a view that's just for you)

### Customization Examples

**Customization of logic**: Making the software do something different than it would normally do.

**Customizations to forms**: Adding a field to a form or changing the order of items on the form, changing a label on a form, or removing fields from the form.

**Customizations to security**: Adding different privileges to a role through code. This can be done through the user interface in all of the Dynamics products, but it can also be done via code. You often want to do it through code when you are creating a new table or column/field/attribute that you know users will need to access.

**Customizations to reports**: Virtually every report is going to need a customization of some variety. Dynamics 365 Customer Engagement and Business Central have reporting "wizards" that allow you to create some basic reports, but they don't look very good without further customization.

**New tables**: If you want to add data where there's not a defined place to store it, you will need to add a table to the system. In Dynamics 365 Customer Engagement, you can do this without code, but you will need to use code in the Dynamics ERP products.

**Integrations**: Each of the Microsoft Dynamics 365 products has services and connection points that can be used to connect to other systems, but you will still need to write code to get the data into the product.

# Requirements

The word "requirement" is very common in the software development space. The term has been in use in the software world since at least the 1960s. I like to define *requirement* as a function or piece of information that is needed to execute or support the business scenario successfully. A requirement may be something that the software already provides, or it may be something that demands a customization. The word "requirement" is a little odd, because requirements aren't always "required" at the time of the launch of the software.

*A Guide to the Business Analysis Body of Knowledge (Babok Guide), 3rd Edition* (International Institute of Business Analysis, 2015) describes a requirement as a condition or capability needed by a stakeholder to solve a problem or achieve an objective. That sounds about the same, so whatever definition you want to use works for me.

An example of a requirement that I've used a few times in the book is the addition of the "legal name" field in our CRM system. We created a requirement to track that name in our system so that we could use the Mail Merge functionality to populate contracts with a company's legal name. Now, you could also say that tracking the company "friendly name" is a requirement as well. That is native functionality, but technically we would have two requirements there—one to track the friendly, or common name, and one to track the legal name. We would put "Contoso" in the common name and "Contoso Ltd." in the legal name field.

## Out-of-the-Box Fields as Requirements

We have a philosophical debate around the company on whether you should track common, native functionality as a requirement. Like the preceding example, the requirement would be to track the company name in a CRM system. Without a company name field, it would be a pretty terrible CRM system, so all CRM systems have that. There are arguments on both sides of the equation, so I will lay them out for you and let you decide if you want to track everything, because I can see value in both sides of the argument:

**Track all requirements**   The reason you would want to track the requirement that a CRM system have a company name field is to make sure that you don't miss it. Yes, you can assume that it will be there, but there's an old saying about what happens when you assume. The thought is that anything you need in your system should be documented so you don't miss it. I understand that argument, as long as you have a quick way of validating it and moving on. If you spend a lot of time validating that a CRM system has a company name field, you are wasting time.

**Track custom requirements** The reason why you want to track just custom requirements is to keep your list of requirements down to a manageable number. Tracking every single common requirement bloats your list of requirements and makes it harder to manage. Sometimes I make the argument: "If you wrote down every requirement for everything, you would never get your software implemented." That said, if you don't write everything down, you may miss something, or an assumption may be made that has a big effect down the line. You may assume that the legal name field is included in a CRM system out of the box, so when it isn't, you miss that requirement and now can't do a function (mail merge legal documents) the way you wanted to do it.

Our typical philosophy on this is that if a company has a list of requirements prebuilt, we will tend toward the approach of writing everything down. If the company has no requirements written down, we try to uncover the requirements during the JPD sessions and write down any custom requirements as we hear them. It comes down to the company's risk versus speed preferences—the more requirements you write down, the less risk of missing a requirement; the fewer requirements you write down, the faster the project goes. Determine what matters most to you and choose accordingly.

## Requirements Link to Processes

The reason why we suggest a process-centric approach to implementations is to make sure that every requirement links back to a process that your company performs. To use my earlier example again, the reason why we ask for the legal name field to be in the CRM system is to run a Mail Merge to create a draft of our legal contracts. When sending out a non-disclosure agreement (NDA), we want to use our CRM system to populate the customer legal name and address fields. We don't have to use CRM to create the NDA; we can certainly do it by hand, but it's much faster to generate it from CRM.

The requirement is tied to the contract generation process. If the contract generation process is taken out of scope, then we no longer need to track the legal name field in the CRM system. Because we can create an NDA by hand, we may choose to remove the contract generation process from the scope of our implementation. If I didn't associate the legal name field requirement to this process, I wouldn't know that this requirement can be taken out of scope as well.

Another reason why it's important to associate your requirements to a process and to a business scenario is so that you know how to test the requirement. We'll talk about it further in Chapter 18, "Testing," but several different types of tests exist. You would do a functional test of the legal name field when it's in the system, but the more important test is to make sure that it works properly when you do your end-to-end testing. If you don't know why you put the legal name field in the system, you might run into a problem when testing the contract generation process. If it does not pull a legal name into the Mail Merge, perhaps the requirement to add the legal name wasn't satisfied. These requirements become the basis for functional design documents and need to be validated during testing.

For each requirement, associate it to a process, which will then associate it to a process group and process category. Generally, you do end-to-end testing at the process or process group level. This connection will highlight for you the need to test this requirement during that testing phase.

# Functional vs. Non-functional Requirements

You can define requirements in a few different ways, but I prefer to keep it to these two categories: functional and non-functional. A *functional requirement* is what you normally think of as a requirement—it's the field that you want added to a form or a specific business task, for example. *Non-functional requirements* can include anything that supports the system. The official definition is a requirement that specifies criteria that can be used to judge the operation of the system, rather than specific behaviors.

*Performance* is typically the most commonly referenced non-functional requirement. Many times, users assume that performance will not be an issue, so it's not specifically referenced anywhere in the requirements of the new system. Generally, you should assume that a modern system is going to perform well, but there are many places where it might not. For example, your volume in an area may be extraordinary, or you may need extremely fast processing in another area, so you should give some thought to defining performance requirements.

Performance expectations might be different depending on what system was used in the past. If you are coming from a DOS-based system, you may be used to one that moves really quickly. If you are coming from a Windows-based system with a server at another location, you might be used to delays between screens. It's important to understand the speed of the current system so that you can set proper expectations on how the new system will be different.

I recommend that you set a performance expectation for each screen and action in the system. Generally, you are going to want to be able to tab between fields instantaneously, and when you save a record, you should be able to move on within 2–4 seconds. If you have to wait 15 seconds for updates after everything you do in the system, you are going to end up with frustrated users. Define your standards up front so that you can have a mechanism to address it if it doesn't meet your standards.

Remember that with cloud-based ERP and CRM systems, the user's performance is often tied to bandwidth and latency from their Internet connection. I suggest that you get statistics from each of your locations to make sure that you know what to expect for performance from each site. You can bring in networking experts to diagnose this for you, or you can take a simple approach by asking users from each location to ping the server to see what the response time is. Figure 12.1 is an example where I pinged MSN.com.

**FIGURE 12.1**
Command prompt example

```
Command Prompt

Microsoft Windows [Version 10.0.19041.572]
(c) 2020 Microsoft Corporation. All rights reserved.

C:\Users\Eric.CORP>ping www.msn.com

Pinging a-0003.a-msedge.net [204.79.197.203] with 32 bytes of data:
Reply from 204.79.197.203: bytes=32 time=29ms TTL=117
Reply from 204.79.197.203: bytes=32 time=31ms TTL=117
Reply from 204.79.197.203: bytes=32 time=33ms TTL=117
Reply from 204.79.197.203: bytes=32 time=79ms TTL=117

Ping statistics for 204.79.197.203:
    Packets: Sent = 4, Received = 4, Lost = 0 (0% loss),
Approximate round trip times in milli-seconds:
    Minimum = 29ms, Maximum = 79ms, Average = 43ms
```

Look at the last value on the screen. That's the average number of milliseconds it takes to get a response from the server. If it's under 100ms, you should have acceptable performance. If the value is 550ms, you are going to have a very frustrated user at that location.

Another key non-functional requirement is the concept of *usability*. Many implementations never realize the value because the system is not very usable. This is, however, a difficult standard to set in advance of the system. One approach is to set a threshold for the number of clicks it takes to complete a process. By "clicks," I mean the number of different buttons you have to press or screens you have to navigate to in order to complete a process. It can be very difficult to map out how many clicks it should take before you get to a process. To keep this from becoming a complete guessing game, I would suggest that you budget time into your project to address usability concerns, so you have the capacity to address situations as they arise.

### Verifying Requirements

We get into this a little further as we show a *functional design document (FDD)*, but as you think through requirements, consider how you are going to verify that the requirement has been met. You accomplish this by writing a test that assesses this functionality, either directly through a functional test or as part of an end-to-end test.

In the FDD, you will note how to test that particular requirement, and you should also note how to test it as part of the end-to-end process. To use the example in this chapter, to generate an NDA with the legal name part of the contract, you will want to state that the NDA must include the legal name in the contract. You should verify the legal name field requirement by seeing that the NDA is properly generated.

## Writing Good Requirements

There is always more work that could be done on a project than there is time to do it. In the next section, you'll learn about how you may have to fight to get and keep your requirements in the project, as there are times when the budget constraints of dollars or time force you to make cuts to requirements that are important to the success of the project.

This is why it's important to take the time to write good requirements. It's one thing to say, "We could use a legal name field in CRM," but it's another to say, "We want to generate legal contracts using the Mail Merge functionality in CRM and to make sure that we're sending contracts with the correct legal name of the business, so we want to track the company's legal name in the system. This should be a text field with 255 characters." That is a requirement that explains both the "why" and the "what" you need. When seeing that requirement, the project owner can look at why this is important to the process of generating a contract. If the process of generating a contract is in scope, then the legal name field needs to be; otherwise, you lose some of the benefits of the generating contract process.

### Requirements Tips

The following are some tips to keep in mind as you write requirements for your project:

**Requirements should be unambiguous**   There are a number of ways in which to write something, and a number of ways in which something can be understood. Good requirements should only be understood one way. Avoid subjective words like "simple" and "user-friendly." These mean different things to different people. Be as clear as possible with your requirements.

**Requirements should be short**   Requirement statements should be just that, statements. Long, drawn-out paragraphs risk ambiguity and confusion. Short statements make for better organization and readability within the requirements document.

**Requirements must be feasible**   If you say that you want to put someone on Jupiter, chances are good that the software cannot do that. The requirement needs to be something that's feasible using the relevant technology. If the technology isn't there to support the requirement, the requirement shouldn't exist.

**Requirements should be prioritized**   As we'll discuss in the "Fit/Gap Analysis" section, you need to prioritize the requirement on a Priority scale of 1 to 4. Prioritization helps make sure that your team is focusing on the things they need to be.

**Requirements should be testable**   I mentioned this in earlier under the "Verifying Requirements" section. Testers should be able to verify whether the requirements have been implemented correctly or not. The test should either pass or fail. Ambiguous requirements make it impossible to determine a pass/fail.

**Requirements should be consistent**   Use consistent terminology. Create a glossary or a style guide if necessary. If you're writing requirements for admin users, don't flip back and forth between "Admin User" and "Administrator." Inconsistency leaves room for confusion.

**Requirements shouldn't give you options**   You can certainly offer two different requirements that would meet the overall goal, but create those as two different requirements so that you can prioritize which one you prefer. If multiple ways exist to satisfy a requirement, that's up to the designer to present those options. A business user or business analyst should just state the requirement.

---

### EXAMPLE OF A GOOD REQUIREMENT VS. A BAD REQUIREMENT

Here's a basic example of the difference between a good requirement and a bad requirement as it relates to sending an email notification of an accepted sales order.

> **Bad**: The email notification must include the relevant information.

> **Good**: The email notification shall include dollar amount, date, payee name, and an identification number.

If you write the bad requirement, you are leaving the developer to guess what the relevant information is. Alternatively, the developer could call you and ask what the relevant information should be, but that takes extra time. It's so much faster and accurate if you put in all the details at once.

---

# Fit/Gap Analysis

We started talking about a *fit/gap analysis* in Chapter 3, "Four Keys to Consider When Buying an ERP or CRM Solution." We discussed making a decision on the software based on the degree of fit—how relevant the software is for your industry. You want to start your fit/gap analysis early in the project, and you should know what some of the high-level gaps are in the software when you buy it.

Plan to catalog all of your requirements as part of this process, prioritize them, and estimate the fits with configuration and gaps. It's a time-consuming effort, but it's critical to remaining on time and on budget for the implementation project. Many projects don't take this step, and they wonder why they go over budget and time.

The fit/gap analysis meeting will be a long one, and it needs to be attended by the business process owners. The overall project owner needs to attend and be ready to make the ultimate decision in the meeting. The project manager should be walking everyone through the process to validate the requirements, priority, and estimate, and then they can recommend cuts. Ultimately, however, it's the project owner's decision as to what gets into the project.

## Fit/Gap Spreadsheet

The best way to track your fits and gaps is to put them into DevOps or a spreadsheet or use a list through SharePoint or Power Apps to track each requirement and how you assign it. Let's go through each of the elements:

**Requirement**: This is the summary name of the requirement.

**Classification**: There are three choices:

**Fit**: This means that the requirement is met out of the box with no further work required. For example, the requirement of a company name field in the CRM system. It has that field, so there's nothing more to do here.

**Fit with Configuration**: This means that the software can meet this requirement, but you have to do something to make it work. For example, ERP systems have a payment terms infrastructure that allows you to set whatever terms you would like. To set up 2 percent 10, Net 30 as a payment term, you have to go into the Payment Terms setup area and set this up.

**Gap**: This is a requirement that cannot be met by the out-of-the-box software. You must add a field, change a report, create an integration, or change the business or program logic to make this work.

**Priority**: This is where you indicate the importance of this particular requirement. The standard priority rating is as follows:

1. **Critical**: This is a field or function that the system has to have for it to be viable. Either it is something that existed in your previous system, or it is one of the main reasons why you are implementing this new system.

2. **Important**: This is a field or function that you are expecting the system to deliver. You may be able to live without it, but living without it means that the system will be more cumbersome or less effective.

3. **Valuable**: This is a field or function that you would like to have because it would allow the system to perform a function that would save the users time, or it is something a few of your customers have asked for. It would be good to add it if possible.

**4. Wish List**: This is a field or function that users would like to see, but it really wouldn't make them more efficient, or it is something that you do on very rare occasions that you would like to automate. These requirements almost never make the cut of what gets done on an ERP or CRM implementation.

**T-Shirt**: This stands for the T-shirt sizing of the requirement. By that I mean is the effort associated with this project small, medium, large, extra-large, or extra-extra-large? It is ideal if you have built out a detailed estimate for these requirements, but you may not have had time to do that at this point. If you can get a detailed estimate, that makes this process much more effective. If not, you estimate based on whatever information you have at the time.

Table 12.1 is a snippet of the fit/gap spreadsheet from an example CRM implementation. Your spreadsheet or list page will be much longer.

**TABLE 12.1:**     Example of a Fit/Gap Spreadsheet

| REQUIREMENT | CLASSIFICATION | PRIORITY | T-SHIRT |
|---|---|---|---|
| Convert Lead to Opportunity | Fit | | |
| Add Legal Name Field | Gap | 1 | S |
| Convert Word Templates to Use Legal Name | Gap | 2 | M |
| Add Legal Agreements Entity | Gap | 3 | L |
| Change Personal View to Include Legal Agreement Status | Fit w/Configuration | | |
| Integration to HelloSign | Gap | 4 | XL |

## Trade-Offs

One reason why implementations fail, go over budget, or go over time is because the company is unwilling to have a hard discussion once the fit/gap analysis is done. At this point, you will inevitably find that your effort level to complete all of the items on the list is greater than your budgeted hours. To get the project done on time and on budget, you will have to make sacrifices, and you will have to tell people that they aren't going to get a feature they want.

The easiest place to start is by looking at the low-priority items. You can generally start by passing on all the Priority 4 items on the list. Next, I suggest that you move to the Priority 3 list—determine which of these are really valuable and which are more in the "nice to have" category. I also look at the T-Shirt size for those items. If it's a Priority 3 item that is XXL, that is a pretty easy cut if you need to remove something.

Where it gets difficult is when you must cut items in the Priority 2 category, and you may very well have to do this. Such items were rated important for a reason; someone will be less productive because they don't have that requirement. The best thing that you can do here is to look at each of the potential cuts and understand what the workaround would be for them. If the workaround is palatable, you would be more likely to postpone that work. Oftentimes, you end up having to make cuts at the Priority 2 level, and it starts to lower the value of the overall implementation when you do that. That is the reason why you want to investigate the complicated and most important features first—you don't want that original estimate to be off by too much or it will result in either going over budget or missing key requirements.

## The Cost of Customizations

I mentioned it at the beginning of this chapter, but there are many components to making a customization, and then there are long-term costs of a customization as well. In Chapter 15, "Customizations vs. Configurations and How You Manage Them," I'll go through more detail of what happens when you make a customization, so in this section we'll articulate the project costs and future costs to a customization:

**Design**: The customization will have to be designed and estimated. You typically do those steps before you decide to move forward with it. This can take anywhere from a couple hours to 80 or more hours to do a detailed design.

**Development**: This is what everyone thinks of when they think of the cost of a customization. You certainly have to interpret the design and write the customization.

**Test Case**: In the design, you should also document a test case—the instructions required to test the customization.

**Testing**: There are a few parts to testing, but the customization will have to be tested over and over again:

**Functional Test**: This is a test to make sure that the scope of the design functions as it should.

**End-to-End Test**: This is when you test the whole process, so this would be part of the overall test.

**Regression Test**: This is when you test the customization after you've made a change somewhere else in the software. This is optional, but it is something you need to do if this process is critical.

**Rework**: You almost never plan for this, but we've found that for every hour you spend in development, you should allocate 1/3 of that time to rework. *Rework* comes from when the customization didn't meet the mark, the requirement changed or was not sufficiently documented, or the code had a bug in it. If you write strong requirements, you reduce the amount of rework that you will have to do.

This is just the work you need to get the customization into this release. If you are thinking about the future, you should focus on the "Regression Test" element. Every time you do another release or apply a Microsoft update, you should run a regression test on this customization. It is preferable to have an automated regression test, but if you're going to do that, you should budget time to develop that regression test.

Each customization will have a different number of hours associated with it based on the complexity of the customization. You just cannot underestimate the cost of these customizations—doing so will put you in a position where you can easily go over time and over budget on your project.

### Cloud vs. On-Premise Software

Customizations cost money in very different ways in cloud software versus on-premise software. In the cloud world, you do a lot of minor updates. If you can create an automated test for your customizations, you can run that routine each time you do an update to make sure that customization will continue to work. If you take the manual test approach, you have to decide if you are going to test it every time you do an update or during certain updates.

In the on-premise world, you do infrequent updates to your system. You may apply a hotfix or service pack, but generally those releases can be somewhat disruptive, and you would have to test your customization in that case. Then the big problem occurs when you have to do an upgrade—you will likely have to redo this customization when you upgrade this software. If you have a different table structure or Microsoft added a feature in that area, chances are good that you will have to spend time on that customization again to make sure that it's compatible with the new software.

In the long run, your customization cost should be lower if you are on cloud software.

## The Bottom Line

**Definition of Out-of-the-Box**   In the beginning of the chapter, we talk about what out-of-the-box means using the software as it was designed by Microsoft.

**Master It**   Which of the following is not considered "out-of-the-box" functionality?

1. Configuration

2. Settings

3. Core system screens

4. Customizations

**Definition of Requirement**   A requirement is a fundamental concept in software design—something you will see a lot of on your implementation project.

**Master It**   Which of these constitutes a software requirement on a project?

1. A process category

2. A function or piece of information needed to run your business

3. Everything you do in the business

4. Showing up to work

**Fit/Gap Analysis**   The fit/gap analysis exercise is where you look at all of your requirements to determine which of them can be met by the software and which require customizations to be built.

**Master It**   Which of the following is not a choice for classification on a fit/gap spreadsheet?

1. Fit

2. Fit w/Configuration

3. Fit w/Customization

4. Gap

**Verifying a Requirement**  When you have completed the configuration and customization of the system, you need a means to identify if the requirement has been satisfied by the new system.

**Master It**  What does it mean when we say a requirement needs to be verifiable?

1. It needs to have a verified priority

2. It needs to have a verified owner

3. It needs to be able to be tested

4. It needs to be verified by another core team member

**Cost of Customization**  Each customization you make to the system increases your short-term and long-term costs of owning the software, so you want to try to use the system out of the box as much as possible.

**Master It**  Which of the following is *not* considered a cost related to a customization?

1. Designing the customization

2. Testing the customization

3. Deploying the customization

4. Training the team on the customization

# Chapter 13

# Conference Room Pilots

This chapter is all about conference room pilots (CRPs).

This is one of the fundamental things that you can do on an implementation to increase your chances of success.

Conference room pilots are a great opportunity to showcase the software and get feedback before you must put the software out into the wild. When done correctly and with the right team members involved, CRPs can be a very positive and beneficial part of the implementation project. If not done carefully, they can shake the confidence of everyone involved in the project.

You will hear about two different varieties of CRPs based on when they occur during an implementation. Many people talk about a CRP as an activity in the sales cycle—where you try before you buy. We tend not to do that because it's unlikely to be tailored enough to be a good experience for potential clients. If we did present something during the sales cycle, we would call that a "hands-on lab." The rest of the chapter will be focused on the CRP that happens in the middle of an implementation. Let's learn all about CRPs and how to make sure they're a positive event.

## AFTER YOU COMPLETE THIS CHAPTER, YOU WILL BE ABLE TO DO THE FOLLOWING:

- ◆ Share with your team the purpose of a CRP
- ◆ Name who should participate in the sessions
- ◆ Pinpoint when a CRP should occur in the overall schedule
- ◆ Explain the difference between a CRP and a UAT session
- ◆ Understand how to get feedback from the CRP and take that into UAT

## The Purpose of a Conference Room Pilot

A *conference room pilot (CRP)* is a session where the client power or end users walk through their processes in the software prior to the completion of the code. That sounds simple, and really it is. The difference between a CRP and using the software is the fact that this occurs in the Create stage of the project so that you can see the software from end to end before you put the wraps on the design and development of the software.

I introduced the iterative sequence in Table 11.1 in Chapter 11, "Designing the Software Collaboratively," and it helps you to understand the flow of the Create stage of the project with CRP being at the end—the final validation. Table 13.1 presents an iterative sequence we laid out earlier. I share it again to reinforce when the CRP occurs.

As you can see in Table 13.1, the CRP session happens after the JPD sessions have been completed.

**TABLE 13.1:**     Iterative Sequence

| JPD1 | JPD2 | JPDN | CRP |
|---|---|---|---|
| Process Group Overview | Demonstrate Process' Happy Path | Demonstrate Alternate Process Paths | Demonstrate Entire Process Category |
| Identify All Processes to be Implemented in Process Group | Use "Demo Data" | Use a Subset of Data | Use Mostly Migrated Data |
| Identify and Document Gaps | Obtain Approval for Demonstrated Processes | Obtain Approval for Demonstrated Processes | Obtain Approval for Entire Process Category |
| Identify and Assign Follow-up Tasks | Identify Alternate Paths and New Requirements | Identify New Paths and New Requirements | |
| | Identify and Document Gaps | Identify and Document Gaps | |
| | Identify and Assign Follow-up Tasks | Identify and Assign Follow-up Tasks | |

The purpose of the CRP is two fold:

◆ You want to get your users working in the software so that they take ownership of their processes and believe that the project is making progress.

◆ You want to validate the design of the processes before you run out of time to make design changes.

You should think of each JPD and the CRP as steps in the process with the goal of getting to the right design and flow. In JPD1, you try to build a foundation from the out-of-the-box functionality, and you determine where the bigger challenges lay. By the end of the JPD cycle, you have all of your designs done, and you believe that you have the right path laid out. The purpose of the CRP is to validate that path or make changes to it if necessary. Ideally, you move through the CRP exercise and say that everything is good. Typically, you end up discovering process designs that need some adjustment from the end user input. You wouldn't have discovered that gap until you got users into the software and doing transactions.

By discovering it in the CRP session, you have time to fix it before your users are caught up in the push for user acceptance and system finalization. The CRP session also gives you a chance to get started on your training documentation—you can consider it a pilot, not only for the system but for your approach to training users on the system.

## How to Organize CRPs

You want to organize CRPs in a way similar to the way in which you organized JPDs. You want to organize your weeks by process category and your sessions by process group. You would say that next week we'll cover Procure to Pay, and we'll have a session on Managing Vendors. You would then schedule all of the relevant process group–related sessions to occur in that week. At the end of the week, you could choose to have one session where you put multiple process groups together to see if the flow works the whole way through—the end-to-end review.

## Common Elements of CRPs

After years of doing this, we have tried many ways to accomplish it, and we have found that the following general guidelines should apply to each CRP session:

**Set up 2- to 4-hour sessions**   If you need to break a process group into multiple sessions, that is fine—it's just that it gets to be difficult to hold everyone's attention in an 8-hour session, and users generally have day jobs that they want to return to.

**Identify your leader or teacher**   The best format for the room or conference call is to have a leader at the front of the room who is guiding the team through the session with the participants following along.

**Make sure that participants are dedicated**   Participants must be dedicated to the process—that means no interruptions from their day job, and they should put their phone away to focus on the activity. They are active participants, working in the software.

**Use the "Test" environment**   There are four common environments in an implementation, as we'll discuss further in Chapter 17, "Environment Management and Deployments." You want to use the Test environment for this exercise because it should have the latest code and your data, and it doesn't require you to elevate everything to the UAT environment.

**All configurations should be tested**   Everything that the users walk through in the session will need to be tested to make sure that the flow works before the session. Nothing is more deflating to users who are seeing the software for the first time than to view a system that doesn't work.

**Use Administrator privileges**   You will need to test with your appropriate privileges before go-live, but at this step of the process, you want to validate functionality, and you don't want to be slowed down by potential security issues.

**Using migrated customer data**   At this stage of the project, you need to start using migrated data so that your users can start to see the processes with data with which they are familiar. If they see the software with real data, it gives them a good sense of how the eventual software will look.

Before you set the schedule for the individual sessions, make sure that you've looked through this list of best practices and validated that you are ready to have the sessions. As I said earlier, if you schedule a CRP session and you're absolutely not ready for it, it can cause serious damage to the confidence of the people on the project.

## CRP Agenda

Each session will have an agenda that fits its process group. You will start with the introduction of CRP and what its purpose is. You want to set expectations with the team on what will be expected of them during the session (that they follow along, or enter transactions, and raise their hand if they have questions or problems) and what success looks like at the end of the session. From there, you jump into the system and walk through the process. You should designate a person who will be responsible for identifying and logging bugs or issues as you go through the session—having someone designated for this activity often keeps the meeting flowing as they will document the problem so you don't spend time discussing or arguing over it during the session.

Let's use the Manage Vendors process group as our example. The goal of the session would be to walk through the activities that take us from creating a vendor to approving that vendor with all of the steps in between. By the end of the session, you should have completed the following steps in the system to get to the point where you were successfully able to approve a vendor:

◆ Create Vendor

◆ Create Vendor Contact

◆ Update a Vendor

◆ Update a Vendor Contact

◆ Vendor Profile Management

◆ Approve Vendors

Once you are able to complete these steps, you have a successful CRP session.

## Logistics

It is best to do CRP sessions in person when you can. Ideally, you have a room with a projector and a big whiteboard, and each user has his or her own computer. When users are spaced out, the helper can come around to each of the users, sit with them, and help them, so it's best if the users aren't packed in too tightly. You can use the whiteboard to write down issues or to put items in the *parking lot*, which is a list of ideas that are worth remembering but not relevant to the matter at hand, if there is something that requires further investigation.

You can do CRP sessions remotely as well. If you do that, make sure that everyone has access to the system ahead of time and encourage users to use the "Raise Your Hand" feature whenever they have questions. The helper can then instant message with that user when he or she has a problem to make sure that you can keep the presentation moving with the rest of the users. It's more challenging, but it can be done; you just want to make sure that you are using all of the conference technology tools available.

## Issues and Questions

What happens if the users run into issues during the session? What should we do if they have questions? These are both good things. If the process goes incredibly smoothly, that's great, but it would be unexpected. You should certainly expect both issues and questions.

Let's talk through how to handle common issues and questions:

**Something doesn't work right**   When a user indicates a problem or an issue, they've likely stumbled across a bug in the software. That's going to happen. At that point, the instructor or helper goes over and asks the user to re-create what just happened. It's possible that the user did something they shouldn't do or that there's a data issue that can easily be fixed. In those cases, you correct the error and move on. If it is a bug in the software, you document the bug and add it to your bug tracking system, such as DevOps.

♦ It gets the training and knowledge transfer process started from fundamentals in the company's users.

If the core team lead is going to run the session, it is advisable to set up a designated CRP training session that occurs before the general CRP session where the functional consultant teaches the core team lead how to lead the session. This can be a time that contributes to delays in the project; if the core team lead sees the system isn't ready, they won't want to show it to their users yet. The project manager will need to be engaged at this point to determine how to adjust the schedule to accommodate a portion that's not ready.

Once the core team lead is ready and trained, they should build a training plan for the session. That training plan can be a documented hand-out for the participants, or it could be something that you show on the screen or write on the board to indicate the steps that the user needs to follow. The session leader will start the CRP session, share their screen, and direct the users through the system. They will stop for questions and issues, but they will try to keep the process moving so that the session ends on time. The core team lead does not have to know the answer to all of the questions, but should write them down for follow up or give them to the project manager or functional consultant to follow up on.

## Helper/Expert

The functional consultant should fulfill the role of "helper" or expert during the CRP session. This means that they are not leading the session, but are sitting in on it and answering questions and addressing issues as they come up. If there's a user who is running behind, the functional consultant would walk over to that user and attempt to help them get back on track.

The goal of the consultant is to support the core team lead in this capacity and should not try to take over and run the session. It's important for the team in the room to see the core team lead as an expert in this part of the solution. The consultant can answer questions and record action items without taking over.

## Business Process Owner

Not many business process owners take time out of their schedule to come to CRP sessions, but they should. This is their chance to validate that the process that they own is going to work well. They should participate in the process flow so that they understand how the system will work at a tactical level.

The most important reason for them to be there is to be able to make judgment calls about any potential process changes. If the business process owner is very confident the process will work well based on participation in the JPD sessions, they could choose not to come to certain sessions. For the session they attend, they need to be ready to make business decisions and chart a clear path for the team.

## Users/Students

Everyone else falls into the category of users or students in the CRP classroom. These should be subject matter experts or IT resources who understand the business process. Their jobs are to

...mmon in its first draft. ...ery common to

**There are questions about the process steps**   If users indicate that the process isn't right or as "what about X?" then you may have to have a discussion with the people in the room to validate if the software was designed correctly to address the process. It's often best to set that aside (put it in the parking lot) until you can get through the rest of the steps and then come back for that discussion.

You want to encourage questions and issues because this is the system setup that the users will be using for the long haul. Encourage them to speak now because issues are much easier to fix at this stage than they would be after you go live.

## CRP Roles and Responsibilities

I find the best way to run a CRP is to have four different roles involved in the session. Each of these roles has a different expectation and goal for the session. You will have the *session leader* who should be the core team lead for this process category. You will have the helper/expert who should be the functional consultant from your implementation partner. You will have your business process owner who will be there to validate the process works well and meets the goals. The largest group includes the subject matter experts and IT resources whose job it is to validate the process. They are the ones whom you should be looking to leave the room feeling confident about the system. Let's go through each of the roles, how they prepare for the session, and how they make it successful.

### Session Leader

You may have expected me to say that the functional consultant should lead the session, and in many cases they do just that. However, the best way to run a CRP session is to have the core team lead run it, for a number of reasons:

- It shows that the company is owning this solution, and it's not a solution handed to them by the implementation partner.

- It forces the core team lead to learn the solution from end to end since they must lead the group.

- It forces the functional consultant to have the solution ready so that it can be used by someone other than themselves (experts in the software can easily navigate through issues, whereas someone new to the software might get stuck).

listen and follow the directions as well as they can. If you bring people to the class who don't understand this process, you'll just be slowing everyone else down.

## Who Not to Invite

You want to be careful about who you invite to a CRP session. You can throw your whole project into a precarious state if you are not careful. You may be thinking, "Clearly you are overreacting. How can inviting the wrong person sink a project?" It's usually not an issue because of one wrong person, but if you invite a few of the wrong people, they can influence leadership into thinking that the project is going the wrong direction.

In a CRP, you will be seeing software that doesn't work quite right and that oftentimes isn't explained very well. The reason why you have to be careful about who you invite is that it's very easy for users who may not learn software quickly to see this software and think that it doesn't work well. Since this is their first time seeing it, when it doesn't work well, they will have a lasting impression that the software is not up to par. They will often share that opinion with their boss and the leadership of the company after seeing the issues.

This is not the right kind of momentum that you want on a project. ERP and CRM projects are already very hard; you don't want to try to finish them facing an uphill battle with negative impressions swirling throughout the organization.

The keys to surviving CRP with a positive impression are as follows:

- **Invite people who want to see the project succeed.** If you invite people who already have a negative view toward the project, you will surely give them more ammunition that the software isn't perfect as you take them through CRP.

- **Invite people who can pick up software quickly.** I'm sure that you all have people in your organization who can understand software more easily than others. If you know someone in your organization is slow to pick up software, you may ask for another person to join the CRP session in their place.

- **Set very clear expectations that the software will continue to get better.** Make sure the users know they are just looking at the first "prototype" of the software.

I wish you didn't have to worry so much about who was invited and how negative impressions can build coming out of CRP, but it's the reality of projects. I've seen too many cases where a failed session, or people who never wanted the project to be successful, can cause negative headwinds against a project coming out of CRP. Be cognizant of this fact as you go into it.

# CRP Place in the Overall Schedule

We have discussed that you should go through your JPD sessions before you get to CRP. You want to schedule CRP when you are code complete or close to code complete with a process category. Because you need to keep the schedule moving, you may have some elements that you can't show in a CRP because it's going to take until the end of the Create stage to finish them. That's not ideal, but it's okay. The reality is not that everything will be fully done for CRP, but you need to proceed anyway in order to get the users into the system and testing it out.

I touched on it briefly earlier, but you want to make sure that you have real data in your CRP sessions. You should have gone through more than one iteration of the data migration by the time you reach CRP. It should coincide with your second iteration (or greater), so you've had a chance to get through Iteration 0 (where you are mostly just trying to make sure that the connections work and that any kind of data is coming over) and Iteration 1 (where you are not worried about the quality of the data, just that the data for most of the entities is flowing), as by the time you reach Iteration 2 of data migration, you should have most of your data coming across and it should be in a usable, yet imperfect, state.

Table 13.2 is a sample Create stage flow for an ERP project showing how to map out the JPDs and CRPs by sprint cycles.

You can see that the CRPs occur at many different times during the schedule. For something more straightforward, like Manage Vendors or Accounts Payable, you would expect there to be fewer customizations, so you could get through those process groups in two rounds of JPD sessions. For EDI, that may take four different sessions, since it requires an amount of integration and potentially an ISV.

## Can You Do a CRP on One Process Group at the Same Time That You Do a JPD?

Yes. You can and you should if you have one Process Group that's ready and another that is still requiring further definition. For those processes that can use primarily out-of-the-box functionality, you should be able to get to the CRP sessions more quickly.

I like to see CRPs done when you are ready to do them. I don't like to see all of the CRPs pushed back to run at the same time right before UAT starts. That doesn't leave you with much time if you have to make adjustments after users get into the system. If there is a problem, I want to know about it as soon as possible so that we can build a mitigation plan for it.

### Entrance Criteria

From here on out in the book, you will hear me talk about entrance criteria and exit criteria. I will define them now, so you know how to think about them throughout the rest of the book.

**Entrance Criteria**  The conditions that need to be met to start a new process. In the example that follows, we will lay out what steps you will need to complete to be ready to enter the CRP process.

**Exit Criteria**  The conditions that need to be met to complete a process. This will become more prevalent when it comes to the end of the Create stage and UAT, but you should define the steps that you need to go through to be done with the Create stage or to be done with UAT.

Let's outline the entrance criteria for CRP:

1. You must have completed the JPD sessions for that process group (anywhere from two to four rounds of JPDs on that topic).

2. You must be code complete with the components that you plan to show. (Again, you may have some bigger components that you are not ready to show—there will be some of those, and you have to make decisions about what you can live without showing.)

3. You should be on Iteration 2 of data migration.

4. You must have the configuration complete in the Test instance for the functionality that you plan to show.

**TABLE 13.2:** Create Phase Schedule

| PROCESS | SPR. 1 | SPR. 2 | SPR. 3 | SPR. 4 | SPR. 5 | SPR. 6 | SPR. 7 | SPR. 8 | SPR. 9 | SPR. 10 | SPR. 11 |
|---|---|---|---|---|---|---|---|---|---|---|---|
| **Requirements Planning** | | JPD1 | | JPD2 | | JPD3 | | CRP | | UAT | |
| **Manage Vendors** | | JPD1 | | JPD2 | | CRP | | | | UAT | |
| **Purchase Orders** | JPD1 | | JPD2 | | JPD3 | | CRP | | | UAT | |
| **Purchase Requisitions** | | JPD1 | | JPD2 | | JPD3 | | CRP | | | UAT |
| **EDI** | JPD1 | | JPD2 | | JPD3 | | JPD4 | | CRP | | UAT |
| **Receiving** | | JPD1 | | JPD2 | | JPD3 | | CRP | | | UAT |
| **Quality** | | | JPD1 | | JPD2 | | JPD3 | | CRP | | UAT |
| **Invoicing** | JPD1 | | JPD2 | | JPD3 | | CRP | | | UAT | |
| **Accounts Payable** | | JPD1 | | JPD2 | | CRP | | | | UAT | |

5. The functional consultant should have trained the core team lead on how to use the software to support this process group.

6. The CRP session should be scheduled, the right people should be invited, and expectations should be set.

7. You have a system to record the bugs.

If you do all of those things going into your CRP sessions, you will have a successful session. If you don't complete any one of those criteria, you are risking the potential for issues in your sessions.

# CRP vs. UAT

I have talked about *User Acceptance Testing (UAT)* in previous chapters, but I haven't fully explained it as I'll do in Chapter 18, "Testing." People who have been involved with software implementations will be familiar with that term, and many may not understand the difference between CPR sessions and UAT sessions. I want to address this now while we're covering CRP sessions so that you know what you should do in CRP and what you should save for UAT. Table 13.3 provides the three key differences between CRP and UAT.

**TABLE 13.3:**     CRP vs. UAT

| CONFERENCE ROOM PILOT | USER ACCEPTANCE TESTING |
| --- | --- |
| In the Create stage before code is complete. | In the Deploy stage after code is complete. |
| The process can be walked through end to end, yet often includes a portion that must be explained or is buggy. | Done when the process can be walked through end to end and should not include any P1 bugs or missing functionality. |
| You will find bugs in this process. | You are still likely to find bugs, but they should be lower priority. |

## How They Are Similar

More similarities than differences exist between CRP and UAT. A few things will happen in both sessions. You will be walking through processes end to end with end users. You are trying to validate the system and find bugs so that you can make the experience better for the eventual end users of the system. The session should be led by the core team lead and supported by the functional consultant.

## How They Are Different

The main difference is the state of completion of the software when you enter the sessions. Your system may not quite be ready by CRP—it should be largely done, but there will often be holes represented by development work that is not yet ready to be tested broadly. In UAT, everything needs to be done and ready to be tested. The Entrance Criteria for UAT stipulate that the code is complete and has passed through a base level of functional testing.

It is frustrating if a process doesn't work end to end in CRP, but you can still keep moving. In UAT, you have to fix that right away. A Priority 1 bug that you find in CRP may be able to be resolved in a week or more, but a Priority 1 bug in UAT requires a much quicker turnaround. Other notable differences between CRP and UAT include the following:

**Security**   In CRP, you give everyone admin rights to do everything in the software, but in UAT you need to do your testing with security in place.

**Environment**   You will use the UAT environment instead of the Test environment when you get to UAT.

**Negative testing**   In CRP, you may not have much time to do "negative" testing. Negative testing is where you purposely do something you shouldn't do in the software—like clicking a button when required fields haven't been filled in.

I'll go into UAT in greater depth in Chapter 18, "Testing," but I wanted to share the difference between CRP while we were on that topic.

# What to Do Between CRP and the End of the Create Stage

The reason that you do the CRP session before the end of the Create stage is that you have time to make changes to the system before you are code complete. You want feedback in CRP because you want to make the system as effective as possible, so please encourage questions, logging bugs, raising issues, and conversations during the process.

In between your CRP session and the end of the Create stage, here are a few things you must make time to do:

1.  Log any bugs that come out of the CRP sessions. The more issues that you can tackle now, the better.

2.  Identify new requirements that come out of these sessions (they may be disguised as bugs). You should determine what priority they have; some may need to get done right away while most should be put in a parking lot for further investigation after you go live.

3.  Test the bugs as soon as the system is ready. You want to clean up as many issues as you can, so validate that the bugs are fixed so that you can have a cleaner bug list as you go into UAT.

4.  Prepare test case, training, and documentation for UAT. Consider CRP a trial run of how you want to train each of your end-to-end processes. If it works well, build your training and documentation content around what you did in CRP. If your CRP session missed the mark, make those changes and come at your training and documentation with a different approach to see if that lands better.

5.  Mark each process group as code complete. As soon as the features have been verified in each process group, you can consider it code complete, which means it's ready for UAT. Keep track of the state of each process group so that you know when you're fully ready for the Deploy stage.

# CRP Goals

Keep in mind the key goals of CRP as you go through all of these steps, with the first goal being most important:

◆ Successfully execute the end-to-end steps of this process group in the software.

◆ Help end users and power users navigate through the system.

◆ Test the migrated data in the system to see how well data migration is going.

◆ Highlight what's working well in the system.

◆ Log bugs for items that need to be fixed.

◆ Look for inquiry screens and reporting that will help validate that the process was followed correctly.

◆ Do some "negative testing" where you make mistakes and see what happens.

CRP can be a great tool for your implementation if you are prepared for the sessions, you have the right people in the room, and you take feedback. CRP can be a disaster if you are unprepared for the session, and it can shake the confidence of the entire project team. I hope this chapter helps you succeed during your CRP events.

# The Bottom Line

**Order of Operations** CRPs occur after the JPD sessions in the implementation and before you start UAT sessions. It's important to do each step in the right order.

**Master It** During which stage of the implementation journey do you find the conference room pilots?

1. Define

2. Create

3. Deploy

4. Empower

**Content of CRP Sessions** The goal of a CRP session is to walk through a part of the overall process from end to end to make sure that the hand-offs between processes work as designed.

**Master It** CRP sessions should be organized by which of the following?

1. Process groups

2. Departments

3. Lines of business

4. Team schedules

**Data Migration**   We discuss data migration further in Chapter 16, "Data Migration—Early and Often," but in this chapter we talk about what iteration of data migration you should use during the CRP cycle.

> **Master It**   What data should be used for testing in a CRP?
>
> **1.** Demo data
>
> **2.** Hand-entered data
>
> **3.** A sample of the migrated data
>
> **4.** The latest migrated data from your previous system

**Understanding Acronyms**   We try not to use too many acronyms on projects, but we do use a few standard acronyms and it's important to understand the order of these events.

> **Master It**   Put these acronyms in their proper order during an implementation:
>
> **1.** CRP-EPR-JPD-UAT
>
> **2.** EPR-CRP-UAT-JPD
>
> **3.** EPR-JPD-CRP-UAT
>
> **4.** UAT-JPD-EPR-CRP

**Benefits of CRP**   In this chapter, we discussed several of the benefits of running through the end-to-end processes before you finish off the Create stage.

> **Master It**   Which of these is not one of the benefits of a CRP?
>
> **1.** Gives you the chance to practice the end-to-end process before code is complete
>
> **2.** Helps with usability by identifying ways to streamline the processes
>
> **3.** Raises the confidence of the team that the solution is getting ready for deployment
>
> **4.** Practices the go-live cutover

# Chapter 14

# Dealing with Challenges Mid-Project

As you've heard me say throughout the book, implementing software is very difficult—it never goes smoothly. When it is done successfully, there will still be moments of anguish and stress, and there will be risks that turn into issues that must be dealt with.

This chapter could fit anywhere in the book, but I put it here as the most problematic time on a project tends to happen toward the end of the Create stage. When you are several months into the project and users aren't getting a feature they want, you tend to see issues, and you should be prepared to handle them.

Since you know you're going to have issues, the goal of this chapter is to teach you how to plan ahead. Many issues are common on projects, so if you know what they could be, you're in a better position to deal with them when they arise.

**AFTER YOU COMPLETE THIS CHAPTER, YOU WILL BE ABLE TO DO THE FOLLOWING:**

- Provide communication and updates throughout the project to keep the project team informed

- Recognize if you may be offtrack

- Foresee common problems

- Manage your risk and issues list

- Mitigate issues when they occur

## THE PROJECT ENTHUSIASM CURVE

Figure 14.1 is a totally non-scientific picture that gives you a sense of the temperament of the team as the project proceeds. I usually see the "Pit of Despair" occurring sometime around the CRP sessions. Sometimes it happens before; sometimes it happens afterwards—especially if you invited the wrong people to your sessions or if you weren't ready for the sessions. The "Risks and Issues" section later in the chapter deals with common issues and how you can move in the right direction if the team's temperament gets really poor.

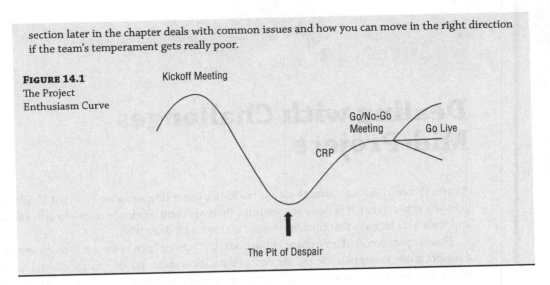

**FIGURE 14.1**
The Project
Enthusiasm Curve

Kickoff Meeting

Go/No-Go
Meeting

Go Live

CRP

The Pit of Despair

## Managing the Project Status

The project manager has the responsibility of keeping all of the stakeholders on the project informed of its progress. After 15 weeks of the project, sending out the project status report can seem like a tedious task to which no one is paying attention. In fact, several tasks that the project manager does throughout the project go from being very new and interesting at first to being routine and ignored as the project goes on. I'm not suggesting that the project manager should bury gift certificates in the bottom of the status report to get people to read it—I think the content needs to be relevant and interesting to make sure that the stakeholders are still reading it.

### Status Report

The *status report* is a weekly report sent to the leadership team and stakeholders that provides an update on the progress of the previous week, an outline of what's coming up next week, statuses on the key elements of the project, and the budget summary. The report itself is about two pages long, with the front page providing the summary and the second page providing detail on what happened during that week and what's about to occur.

The header typically contains project information that doesn't change week to week, such as the project name, the executive sponsor and other roles on the project, the date of the report, and the expected go-live date. This part of the report will remain consistent throughout the project with the exception of major role changes.

The *executive summary* of the report is where you give your high-level status of the project and where you provide a status on eight key elements on the project. For each of these eight elements, you should rate them as Green, Yellow, or Red. Let's discuss each of the elements first, and then we'll talk about how to rate them with the appropriate colors.

## EIGHT ELEMENTS OF A STATUS REPORT

1. **Overall Project Health:** This is the summary of the elements of the project. In the report, this is where you provide the 10,000-foot view of the state of the project.

2. **Budget:** The status of the actual money spent versus the budgeted amount at this point of the project. You should also project the final amount (Estimate at Completion) and how close that is to the full budget.

3. **Schedule:** The status of the progress toward the go-live date compared to the planned project schedule. Even if the go-live date has changed, if you are on track to meet the currently identified go-live date, this would be on track.

4. **Scope:** The status of scope relative to the original scope. This typically measures how many change requests are outstanding and how many changes have been requested but haven't been addressed yet. It can also measure the impact of the scope changes on the project budget and schedule, but those are best represented by the first three elements.

5. **Resources:** The current state of the people on the project and the coverage of the roles needed to be successful.

6. **Risks:** The potential issues that may surface on the project.

7. **Issues:** The issues that have surfaced and their impact on the ongoing state of the project.

8. **Stakeholder Engagement:** This is related to the change management side of the equation. It measures whether your resources are coming to the schedule meetings and focusing on their deliverables.

Each of these elements will receive a color that provides the status at a glance. After you present your color, you should write a one- to two-line summary of that element. If you rated it Red, your audience will be expecting some explanation for why it was Red and what you're doing to get it back to Green.

## Colors on a Status Report

In theory, the colors used on a status report should be pretty straight forward. *Green* means that the project, or the element of the project, is "on track." If you have a budget of $1M and you are halfway through the project having spent $500K, you appear to be on track and that budget element should be listed as Green. *Yellow* means "at risk." To use the same example, if your budget is $1M and you're halfway through the project having spent $525K, you may be able to reduce some future spending to get back in line with your original budget. If you can cite how you can reduce your spending trend, you could put this status to Yellow, indicating that you see a risk and you have a plan. Once you've proven that you can lower your weekly spend so that you can be on target for a $1M budget, you can set the status back to Green. *Red* means "offtrack." To continue the budget example, you are halfway through the $1M project, you've spent $600K, and your trajectory has you spending $1.3M to complete the project. That is a big concern for the project, and it must be dealt with. We'll talk about how you might handle it later in the chapter, but you would adjust your status back to Green if you either: (1) decrease your spending back to the point where you are on track to come in at a $1M budget or (2) you have issued and approved a change request to increase the budget up to $1.3M.

I wrote a blog recently about how there seem to be many different definitions of what "Yellow" or "Red" mean on project status reports. In reality, status reports should not stay Red for long; if there's an issue, you either fix it relatively quickly or have to reset expectations on the project to accommodate your new reality. Once you do that, the status should go back to Green.

---

## COMMON PROJECT SITUATION EXAMPLES

Here are some common project situations and how I would rate the status of the elements of the project:

### SITUATION 1

The project just began, and everything is off to a good start, but you don't have your project measurements and milestones in place yet.

#### COLOR: YELLOW

**Rationale**: Most people put it to Green, but at this point you don't know yet if you're on track or not. If the project has properly built-in tasks and milestones, and you've hit all those milestones so far, it should be Green. I've also seen people put this to Red because they don't know if the project is offtrack. If you knew it was offtrack, you'd choose Red, but since you don't know, it's Yellow.

### SITUATION 2

On your eight-element scorecard, you rate seven as on track (Green) and one as at risk (Yellow). How should you rate your overall project status?

#### COLOR: GREEN

**Rationale**: If the one area is in serious trouble, you would have to flip the overall status to Yellow, but if you believe that it can be put back on track soon, I'd recommend that you stick with Green, address that particular situation quickly, and get back on track.

### SITUATION 3

Several components of the project are at risk, and one of the eight parts of the project is offtrack and threatens the project as a whole.

#### COLOR: RED

**Rationale**: I've seen many people make up the color "Amber" to use for this state. While I appreciate the creativity, it's not one of the options, so you should pick Green, Yellow, or Red. Generally, if a portion of the project is fully offtrack, you should set the color to Red. It's especially true if many other parts of the project are at risk. If everything else were going perfectly and one area was offtrack, it would still be Red, but you could make an argument for Yellow at that point.

### SITUATION 4:

A portion of the project is not going to meet its timeline; therefore, your "schedule" element is Red.

#### COLOR: RED

**Rationale**: This is where the value of "Red" comes in. You can use it to signal to leadership and the project team that a portion of the project is offtrack, and you need to come up with an alternate plan.

**SITUATION 5:**

A portion of the project is not going to meet its original timeline, but a new timeline has been established, and the project is on track to hit that timeline.

*COLOR: GREEN*

**Rationale**: This is the example that makes me passionate about this subject, because no one seems to handle this correctly. It does no good when people leave a project in Red status forever. It's like the boy who cried wolf situation; if the project is always Red, stakeholders start ignoring the status reports because they are tired of constant bad news. One of the first clients I worked with had nearly all of their projects in Red status all of the time. Red stopped meaning anything other than everyone in the room thought the IT team was inept. When a project misses its timeline, the project should be Red until a new timeline is established. Once the project is on track for that new deadline, the status should go back to Green. It is counterintuitive to put a project that is past its original deadline at Green, but once the timeline is reestablished, the best thing for everyone involved is to adapt to the new timeline and work like crazy to make sure it happens.

## Managing Your Budget

As the budget goes, so goes the status of the project. If the budget is offtrack, chances are very good that the entire project is offtrack. People on the project may not think it is, but when you run the budget versus the actual report and see that you are spending 25 percent more per week than expected, you can start to see that you have a problem which you'll need to address.

It's important for the project manager to establish a regular rhythm for tracking the budget and presenting it to the leadership team. The project manager should track the budget on a weekly basis so that they can find small problems before they become big problems. Many projects do a monthly budget review, and that enables the project to be pretty far offtrack before a problem is discovered.

Here are some key terms for you to learn about project budgets:

**Budget**  The initially established budget for all of the activity on the project. Depending on how you work with your implementation partner, this may include the partner's costs (consulting costs and travel) only, or it could include the partner costs plus ISV costs and internal costs. Oftentimes, the partner prepares their budget, and the company manages another budget that includes those other costs. You need to have a budget that includes everything to see the full picture as you go along on your project.

**Actual**  This is the actual spend-to-date on the project from all of the sources you are tracking.

**Forecast**  This is what you expect to have spent on a week-to-week basis. Once the project starts, the budget remains the same, but the forecast may change depending on the activity. It could be that you forecast a lower weekly run rate at the beginning of the project and a higher run rate at the end. This is your expected weekly spend based on what you think the project needs to be successful. You shouldn't just try to aim to hit your overall budget number; you should base it in reality so you know what you may end up spending on the project overall.

**Earned Value**   I introduced this concept in Chapter 5, "Organizing Your Team for Success and Project Governance," and it is rarely done on projects, as it can be difficult to assess. *Earned value* is the value of the work that has been done to this point on the project. The only way that you can assess this on an implementation project is to break the activities on the project into tasks and lay them out into sprints. If you appear to be getting more done on sprints than expected, you are net positive on earned value; if you are not hitting your sprint goals, it is likely that the project hasn't gotten the value it should have by this time in the project.

**Estimate at Completion (EAC)**   The *Estimate at Completion (EAC)* figure starts as the overall budget, but it changes throughout the project as the actual costs come in and the forecast changes. The formula for this is pretty straightforward:

EAC = Actual cost + Forecasted costs

This number is not used as often as it should be on projects. To calculate this correctly, you need to have broken the project out into sprints or blocks of time so that you can forecast each week of activity on the project. Once you've done that, you need to compare your actuals to the forecast and continually update your forecast based on the number of resources that you will need at a given time during the project. If you keep those numbers up to date, you can calculate your EAC. You should be comparing your EAC to your budget to know if you are at risk or offtrack. If your budget was $1M and your EAC is $1.05M, you are at risk and need to trim resources to get your forecast back on track. If your EAC is $1.3M, you are officially offtrack and have to do something to get your costs in line with the original budget, or you have to change your original budget.

**Estimate to Complete (ETC)**   The *Estimate to Complete (ETC)* is the amount of money it will take to complete the project from where you currently sit. It requires the same information as the EAC calculation:

EAC – Actuals = ETC

It is basically the sum of your forecast. This is good to calculate, but it's the EAC value that is most important to understand.

**Variance at Completion (VAC)**   The *Variance at Completion (VAC)* is the difference between the EAC and the budget. The formula is as follows:

VAC = EAC – Budget

Everyone computes this number, but it is oftentimes not represented on the status report because the difference is usually obvious. In my examples in the EAC section, one VAC is $50,000 and the other VAC is $300,000. The higher the VAC, the bigger the budget problem.

You should have a budget spreadsheet that captures the preceding information, and you must update it on a weekly (or bi-weekly) basis. To manage the project expenses successfully, you should follow these four steps:

**1.** Lay out a forecast for the entire project right away. When you go to the kickoff meeting, you should have a spreadsheet with a week-by-week forecast that shows you hitting (or better yet, coming in under) the budget number.

2. Update the actuals on a weekly basis.

3. Update the forecast on a weekly basis. This is not commonly done on projects, and it's one of the main reasons why projects go over budget. You must estimate your future resource costs every week to be able to see where your EAC ends up. If you are earning value at the same rate that you spend money, the EAC and budget should remain equal.

4. Raise an issue anytime you have a VAC. To stay on budget, you have to identify causes for exceeding your budget and try to mitigate those issues as quickly as you can.

The project manager and the project leadership team members (executive sponsors, project owner, and engagement manager) should be looking at the variances on a bi-weekly basis and addressing issues as soon as they arise. If you are a project leader and you are not watching the budget closely, you are not doing your job.

## Project Pulse

At Stoneridge Software, we started using a service called OfficeVibe (officevibe.com) several years ago to take the pulse of our team on a frequent basis. The service sends a survey to our team members every week asking 5–10 questions about how work is going. The survey takes about two minutes to fill out, and it provides really good feedback to our leadership team. Employees can share anonymous feedback and get responses back from leaders without having to look like they are complaining.

After seeing how effective this was, we thought that it would be a good idea to implement a rapid survey process for our implementation projects as well. Change management best practices also suggest that you take polls of your team members to measure their engagement. If you use sprints, you should conduct a retrospective at the end of each one to see what you could be doing better as well.

Incorporating all those thoughts, we now send out a three-question survey at the end of each sprint to take the pulse of implementation team members. We ask the following questions:

1. On a scale of 1–10 (10 being the highest), how satisfied are you with the work completed on the most recent project deliverable or sprint?

2. On a scale of 1–10 (10 being the highest), how satisfied are you with the overall project and the progress toward the success criteria?

3. Please share any additional feedback you have on the latest project deliverable/sprint and project overall, with praise for what's gone well and suggestions for what could be done better.

We recommend that you review the results of the survey every two weeks at the leadership meeting to see if there are trends or risks that could impact the overall success of the project. It's a great way to spot small problems before they turn into major issues.

# Risks and Issues

Risks and issues are closely associated, but they are not the same thing. A *risk* is something that may cause a future issue on a project. An example of a risk is the possibility that the ISV you selected for your sales tax reporting system can't get the resources to put on the project in time relative to your go-live date. An *issue* is something bad that has happened that you now need to address. An example of an issue is when the Sales Tax ISV can't get a resource for your project, and you now face the options of (1) pushing back your go-live date, (2) going live without the sales tax functionality, or (3) finding a different ISV provider who can get the work done in time.

These definitions are pretty simple, and in the next section I'll use common challenges to show you how to deal with these risks and issues as they arise on the project. It's important for everyone on the project to know what risks and issues are, and it's critical that the project leadership team discusses them on a weekly or bi-weekly basis.

## Risk Register

A *risk register* is a common tool in project management—it's a tool that you can use to track the risk, the likelihood of it occurring, the severity if it does occur, who "owns" the risk, and what your mitigation plan is for it. Figure 14.2 is an illustration of a risk register.

**FIGURE 14.2**
Risk register

| Risk | Likelihood | Impact | Score | Owner | Response |
|------|------------|--------|-------|-------|----------|
| Key person leaves project | 3 | 4 | 12 | Bob | Retention plan/bonuses |
| Change requests are exceeding contingency | 2 | 4 | 8 | Bob | Request addition contingency or take harder line on changes |
| Integration solution not working | 2 | 5 | 10 | Ted | Need to consider other alternatives early on |
| Data migration not complete in time for UAT | 3 | 4 | 12 | Ted | Start data cleansing earlier – bring in other resources to move it along |
| Developer never completes tasks on-time | 2 | 4 | 8 | Ted | Impact to project schedule |
| Not getting right people to meetings | 4 | 5 | 20 | Bob | Expectations need to be set from the start |

I'll explain each of the columns so that you have a better sense of how this works. Typically, the likelihood and impact values range from 1 to 5, with the higher number indicating the greater risk to the project. Let's talk through each column:

**Risk**   This is the potential issue as best as you can define it. Anytime a key person leaves a project, it creates an issue for the project, so you could articulate a risk for every single person who could potentially leave the project, or you can just list one risk that covers any person leaving the project.

**Likelihood**   This is your rating of the chance that this risk may become an issue. Let's use the top risk as an example. If you rated the likelihood of a specific individual leaving the project, it would probably be 2. If you rated the likelihood of anyone leaving the project, it's probably more like 4 or 5. If the project duration is shorter, it may be as low as 3. If you rate something as a 1, it should be very unlikely to happen. If you rate something a 5, it's going to happen; it's just a matter of when.

**Impact**   This is severity of the issue once it does occur. Let's say that you are concerned about a potential change to Judy, the project owner. Since she is accountable for most of the people on the project, if she is not involved, that's a big risk. Let's say Judy is up for a promotion that would take her to a new location and force her to relinquish her role on the project. That would be a 4 or 5 impact because it's hard to find someone to fill the project owner role in the first place, and the transition effort would be large once you found someone.

**Score**   This is simply the result of multiplying the likelihood times the impact. The higher the score, the more concerning the risk. You should identify those risks that have the highest score and talk about them in your leadership meetings.

**Owner**   The owner is the person who would be responsible for managing through the issue if it were to occur. This person also keeps track of the risk and does what he or she can to avoid the risk inasmuch as it can be controlled.

**Response**   This is the mitigation plan for that particular risk. When an issue is in the "risk" stage, the mitigation is focused on avoiding the occurrence of the issue. When the risk becomes an issue, the mitigation is what you are doing to address it. If Judy, the project owner, takes her new job, you need a plan to backfill and train her replacement as quickly as possible.

The risk register should be maintained on a weekly basis, and the project leaders should review it at their weekly or bi-weekly meeting to see what risks have the highest scores and if the mitigation plans need to be adapted. You don't have to spend five minutes talking about every risk on the list; just focus on the ones that are lacking a mitigation plan or the ones where the likelihood or impact are increasing.

### Issues vs. Bugs

One common source of confusion in discussion of risks and issues is when people mix up a bug and an issue. A *bug* is a software defect where the software does not do what the requirement says it should. You will encounter many bugs on the project, and those should be tracked in your task management tool, preferably Microsoft's Azure DevOps. An issue may be a bug, but it usually is a broader project problem.

It gets confusing when issues are related to bugs. For example, if you have two P1 bugs, this may cause an issue for the project timeline. If those bugs are preventing you from getting through your UAT sessions, that becomes a project schedule issue. To mitigate it, you would review what resources are assigned to those bugs and see what you can do to increase resources to get them fixed faster. Most of the time issues are related to the elements of the project score-card, like budget problems, scope problems, resource problems, or engagement problems.

## Common Project Challenges

I wish I could provide an exhaustive list of all of the challenges, but so many things could go wrong, it's impossible to guess. Let's use Figure 14.3 as an example of common issues and break them into Table 14.1, where we categorize them into the type of issue and discuss mitigation plans.

**FIGURE 14.3**
Mid-project challenges

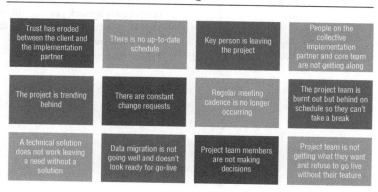

## Mid-Project Challenges

| | | | |
|---|---|---|---|
| Trust has eroded between the client and the implementation partner | There is no up-to-date schedule | Key person is leaving the project | People on the collective implementation partner and core team are not getting along |
| The project is trending behind | There are constant change requests | Regular meeting cadence is no longer occurring | The project team is burnt out but behind on schedule so they can't take a break |
| A technical solution does not work leaving a need without a solution | Data migration is not going well and doesn't look ready for go-live | Project team members are not making decisions | Project team is not getting what they want and refuse to go live without their feature |

**TABLE 14.1:** Mid-Project Challenges Mitigation Plans

| ISSUES | ELEMENT | HOW TO PREVENT | MITIGATION PLAN |
|---|---|---|---|
| Trust has eroded between the customer and implementation partner | Overall | Communication and difficult conversations—the parties have to agree to be open and address concerns with one another. | The parties need to get back together and put their concerns with the other party on the table so that they can work through them and rebuild trust. |
| There is no up-to-date project schedule | Schedule | The project manager should be reviewing this weekly and making updates as necessary. | The project manager needs to meet with the project leadership team and make the updates. This may take several hours, so it needs to be prioritized. |
| Key person is leaving the project | Resources | You have to take the pulse of everyone on the project to see how they are doing and work with each individual to make sure that they are content with their role. | It depends on the role, but you need to backfill that resource and have the current resource train the new person as quickly as possible. You may have to adjust the schedule to accommodate delays coming from an untrained resource. |
| People are not getting along between the partner and core team | Overall | A trust-building exercise at the beginning of the project is a good way to start—from there, the parties need to communicate and be open with each other. | Get the parties together and talk through the concerns. Involve the leadership team to help. If there is a particular personality conflict, see if you can separate those people. |
| The project is trending behind schedule | Schedule | During your sprint reviews, compare the work completed to the expected output; if you are consistently behind, you should see that your project will trend behind schedule. | Consider your options to speed it up by adding more resources or finding more efficient resources. If you can't, you will likely have to push back the go-live date. |

**TABLE 14.1:** Mid-Project Challenges Mitigation Plans *(CONTINUED)*

| ISSUES | ELEMENT | HOW TO PREVENT | MITIGATION PLAN |
|---|---|---|---|
| There are constant change requests | Scope | Conduct a thorough review of the potential in scope items before you get to the kickoff meeting and lock in the budget. If it happens after that, try to find them at once so that you can address them with one bigger change request. | Dive into the bigger issues early in the project to find those areas where scope may expand. If you get constant change requests, work with the leadership team to get sign-off to keep moving forward. You will likely have a schedule impact from all of this additional scope. |
| Regular meeting occurrence is no longer happening | Overall | Project manager should make sure that the originally defined meeting occurrence is happening. If not, raise the issue to project leadership. | Get the meetings back on the calendar and highlight the importance to all participants. |
| The project team is burnt out, but the schedule doesn't allow for a break | Stakeholder Engagement | This happens when the project manager hasn't planned out events ahead of time or when the project team is constantly bringing up changes or rare scenarios. In either case, the project team is not getting their work done in the time frame expected. | Get the schedule updated and impress upon the team the need to stick to it. Come to meetings that get derailed and lay down rules to make sure that they stay on track. If you can't move at the pace that you originally envisioned, push the go-live date back. |
| An important technical solution is not working | Issue | Early in the project you try to find solutions for big problems and sometimes the solution envisioned does not solve the problem. You want to find this out as soon as possible so you can start on another potential solution. | Assess the priority of the solution, and if it's of lower importance, take it out of scope. If it's important or critical, you should add resources to try to find the right solution as quickly as possible. If all else fails, you will have to push the go-live date back. |

You can see that in most cases, if the issue goes unmitigated, it will push back the go-live date of the project. Whenever you push back the go-live date, it increases the costs as well because you have to keep all of the resources on the project engaged, and their time costs money. This is a good illustration why many projects go over time and over budget.

## PSYCHOLOGICAL SAFETY

No one likes bad news. No one likes to be the one to tell someone else bad news, and no one likes to hear bad news from someone else. It's human nature to want to avoid telling bad news. There is one thing worse than communicating bad news. It's not communicating bad news and hoping that the issue goes away—but the issue actually gets worse. Imagine an extreme example. You are a doctor who performs a test on a patient and discover that they have Stage 1 cancer. Stage 1 cancer is a small, invasive mass or tumor that has not spread to the lymph nodes and is generally very treatable. Imagine that you don't want to tell your patient the bad news and you hope that it doesn't spread. When you check on the patient again in two years, it is now Stage 4 cancer, which is very bad and usually uncontrollable. Now this patient cannot recover because the cancer has spread too much.

No doctor would ever do that, thankfully. We are definitely not dealing with life or death in an implementation project, but an illustration like that shows the gravity of the unwillingness to share bad news. You need to be willing to share bad news early—if it ends up getting resolved on its own, that's great.

### CREATING AN ENVIRONMENT WHERE PEOPLE CAN SHARE BAD NEWS

The reason why people are reluctant to share bad news is the reaction they receive when they share it. Often, that reaction is one of blame and shame, and the sharer does not want to feel those emotions unless it's absolutely necessary. As a leader, you should encourage the sharing of risks or issues as soon as they may exist so that you are ready to mitigate them.

Let's take the example from the potential issues list earlier where data migration is offtrack and is now affecting the project timeline. When the project manager checks in with the data migration, she finds that they are struggling with data cleanup and running a week behind schedule. She could sit on that information and hope that the team turns it around, or she could raise the issue to the project leadership team. If she raises the issue and the executive sponsor says, "I can't believe that you don't have those idiots under control. Get your act together and get them moving, or I'll find someone who will," the project manager is going to be reluctant to share bad news in the future if the project leaders respond with blame and threats.

Even small facial reactions can give away your opinion on a subject. If you tell the project leaders that Bob, the lead functional consultant, is leaving the project and the executive sponsor winces or turns around in her chair in frustration, you have to absorb that reaction. It can be very hard to do, but the best thing to do is take a deep breath, digest the information, and think through the appropriate response. As a project leader, you need to reaffirm your team and be a problem-solver for your them. You have to take the news in stride (throughout the book I have said that there will be problems) and put a productive spin on the news—whatever it is. If you can establish a pattern of trying to find solutions and not placing blame, you will hear bad news fast and deal with it before it becomes terrible news.

## THE FEAR OF THE UNKNOWN

In my experience, people on implementation projects often fall into one of two states: they are over-tasked or overwhelmed. If they are overtasked (they have more on their plate to do than the hours needed to get that work done), that is a problem that a project leader can help solve. If you see an overtasked resource, you can (1) get another resource to take on some of that work, (2) free up that person's schedule in another way to allow them more time to get the work done, or (3) de-prioritize some of the work so that the workload is lessened. A person who is overtasked may be frustrated by the amount of work to be done, but it is a manageable state.

A resource who is overwhelmed is a different problem entirely. Usually someone is overwhelmed because they don't know everything they have to do, and the reality is either that it's more than they can get done well or that they perceive it's more than they can get done well. You are overwhelmed because there are unknowns, and the fear of the unknown is what leads to stress.

That is why it is so important for the project manager to lay out for the team what needs to be done and when. If you use sprints and you estimate tasks reasonably well, you should be able to avoid your team becoming overtasked or overwhelmed. Don't assign someone 120 hours' worth of work to do in a two-week sprint; otherwise, they will be overtasked.

To avoid overwhelming someone, tell them what is expected of them in clear language. If there is an unknown in the future, try to make it known as soon as possible. If it's a technical issue that has not been discussed yet, set up time in the next sprint to discuss it and identify potential designs for that problem. Once the team knows about potential solutions, the fear of the unknown decreases and you can get back to being productive with the tasks laid out before you.

To be an effective leader of an ERP or CRM implementation, you need to understand psychology and you need to know how to motivate your team. You need to be able to accept bad news, manage risks and issues, and communicate the path to success to your team on a regular basis. It sounds simple, but it is difficult to do when you are balancing other responsibilities or dealing with the massive amount of information that comes out in an implementation like this.

## The Bottom Line

**Issues vs. Bugs**   I discussed the difference between issues and bugs in this chapter. Issues can be bugs, or they could be problems with scope, resources, or budget.

   **Master It**   What best explains bugs in a project?

   **1.** They are technical issues with the expectation that there will be many in a project.

   **2.** They are personnel/non-technical issues.

   **3.** They are the same thing as an issue.

   **4.** They are microscopic mites that infect one's hardware.

**Color of Your Status Report**   For each of the core elements of the project, you should report the status weekly as either Green (on track), Yellow (at risk), or Red (offtrack).

**Master It** Status Report Situation: The project has just begun, and everything is off to a good start, but you don't have your project measurements and milestones in place yet. Which status color should the overall project be tracked as?

**1.** Green

**2.** Yellow

**3.** Red

**4.** Orange

**Risks and Issues**   For each of the core elements of the project, you should report the status weekly as either Green (on track), Yellow (at risk), or Red (offtrack).

**Master It** Status Report Situation: Several components of the project are at risk, and one of the eight parts of the project is offtrack. Which status color should the overall project be tracked as?

**1.** Green

**2.** Yellow

**3.** Red

**4.** Orange

**Project Challenges**   An infinite number of challenges could occur on your project. Project managers should identify possible challenges and put them on the risk register so that you can start to build mitigation plans.

**Master It** Which of the following are mid-project challenges?

**1.** Key person is leaving the project

**2.** Project team members are not making decisions

**3.** The project is trending behind

**4.** All of the above

**Psychological Safety**   No one likes to hear bad news, nor does anyone like to share bad news. Unfortunately, bad things will happen on implementation projects, and it's important to create an environment where you can effectively deal with the bad news quickly.

**Master It** Psychological safety is a key component to keep a project moving forward successfully. Which of the following are ways to support safety within a project?

**1.** Establish a pattern of always trying to find solutions, not of placing blame

**2.** Take a moment between hearing something and reacting to it to choose the right decision

**3.** All problems are team problems, not problems for individuals

**4.** All of the above

# Chapter 15

# Customizations vs. Configurations and How You Manage Them

There tends to be a lot of confusion on projects about the difference between a customization and a configuration. From a cost perspective, configurations are good, and customizations are expensive, but it isn't as straightforward as that, as you'll see in this chapter.

As the world sees more low-code, no-code platforms, more and more problems can be solved without having to open a development environment. That makes software implementations faster, but it certainly can't solve all the problems you are likely facing.

### AFTER YOU COMPLETE THIS CHAPTER, YOU WILL BE ABLE TO DO THE FOLLOWING:

◆ Explain the difference between customizations and configurations

◆ Track your configurations

◆ Take a customization through the design flow

◆ Articulate the steps developers follow to create customizations

◆ Push the customizations through testing and release

## Customizations vs. Configurations

We will get to the question of when to use customizations versus configurations, but it's important to start by going through several definitions of concepts that are commonly used in software development projects—especially ERP and CRM implementations.

### Customization

A *customization* is a code change of any variety within the application. This is usually something that is visible within the software, but it could be a change to the underlying logic. You can make customizations to forms within the application by moving fields around, adding fields, or changing labels or columns on a grid. You can, and will, make changes to reports by adding images, pulling in additional data fields, and reorganizing the way that the data is represented.

## Configuration

A *configuration* is a setting made in the *user interface* of the software that affects how the application works. They are sometimes called "switches" or "dials" colloquially, because they are different settings that you can flip from one thing to another. Nearly every module or area of the product will have a parameter area where you can set a number of configuration settings.

You will sometimes create a distinction between two types of configurations: parameters and reference data. A *parameter* is typically a setting that you can turn on or off. An example of a parameter setting in Microsoft Dynamics 365 Customer Engagement is the auditing setting. You can change the parameter at a system level to indicate if you want to allow auditing in the system. Then, on each entity you create, there is a checkbox indicating whether you would like to turn on auditing for that particular entity. This is a parameter because you can turn it on or off.

A *reference data configuration* is when you populate some data in the system that could change the system's behavior in one way or another. Reference data configurations are explained in greater detail in the upcoming sections.

---

### NO-CODE CUSTOMIZATIONS

In Microsoft Dynamics 365 Customer Engagement or Model-driven Power Apps, you will find that you are able to make many customizations within the user interface without having to write code. You will also find that you can use JavaScript to write functions within the user interface that would otherwise typically require customizations to be written by a developer. These fall into the strange category of "not really a customization," because the changes can be made by a non-developer, and it's "not really a configuration," because you can generate errors if you make mistakes in the code.

Certainly, if you have the opportunity to create entities/tables and attributes/fields without having to write code, that is a great thing that will save the project time and money. In CRM projects, you certainly want to take advantage of that and do as much through the user interface as you can. You should still expect to have to do some amount of customization work, though, as customized logic will typically require code.

Microsoft is advancing the *low-code, no-code strategy* with its development of the Power Platform. The *Power Platform* includes Power BI for reporting and business intelligence; Power Apps, which allow you to build tablet and mobile apps without code (or without much code); Power Automate, which is a workflow engine that can be used to perform an action upon a trigger; and Power Virtual Agents, which allows you to create bots to provide chat responses to customers or prospects. All of these systems were designed to provide a significant amount of power to the user without requiring custom development.

---

## Integration

An *integration* is a connection to another system that does not run in the same database. I make this distinction because many of the Microsoft Dynamics–related ISVs do run in the same code base and database. An integration is an outside system where data has to be exchanged with another platform via an API (application programming interface) or some type of data exchange.

Most every integration will require code—sometimes on both sides and sometimes just on the Dynamics side—to make it work. You will need to receive a piece of data from the integrated solution and do something with it. You may receive an invoice from another system that you have to register against one of the customers in your database. In that case, you would write logic to match the data you receive with the data in your system. If the data doesn't match, you would have to write error-handling functionality to decide what to do in that case.

If you have many integrations in your deployment, plan to budget a considerable amount of time and money for custom code development.

## Master Data

*Master data* is non-transactional data that's stored in the system. Another way of describing it is data about the business entities that provides context for business transactions. Your master data will be the core information that makes the system run—your customers, vendors, chart of accounts, items, warehouses, and employees. This information is foundational to everything you do in the system and typically where you want to start with your data migration efforts.

It's always good to start your implementation effort by getting clarity on the structure of your master data. If you know how you want your customer data to be tracked in the system, it provides a building block for how you do orders and invoices later. If you haven't settled on your master data, any work that you do in areas that depend on it may need to be changed later.

**NOTE**    Making a late change in the structure of your master data will set your project back weeks or months.

## Metadata

*Metadata* is data that provides information about other data. Yes, that sounds confusing, doesn't it? It is the data structure, so it is a table that tells you what columns or options are available in a table you use in the system. I will use the term "entity" or "table" to refer to a data structure that holds other data in the system's database. For example, we created a new entity in our CRM system called Legal Agreements. We use it to track any legal agreements that we have signed with our customers. This entity has several fields or attributes in it like the associated account, who signed it, when it was signed, and a link to the document repository where the signed contract is stored. All of this structure is considered metadata. There is a table in the CRM system that tracks these entities and attributes. This is how the system is able to allow a non-developer to create data structures without custom code.

## Personalization

These are often confused with configurations, and technically, *personalizations* are configurations. They are just configurations that are saved to a user's profile and specific to that user. In the Microsoft Dynamics 365 systems, an example would be a grid view. You can typically change what fields show on that grid, and you can save that personalization, so the next time you come into the system you see the fields you want to see.

## Reference Data

*Reference data* is data that you have in the system to classify or categorize other data. Most areas of the product have some type of reference data that is used to provide a baseline of data or options that you can change in the system. Common examples include units of measure; country, state, and ZIP codes; calendars; payment terms; and number sequences. If there is any debate on these items, just like master data, you want to have that debate as early as possible so that you can lock these building blocks in as future functionality will build on this base.

## When to Customize vs. Configure

If possible, and if you have the options, you always want to choose to configure your solution instead of customizing it. If there's a change you want and it's not something that can be configured, you will need to customize it. When you customize it, you can choose to build in configuration options so that different users or companies could change the configuration later, but to get that capability you'll need to do a customization.

Customizations are needed when any of the following conditions are met:

◆ The system lacks the functionality you seek in a particular area.

◆ You are integrating to another system.

◆ A report requires a modification that can't be done within the user interface.

If you can make these changes with the base functionality of the system, you should—it's much easier to manage that way. The other option that you have if the system doesn't have the functionality is to decide not to do the customization and to use a workaround that would be available in the core system.

## Why Choose to Customize

As mentioned in the previous section, many times you need to customize the system because it lacks the functionality to do something that you need to do in its base functionality. You knew this, and you bought the system anyway (all systems will lack some functionality). In order to perform your standard process flow, the system needs a customization to fill the gap.

Many people choose to customize a system when a non-customized option is available. This may sound strange because that customization will be more expensive. You would do this when you purposely want to do something different than the standard system functionality. You would do this because what you are doing constitutes your "secret sauce" or something that you do better than your competition.

You should not choose to customize the system if you are modifying a standard process just because it's the way you've always done it and you don't want to change. If that way provides significant value to your business, go ahead, but most of the time when I hear this, it's just an excuse not to change. Many companies have legitimate reasons to customize and should do so; you just want to make sure that you know the "why," and the why is not just to avoid change.

# Tracking Configurations

It sounds like a great idea to use configurations whenever you can—it is, but just because you use configurations doesn't mean that there's no work associated with them. It is a common misconception that because something requires a configuration, it requires no time at all.

Implementation teams can get into lots of trouble if they don't have a good approach to managing their configurations. Imagine if you wanted to set a configuration to one thing and another user didn't get that message and changed that configuration. Or you thought that the configuration was set to X in your Test system and you find that it's set to Y in your UAT system. When you have an error or a strange problem due to mismatched configurations, it can be very difficult to solve.

You have three common ways to track configurations on implementation projects. Let's discuss each of these options.

## Configuration Tracker

A *configuration tracker* is pretty simple—it's a spreadsheet where you can track the parameters and basic configurations that you have put into place in the system. You typically create a tab for each module or functional area, and then you list the configuration decision and what value you entered.

You want to have one central configuration tracker that is updated by the various functional consultants and any core team members who might be making changes. You don't want to change any values until you have agreement that this is the setting you want to use. Once you change it in the Test environment, you use the configuration tracker as a way to check in this configuration to indicate that it's final.

## Gold Environment

The *Gold environment* is often used in addition to the configuration tracker. The reason it's called a "gold" environment is that this is a separate instance of Microsoft Dynamics that you set up just to track configurations. You would use this environment as the base layer for future environments because you know the configuration is correct, so you would start with this, then add the migrated data, and you'd have a clean environment ready to test.

You may decide that you can't afford to maintain an environment just to track configurations, so another similar option would be to use the UAT or Production environment as a temporary "gold" environment where you track configurations. The Production environment is a good place to store the configurations (if you are not otherwise using it), so you can copy those values back down to the lower environments when you need them. You would make a backup of the Production environment and use that as the base layer for future environments.

If you are already live and can't afford an environment for tracking configurations, you will need to re-enter configurations each time you establish a new environment. In this case, you will want to use the configuration tracker to validate that the configurations are correct.

## Lifecycle Services

Microsoft has a service platform called *Lifecycle Services*, available at lcs.dynamics.com, which provides tools to help drive more predictable implementations. It is primarily used for Dynamics 365 Finance and Supply Chain Management, so the functionality for the other Microsoft Dynamics 365 solutions is limited at this time. You would set up an instance of Lifecycle Services for your implementation to take advantage of these capabilities.

Inside your Lifecycle Services instance, you would use the Configuration and Data Manager option to create a package of configurations. You can use this system to deploy packages to each new environment to make sure that you have a set of consistent configurations.

# Functional Design Documents

The standard way to express a design in an implementation project is through the creation of a *functional design document (FDD)*. An FDD is a part of a set of software specifications that outlines the features of the system from the user's point of view. The FDD is written by the functional consultant with consultation from the core team lead, other consultants, and the developer. It contains six sections, so let's talk about each.

## Overview

The first section is the overview, and this describes the reason why this design is being created. The idea here is to provide a business reason that clearly explains why it was important and what gap this solution is filling. This starts with the requirement that needs to be met and where that requirement exists in the process catalog. This should be a paragraph or two so that the reader understands why this work should be done.

The next part of the overview is where the designer explains the design plan in plain language. This isn't where you identify the tables and objects to be changed; it's an explanation of what needs to be done to address the requirement that you outlined.

The final part of the overview contemplates the audience for this document—generally the core team, subject matter experts, business process owner, and the developer and solution architect from the implementation team.

## Modification

The second section is the modification. You start by articulating how Dynamics 365 works out of the box. This way, the reader has a baseline from which to see what is changing. The first part of the section describes the tables and entities that are involved in the provided functionality today, so the developer knows where to start and how it normally works. The second part shows the updates—what needs to change in that data structure or report or logic to accommodate the requirement that needs to be met. This can be a more technical chapter, where the designer explains what objects should be used and how they should be changed. The more detailed the writer can be here, the easier it is for the developer to get the code right.

The technical guidance section comes next, and that's where you articulate the security that should be associated with this change. If you create a new entity/table, you will need to assign security to that table, or no one (besides system administrators) will be able to see it. You would also talk about any data migration changes that are necessary to support this change. If you already started on the data migration and now you have new data to import, you will have to let the data migration lead know that their mapping will need to change to accommodate this new table or field.

The last part of this section is where you provide a risk assessment. This is where you identify possible risks associated with this change. There are always risks related to bugs and proper testing, but you want to think about additional risks, such as the business process change, training needed for the new process, and the acceptance of the new process.

## Testing

The third section is testing. This covers what testing should be done to validate this change. You would suggest the best way to do functional and end-to-end testing for this change in this section. If you are building test cases to support this process, you can identify the steps that should be included in the test cases.

## Development Quotation

The fourth section is the development quotation. This contains the work estimate related to this change. It should include the development and testing hours so that all parties understand what impact this change is making to your overall project budget.

## Revision and Sign-off

The fifth section is about revision and sign-off. This is the section where the customer signs off on the design. Before you spend 40 hours designing something, you want to make sure that the organization wants this customization. There is always some work involved to estimate the total effort for a customization, so you would use the T-shirt sizing exercise to help the decision-making around whether you should do the customization. If you give it the green light, you would break down the development estimate once you complete the design so that you can have a more accurate representation of the work involved. It's always possible for the business process owner to decide against doing the work if the design reveals that it involves considerably more hours than originally expected.

When the design is complete, the core team lead or business process owner needs to sign off on the design approach and estimate as outlined in this document. To keep the project moving, you should respond within 2–3 business days. If you don't, one of two things happens, and they are both bad—either the work gets delayed because it's not approved or the work starts without approval and the approval comes after the code is delivered. If the approval comes much later, it is more likely that the code will need to be reworked because it didn't meet the expectation of the user. You don't want to push more work to later on in the project. That kind of thinking easily leads to project delays.

In this section, you outline each of the different versions of the document where you may end up making several revisions after you get feedback from a wide variety of parties. It's helpful to see the versioning related to each of those changes.

## Updates

The sixth and final section is any updates that are made after approval. This section is often neglected because there's a tendency to consider a design done once it's been approved. Even if the design concept is changed after the code was developed, there isn't often a big push to go back and make the changes in the FDD. It's great if you do, because the FDD becomes a historical reference document that you can use years from now to understand the requirement and design approach for the problem. If it's out of date, it becomes far less useful.

If you end up changing or adding to the design in the future, the best practice would be to come back to this original FDD and use this section to highlight the changes.

## Design Complete

Once the FDD is written and approved, it goes into the development process, which we'll discuss next.

# The Development Process

Once you have created and approved the FDD, you will hand the document to the developer who will take it on the next leg of the journey.

Figure 15.1 gives you an idea of the steps in the development process.

**FIGURE 15.1**
Developer activity

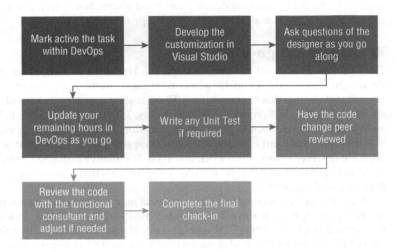

## Develop the Solution

The first step only takes a minute, so I didn't create a section heading for it. Step 1 is to go into DevOps (if you're using it) and mark the development task as active. Next you start developing the customization in the appropriate development environment. In most cases, that will be Visual Studio, but it may be different if you are developing a JavaScript customization in the UI of the Power Platform, for example.

I'm not a developer, and I don't play one on TV, so I won't go into exactly what you change as you open up the proper files on your machine. I will just skip ahead and say that once you are done making the changes to add the field, change the UI, change the report, connect the data and/or change logic, the customization is ready to move on to the next step. As you develop, you may have questions about the FDD or the design concepts—you may want to reach out to the functional consultant for clarifying questions. I suggest the more conversation, the better. It's much easier to ask questions while you have the code pulled up than to finish something, promote it to an environment, and then start asking questions.

As you complete your development, you should make updates to the task status in DevOps. If you are working on a 20-hour customization and you are 8 hours into it, you will want to put 12 hours into the Remaining Hours field at the end of the day so that your project manager has a better idea of how much work is left on that particular task.

## Unit Test

A *unit test* is a test to determine if the entire code or elements of the code work execute as intended. The unit test is often written at the same time the code is written and used by the debugger to run an automated test on the code. The idea is to be able to send a value to the system and get a Pass or Fail result. The goal of unit testing is to isolate each part of the program and show that individual parts work correctly. It is typically written in a different project and then passed to the original customization .

In most implementations, developers do not write automated unit tests, but they should determine a means for running a unit test against their code. Unit tests take extra time, and oftentimes you don't have the framework in place to run them in an automated fashion. The decision to write unit tests pits the short-term cost against the long-term value of automating testing. If you are intending to automate testing as much as possible so that you have less risk when you do future updates, you should write unit tests on your key customizations.

Developers would write the unit test and use their experience to know whether they need to write one or multiple tests. You put unit tests on logic, and you are trying to make sure that the test can result in a Pass or Fail output.

Most unit tests are connected to builds, so they are typically automatically run when you deploy as a new build. With automation, you can stipulate to execute the unit tests at each deployment so that you will know if any new code may have broken this existing code where you built unit tests. Unit tests will not find everything, as they don't test for data or process flow, but they will help you catch events where a change in data or logic somewhere else might break this piece of code.

## Code Review

The idea of a *code review* (sometimes called a *peer review*) is to have another developer review the code to see if best practices were followed and the logic is well represented. It also helps to educate the second developer on what was done and to give them an opportunity to find obvious defects that might have been missed by the primary developer.

The code review can happen interactively or after the code is checked in; it's usually the latter. If a developer is struggling with how to do something, they will likely reach out to a peer to get some advice. That's not really a code review, but the other developer might review the code while they are in there. Typically, the code is checked in, and the developer reaches out to their designated peer to do a code review. Code reviews are typically done by a peer or a mentor—you normally wouldn't ask a junior developer to do a code review.

The reviewer will put comments in the code and/or send an email with the suggestions or specific guidance from the code review. Comments sometimes point out a better way of approaching a problem that could be taken as a suggestion, and at other times the reviewer may indicate a security threat with the way the code is structured that needs to be fixed. Ultimately, the code quality is the responsibility of the team and the original developer, and the code reviewer should work with them to make sure that the code operates as efficiently as possible while solving the problem it was intended to solve.

## Functional Testing (Part 1)

The best-practice way to validate a customization is to have the functional consultant log in to the developer's environment and have the developer walk through what they've done. This is a good way to validate that the functionality meets the design before you go through the effort of deploying the customization. If something is not right, the functional consultant and developer can talk about it right then and there and potentially make the change at that time. It makes the whole process go more quickly if the functional consultant and developer can get together quickly and test it in the development environment.

Functional testing can certainly be done after the development is fully done and checked in, but we have found that this way is more efficient because you can make changes to the system before the code is checked in.

### Finishing Up

Your code has finished functional testing, and it's ready to be considered code complete. When you are done with the development, you will check the code into your source control, which is generally Azure DevOps, and it's usually connected to your instance of Visual Studio. It may take some time for the code to get checked in, so while that's being done, it's a good time to go into the DevOps task and update the status. You typically update the status to Closed to indicate that your particular task is closed out, and then you enter the total number of hours and clear out the Remaining Hours field. Now you have reported on the status of your activity, so you don't have to send an email to the project manager or functional consultant to let them know that you're done.

## After Code Complete

Your developer has finished the customized code and checked it into the appropriate source control tool. What happens next?

### Deploying the Code

We will spend all of Chapter 17, "Environment Management and Deployments," talking about environments and how code gets deployed between the various environments, so I will keep it brief here. The technical consultant or IT Operations resource will take the code from the source control tool and deploy it to the relevant environment (most likely the Test environment).

Once the code is deployed successfully, the technical consultant will let the team know that the customization is ready to be tested in the Test or UAT environment. If any errors occur in the deployment, the technical consultant will try to troubleshoot them and potentially work with a developer to resolve those issues.

### Functional Testing (Part 2)

Once the code is deployed, the functional consultant will take another pass at testing to make sure that the code for this particular design works as intended. If you did this during the code development process, you should still do it again once it's been deployed. The reason for the re-test here is that it can be tested with the appropriate configurations and data in place. It may have worked well in the developer's environment with fake data, but it might not work when it's intermingled with real data.

Once the functional consultant has indicated that the test has passed, she will often pass it on to the core team lead and a small group of subject matter experts to validate the test from the customer's point of view. This is a good step to do as the core team lead should have a good perspective on whether the design meets the need of the business process.

### Preparing for CRP and UAT

Once it's been tested and passed, the next step is to prepare for end-to-end testing. You can certainly take a more process-based test pass on this code and run through several steps to make sure that it fits into the process flow well. That is what you will do during CRP and UAT, so you will need to do this while you prepare for CRP and UAT testing, and the sooner you can do it, the better.

The big, key task that you need to do before CRP and UAT is to prepare training material on this subject. You can write up instructions on the steps required to complete the action outlined in the design and put that into the broader training material. Another suggestion is to record a video of the activity and talk through what is happening while you show what you're doing in the system. This will allow you to share that snippet with the rest of the team and incorporate it into your eLearning.

## The Lifecycle of a Customization

Let's pull everything together that we've learned from the past few chapters about how a request goes from the requirement stage to a fully tested, ready customization in your production system. We've talked about each of the steps in some detail, but it's helpful to see it all come together.

Figure 15.2 gives you a good idea of the steps involved to go from a requirement to working code in your system.

**FIGURE 15.2**
Lifecycle of customization

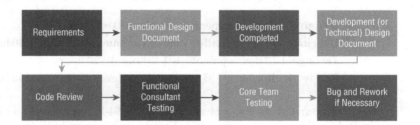

I note in Figure 15.2 that the Development Design Document (DDD)—sometimes called a Technical Design Document (TDD)—should be written after the development work is done, and that is the typical practice. For a large or complex change, it is often worth developing the DDD first and walking through it with the team before development to make sure that everyone agrees with the plan of attack. In that case, the developer would go back and edit the DDD after the code is developed to make any adjustments.

### Managing These Tasks

Microsoft's Azure DevOps (DevOps) is the recommended tool to use on implementations to track all the activity on the project. You can go crazy and track every time someone goes to the bathroom, but that's overkill that will result in more project management burden than value. You generally want to manage DevOps tasks at the 2-hour or more level because managing every 15-minute task is overwhelming.

For the steps in the customization process, we typically track the Requirements step as part of the JPD sessions. You will track JPD sessions in DevOps, but not a specific generation of one requirement. If that requirement leads to the need to build an FDD, you will create a design task and assign it to the functional consultant who covers the process from meeting with the core team to ask more questions, to investigating options, to building a draft document, to reviewing that document with the core team, and through getting approval on the document. That task requires several steps, but you would create one DevOps task called "Design" that would incorporate all of that, primarily because it's led by one person.

For the Development work, you would aggregate the development activity plus the DDD and the code review into one task for the developer to complete (even though the developer may reach out to a colleague for the code review).

For the Testing work, you would create a task for the functional consultant to run a functional test and to create a test case for the system. At that point, the core team testing falls into another effort bucket, such as CRP or UAT activity.

If there is a bug or rework needed on the customization, you would create a fourth DevOps task to assign that work back to the developer.

Each task needs to be estimated and assigned to the right person in DevOps. As a rule of thumb, you index the work effort based on the estimated development time. If the development time is 40 hours, you typically reserve 50 percent of the time for design and 50 percent for testing, and then you allocate 35 percent for potential rework. This is just a rule of thumb, and the best thing to do is to ask each party to estimate their effort level.

If you are doing the math in your head right now, you can see that what seems like a 40-hour customization will be a lot more work than that. Let's do the math together:

$\textbf{Design} = 1/2 \text{ development cost} (40 \text{ hours}) = 20 \text{ hours}$

$\textbf{Development} = \text{Originally estimated amount of 40 hours} = 40 \text{ hours}$

$\textbf{Testing} = 1/2 \text{ development cost} (40 \text{ hours}) = 20 \text{ hours}$

$\textbf{Re-work allocation} = 35 \text{ percent of the development cost} (40 \text{ hours}) = 14 \text{ hours}$

Now your 40-hour project has turned into a 94-hour project. You can see how hours build up quickly in the customization world. That doesn't even include time for testing and for future testing that you would need to do as you update the system over time.

Figure 15.3 shows an example view of DevOps related to the design of a 1099-PATR (patronage) form with each task and the estimated hours per task on the right.

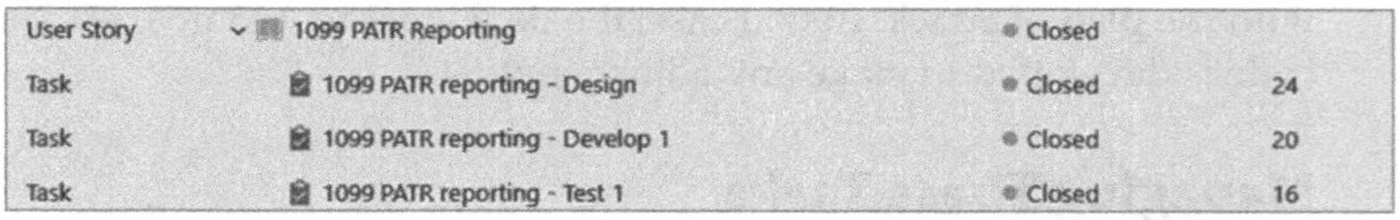

**FIGURE 15.3**
DevOps example

| User Story | ⌄ 1099 PATR Reporting | ● Closed | |
|---|---|---|---|
| Task | 1099 PATR reporting - Design | ● Closed | 24 |
| Task | 1099 PATR reporting - Develop 1 | ● Closed | 20 |
| Task | 1099 PATR reporting - Test 1 | ● Closed | 16 |

## Wrap-Up

With this and the discussion of whether to customize the system, you should have a good idea of what you are getting yourself into with any customization you make to your Microsoft Dynamics 365 system.

# The Bottom Line

**Commonly Used Definitions**   In implementation projects, participants should know commonly used terms so that they understand exactly what's being discussed.

**Master It**   Which of these is a definition of configuration?

1. Code change of any variety within the application

2. Individual user changing columns on a grid

3. Data that provides information about other data

4. A setting made in the user interface of the software that affects how the application works

**Customization vs. Configuration**   One of the big decisions you will face on projects is whether to use configurations or customizations to achieve what you want in the system.

**Master It**   When should you choose to customize the system?

1. An ISV exists that provides all of the necessary functionality

2. The system lacks functionality that you need in a particular area

3. Users want to modify a standard process because that's what has always been done

4. To automate entering configurations

**Configuration Tracker**   Three common ways exist to track configurations, so make sure that you know what has been changed and in which environment.

**Master It**   Which of the following is not one of the ways to track configurations?

1. Configuration tracking spreadsheet

2. Lifecycle services

3. Personal notebook

4. Gold environment

**Customization Lifecycle**   The lifecycle of a customization consists of eight common steps that take the idea from a requirement to a live, working customization.

**Master It**   Which of these is not a step in the lifecycle of customization?

1. Functional design document

2. Development completed

3. Code review

4. Joint process design

**Project Activity Tracking**  When developing customizations, you want to log three different tasks in your Azure DevOps system to manage the effort related to the customization.

> **Master It**  Which three DevOps tasks are tracked related to the lifecycle of the customization?
>
> 1. Design, development, test
> 2. Requirements, design, approval
> 3. Development, code review, deployment
> 4. Unit test, regression test, end-to-end test

# Chapter 16

# Data Migration—Early and Often

ETL is an acronym that's used all of the time in data migration, and I must say I heard it at least 100 times before I really understood what it meant. It's one of the most useful acronyms that you can learn because it tells you the important steps that you need to follow to be able to move data from one system to the next.

This chapter focuses on the process of moving data from your current system to your new Microsoft Dynamics 365 system—a process called data migration. We'll go through the *E* (extract), *T* (transform), and *L* (load) steps and validate the data so you know that you have accurate data in the new system.

Figure 16.1 outlines these three data migration steps.

**FIGURE 16.1**
Three steps to
data migration

### Three Steps of Data Migration

| **Extract** | **Transform** | **Load** |
| Pull data from existing system | Change the data from the old structure to the new structure | Import the data into the new system |

## AFTER YOU COMPLETE THIS CHAPTER, YOU WILL BE ABLE TO DO THE FOLLOWING:

◆ Prepare your data migration plan

◆ Extract data from your current system

◆ Transform the data from your current system to the new format

◆ Load data into the new system

◆ Validate the data's accuracy

All the way back in Chapter 2, "What to Do Before You Begin a Project," I talked about how important the cleanliness of your data is to the success of your system. Many, many times I've seen companies go live with data that they believe is clean, only to end up dealing with significant issues arising from the cleanliness of the data. The hard thing about data issues is that you think it's a software bug, but it really isn't. You see an issue and try to write code to solve it, only to realize that you have an unexpected Null value in your data that was causing your issue in the first place.

The other big concern about the data migration process is how it impacts the timeline of your project. You cannot go live without good data in the system; you can go live without a particular customization, but if you don't have your customers and their open balances in the new system, you can't go live. Also, the experience of the users is greatly affected by the readiness of data migration. If you run a CRP using the standard bicycle parts data, your users will not have a very good experience. The experience will be much better if they are working with data with which they are familiar.

## Data Migration Plan

The title of this chapter is "Data Migration—Early and Often." In the historical Waterfall approach to implementations, data migration would start after all of the code has been designed and developed, but we have found that to be way too late if you want data migration to be successful. Data migration needs to start very early in the process. You should analyze your approach before the kickoff and start building your data migration right away after the kick-off meeting.

### Proactive Cleaning

In Chapter 2, we discussed how important it was to have clean data. This is a process that you can start at any time—even before you choose your new ERP or CRM system. If a project team member ever says to me "I have time to work on the project, but I don't know what to do yet," I like to respond by suggesting that they get involved in cleaning the data. It seems like you can always find work standardizing your data.

The best way to attack cleaning your data is to develop a *rule book*. This rule book sets the standards for how text data should look in your system. For example, if you have McDonald's locations in your system, you may want to create a naming scheme on how you reference them. Perhaps you want to list the McDonald's that is in the Illinois Center on Michigan Avenue in Chicago as "McDonald's - Chicago - Michigan Avenue." If that's the naming convention you use, all McDonald's locations should be listed the same way with hyphens between the name, the city, and the avenue. If you want your new system to have naming conventions like this, you can change the data in your existing system so that it's ready when you import it.

Another part of the rule book would be how you handle duplicates. For example, what do you do if you have two McDonald's in your system today? If you import them into your new system with the same name, your system will not know whether it's the one on Michigan Avenue or the one on Wabash Avenue, and it may map the historical data to the wrong location. Look for duplicates in your existing system so that you don't import problems into your new system.

Another data preparation activity is to pick the master system if you have data coming in from multiple, different systems. Oftentimes, the reason why you're doing an ERP or CRM project is because you don't have a single source of truth for your master data, so if that is your reality, you should determine the source that you will use during the data migration activity.

If the data in that source is incomplete, you should try to pull the full picture together in the current system so that the import runs more smoothly.

Many times, I've seen customers who don't have a full dataset in any of their systems today for a given piece of data. If you ask the sales team, "Where are you tracking your conversations with prospects today?" one might answer "In the notebook in my car," while another will say "In my head," and still another will say "In OneNote." Good luck compiling that data together easily. If you have incomplete data that you need to put into your new system, you are going to have a project on your hands to prepare the data from these various systems so that you can use the functionality within the new system well. If you don't pull this information together, you are putting more pressure on the project team to cobble together data before you are ready to go live.

## Before the Kickoff

In the period before the kickoff meeting, you want to take stock of the current state of the data that you want to migrate into the new system. For ERP projects, generally you are always going to move over the following data from these different classes of data, as outlined in Table 16.1.

**TABLE 16.1:**    Data Migration Classes

| MASTER DATA | SUMMARY DATA | OPEN TRANSACTIONS |
|---|---|---|
| Customers | Ending balances per account | Open quotes, orders, or invoices |
| Vendors | Inventory balances per location | Outstanding balances to collect |
| Chart of Accounts | | |
| Items | | |
| Sites/Warehouses/Locations | | |
| Employees | | |

I'm sure that you will have more data to import than what I listed in Table 16.1, so you want to start asking questions to determine all of the data sources that you will need for your new system. You might not know all of these until you know how the new system works, but you should write down all of the obvious data sources pre-kickoff so that you can start to build a plan to import that data.

Once you have the list as complete as you can make it, you should assess the state of the data in your current system. You want to ask yourself questions like the following:

◆    Where is that data?

◆    Is the data clean? (Does it follow the rule book mentioned in the previous section?)

◆    Who is the owner of this data?

◆    Do I have resources who can get the data ready to be imported?

This step is really important to the success of data migration. You want to make sure that you have the data ready for the migration process. The sooner you can get started on this, the sooner you can be in a position to import this data into your new system so that you can start using it in CRP sessions and you can validate how accurate it is.

---

### How Much Data to Migrate

The more data you migrate, the more history you will have in your system. The more data you migrate, the more it will cost. These are the two poles pulling you in one direction or another as you determine how much data to migrate. In Table 16.1, I listed the data that really has to be migrated for you to have representative data in Microsoft Dynamics, but you could migrate many more data elements if you so choose.

The biggest decision comes around how much transaction history to bring over. It would be great if you brought over the past three years of history into the new system, as you can then look up activity for your customers and you will know the source of all of your balances. There are two problems with this:

◆ That's a lot of data to bring over.

◆ It gets harder and harder to validate your data the more you bring over.

If there's a transaction from two years ago that is one-sided (it has a debit but no credit or vice versa), now you're either importing a problem into your new system or having to hunt down the problem during the implementation project and resolve it before you import it. If your data is clean, then you are in a better position to import more data.

The generally accepted standard is to import open transactions and to leave all of the historical transactions behind. To keep things current, you would bring over beginning balances for each account, and you would bring over the outstanding transactions associated with each account. If you don't do this and a customer makes a payment, you wouldn't be able to tie it back to a transaction. You can get away with that, but it will make your controller crazy because there isn't a way to tie out all of the transactions.

I recommend that you start with the plan of bringing over open transactions, and you can decide from there if you want to bring in more history. Make sure that you factor in the cost of that plus the potential performance or data costs that stem from having all of that data in your system. Having a cloud-based ERP or CRM solution is great, but since you are not in control of the hard drives, Microsoft imposes soft limits on the storage that you are allowed, and any storage you need over that amount will cost an extra amount each month. Be sure to factor any potential additional storage costs into your decision to bring over more history.

---

## Data Migration Tool

Once you have a general idea of the data that should be migrated, you should investigate and determine the right tool to use for the migration. The tool you choose will end up affecting how you extract, transform, and load your data. Several tools are available that have prebuilt features to help you extract, transfer, and load data into Dynamics 365, so if your source is something like QuickBooks or Salesforce, you may be able to acquire a tool that gives you a big head start.

If you can take advantage of one of these tools, you should do that. Some of them are not very customizable, so if you need to add a few new fields to the transformation, they may not work for you. Test them out to see how flexible they are before you sign on the dotted line.

If you can't take advantage of a prebuilt tool, you will need to put together a solution using a database, a data warehouse, or Excel. Excel is the most widely used data migration tool, so don't be concerned if you have to go this route—you will have a good amount of work on your hands, but you should be expecting that anyway.

## Iterations

Let's first explain what I mean by a data migration iteration. A *data migration iteration* is an attempt to extract the data from the source system, transform it into the format needed for Dynamics 365, and then to load it into Dynamics 365 and validate the data. An *iteration* is the process of following those steps successfully, so that you end up with data in Dynamics 365. The quality of the data that results in your system will improve with each iteration.

You should plan to run through four or more iterations of data migrations during your implementation project. Identify your preferred number of iterations and their purpose, and then schedule when you want this activity to occur. Each iteration, before your go-live migration, should serve as an opportunity to refine the process and make it better.

Figure 16.2 shows the main activity that occurs in the data migration workstream. You start by working on building the right mapping between your current data and the format used inside Dynamics 365. Once you complete that, you get to the point where you can test the process by running through iterations.

The first iteration (*Iteration 0*) is considered the technical preview. In this iteration, you don't really care how good the data is that you are moving to Dynamics 365; you mostly care that you can get it there. The goal is to validate that the technical connections work—you can extract the data, transform it, and load it (remember the acronym ETL). You will have some parts of that process fail as you go through it, but if you can get some amount of data into Dynamics 365 in Iteration 0, you have succeeded. When Iteration 0 is complete, you don't run out and tell the project team that there's data in the system to use—you just share that you have successfully connected the systems to the point where data can come over, and you are getting ready for a more successful run with Iteration 1.

The second iteration (*Iteration 1*) is the first public data migration activity. The previous iteration was called Iteration 0 because it's not necessarily for public consumption—it's a proof exercise for the technical team to show that they can move the data. This iteration is your first attempt at pulling data over that you may consider using in the new system. Each time you go through one of these iterations, you should be writing down what you've learned so that you can make changes and improve each iteration. One thing that you learn when you do data migration is persistence. Oftentimes, one little mistake will cause the whole migration to fail, so you learn pretty quickly that you need to make that change and document it, so that you don't make that mistake again.

In Iteration 1, you take the data and move it through the *ETL process* to the Dynamics 365 system. The data is not going to be perfect, but it should be good enough that most of the data elements move over and have representative data. You want it to be in a state where the project team can understand and use the data with the caveat that it won't all be there, and it won't be perfect. You should look to bring in subject matter experts who really know the data after each iteration, but specifically after Iteration 1. If you can catch an error right away, you won't have to see it over and over again with each subsequent iteration.

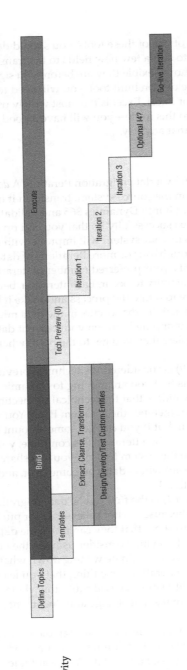

**FIGURE 16.2**
Data migration
workstream activity

Iteration 1 is typically associated with your JPD3 timing. Because it's being done before design is complete, there may be some entities that are not part of the migration, and there may be some mapping that will change once further adjustments to the design are made. The good news is that it should show the users how the system will work with a sampling of their data and not the very incomplete dataset you've used in JPD1 and JPD2.

*Iteration 2* takes the learning you have from Iteration 1 and the design changes stemming from JPD3 and puts you in a good position to put representative data into the new system. At this point, you should have what you need to make a good effort on the migration so that you can show this data off during your CRP session. As I mentioned in Chapter 13, "Conference Room Pilots," it's important that CRP presents the system as if it is nearly ready for production so the users don't lose faith in the capability of the system.

*Iteration 3* of data migration can be the last test migration before you are ready to go live. Iteration 3 is tied to UAT, so it should be done when the code is complete so that your data mapping can be completed as well. You may find bugs in Iteration 3, but they should be minimal and something that you can fix fairly quickly. If you have an expectation for UAT, have a similar expectation for the quality of Iteration 3 of the data migration. You will use the UAT process to validate the data, so this will be your first big test of the data validation activities that you will need to do when you go live.

You may choose to do another iteration after Iteration 3 if you see the need. This would give you a chance to fix any issues in Iteration 3 before you conduct the go-live migration. If you experienced minimal issues in Iteration 3, you probably don't need to do this. If you experienced several, or if you just have the time, you should consider running an Iteration 4.

Your *go-live iteration* will be the final one, and it will occur the weekend of go-live, or the cutover. This is the ultimate goal of the data migration workstream, so remember to build on everything you do so that final data migration can be flawless—it needs to be, or you will experience issues after you go live.

Figure 16.3 gives you a sense of how the iterations map to the key milestones within the functional side of the project.

**FIGURE 16.3**
Data migration
iterations

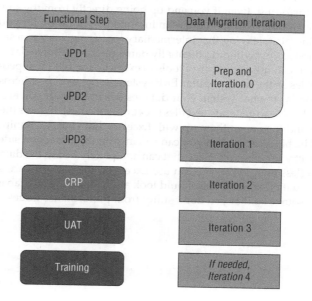

## Data Migration Iterations

| Functional Step | Data Migration Iteration |
|---|---|
| JPD1 | Prep and Iteration 0 |
| JPD2 | |
| JPD3 | Iteration 1 |
| CRP | Iteration 2 |
| UAT | Iteration 3 |
| Training | *If needed, Iteration 4* |

# Extract

Extracting is the first part of the E (Extract), T (Transform), and L (Load) process. *Extract* means to take the data out of your source system or systems. The extract process shouldn't be particularly challenging—the transform process is the hardest of the three, but you need to make sure that you know where the data is coming from so you can put it in a place where you can transform it.

## Finding the Data

I mentioned it in the "Proactive Cleaning" section, but the trickiest part of the extraction process is to find the data you need to extract. To do this, you will need to catalog all of the sources of data that you might need in the new system. If you are moving from one ERP to a Dynamics 365 ERP or moving from a CRM to Dynamics 365 Customer Engagement, you may think this is very straightforward and easy. It might be, but you need to understand all of the data that should be moved.

You want to take a look at the process catalog and see all of the items that were marked in scope. As you view that list of in-scope items, you should have a good idea what data needs to be in the system to support those processes. If all of the data is in your current ERP or CRM system, that's great. That is rare, however; oftentimes, you will have data in multiple, different systems that you need to extract to put into your new system.

Once you know all of the processes in scope, you can start mapping the data sources to the entities in Dynamics 365 that will host the data. This data migration map is critical to this exercise. You can use an Excel spreadsheet to track this for simplicity's sake, but you should have a four-column spreadsheet that includes the data table/entity in Dynamics 365—its friendly name and its technical name—and then a column for the source system and the technical name of the data inside that source system. If more sources than the primary one exist, add another line to the spreadsheet to indicate that it will require two steps to get the data moved over.

## Extraction Tools

Most of the time when you extract data, you will need to find a place to park it as you get ready to transform it. Even if you end up going directly from the source to the target without a system in the middle, you should use an intermediary location for your data as you build your transformation plan. Having that intermediary location gives you a sandbox where you can test transformation scripts without potentially damaging live, source data.

You can use a number of tools to extract data, but most people end up using the tool that also doubles as the most popular ERP system in the world—Microsoft Excel. The tool for this job depends on what system your data resides in today. If you are using an older system, you may only be able to generate text files (.txt or .csv files). If that's the case, your best bet is to extract .csv files and then open them up with Excel so that you can manipulate them from there.

The biggest problem you can run into on the extraction side is making sure that you can extract your data to a place that can adequately house the data. If you have a small amount of data (less than 1 GB), you can use Excel and the performance should be acceptable. If you have more data than that, you should look at provisioning a database to serve as your intermediary data source so that you don't suffer from performance issues.

The reason I recommend Excel is that it's easy to manipulate the data if you have it in Excel. You can filter data, you can sort to find duplicates, and you can run "Find and Replace" if you need to change certain data in the system. It gives you a lot of flexibility to transform the data, and every system is going to allow you to load the data from Excel. All of the Microsoft Dynamics 365 tools have deep integration with Excel, so you can use it to load data in those systems easily.

One final suggestion here is to take advantage of data residing in a data warehouse if you can. A data warehouse has typically already aggregated and normalized the data, and it often contains data from multiple, different sources. You can do a lot of pre-work for your data migration in your data warehouse if you have one.

---

### WHAT DOES IT MEAN TO "NORMALIZE" DATA?

In software, you will sometimes hear the words "normalize" or "de-normalize" when it refers to data. When you normalize data, you attempt to reduce data redundancy and improve data integrity. You are generally looking to create a more efficient design of the database that allows for more flexibility in the data. A common example is to use numbers as a way to point to text data, rather than storing the text data in the database tables. This can improve data flexibility and performance. Here is an example to explain this.

Let's say that you have an option set in CRM that tracks the status of an order. The options could be Open, Backordered, and Invoiced. You could store those three words in your database in the order table. That is how a denormalized system would do it. The problem comes when you want to change the text on one of those status labels.

Let's say that now you want to change Backordered to Awaiting Inventory. If you change your system to allow the entry of Awaiting Inventory, you now have two different representations of the same data in your system. If you search for all of the orders awaiting inventory, you will not find the ones that were previously labeled as Backordered, even though the statuses are the same.

A normalized system would use an integer value in the order table to represent the status. Open = 1, Backordered = 2, and Invoiced = 3. You would have a separate table to store the label associated with each of those integer values. This gives you two advantages:

◆ It makes your system faster because it's faster to retrieve integer values than text values.

◆ It gives you the ability to change labels without fundamentally changing your data.

The downside comes on the reporting side. If you try to query your database to pull up all of your orders, you will see that several orders have a status of 2. You will not necessarily know that those orders are on backorder because the integer won't be translated to a text value. You will have to join another table with your query to get the text value. This process is referred to as "de-normalizing" the data, and it's a common practice in reporting. Data warehouses have already de-normalized the data from multiple sources, so it makes them easier to use as extraction points for data migration. If you try to extract normalized data from your previous system, your value of 2 might mean something else in your previous system.

# Transform

This is by far the hardest part of the data migration journey. In this step, you need to map the data from the source system to the destination system. Many fields will be consistent between the two systems, so they won't require transformation work, but many fields will not be consistent, and that's where the real work comes in. You'll also need to spend considerable time with data coming from two different sources. Hopefully for your sake, you don't have too much of that.

## Mapping the Data

*Mapping the data* is the process of taking a field in your source system and mapping it to the destination system. Let's use a complicated example. You probably want to bring over your historical part numbers to the new system. You probably don't want to use your historical part numbers as the official part numbers in the new system; you are better off allowing the system to generate new numbers. However, you want to track those numbers, so you map the Item ID (or whatever it's called in the old system) to a table in Dynamics that stores historical ID numbers. You would need to find where to map it to in the new system and then decide if you need to transform that particular value. In this case, you wouldn't have to transform that value, so it's just a matter of populating the new field with the historical field.

It can be easy to map the data if the source and destination tables have the same fields in them, but you will not be that lucky. During the migration process, you will have to put values in all sorts of different places, so get ready to do some detective work so that you can make sure everything is mapped correctly.

## Mapping Tools

I typically see four ways that customers will map the data between their source and destination systems: Excel, a specific mapping tool, a general data migration tool, or using code:

- **Excel.** This is the most common solution, but the one most prone to error. This is the cheap way to migrate data because you just dump your data out to Excel, build a mapping tool in another Excel spreadsheet or OneNote that tells you which data goes where, and then build a new workbook that puts the data in the right place to be loaded into the new system. You would then use Excel formulas to do any transformations. This is what most people do, and it can work; it is very manual, and it is subject to mistakes. You will find that you will forget to map a field, or you'll map a field incorrectly and it may be hard to find your mistake. If you use this method, be prepared to do many different iterations.

- **A specific mapping tool.** If you use a specific data migration tool, like the QuickBooks to Microsoft Dynamics 365 Business Central tool, it will provide the default mapping for you. That makes it a lot easier to find the fields that need to be mapped and to see where they are going. This is good way to transform the data, except for one, very often overlooked wrinkle. The problem with this solution occurs when you have data that you need to map to a new field that doesn't exist in the mapping tool. If you have customized your system and added a new field to Dynamics, this mapping tool doesn't know about it, so it doesn't tell you how to map it from your source system. Many of these mapping tools don't have a mechanism for adding a field to the destination system to map to it. If the tool does, then you're in good shape.

The key is that you want to find out this information before you get too far into it. I've seen many times where customers select a tool thinking that it will do all of the mapping for them, and then they end up with a mess because they can't migrate into a custom field.

◆ **General data migration tool**. If you use a generic mapping tool, like Scribe or Kingswaysoft, you have a system that gives you a nice framework for mapping the data between the systems. These tools will tell you what the destination field should be, and as you load your custom data into the source side of the system, you'll be able to determine how you want to map the data between the two. It will give you tools to do that transformation as well. These tools are designed to be flexible, so they will allow you to add custom fields to the destination side. These are good solutions, especially if you can use one of their prebuilt maps.

◆ **Code to map your data**. If you use code to map your data, this is a very well-organized way of conducting the migration. The challenge with this is that it requires a developer, and it will take them significant time to build up all of the mapping between the systems. If you have access to such a person, you should consider this option. As you will see in the next section, you often have to transform or manipulate the data in a field, and a developer can write code to do that, so you don't have to rely on Excel formula manipulation to get there. When taking this approach, make sure that you add lots of meaningful comments to the code so that it is easy to see the source system definition, the destination, and the logic you used to map the data between them.

## Transforming Mapped Data

This is the trickiest of the tricky parts of the implementation. The source and destination fields match, but the values in the tables don't match. A common example here is order statuses for sales orders. Let's say that the order statuses in the source system are New, In Progress, Invoiced, and Canceled. In Dynamics 365's CRM system, sales orders have five default states: Active, Submitted, Canceled, Fulfilled, and Invoiced. Since the two status options are different, you now have to map your existing data to the new statuses (or you can change the status options in the new system, but I don't recommend you do that with something as important as sales order statuses). You first have to make the business decision about how you want to map it before you do the data migration work to map it to the new system.

Another challenging part of the transformation happens with different data types. You may struggle to get fields with date values out of the current system and into the new system. Dynamics 365 uses the Universal Time Code (UTC) to store its data, so if you want to import the accurate time, you may have to convert it from your time zone to UTC. You may store decimals at a precision of 4 in the old system, and you need to convert it to 2 in the new system—now you have to come up with a rounding or truncation plan that could leave your data off by a number of pennies.

You will find yourself facing these scenarios several times as you go through the data migration process, so it's important to get deep into the system so you'll discover these issues early in the design process. The sooner you can discover them, the faster you'll have the full picture of what needs to be done on the project.

# Load

The next step in the ETL process is to load the data into Microsoft Dynamics (the destination system). If you have done all of the hard work in extracting and transforming the data so that it meets the definition of the destination system, loading the data into the system is pretty straight-forward. If you used a prebuilt migration tool, it will come with a solution for loading the data, so, in that case, you just click a button to load it. If you are loading the data using the Excel method, you have a few issues to watch for.

## Order of Operation

The biggest challenge with loading data by hand is defining the order by which you load it. I have personally made this mistake many times where I try to load data that depends on other data existing, only to realize that I hadn't loaded the dependent data first. If you are loading Contacts into CRM, you need to load Accounts first so that the contact can be associated with an account. When building your load order, you should start with default data (the data that doesn't change); always load default data first, then master data, and then load transactional data after it. You may have to set aside the order in which you load the master data as well so that it serves as a building block.

Make sure you have a plan built out that shows the order in which the data is loaded. That's a key step to save you from having all sorts of data inconsistencies.

## Load Time

The other variable to consider in the load process is how long it's going to take. During the early iterations, you should start tracking the amount of processing time for loading the data into the new system. In the Microsoft Dynamics 365 solutions, loaded data typically has to run through some business validation in the system, and that can take some time. The project manager needs to know how long this process will run so that they can adequately plan on when the activities should occur and how long the final cutover will take.

# Validating the Data

Once the data has been imported, you now must go through the painstaking process of validating it. The reason why you do so many iterations is so that you can find issues in the early runs and make changes to the system to make sure that your data will be right when it comes time to go live. Validating the data after each iteration is an important step in the overall success of this workstream. You want to write out a formal test plan for the validation process so that your users don't fall victim to confirmation bias, seeing what they expect to see.

Table 16.2 outlines the three levels of validation which you should go through as you assess the cleanliness of your data:

◆ *Technical validation* to make sure that the data successfully came over.

◆ *Business validation* to make sure that the data mapped correctly.

◆ *Functional validation* to make sure that the data is usable in the new system.

Let's dive deeper into each of these validations.

**TABLE 16.2:**    Three Levels of Validation

| TECHNICAL VALIDATIONS | BUSINESS VALIDATIONS | FUNCTIONAL VALIDATIONS |
| --- | --- | --- |
| Typically performed by those building the transformations | Performed by the core team | Performed by the core team |
| Data visible, record counts proper, data adheres to standards | Source and target data should match. Example: Does open AR in D365 line up with open AR in source system? | Can you perform functions in the target system with imported data? Example: Does a cash discount process properly on an imported payable? |

# Technical Validation

The technical validation is performed by those people building the transformations—the data migration team. You would perform this validation step before sharing with the rest of the team that the migration process is done. You would want to define a series of checks that you want to use to validate the data before you do this validation.

Examples of technical validation would be as follows:

◆ Master data visible in the destination system—customers, products, and so forth.

◆ Beginning balances loaded in the destination system.

◆ Open transactions loaded in the destination system.

◆ The record count between the source and destination system is the same for master records and transactional data.

You don't have to test to make sure that the system works, but you need to validate that the data appears correctly in the new system and that the right number of records came over.

## Business Validation

There is a fine line between business and functional validation, but it's a line worth delineating. Most subject matter experts who haven't been heavily trained on the system can likely conduct a business validation, whereas the functional validation is best performed by core team members who really know how the destination system should function.

To conduct the business validation, you pull up the source and the destination system and compare the two. Go find a customer in the source system, look at the information about that customer and their open transactions, and then compare that information to what is in the destination system. You will do a series of spot checks to make sure that the data is consistently accurate.

In this step, you will also run reports to make sure that the data is the same between the two systems. Run the AR aging report to make sure that's correct. Run a customer summary report, a sales report, and so forth. Before you begin this process, make sure that you have documented several reports that you want to use as validation.

### Functional Validation

The functional validation is run by the core team—it is the process of running through transactions in the system to validate if the imported data works as designed in the system. This is particularly important in areas like sales and purchase orders or more advanced functionality.

From a schedule standpoint, you can use your JPD, CRP, or UAT session as a functional validation step for your migrated data. If you build the schedule to have your data migration iterations precede these key events, you have a built-in opportunity to do functional validation without having to schedule another task to accomplish it. If you take this approach, you just have to educate the team that the issue that occurred in one of those sessions could be stemming from a bug, or it could be coming from bad data. You just need to make sure to investigate both options. You don't want to create a code fix for a bug only to find out it was bad data that caused the issue.

## Go-Live Iteration

Once you've worked through your four or five test iterations, you are ready for the real thing. Before the go-live iteration, it's always a good idea to run another mock cutover as a final test that the process is working and as a way of determining how long it will take to run the real data migration. Depending on how much data you are bringing over, your data migration activity may take four hours, or it may take four days. The project manager needs to know how long the data migration will take to be able to build the cutover plan. It may even impact the entire business if the data migration takes four days. I've seen many cases where a business will shut down operations earlier than 5 p.m. on Friday so that they could start the migration process early and give themselves time. When building your go-live schedule, make sure to leave enough time for the technical, business, and functional validation to assure that everything comes over correctly. Also, build in extra time just in case you have to run it all over again.

My typical suggested schedule is to start the cutover Friday at 5 p.m. by going through your initial preparation steps and then kicking off the data migration as quickly as possible. You can then allow the data migration process to run overnight so that you can maximize processing time while people are sleeping. You then set up your validation steps to occur on Saturday, and you give yourself time to run it all over again if there was a big problem.

After you go live, your data migration team isn't completely done—you shouldn't have a lot of activity left to do, but you should stay close to the project for the first week or two to make sure that data issues aren't cropping up after go-live. You may also be needed during the first month's end—it's really hard to simulate a month end, and there may be underlying data problems that rear their heads during that time. As a general rule, the data migration is complete once you go live but, as I mentioned in the introduction to this chapter, data problems in the system can be really difficult to troubleshoot, so it's good to have this team available to help with those if they arrive.

If you follow the steps outlined in this chapter, you can move through this process with a game plan and set yourself up for success with clean data in the new system. You probably have never had clean data in the system before, so this could lead to much greater levels of productivity when the data is right.

# The Bottom Line

**Core Concepts**    The acronym ETL actually describes the important steps in the data migration process, so it's a key term to know.

**Master It**    What does the abbreviation ETL stand for?

1. Extract, transition, logistics

2. Enter transactional, lines

3. Extract, transform, load

4. Export, troubleshoot, load

**Data Cleaning**    "Garbage In, Garbage Out" is a phrase that you will hear a lot on projects. You want to put a good amount of effort into making sure that there's no garbage when you are migrating data.

**Master It**    When should you start data cleaning on a project?

1. As soon as possible

2. After JPD1

3. Before CRP

4. Before UAT

**What Should You Migrate?**    One of the most difficult decisions to make in the data migration process is how much data to migrate. The more data you migrate, the more history you have in the new system, but that effort takes time and money.

**Master It**    In which of the following cases would it be a good idea to migrate all transactional history?

1. You have 4 TB of data

2. Your previous system will soon no longer be accessible to you

3. You can query your previous data

4. You have significant data issues with your previous transactional data

**Understanding Transformation**    After you extract the data, the most challenging part of data migration is to transform the data so that it's ready to be loaded into Microsoft Dynamics 365.

**Master It**    What happens in the transform step of data migration?

1. You clean your data

2. You load the data into the new system

3. You run Iteration 3 of the data migration effort

4. You map your source data to your target system

**Iteration Timing**    During the project, you want to do several runs or iterations of data migration so that you can keep refining your process and making it better. You want to associate these iterations with major events on the functional side of the project.

**Master It**    Which data migration iteration typically lines up with UAT?

1. Iteration 0

2. Iteration 1

3. Iteration 2

4. Iteration 3

# Chapter 17

# Environment Management and Deployments

This chapter should be really short—we're in the cloud with Microsoft Dynamics 365, so there shouldn't be any technical activity on this project, right? It is significantly easier to manage environments in the cloud than it was in an on-premise world, but the effort level didn't go down to zero. As with everything we've covered in the book, if you have a plan and execute against it, you will be able to have a great foundation for your implementation.

We will start by defining the different environments that you may need, and then we'll talk about how you can manage those environments and move code between them. We'll finish up by talking about security, which isn't necessarily associated with environments, but it typically falls on the technical consultant, so we'll cover it here.

The technical side of an implementation can and should go very smoothly, but it can cause the implementation many headaches if you don't do it right. Let's make sure that it goes as smoothly as possible.

## AFTER YOU COMPLETE THIS CHAPTER, YOU WILL BE ABLE TO DO THE FOLLOWING:

- Build your environment plan
- Distinguish between the types of releases
- Use DevOps to deploy your code to the various environments
- Develop your security strategy

---

### THREE KEYS TO SUCCESS IN MANAGING ENVIRONMENTS

1. Make sure that you have a well-documented plan.
2. Train your team to make sure that they understand this content.
3. Don't skimp on environments.

---

# Types of Environments

You will need at least two environments to manage your Dynamics implementation; how many more you need depends on how many developers you have and how many different connections you need to make. I have seen Microsoft Dynamics 365 Finance and Supply Chain Management implementations with 20+ environments, which seems like a lot. It is possible that many environments are needed if you have a lot of developers and integrations.

Figure 17.1 is a map of the typical environments and how data would flow between them. You do not necessarily need all of these environments, but this shows you how many environments can be required and how they would be arranged.

**FIGURE 17.1**
Environments and necessary steps

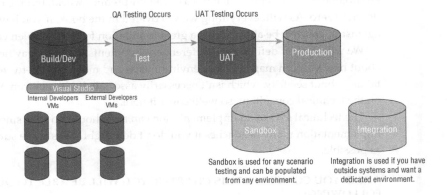

Let's dive into an explanation of each of the environments, so you can understand which ones you might need on your project.

## Developer Environments

The different Dynamics products will have different needs for *Developer environments*, but as a general rule, each developer should have their own environment for developing customizations. This can get to be a lot of environments if you have many developers on the project. Microsoft can provide you with additional environments so that you can work with your implementation partner to provision these environments as you need them. The good thing about cloud environments is that you can decommission them whenever you are done with them.

You can also provision a virtual machine (VM) in the cloud or on-premise on a server that you manage for Finance and Supply Chain Management developers. (This doesn't work for Business Central or Customer Engagement, as the code is different for on-premise versus the cloud.) With these environments, you can run scripts in Azure to turn the VM on and off every day. For example, you can run a script to turn on the environment at 7 a.m. and turn it off at 7 p.m. every day. This saves a lot of money over time because you are not consuming as many computing cycles.

One of the challenges with managing multiple developer environments is making sure that you have the latest code and configurations on each developer's environment. You don't always have to worry about configurations in a developer environment because they may not be coding in an area that is using certain configurations. This is when it's good for the functional consultant and developer to work together to make sure that the necessary configurations are in place.

If you're using DevOps, you can grab the latest build from the centralized location so that you can make your changes with the latest code in place. Once you make changes, you would check them into DevOps so that those changes can moved to the other environments.

## Build

The *Build environment* is the place where all development activity converges. Developers submit code to a check-in gate. Builds are executed by that check-in gate on the Build environment. You have many options here, depending on the level of professionalism that you want in your development. Most of the time, you are trying to get the code as fast as you can. In those cases, you would use this environment to aggregate the development and check it into the official build that gets migrated to the other environments.

If you are looking to put quality measures in place before code is included in the build, this is where you would run unit tests. We discussed these in Chapter 15, "Customizations vs. Configurations and How You Manage Them," but if you are having your developers write unit tests, the build environment would run those unit tests against the code before allowing the new code to be included in the official build. If the code does not pass the unit test, the check-in is rejected, and a notification is sent back to the developer.

You can also run what's called *code coverage* in the Build environment. Code coverage is a means of validating what percentage of your code has a unit test running against it. If you wrote 100 lines of code and the unit test tested 90 lines, you would have 90 percent code coverage for your unit tests.

The Build environment can become a bottleneck if you have a lot of development going on and you're running a lot of tests before allowing code to check into the build. Normally, you would not be too concerned about the specifications on a build environment, but if you have several developers and you are running many unit tests, you may end up with your developers waiting on the build server queue for hours. If that's the case, you can consider increasing the specifications on that VM to make sure that it can move through all of these operations more quickly.

## Test

The *Test environment* is the most active environment in the early and middle stages of the implementation project. The Test environment is where the functional consultants and core team members are testing all different types of activities in the system. Here are the common elements that are tested in the test system:

◆   Core functionality as shown in JPDs

◆   Configurations

◆   Customizations that have been built in the development environments

◆   Data that has been migrated

◆ Integrations to other systems

◆ CRPs run from this environment

The Test environment is where everything comes together for the first time. The Build environment will have the latest code, but it will not necessarily have the configurations that you need, and it won't have migrated data. This is where the functional consultants and core team members do the bulk of their testing in the effort to get the solution ready for the UAT environment.

## Sandbox

*Sandbox environments* are optional, so you can have anywhere from zero to five or more. They can have different purposes, and I call them Sandbox environments because they aren't necessarily part of the standard flow of build to test to UAT to production—they are outliers that are used for a specific purpose. Here are some examples of Sandbox environments:

**Production copy**   This is actually an important environment to have if you are already live, but you have another project coming up through the build-test-UAT pipeline. If you are live and have a problem, you need an environment available to create a fix when necessary. If you don't have this environment, you would have to use your UAT environment. If you are developing the next version of code in that environment, however, you don't want to release it before it's ready. This is a very valid reason for a sandbox environment, so I strongly suggest you invest in one in this case.

**Validation of core functionality**   If you have a lot of customizations in your environment, you may want to have a Sandbox environment available that has no customizations on it. This way you can troubleshoot issues there to determine if they are core Microsoft issues or if they are issues with your customizations.

**Consultant playgrounds**   You may want to have an environment where your consultants or core team members can "play around" with other solutions. In that case, they can change settings without disrupting other people. This comes in handy during the middle part of implementations when you have users in the Test environment running CRPs, and you don't want to disrupt that; yet, you still have something you want to test.

**Data migration**   You may want another environment for repetitive testing of data migration loads. This way you can run many iterations without disrupting CRPs or other testing in the official test environment.

**Integration**   You may want to have one or more integration sandbox environments depending on how many integrations you have. This again gives you the chance to integrate data into a segmented environment so that you don't disrupt CRP or other testing in the official test environment. Once you have validated that the integration works as desired, you would point the integration to the test environment so that you can try it out there.

**UAT**   The *UAT environment* stands for *User Acceptance Testing environment*, but it is almost universally never called anything but UAT. It is called the UAT environment because it is used for the UAT process during an implementation. The lifecycle of the UAT environment consists of three parts, and this should give you an idea of how it's used:

**1. Pre-UAT phase**   You would typically stand up the UAT and Production environments sometime early in the Create stage so that you have them ready for future use. Once set up, you would use the UAT environment as a "Gold" environment, as I discussed in Chapter 15 when talking about how to manage configurations. You put your configurations there once you have collectively agreed on the setting you want to use in production. Before you go into UAT, you would lightly use this environment, mostly as a proof point for data that you believe to be clean or configurations that you want to validate in another, clean environment. You will make backups and restore clean versions of this environment frequently if you use it like this.

**2. Deployment phase**   This is what the UAT environment was built for—to be used as the final test environment before you are ready to go live with this code. The UAT environment is used for running the UAT process, so you would take your customizations, configurations, and integrations, deploy them here, and run your data migration to populate the data in advance of UAT. You would then conduct testing here, inviting in a larger group of users than had previously used the test environment. Once UAT is complete, you would use this environment for end user training as well. You would also conduct performance testing in the environment while running through UAT and end user training, as this environment should be designed with the same specifications as the production environment.

**3. Post go-live**   After the deployment phase, this is your production copy to test any fixes that need to go into production. If you have an error in production, you would troubleshoot it in your test environment, and when a fix looks good there, you would deploy it to the UAT environment for a final test before you move it to production. You test it in the UAT environment because you want to see how it works when you simulate the activity that you would take in production.

If you have a very small implementation, you can consider foregoing the UAT environment, but if you do that, you won't have an environment where you can simulate deploying code before you get to production.

**NOTE**   The biggest value of a UAT environment is the chance to test the population of customizations, configurations, integrations, and data in the same way that you would populate the production environment.

## Production

Everyone needs a *Production environment*. This is what your users use when the system is live. I suppose this is the only environment that you must have, but you don't want to live in a world where you only have a Production environment. Figure 17.2 is a common joke for people in IT working on a Production environment.

The lifecycle of the Production environment starts early in the Create stage when you first build a clean environment. You may use it as your "Gold" environment to keep your configurations, but I suggest you use UAT for that and leave production alone until you are ready to go live. The first time that you should use your Production environment is when you do the mock cutover a week or two before you go live. This is where you test everything that you would want to do in a real production move, even though you clear out the environment afterwards. Then next time you would use it would be at the go-live.

**FIGURE 17.2**
Production envi-
ronment joke

I Don't Always
Test My Code
But When I Do
**I DO IT IN PRODUCTION**

The Production environment should be sized appropriately to make sure that the system will perform to expectations once all the users get on the system. You would try to use the same specifications between the UAT and Production environments and do performance testing in the UAT environment.

## Environment Plan

Now that you understand the types of environments and how they are used, you want to put together your *environment plan*, which is a document that will guide you throughout the implementation. This is something that you should put together prior to the kickoff after explaining the different environment types and understanding your risk tolerance. The more environments, the lower the risk of a technical issue; however, more environments cost more money. Your IT leader should make the decision factoring in all of the options early on so that you can plan appropriately.

In your environment plan, you would have a diagram, such as the one outlined in Figure 17.3, which identifies each of the environments and what type of subscription you are using to set up this environment. Figure 17.3 does not specifically call out a Production copy environment, as it assumes that you are in the process of your first deployment. If you have the system live, you should invest in a Production copy environment as well.

### Types of Releases

Another thing to consider as part of the environment plan is your *usage plan* for each of these environments. You want to set out which environments are used for which activities on the project. Even though I laid out the recommended course in the preceding text, it is uncommon to see it used like that.

**FIGURE 17.3**
Environments and types
of subscriptions
*Source:* Craig Conzemius

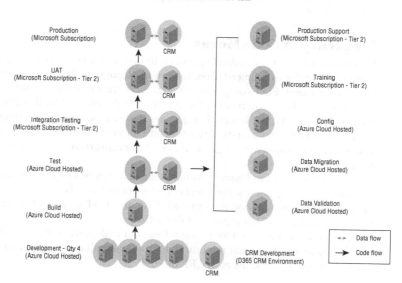

As part of this release plan and cadence, you want to understand what the different release types are and how frequently you do them. Table 17.1 will come up again after go-live, but it's important to think this through in the early stages of the implementation so that you can determine how frequently you want to do each type of release.

**TABLE 17.1:**    Implementation Releases

| RELEASE TYPES | RELEASE FREQUENCY |
|---|---|
| **Lower Environment** | **Definition**: Moving code to the Test or UAT environments or a Production move before you're ready to go live.<br>**Considerations**: Make sure configurations can move easily between environments. |
| **Go-Live** | **Definition**: Full deployment to the Production environment when all of the code is ready and tested for end users.<br>**New Environment**: Code can be moved ahead of time, but data migration needs to be done at one point.<br>**Existing Environment**: Code can be moved ahead of time if tested—be careful on backups and restores. |
| **Hotfix** | **Definition**: Post go-live patch that solves a small number of issues.<br>**Considerations**: Not typically thoroughly tested; should be used to resolve Priority 1 issues only; introduces risk and requires unplanned downtime. |
| **Enhancement** | **Definition**: Post go-live production release including new features and bug fixes.<br>**Considerations**: This should be planned for regular intervals post-release—everything should be well tested. |

Once you understand the different types of code moves, you can set a path for how frequently you run them.

## Frequency of Code Moves

It's important to set a standard approach to how often you move code to your various environments during the implementation. Like many things on the project, you have to discuss the trade-off between the two options. On one side, the more frequently you deploy code to test or UAT, the more fixes you have in the system. On the other side, the less frequently you deploy code to test or UAT, the fewer changes you have in the system. If someone tested the environment on Tuesday and you deploy new code on Wednesday, you don't know for sure that what you tested on Tuesday still works. This is the conundrum—the more releases you do disrupts testing.

The best suggestion I have is to use your sprint cycles as your default code-move cadence. After every sprint, deploy the latest code to test or UAT. This gives the project team a predictable calendar, and you can then line up your CRP and UAT sessions to occur when sufficient testing has happened on the latest build of the software.

You certainly may need to do more frequent code moves than that if you have an event for which you must plan—just remember to give yourself a few days in advance to test that build before you spring it on users in CRP or UAT.

## Populating Configurations and Master Data

As you build your project test release schedule, you should also determine your plan for populating all of the contents of the release. The build process will give you your code, reports, integration code, and security (if you have built it into code or configuration). However, it does not give you your configurations, master and reference data, or your transactional data. Also, if you have an integration with another system where code needs to be changed, you will have to coordinate activity in that system as well. Figure 17.4 provides a reference to what does or doesn't move between environments with the code package.

| FIGURE 17.4 Environments in code packages | **What Does and Does Not Move Between Environments in Code Packages** | |
|---|---|---|
| | DOES | DOES NOT |
| | ▐▌▌ Custom Code | ⚙ Configurations |
| | 🗎 Custom Reports | 🔍 Master Data |
| | ▦ Integration Code native to D365 | ▦ Transactional Data |
| | ⚷ Security | ▥ Integration Code on Other Platform |

To do this, identify where you are storing your configurations: either in the "Gold" environment or re-entering it each time. Next, determine how you are populating data—in the early part of the release, you may have a temporary solution where you enter enough master data to do basic testing that you want to import. As you get further along, you certainly would use your official data migration process to populate your master and transactional data.

You should have a written plan for all of this so that the project team knows how this will work throughout the implementation project. It really keeps you from having to repeat your plan and process throughout the project.

# Deploying Code

The process of deploying code is a little different among each of the three Microsoft Dynamics 365 products. Since this isn't meant to be a technically focused book (and because the technology changes quite frequently), I will concentrate on the general process of moving code between environments rather than the specific steps for each product.

The first place to start is to visit Microsoft's website for the latest documentation on Dynamics 365 at docs.microsoft.com/dynamics365. If you want a deeper look into each specific product, I would recommend the following books:

◆ For Business Central, I recommend *Mastering Microsoft Dynamics 365 Business Central* by Stefano Demiliani and Duilio Tacconi (Packt Publishing, 2019), which explains how to use extensions and DevOps tools specifically related to Business Central.

◆ For Customer Engagement, I recommend *Mastering Microsoft Dynamics 365 Customer Engagement* by Deepesh Somani (Packt Publishing, 2019), which is also more focused on developing and customizing solutions in that product.

◆ For Finance and Supply Chain Management, I recommend *Implementing Microsoft Dynamics 365 for Finance and Operations Apps: Learn best practices, architecture, tools, techniques and more* by JJ Yadav, Sandeep Shukla, et al. (Packt Publishing, 2020).

Generally, once the code is packaged into extensions, packages, or solutions, you would import that code package into the environment you want to use. This could be the Test, UAT, or a Sandbox environments if you are moving code in a pre-production environment. For production releases, you will generally deploy the new code to UAT first, then test it, and then deploy to production after that.

## Application Lifecycle Management

You will hear the term *application lifecycle management (ALM)* used to describe the management of applications including governance, development, and maintenance. You could consider everything in the implementation part of ALM, but it generally is more focused on the management of the code through the process.

Azure DevOps is an ALM software suite, so it provides you with the tools that you would need to manage the software development process all the way from requirements to customizations to deployments to bugs and hotfixes.

**NOTE**  The term DevOps is more universally used in software development that combines the software engineering efforts (Dev) with the software operations management (Ops). It is a term used more broadly than just in Microsoft-related development projects.

## Environment Flow Using DevOps

Figure 17.5 highlights the general flow for using DevOps in the various products. The process goes as follows: First, the developers check their code into DevOps; then, the build server runs its unit tests or automated tests to validate that the code is ready to be packaged. It is then deployed to the build server, where you create a deployable package, called a *changeset*. That changeset is then deployed to the new environment.

Deploying code in a labeled changeset allows you to trace an error that might have occurred in the environment. If it occurred only after a new set of code was deployed, you can look to see what code is part of that changeset so that you can narrow down where to search for the bug.

**FIGURE 17.5**

DevOps to environments

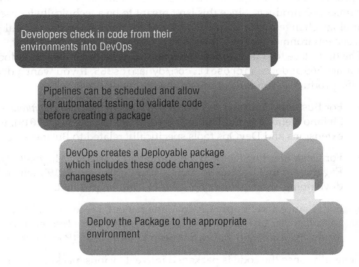

## Rollback

One word you hope never to use on a project is *rollback*. This is the process of rolling back a release to a previous version because there was a problem with the latest release package. It typically comes up once in a while on a project where you have to consider rolling back to a previous release. DevOps provides you with tools to roll back the code, so that's generally not the hard part.

If you have to roll back a build in the development process, that's not a big issue because you probably haven't created too much bad data, and if you did, you can rerun the data migration to clean up any issues.

The difficult part of a rollback comes when you have created a data problem in production with the problematic code. If you have made changes to the data since the new code went out, you have three options, and none of them are great:

**1.** You can tell the users that whatever they entered between now and the previous backup will have to be re-entered.

2. You can run queries to try to determine what data has changed and attempt to re-insert the data after you restore the backup. This is a lot of work and can cause more problems than it solves if it's not done correctly.

3. You can choose not to restore the backup, redeploy the previous code, and manually fix any data problems that might exist in production. Again, this can cause problems in the future if it's not done correctly.

You generally want to go through an exhaustive testing process so that you don't ever have to utter the word "rollback" during your implementation project.

# Security

Each Microsoft Dynamics 365 product approaches security a little bit differently, but there is common terminology that is important to know. If you'd like to dive deeper into the security for your products, I recommend the books listed earlier in the "Deploying Code" section.

Security in each of the applications can be very granular, and you can create an unlimited number of roles to manage the distinct access in the system. This presents both an opportunity and a challenge, as you have the opportunity to make this system very complicated. If you do, however, that will bring its fair share of challenges to the maintenance of the security structure.

## Definitions

Let's start at the most granular level of security and build ourselves up to the top. The most granular security level is called a *privilege*. A privilege is what controls whether you can access an object, and if you can, what you can do with that object or a record. You generally think of privileges as create, read, update, and delete, but Microsoft Dynamics can include other privileges as well, such as append, append to, assign, and share. To keep from getting too complicated here, let's just say that we have the privilege to create, read, and write a customer record, but we can't delete it.

Many privileges can be combined into roles. You can create as many roles as you want, and you can assign multiple roles to a user for each company or business unit. Since roles are additive in Microsoft Dynamics, if you give a user 10 privileges in one role and give them 20 more privileges in another role, they will end up with 30 privileges (assuming that the privileges don't overlap).

Beyond roles comes the concept of companies or business units. Within Microsoft Dynamics, you have the ability to run multiple different business entities on the same instance of the software. You may not want every user from each entity to see another's activity, so you can assign different roles in different companies or business units, and you can also restrict a user from logging in to a company or business unit by removing their access.

Microsoft Dynamics 365 Customer Engagement has a security concept of "teams," which allows you to group users together to manage permissions or have certain records owned by a team instead of an individual.

**AUTHENTICATION VS. AUTHORIZATION**

Modern security has two concepts that are important to how you log in to a system that are very similar but mean different things when it comes to security.

*Authentication* is the process of confirming your identity; that is, when I log in to a system, I have to tell the system "This is Eric Newell, trying to log on." Once the system confirms my identity, it then attempts to determine what I am authorized to do in that system.

*Authorization* is the act of granting permissions or privileges to take action in the system. When you first set up a user in Microsoft Dynamics 365 Customer Engagement, you will often see how a user can log in to the system, but as soon as they get in, they are presented with an error saying that they are not "authorized" to access the application. By default, users are not assigned a security role, so they may be licensed or authenticated to the application but not authorized to do anything inside the application.

Many more distinct security concepts in each application are addressed in more product-focused literature.

## How Best to Manage

My recommendation is to try to create many roles with a limited number of privileges and then try to assign multiple roles to the users who need them. If you try to create a custom role for every different user, you will end up with too many to manage. It is complicated to manage multiple roles for a user; it makes it more difficult to troubleshoot a missing permission if they either can access something that they shouldn't be able to access or can't access something they need to access.

You want to try to manage security roles and privileges in solutions or using code if you can. You want to do this so that you can move security roles among environments easily. It can be a lot of work to have to set up security over and over again each time you do a new deployment, so be sure to package them up if you can.

**WARNING**    Dangers are inherent in the SysAdmin role. Every product has a system administrator role that gives that user authorization to do anything within the system. In the beginning when you only have a few people in the system, you want to give them the SysAdmin role because you don't want to run into security issues in the early parts of the implementation. This changes as you get to your CRP sessions. If possible, you want to give users a broad security role at the time of CRP. You don't want them to have the SysAdmin role—generally you only want people to have that role if they understand it and fear what they can do with it. This keeps them from making mistakes with the role.

Once you get to UAT, you want to limit the SysAdmin role to as few people as possible. The only people who should have access to it would be your lead IT Operations person as well as a system account. The system account would have a password that wouldn't have to be reset, and the system account could be used for integrations as well.

Many customers break this rule and end up with many SysAdmin users even after they go live. You are just inviting problems if you do that. Most of the problems come from well-intentioned users who accidentally make a change in production. The users often don't understand that they can change a parameter or give too much security to another user, and those issues can be difficult to track down. Be very careful about who has SysAdmin access!

# The Bottom Line

**Understanding Environments**   Four core environments are recommended for most implementations so that you can move your code from development to production while providing
adequate means for testing.

> **Master It**   Which of these is the lowest-level environment?
>
> **1.** Build
>
> **2.** Test
>
> **3.** UAT
>
> **4.** Production

**Environment Usage**   In this chapter, we explain how each environment is used and when it
is used. Each environment has a certain function that project team members need to
understand.

> **Master It**   Which of these is the closest environment to production?
>
> **1.** Build
>
> **2.** Test
>
> **3.** UAT
>
> **4.** Sandbox

**Code Moves**   During code moves, it's as important to know what moves between environments as what doesn't, so you can plan for how to handle that information.

> **Master It**   Which of the following does not typically move between environments
> through packaged solutions?
>
> **1.** Custom development
>
> **2.** Custom reports
>
> **3.** Security
>
> **4.** Data

**Types of Releases**   Four different types of releases happen during the implementation
project and after you go live. Each has a different process from the release, including different
environments that would be used.

> **Master It**   What would you call the type of release used when you move code from your
> build server to UAT?
>
> **1.** Lower environment
>
> **2.** Production

**3.** Hotfix

**4.** Enhancement

**Environment Plan**  We discuss many elements of the environment plan in this chapter. The environment plan is your guide to what environments are needed and how you use them.

**Master It**  Which of the following elements shows up on an environment plan?

**1.** Project schedule

**2.** Change request deployment plan

**3.** Functional design document

**4.** Planned environment outline

# Chapter 18

# Testing

We have now officially made the shift into the Deploy stage of the Client Journey, or the Deployment phase of the implementation steps. Like most everything we've covered thus far, not all testing happens in the Deploy stage—much of the planning and functional testing should occur before the Deploy stage. Since most of the activity happens in the Deploy stage, I thought it best to tackle testing at this step of the journey.

This chapter is full of definitions, as many more flavors of testing exist than I had envisioned when I first learned about this. You want to make sure that the project team knows exactly what they are testing, when they are doing it, and how they are doing it to be sure it's done effectively.

Testing is key to the success of the project. Testing can also be a never-ending task that drains too much time and money from your implementation budget. Like many aspects of the project, your goal is to find the happy medium that provides you with good testing coverage without having to root out every single Priority 4 issue.

We have addressed the user acceptance testing (UAT) activities briefly in previous chapters with discussions of how UAT differs from a CRP session. In this chapter, we'll dive deep into the UAT process so you know how to get ready for it and execute on it successfully.

## AFTER YOU COMPLETE THIS CHAPTER, YOU WILL BE ABLE TO DO THE FOLLOWING:

- ◆ Define common terms used in testing

- ◆ Articulate what work should be done before the Deploy stage

- ◆ Set your UAT entrance and exit criteria

- ◆ Conduct effective UAT sessions

- ◆ Manage testing activity after UAT

## Definitions

Not everyone loves testing. In fact, that's pretty generous; most people don't like testing. However, there is a rare breed of individuals who love it, and your goal is to find them and put them to use on this very important step. Let's look at common testing terminology so you understand which types of testing are most important to your project.

## Types of Testing

If you Google the different types of testing possible, you get a list of about 30 different types. That is more than I have ever used, so you don't need to know all 30, but I think you should consider the following types of testing when building the plan for your project. You can broadly categorize testing as functional (related to the functionality in the system) and non-functional (how the system operates instead of what it does). After each type of testing, I'll indicate if it is functional or non-functional:

**End-to-end or process-based testing (functional)** *End-to-end testing* walks through an entire process to test multiple use cases or processes. This is what we will do in CRP and UAT sessions, and this is something that needs to be done on projects to make sure that all of the parts fit together.

**Functional testing** *Functional testing* is both a class of testing and a specific type of testing based on analysis of the specification of the functionality of a component or system. This is what the functional consultant and core team lead do when code is written by the developer. They test it to make sure that the functions work as designed.

**Integration testing (functional)** *Integration testing* is performed to expose defects in the interfaces and interactions between integrated systems. This is work done by the architect or consultants working with integrations to make sure that the connection works and that data is passing as it should between systems.

**Load or performance testing (non-functional)** *Performance testing* is where you simulate multiple resources hitting the system at the same time. Many implementations don't do load testing, and much of that is justified. If you have a small number of users (less than 50) with a small amount of transactional load (less than 500 transactions a day), chances are very high that your system will perform just fine. If you have hundreds of users and thousands of transactions a day, I recommend that you develop a plan to make sure that your system will perform well under load.

**Non-functional testing** *Non-functional testing* is testing that does not specifically cover functionality in the system; instead, it covers how the system operates. I mentioned several examples of non-functional testing in the types of testing: load/performance, usability, and security. These are all important types of testing to weave into your overall project plan, and it can have a negative impact on the success of the system if they are not considered.

**Regression testing (functional)** *Regression testing* is done on a previously tested component once changes were introduced elsewhere in the system. I will talk about the trade-offs in more detail in the next section.

**Security testing (non-functional)** *Security testing* checks a variety of roles to make sure that their security is set up properly. You can incorporate this into your other training activity if you choose, rather than running a specific testing session for security. The important part is that you remember to test security before you go live.

**Unit testing (functional)** *Unit testing* involves code written to test the functionality just developed. We discussed this in great detail in Chapter 15, "Customizations vs. Configurations and How You Manage Them," as it is code that should be used by the developer to validate that elements of their code return the expected results.

**Usability testing (non-functional)**   *Usability testing* is designed to determine how easy the interface is to use. This is similar to security testing in that you don't often set aside a session on usability testing, but you need to be looking out for it as you do end-to-end testing. Ideally, you provide feedback on usability in CRP sessions so that you have time to make adjustments before you get to UAT.

**Use case testing (functional)**   *Use case testing* walks through all of the components of particular use cases. This is similar to end-to-end testing, but use cases are detailed, specific activities that you need to confirm in the software. These often span different process groups, so you want to make sure that the parts work together even if you have to move around the application to test all this.

With all these types of testing, you should decide which are important to you and how you want to incorporate them into your project plan. Generally, unit, integration, and functional testing start in the Create stage as you develop new code. Use case and usability testing should start during CRP. Security, load, and end-to-end testing primarily occur during the Deploy stage, but you can always start them early. We'll talk more about regression testing in an upcoming section.

## Common Testing Terms

Before we get deeper into the chapter, let's cover some of the common terms that you will hear during the testing process:

**Bug or system defect**: A *bug* or *system defect* is a flaw in the system that causes a failure. We've discussed this earlier in the book, but bugs come up more frequently in the Deploy stage.

**Blocker (dependency)**: A *blocker* is bug that is blocking the ability to complete another test. You will hear this term earlier in the project as well, but it comes up more frequently during testing. You may hear the term "blocking bug," which means that a bug that is preventing you from accomplishing a process that you need to complete.

**Fail**: A *fail* is a test that does not complete all criteria. When you test something and one part of it doesn't work, you give it a "Fail" rating and explain what failed.

**Pass**: A *pass* is a test that meets its expected result fully. When you test something successfully, you give the test a "Pass" rating.

**Test automation**: *Test automation* occurs when you use software to perform a test. This doesn't necessarily mean the same as regression testing—you often use automation to run regression tests, but you can use test automation to test new parts of the system as well.

**Test case**: A *test case* involves a scenario in the software that you want tested. This usually includes step-by-step instructions on how to complete the scenario.

**Test plan**: A *test plan* is a document describing the scope, approach, resources, and schedule of test activities.

**Use case**: A *use case* is a sequence of transactions in a scenario a user follows in the system.

We will talk about these terms further as we get deeper into this chapter.

# Pre-Deploy Stage Activities

In the chapter opening, I mentioned how most of the testing occurs in the Deploy stage, but you can make the process go much more smoothly if you prepare for it in the Align and Create stages. Let's talk about how to be get ready early for a successful Deploy stage.

## Testing Strategy

The best thing that you can do for your testing strategy is to develop it early. It should be built before your kickoff meeting. Almost no one does this, but if you do, you won't regret it.

A typical testing strategy document contains the following contents:

**Testing goals and objectives**: This is where you cite the overarching goals of your test plans and set the direction for the level of testing that you plan to build into this strategy document.

**Scope**: The *scope* is where you articulate what types of testing will you do and what testing you are not planning to do.

**Test execution**: *Test execution* indicates what system will you use to track testing activity where you store your test cases and test runs. This also includes how test cases and scripts will be stored and the process for executing tests and collecting results.

**Defect management**: In *defect management*, you identify your priority and severity definitions so that everyone on the project has a good idea how to classify bugs as they occur. You should also define what type of bug it is—data, configuration, process, code defect, or a non-functional bug (security, performance, usability, and so on).

**Resource plan**: Your *resource plan* answers who will serve as your project's test manager and your testers. You will clarify the expectations between your project team and the implementer's team when it comes to testing.

**Environments**: You should have previously defined *environments* in your environment plan, as discussed in Chapter 17, "Environment Management and Deployments," but you would identify what testing will occur in which environments in your testing strategy.

**Deliverables**: *Deliverables* is where you lay out your expectations for artifacts related to testing, such as the testing activity by phases and expectations for the quality and amount of test cases and scenarios.

**Meetings**: This is the suggested meeting schedule related to the testing process—what meetings you should have in the Create stage and how those meetings escalate in the Deploy stage.

**Risks**: Identify potential *risks* that may impact the amount of time you have to conduct testing and how you plan to mitigate those risks. You may think that everyone thinks thorough testing is critical to a project, but sometimes when time gets tight, project leaders are willing to cut corners on testing. You should decide early on how many corners you would allow to be cut.

**Testing schedule**: The *testing schedule* is your chance to lay out each of the testing activities and when they should take place on the project. You first define the types of testing that will be done and the goals you have for each type of testing. Then you describe the entrance and exit criteria and means of measurement for success. You lay out a schedule for when these activities will occur in your project plan and assign an owner for each.

**Reporting**: *Reporting* is where you lay out the reports that you will share with the project team on the progress of testing. All of these reports can be generated from Azure DevOps. The common reports you should share include the following:

◆ Number of test cases written versus your target

◆ The number of tests run—you actually show three columns here—tests passed, tests failed, and tests not run. It is important to track which tests have not been run so you know that potential bugs still exist.

◆ Activity by tester—so you can make sure that everyone who is assigned to test is following through on their commitment.

◆ Defect tracking—number of Priority 1, 2, 3, and 4 issues.

**NOTE** You may look at this list and say that it's way too formal for your small project—and maybe it is. If you are running a small project, you can certainly scale back on a formal testing strategy, but you would still need an informal testing strategy. You still want to make sure that you are testing the key elements of the solution before they go live, no matter how small the project.

This testing strategy document should be reviewed and signed off on by the project leadership team in the early stages of the project so that everyone has the same expectations for testing on the project.

## Unit Test and Regression Tests

Chapter 15 covered unit testing in great detail, so I won't re-explain it here other than to say that you should know what your plan is as you start to budget for the project. If you ask your developers to create automated unit tests, you are adding another 25–50 percent to the cost of development, plus you must have the infrastructure to run these tests on the build server. If you want to make that investment, plan for it before the kickoff meeting.

One of the most common, difficult questions I hear is this: "How much regression testing should I do?" Try to remember Goldilocks as you come up with your regression testing plan. Using no regression testing will lead to problems—as much as you don't like to think it can be a problem, when you make a change in one part of the system, you may negatively affect something that worked successfully in another part of your system. You can also spend so much time running tests on all areas of the system that you chew up valuable time testing something that has a 99.5 percent chance of working. If you think about how often you will make updates in the future (you will need to make at least two per year), you can start to see how investing in automation can save lots of time in the future. You want to use automated testing as much as you can without spending too much time in areas that you wouldn't otherwise manually test after each update. You will likely need to employ a combination of automated and manual testing for each update you make. Start by testing more, and after a few updates if you haven't encountered issues, you can slowly back down on the amount of testing you do.

With a cloud-based solution like Microsoft Dynamics 365, you can avoid a major upgrade in the future because the software is continually updated with new features and new fixes many times each year. From a total cost of ownership perspective, this will save you a lot of money over the years, as you only have to handle small updates instead of a large upgrade cost at some point in the future. The trade-off is that due to these frequent updates, you will need to run regression tests more often than you would in an on-premise world.

Whenever possible, try to incorporate automation into regression testing. In Microsoft Dynamics 365 Finance and Supply Chain Management, you can record your activities in the system with a tool called *Task Recorder*. You can then save those recordings, and the system will play them back for you. This was originally meant to be a training tool for end users, but it can also be used to create automated testing. There is also a tool called *regression suite automation tool (RSAT)*, which can be used to run these recordings through automated tests. You can create test plans in DevOps and run these tests to uncover issues. Incorporating some type of automation into your regression testing allows you to have much more coverage without having to have users do manual testing.

What should you test manually? As little as possible, ideally. If you don't have automation coverage on your tests, you should still make an effort to run manual tests on those areas of the system that must work successfully. If you think there's any chance that the code near them has changed, you should try to run manual tests on whatever is most important to the system—it could be sales orders, purchase orders, work orders, and so forth. Focus your manual regression tests on the most critical areas to your business and the areas that are most highly customized; those tend to run the biggest risk of affecting your business.

## Developing Test Cases

As mentioned in the "Definitions" section, a *test case* is a set of input values, execution preconditions, and expected results and post conditions developed for a particular objective or test. I often describe it as a use case or scenario that you want to make sure works in the system. That seems to resonate better with less experienced testers.

To develop a test case, you simply write out each step the user needs to test in the system. Azure DevOps has a work type for test cases, and it makes it easy to track the steps so that you can identify where the process may have failed. Figure 18.1 is an example of creating a test case with the associated steps.

**FIGURE 18.1**

Creating a test case

| Steps | Action |
| --- | --- |
| 1. | Click on Customer Sites and select a Customer Site |
| 2. | Click on the Crop History Tab |
| 3. | On the soil sample subgrid click +New Soil Sample. |
| 4. | Type in the Sample Identification inside of the *Sample Identification* field, |
| 5. | Fill out any other fields you would like |
| 6. | Click Save |

If you are using Microsoft Dynamics 365 Finance and Supply Chain Management, you can use the Task Recorder tool to generate test cases simply by recording the steps that you take within the product. If you don't have that tool, I suggest that you open up the system on one screen and DevOps on another and write instructions for each thing that you do within the system.

The keys are to creating a test case are as follows:

◆ Make sure that the steps are easy to follow.

◆ Make sure that you cover the important process steps with test cases.

You want to make the steps easy to follow because you want to engage many users in running tests, and they may not be very familiar with the system. Make sure that you're writing test cases with the novice user in mind. You also need to go back to your process catalog to identify the use cases and scenarios that need to be tested. You should identify the out-of-the-box tests that you need to run and when you write an FDD and outline the test cases that need to be developed to support the new customization. Make sure that your functional consultant and core team lead meet to review the test cases that are needed for each process group so that you can assign them and validate that they have been created.

## UAT Entrance Criteria

We've covered entrance and exit criteria before in Chapter 10, "Factors for a Successful Project Kickoff," and Chapter 13, "Conference Room Pilots," so I won't repeat the definition here. Just like going into and out of CRP, you need entrance and exit criteria for your UAT sessions.

As you are thinking about your entrance criteria, consider your pre-UAT checklist. Many items on the entrance criteria should be part of the pre-UAT checklist as well. Let's cover the entrance criteria portion of the pre-UAT checklist first. I suggest your entrance criteria for UAT should be as follows:

◆ Your code should be complete—this means written and functionally tested.

◆ You should not have known Priority 1 issues that prevent you from completing core functions in the system. You can still enter UAT with Priority 1 issues, but you should balance your schedule so that you are not running users through testing of an area of the system which you know won't work well for them.

◆ All configurations must be in place and able to be easily imported into the UAT environment.

◆ The UAT environment must be ready, which includes the following:

  ◆ Data migrated into the environment

  ◆ Integrations connected to the environment and working

  ◆ Security set up as you plan to use it when you go live

Now let's cover the other pre-UAT checklist items:

◆ The project manager should have mapped out each of the UAT sessions and their schedule. You may have to adjust the schedule if you have a Priority 1 issue that is preventing a positive session in a particular process group.

◆ The project manager should determine the exit criteria and who is responsible for signing off on each element of the solution.

- The project team should be aware of the plan for UAT so that they can support the activities that will occur during the Deploy stage.

- A session on "How to Test" should be recorded and made available to everyone who will be participating in UAT. This session will include an explanation of the items in this chapter, including the definitions used in testing, when to log a bug, and how to log it.

- The UAT kickoff session should be scheduled and put on the calendars of everyone who will be participating. The "How to Test" session can be a part of the UAT kickoff, but it should be recorded for those who cannot attend.

## UAT Exit Criteria

It is highly recommended that you determine the exit criteria before you get into UAT—the best-case scenario is to determine this as part of the testing strategy in the very beginning of the project.

You won't be able to exit your UAT sessions with no Priority 1 issues. It would be great if you did, but that's unlikely given that you could discover one of those issues on the last day of UAT and there wouldn't be enough time to get it fixed before UAT ends. The exit criteria related to UAT typically are truly criteria for moving to production, which we'll address in Chapter 20, "Going Live."

The true UAT exit criteria should be more focused on accomplishing all of the tests you set out to complete. The exit criteria should be as follows:

- All UAT sessions were successfully completed, and the end-to-end processes were tested.

- All test cases were executed.

- Integrations were tested and connections worked.

- Load test was completed.

- Security was in place for all users.

From this point until you go live, you will be working to resolve bugs in the system, so you want to make sure that you have a good process for that and that you can avoid disturbing the end user training that is coming up next.

# UAT Sessions

The UAT sessions are a critical part of the overall success of the project. For many users, this is their first chance to look at the software, and this is your chance to get in as much testing as possible before you go live on the new software. Setting proper expectations and meeting them is key to the success of these sessions.

## Purpose

Let's walk through the specific purpose of the UAT sessions to identify the key objectives that you want to accomplish during these sessions. The UAT sessions typically seek to verify that the system is ready for go-live, so the key objectives are as follows:

**Verify that the business processes are ready for go-live**   Run through all of the processes that are in scope for the implementation to make sure that they work as designed.

**Verify that data migration supports operational needs**   Make sure that you have the process in place to extract data from your current systems, transform the data into the format needed for Microsoft Dynamics, and load the data into Microsoft Dynamics.

**Verify system configurations**   You will typically address this by running through the end-to-end processes, but you want to make sure that you have documented all of your configurations and you can validate that they are set correctly when you run through the processes.

**Verify integration readiness**   Make sure that all of your integrations are connected and passing data back and forth and that the data is what you want in your Microsoft Dynamics system.

**Verify security setup**   Validate that users can access what they need to and that they can't access areas of the product that they shouldn't.

In short, the goal is to test the system thoroughly so that you know what you will have in production when you go live. You will not fix every issue that arises in UAT, but you need to fix the most important ones.

## Additional Benefits of UAT Sessions

One of main tangential benefits of UAT sessions is the opportunity to introduce many new users to the system. This isn't your end user training, but for many users it's their first opportunity to spend significant time in the system. Just like I warned in Chapter 13 on CRP sessions, bringing many new users into the system can be a blessing or a curse depending on how you handle the situation. It's critical to have a professional session with the key processes working, otherwise you might inadvertently convince the new users that the system doesn't work or isn't ready for go-live. You want to set expectations that the system will perform the key functions they need, but they will experience some bugs in the system. If you can set expectations well, you can introduce them to the system and get the feedback you need.

Another tangential benefit of the UAT sessions is that you can test out your test cases. This may seem obvious, but there's value in having accurate test cases for the long haul, and this is your chance to make sure that they are working well so that they can be used for future regression testing as well. This activity typically happens after the UAT sessions are over, but it's a good chance to do a retrospective on how good the test cases were so that you can refine them and reuse them in the future.

Finally, you can use the UAT sessions as a dry run on your end user training materials. Since you are introducing new subject matter experts to the system, you can walk them through the flow you plan to use in your end user training. As you walk through the process flow, take notes on what the team understood easily and what was difficult for them to understand so that you can make those adjustments before you get to end user training.

## UAT Roles and Responsibilities

Before you engage in the UAT sessions, make sure that you know who is responsible for what. Both the partner and customer have key responsibilities in UAT, and it's ultimately the business process owner who will sign off that their process flow is well represented in the system. Thus, it's key that they participate in the system and collect feedback from their core team leader and subject matter experts.

From the partner side, the solution architect is responsible for making sure that the overall flow fits together, and that the solution is ready for UAT. The functional consultants from each area will validate their areas and coordinate with their related core team lead to make sure that the process categories in their scope are ready. The technical consultant needs to get the environments ready, connect any integrations, validate any ISV solutions, and set up security in the UAT environment. The project manager sets the agenda for the sessions and makes sure that the team is prepared for what is going to happen.

The UAT sessions are typically led by the core team leader for that particular business process area. This is the same person who will have led the CRP sessions, so this is another opportunity to refine the training plan that they debuted in CRP with the updated code that is close to ready for go-live. The core team leaders need to understand their responsibility to make this a great session for their subject matter experts and to partner with the functional consultant to make sure that the system is as ready as it can be and that the core process flow works as expected.

The business process owners need to sit in on the sessions as they ultimately need to sign off that the processes are ready for go-live. Their subject matter experts will be attending the sessions and running through the tests, and they need to be prepared to speak up about challenges they see with the new system. The business process owner needs to understand that not everything will work perfectly in the new system and set expectations with their team that some amount of lower-priority bugs will still exist when you go-live.

Your IT team can support the technical consultant in getting all of the environments ready. This is a good time to transition responsibility for the environments from the technical consultant to the IT Operations team internally so that you have the resources on staff to manage the solution on your own long-term.

## Executing Your Test Plans

During the sessions, you will be executing all of the test plans that have been created to test each process end-to-end in the system thoroughly. Prior to UAT, you want to confirm that you have good coverage for all of the test cases needed so that you don't end up missing a key portion of the system testing you need to do.

In the sessions themselves, the core team lead will introduce what is going to be tested and walk through the process in the system end-to-end, showing what each user needs to go through to make it to the end of the process in the system. Then they will show the test cases associated with this process flow. From there, they turn it over to the session participants to run through those test cases. Running through a test case is simply known as a *test*.

For each test, the user will give it a rating of Pass, Fail, Blocked, or Not Applicable. The test must successfully run all the way through from start to finish correctly to receive a Pass rating. If there is anything that doesn't work along the way, that is reason to give the test a Fail rating. (If there is confusing wording in the test case explanation or something that isn't quite right about the test case, I prefer users to pass the test but provide feedback to the core team lead that the test case language should be adjusted to be more accurate.) The user would identify the test as Blocked if they are unable to run the test due to a bug somewhere else in the system. This doesn't mean that this test case doesn't work; it means that you don't know if it works or not. The final status option is Not Applicable, and this would be used to indicate that this particular user shouldn't have had this test case assigned to them.

If you are using DevOps, each user should see a list of tests that they need to run and then they can update the status after they run through each individual test. The project manager or test manager reviews the DevOps status of each of the tests to provide reporting to the project leadership team on the success of that day's testing. They would also share some analysis of what went well and what went poorly and perhaps make adjustments to the testing plan for the next day to reflect any course changes that might be needed.

## Tips for the Sessions

To get the most out of your UAT session, I suggest a few tips to make sure that they run as smoothly as possible:

1. **Set expectations at the beginning of each session.** You will be tired of hearing yourself say this at the end of the sessions, but set expectations that the core process should work even though the users will experience bugs along the way and they will have tests that do not pass. That does not mean the system will be a colossal failure when you go live—this is the reason why you are doing the testing now, so that you can find issues before you go live. You should also do the following:

    a. **Identify roles and responsibilities.** Introduce the role of the core team lead and indicate that the business process owner has ultimate responsibility for the process flow here. Tell the users that their role is to execute the test cases and provide feedback about the experience.

    b. **Introduce the purpose of the UAT session.** Start with the overall goal of UAT, but then specifically identify what you want from this session.

    c. **Walk through the agenda for the session.** Identify what you plan to cover in the session and make sure to mention what is not in scope in the session as well. You don't want users straying off to test functionality outside of the process area during your session as that is distracting to the ultimate purpose of this session.

    d. **Ask for undivided attention.** Ask everyone to put their phone down and close out of their email so that they can focus on executing these tests. There will be breaks throughout the session where they can attend to their day jobs.

2. **Run the sessions for no longer than six hours a day.** To follow on from the last point, if you are asking the team for their undivided attention, you should be sure that they have time throughout the day to attend to their day job and their personal lives as needed.

    a. **Keep your stand-up meeting in the morning before the session begins.** This gives the team a chance to get caught up on the events of yesterday and to be made aware of any key change that might impact the day's events.

    b. **Run a three-hour session in the morning.** Give yourself a little time before the session starts to make sure that everything is working. This is especially important if you made a new build the previous night.

    c. **Run a three-hour session in the afternoon.** This gives everyone time to catch up on their day jobs over lunch and step away from the computer screen for a time.

    d. **Book 30 minutes after the session for the functional leads.** This is the time that the team can use to log any bugs that occurred during the session, to debrief on how it went, to adjust any test cases, and to prepare for the next day's session while the memory of the previous session is fresh.

3. **Session flow**. Provide an overview of the business process and a quick run through of what they will see in the session to set the stage for attendees.

   a. **Focus on critical processes**. Don't spend much time on exceptions—you can note them, but make sure that the common path works first.

   b. **Call out handoffs to other processes**. If this process is intertwined with another one, make sure that you identify the connection and note it for further testing. To keep the sessions focused, you want to make sure not to cover disparate processes in a session, but reality dictates that there are cases where you need to hand a transaction off from one process to another. Make note of it so that you can be sure it's tested at some point during UAT.

   c. **Capture issues in adequate detail for follow-up**. When someone finds a bug, note information such as what they did before they got to that particular screen, if it relates to migrated or integrated data, what security role they had at the time of the bug, and what configuration was in place where the error occurred. All of these questions will greatly improve your troubleshooting time when you go to tackle the bug.

   d. **Don't deviate from scope**. Stick to the end-to-end process that this session is supposed to cover. If the users complete their testing early, you can have them do some exploratory testing until the prescribed ending time. You could ask them to do some "negative testing," where they test what happens if users make a mistake in the system.

   e. **Create a parking lot**: Use a whiteboard to record any ideas or feedback that comes up which is not specifically related to the testing occurring in the session.

4. **Daily recap**. After that 30-minute functional lead meeting at the end of the day, connect with the project manager so that they can take down the notes and action items from the session.

   a. **Send out a recap of the day's testing activity at the end of the day**. This keeps the project leadership team informed and sets the stage for a productive session the next day.

   b. **Review the parking lot items**. Try to identify any issue that requires more immediate attention.

   c. **Review the bug list by process category**. Do this to see if you have a process that needs a lot of attention.

   d. **Provide an update for issues resolved by process category**. This way, you can test out the fixes in the upcoming sessions.

## Post UAT Testing

As you can imagine, you don't walk out of UAT with no bugs in your system. It would be great if that were true, but it will not be true, so you need to have a plan for how to handle these issues as you try to get training done and prepare for go-live.

## Issues List

You will be tracking and logging bugs as you go throughout the UAT sessions and updating the team daily with the latest information, but once UAT is done, you will want to take the time to update your issues list with the key project-wide issues that must be addressed. Issues and bugs are different, but at this time of the project, a Priority 1 bug is an issue, so it needs to go on the list. Your issue list should include those Priority 1 bugs and other work that needs to get done in a short period of time. This would also include any integration connection issues, security issues, data migration issues, or configuration issues.

Just as you maintain it throughout the project, you should update your issues list to make sure that your issues are prioritized and assigned with a target delivery date. The main difference between the issues list during the middle of the project and the issues list at this stage of the project is the urgency level. Now you have very little time to clean up these issues before you get to your end user training and go/no-go decision.

Many issues may be resolved during or shortly after UAT, and the business process owners should test the resolution of these issues. As you build your issue resolution plan to get the key issues completed before your go/no-go meeting, make sure to include a testing plan for the resolution of the key issues.

## Process Sign-Offs

For each of the process groups, you should ask the business process owner to sign off on the process flow and the testing results. This does not mean that the process has to be bug free—it just means that they are affirming that the process allows them to achieve their business goals. You want to collect the results from these sign-offs so that you can share this with the project leadership team.

You need to remind the business process owner what happens if they don't sign off on the processes at this stage. You are now very late in the project timeline, so it's hard to change course at this point. Any major objection here will threaten the release timeline. If you have a major objection, you probably missed many warning signs along the way that the process didn't meet the needs of the business, or you've put someone in charge of an area who doesn't have the right mindset or understanding of the project. You will need to escalate the issue to your executive sponsor if there is a major objection.

For minor objections to the process flow, those need to be dealt with swiftly or pushed to a future release after go-live. You will have to look at the overall workload between now and go-live to see if you can make the changes in time. That's how you'll decide what course to take. These can be very difficult conversations, but they are ones that need to happen at this stage of the game.

## Scenario Recaps

After the UAT sessions, you should provide an update on the end-to-end processes and scenarios to let the project team know which ones received passing scores on all of their tests and which ones have failed tests. You also want to indicate which processes have received official sign-off from the business process owner. If you have people dedicated to building the training content, you can have those people work on content in the process areas where the tests passed and potentially wait on those areas that had failures until they get resolved.

It's reassuring to the company leadership to see that the scenarios passed in most cases as well—this helps them to see that the project is moving in the right direction. All along, you should be setting expectations with leadership and testing that issues are expected (even encouraged) during UAT. It's a sign that the testing has been thorough. Even with that said, the company leadership can get very nervous over any issues at this point of the project, as no leader wants to see the company go live on software that will cause customer satisfaction issues or shipping delays.

## The Bottom Line

**Understanding Definitions**   Many different types of tests exist, as discussed in the early part of the chapter. Make sure that your team knows the common types of testing so that they can distinguish what type of testing is needed.

**Master It**   What is the term for code written to test the functionality just developed?

1. Load testing

2. Unit test code

3. Use case testing

4. Security testing

**Key Terminology**   Educating the team on the terms used during the implementation and the UAT sessions is key to keeping everyone on the same page throughout testing. You should introduce key terms in the UAT kickoff meeting.

**Master It**   Which of the following is a sequence of transactions in a scenario a user follows in the system.

1. Use case

2. Test plan

3. Test case

4. Pass

**Functional and Non-functional Tests**   It's easy to remember to run the functional tests, as that is what the users will see in the new system. It's equally as important to remember to run non-functional tests, as that will affect the quality of the new system.

**Master It**   What is an example of non-functional testing?

1. Unit test

2. Regression test

3. Performance test

4. End-to-end testing

**Roles and Responsibilities**   It takes a concerted effort by the project team to make it through UAT successfully. The end goal is to get sign-off on the processes that you ran through during the testing sessions.

**Master It**   Which project role is responsible for signing off on the process at the end of UAT?

**1.** Core team lead

**2.** Business process owner

**3.** Executive sponsor

**4.** Project manager

**Exit Criteria**   At the end of UAT, it's important to look back on the goals that you had for the UAT sessions and to review the exit criteria that you set going into it. You can consider UAT complete only when those criteria have been met.

**Master It**   To exit UAT, which of the following conditions must be met?

**1.** All Priority 3 issues must be resolved.

**2.** All test cases must have been run.

**3.** All Priority 4 issues must be prioritized.

**4.** All Priority 1 issues must be resolved.

# Chapter 19

# Training for All

People like systems that they know. It doesn't matter how good the system is—if they know it well, they will like it better. I've told this story many times, but at my first professional job, we were on an old (even for that time) mainframe, and I was a 21-year-old kid coming out of college having used PCs and Macs. I was tasked with retrieving all of the natural gas consumption for one of the towns that we supported. I went to the accounting team to ask how I would pull this information. They said, "Oh, that's easy. You just go to the mainframe and type **BTLHNM13**." I said sarcastically, "Of course, I should've realized that." I never really did learn that system in the three years I was there. They were getting a new accounting system when I left, but the accounting team was against it. They were against it because they liked their current system—not because that system was good, but because they knew it well.

You are going to face this same uphill battle when you try to roll out a new system to your team who has grown to like their existing system. They probably don't like a few things about it, but because they know it so well, they are very attached to it. There's actually a part of the brain (the amygdala) that is naturally resistant to change. You have a lot to overcome to get them to love the new system.

The good news is this: It can be done. You just need to attack the problem in the same way that they have come to love their existing system; you must get them to know the new system so that they will love it.

In this chapter, we will talk about training and learning throughout the entire project with a focus on how you should put together your end user training plan to achieve maximum benefit. The ultimate goal is for your users to hit the ground running on Day 1 of the new system. No matter how well you train them, there will still be problems in the first few weeks of working with the new system. However, you can minimize those problems by taking a thoughtful approach to training throughout the entire project.

Since we recently covered environments, I should mention that end user training activity should generally happen in the UAT environment. I have seen people run through training in production, but then you have to be sure to restore backups to keep these test transactions from clogging up your live system.

**AFTER YOU COMPLETE THIS CHAPTER, YOU WILL BE ABLE TO DO THE FOLLOWING:**

- ◆ Increase the team's familiarity with the system during the interactive sessions
- ◆ Define different learning modalities

- Prepare materials for training
- Explain the value of a Learning Management System
- Articulate the best end user training models

## Learning During Interactive Sessions

One of the major goals of an iterative and interactive implementation model is to get users into the system as much as possible, even before you get to end user training. In a pure waterfall approach, users give requirements and suggestions, but they often don't see the software again until it has been built and you are in the Deploy stage. We did things that way during the first few years at Stoneridge Software, and it does not work very well. When the users first see the software, they find all kinds of things that they don't like, and you don't have enough time to make the changes while still hitting your deadlines. Also, users are less likely to adopt the solution because they have had so little exposure to it.

In the previous chapters, we talked about the dangers of showing users software that does not work right; that's the biggest downside to the iterative model. You must set expectations with users and only share non-working software with those users who will be able to see through the problems to realize the opportunity that the software will bring.

Let's look through the interactive sessions that have happened up to this point in the implementation and consider how they help users to learn the software.

### JPDs

The training goal during *Joint Process Designs (JPDs)* is to get your core team lead and key subject matter experts comfortable moving around in the software. At the time, they are not seeing the finished software, so you don't want them to focus too much on what each function is in the software. The best way to help this land with them is to focus on navigation training. They should know how to find the key functions in the software. Specifically, they should know how to use favorites, perform searching, filtering, sorting, exporting to Excel, and changing grid views, to name a few. If they walk away with a good idea of where to find things in the software at the end of the JPD cycle, that's terrific.

During JPDs, you want to be careful how many users get access to the system to play around on their own. I would limit it to the core team leads because they should have seen the menus and core functions. The average subject matter expert has not learned enough to be able to explore the system independently. They will end up frustrated because they cannot do what they want to do, and that could spill over into the overall opinion of the product and project.

### CRPs

During *Conference Room Pilots (CRPs)*, you want to get users into the system and get them comfortable with how it works. For the subject matter experts, this is their first time working in the software with their hands on the keyboard. You must remember that and make sure that they have the training necessary to be successful. The scope of CRP does not cover the whole product, so you don't have to teach them as much as you would in the full end user training, but you have to think about what background a first-time user would need in order to feel confident during the training session.

It is crucial that you start CRP with navigation training, so the users know what the key buttons mean and how to get back to the area you are showing them. As the users get into the function, it is also imperative that the instructor walk them through the software first before engaging the users to try it out themselves. Explaining how the Dynamics solution works as you go through it helps the users get comfortable with the software.

At the end of CRP sessions, you should now have a sizable number of users who understand the navigation and have some familiarity with their area in the product. This is important because you need these users to be advocates for the software and play their respective roles in the eventual end user training plan.

CRP is a good time to give your training content a test-drive. If you have a plan for how you want to train users on this process group, try it out in CRP. After the CRP session, send out a survey to get feedback on how well organized the training was. Take some learning from the feedback you get on those surveys.

## UAT

As mentioned in Chapter 18, "Testing," the goal of UAT is to find any system issues to make sure that the system is ready for production. A key ancillary benefit is the opportunity to provide further training of the users in the system. Like CRP, you will be introducing new users to the system at the time of UAT, so you want to make sure that they have an idea of how to navigate the system and use basic features. Anytime you have new users in a UAT session, you should start with the navigation training.

After that you will be taking UAT users through more complex steps, so again, first you want to walk them through how it is supposed to work. If you just send them in to find bugs without knowing how the software works, you will face two problems:

◆ They will think that everything they do not understand is a bug. This results in a lot more bugs recorded that are not actually bugs.

◆ They will find the software frustrating because they do not know how to complete the process.

If you only remember one thing, remember that each time you introduce new users to the system, you must take them through a session of navigation training, so they understand the system and how to get around in it. The more people who have that background when it comes to training the masses during end user training, the more helpers you will have for those first-time users. You want to identify champions for the software who can understand it well and are willing to train others. You want to highlight these champions as the model you want others to follow during training.

## Learning Modalities

Twenty years ago, training required the instructor to hop on an airplane or get in a car and drive to every different location to conduct in-person training. The world has changed with the broad adoption of the Internet and Internet-based training. We saw this even more in 2020–21, as the world moved all meetings to remote get-togethers in response to the COVID-19 pandemic. This has created a new language in the educational world related to the modalities or ways that training is delivered. The common language today breaks it into three delivery models: in person, synchronous, or asynchronous, as outlined in Figure 19.1. They used to be known as classroom, online, and eLearning. They mean the same thing, but the newer terms are a bit more descriptive.

**FIGURE 19.1**
Learning modalities

Learning Methods

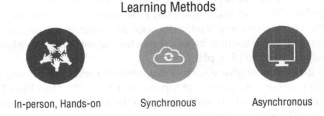

In-person, Hands-on    Synchronous    Asynchronous

Let's define each of these different types and then compare when to use each modality.

## In-Person, Classroom Style

In-person, classroom-style training is a form of *synchronous learning*, because the teacher and the attendees are working together in real time. It is sometimes called "immersive" because of the in-person nature of the training. If you can get them all in one room, it is the best way to train users. The reasons why it is the best method are as follows:

◆ The users can have machines ready with the software laid out for them.

◆ They can have an instructor in front and a helper in the back to work through issues when they encounter them.

◆ They can raise their hands or blurt out any questions that they may have.

◆ The instructor can see them and read their body language.

◆ Attendees pay greater attention when they are in person.

The other modalities have some advantages, but none are as great as being in person.

Of course, the big problem with getting everyone there in person is the cost. If you have users on different continents, this includes flying people around the world to conduct these training sessions. The costs are high, and it requires a major time investment. If you have users at great distances from the home office, I suggest that you do a "train the trainer" session where you train those users in one location at one time and then send them back to lead the training in their regions. This distributes the training, saves money in the long run, and still achieves the goal of having in-person training.

Another problem with any kind of synchronous training is getting everyone together at the same time. End users will have day jobs that they need to do, so they may not be able to get away to attend the training all at the same time. In cases like call centers, you divide up the training into three parts to make sure that you still have coverage for the phones or incoming chat requests. To keep your project on track, you will often need to disrupt operational schedules to get the training done on time. If the operation leaders do not support the new system initiative, you can get pushback that could potentially delay your project timeline.

As I mention later in the chapter, users learn best by distributing their learning across multiple sessions, as opposed to having one big training event for all of the content. Because of that, I suggest a mix of asynchronous, synchronous, and in-person learning, even if you are in close proximity and do not have a great deal of expense associated with getting everyone together. You can assign people to watch videos on their own time, and that eases the burden of trying to get everyone scheduled for a meeting at the same time.

## Remote, Synchronous Training

*Remote, synchronous training* (which I will call synchronous from here on) is instructor-led training not done in a classroom-style setting. It constitutes a meeting set up on a conference call platform where everyone can join from whatever their current location might be. Since it is instructor-led, you still have to schedule people to join the training at a given time, but you don't have the cost of getting everyone together in the same room.

Synchronous training should be part of every training plan because it can be focused on a set of common users. Imagine that you need to train month-end procedures to all of your controllers. You may have 10 controllers all over the country. Rather than pulling them all together in person, you can set up a conference call for them to attend from whatever location is easiest for them. Use synchronous training to train users with similar roles who happen to be distributed across the company's geographical locations.

---

### IMPACT OF COVID-19 ON REMOTE TRAINING

2020 marked the onset of the COVID-19 pandemic, and with that businesses tried to conduct all of their activity remotely. For technology-savvy businesses, the impact was not dramatic. For businesses used to doing everything in person, this represented quite a change. Schools faced a similar transition as classes that had been held in person now needed to be conducted through a video conferencing tool. This led to a forced learning of these tools—with mixed results.

Many implementation activities that had been done in person now had to be done via conferencing tools, including training. The biggest problem with training via video conference is that the teacher can't easily tell if the user understood what was being taught. In person, you can walk around the users' computers to see who has completed the task. In a video conference, you would have to ask everyone to share their screen to validate that they completed the task. If you have 10 people in a class, that can really slow down the flow of the training.

The best way to address the problem of monitoring progress remotely is to do more sessions with fewer attendees. People are often intimidated to raise their hands and say that they are falling behind in a group of 10. If it's one on one, or one on two or three, you can have the user show their progress as you move along. You will have to budget more time for training, but the users will be even more confident in the system having received additional individual attention.

---

Table 19.1 compares the benefits of in-person versus online synchronous training to help you pick the right modality for your business.

**TABLE 19.1:**    Benefits of In-person vs. Online Synchronous Training

| AREA | PROS OF IN-PERSON | PROS OF SYNCHRONOUS |
|---|---|---|
| Scheduling and Attention | You tend to get higher attendance because there is a strong expectation that everyone attends in person. During the class, you can monitor the attendees to make sure that they are paying attention. | It is much easier to arrange, as you do not have to consider travel schedules. Attendees can get back to their day jobs as soon as the training has concluded. |
| Asking Questions | Attendees are more willing to ask the instructor questions in real time. | Attendees can raise a virtual hand to ask questions, so the question period is more contained. |
| System Setup | Computers can be set up with the right screens, and everything is ready for the attendees to be successful. | When sending out preparation instructions, the work is distributed to the participants, requiring less administrative overhead. |
| Helping Slower Learners | Another trainer can walk around the back of the room looking at the progress on attendees' screens and help those who are falling behind. | You can set up separate sessions whereby those who struggled in the session can get one-on-one time. This makes it so that you only need one instructor for each session. |
| Technical Comfort | Less technical personnel feel more comfortable with someone there to lead them. | Some attendees feel better not having someone watch everything that they do. |

I typically recommend in-person when it is possible. The other value of in-person is that training seems more important when the company is willing to invest the time and energy to bring everyone together in one location. It is very important. All attendees should not only understand that, but feel it. You should have two leaders in the classroom with the core team leader training the session and the functional consultant or another expert walking around assisting the users.

### SHOULD YOU MIX IN-PERSON AND REMOTE LEARNERS IN A SESSION?

It happens very frequently, but I do not recommend it. In my experience, every time it is done, one of the user groups ends up frustrated. If you cater to the in-person audience (which is the easier thing to do because they are in front of you), you sometimes end up ignoring the online users. Even if you don't ignore them, it's hard for them to get their questions in as the moderator has to stop and specifically ask them for questions. If you do a great job of incorporating your remote users, you will spend time working on technical issues—audio issues, forgetting to share your screen with the remote users, and so on, and any time you spend on those issues takes away from the focus of the audience who made the commitment to show up in person. You can pull off a mixed training, but you must work out the technical kinks in advance, and the leader needs to specifically ask for questions from the remote users to keep them engaged.

## Asynchronous

*Asynchronous training* is a fancy word for eLearning or recorded training sessions or forms of documentation. This is content that the user can consume whenever they want. It does not have to occur at a given time, although sometimes asynchronous content is used as a supplemental resource to a synchronous training.

I will cover the different types of content and when to use them in the upcoming section. Every good training plan should include a good amount of asynchronous content, so make sure that it is part of your plan as well.

## Building Your Training Content

When I hear people talk about training content, they usually just mean the training material designed for end user training. If you step back and think about it, that is only one part of the puzzle when it comes to what helps people learn. I encourage you to think more holistically about all of the content that can be used as part of your overall learning strategy.

## End User Training Content

The *end user training content* may consist of many different formats. Some projects have hired consultants and have asked them to create step-by-step instructions for everything that needs to be done inside the system. You want that content, but it can be an expensive way to put it all together. Others put together no content and have their instructors "wing it" when they show up for the training sessions.

The happy medium is where you define your content approach ahead of time and break out each role into a training plan that works best for that role. For example, you need to train salespeople on how to manage opportunities in CRM. If you spend hours writing up training content for them, upload it to a document repository, and ask them to take the training on their own time, you will not get satisfactory results. You may be able to take that approach with a more diligent and detail-oriented group of users, like accountants, but that approach will not work for the stereotypical salesperson.

For salespeople, you want to try to organize an in-person (or at least synchronous) training plan, and you want to use examples and tell stories. You also want to highlight how they are incented to fill out the system correctly (it is always a good thing to tie commissions to filling out the necessary information successfully in a system—if you don't, good luck getting your salespeople to use the system). You may want to record a video for future reference on what steps they should follow to use the system, but personally, I would not write a lot of documentation to train a sales team.

For accountants, I would write documentation—I would send it to them in advance, and then I would schedule a synchronous training session to review the content and answer any questions they may have. Make sure that they know where the content is so that they can reference it at any time. Also, make sure the document is thorough, as they tend to dislike imprecise documentation.

As you can see by these examples, there is not a one-size-fits-all approach to end user training content. You should present users a mix of reference material and synchronous training, but the balance of that content and the approach will be different based on the types of learners you have in these different roles.

## Product Help Content

All Microsoft Dynamics products include Help content in the solution, so you can reference that content to help explain how to use that function on the screen. This content is designed to tell you the steps to follow for that screen, and it is only designed for telling you how to use an non-customized version of that screen. If your screen has many customizations, the product help will be confusing to the end user. When it comes to the product help, I advise one of three approaches:

◆ **Ignore it**. If you have a highly customized system, you may create more confusion if you try to have your users use Help content that is generic.

◆ **Use it as is**. If your system does not have many customizations, it can be a good reference for your users. I typically recommend walking your power users through the Help system so that they understand it, and then they can share it with those who might find it beneficial. There is a lot of content out there, and you are unlikely to be able to review it all, so it can be dangerous to tout it as a solution if you are not familiar with everything that is available. Again, it is designed to tell you "what" to do and not "how" to do it, so the users may be frustrated by the fact that they are not getting an explanation of how to use the system in Help.

◆ **Fully embrace it**. This is the least common approach, but one that you can consider. In this model, you tell the users to use the Help content, and you spend time customizing the Help content to be relevant to how you use the system and your customizations.

My recommendation is that the project team meets regarding the training plan, which should include a decision on how to use Help content. Figure 19.2 outlines this Help content. Be intentional about the path you choose so that this does not create confusion for your end users.

**FIGURE 19.2**
Microsoft Dynamics 365
Help documentation

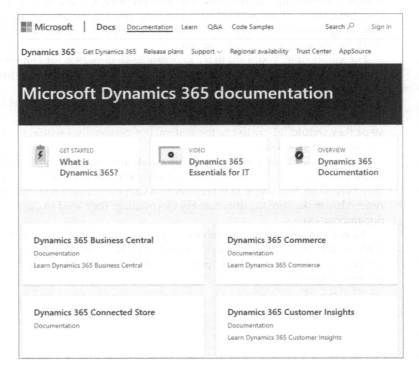

## Microsoft Learn

Microsoft introduced a learning platform called *Microsoft Learn*, which spans all of its products. The Learn home screen is shown in Figure 19.3. This is a good system, which allows you to build learning paths, work toward certifications, and watch live and recorded events. There is a mountain of great content here as well.

**FIGURE 19.3**
Microsoft Learn
learning platform

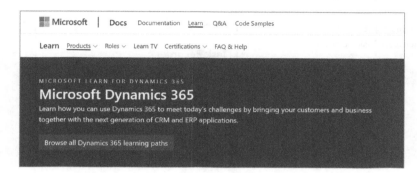

This is a great place to start for your project team. They can watch videos on the out-of-the-box functionality in the system and develop real expertise with the product. The danger with Microsoft Learn is that project leaders see this and think "my training problem is solved." It is intended to be a resource for your team and not the solution for your implementation's training plan. The content available is not specific to your implementation, and it does not contain any of the "how" or "why" you do things the way that you do. Use it for what it is intended—a great way to provide background to your project team.

## Recording Sessions

It used to be that creating a video that combined audio and showed the steps that users must take on the screen was difficult. Now, all you need to do is set up a meeting using your conference calling tool of choice, click to record the meeting, and voila, you have a *recorded video*. It has become so easy that the problem now is having too much content, which makes that content more difficult to organize.

I suggest that you take advantage of the ease at which you can record a training session. While reference documents are helpful, people are visual learners, and it is easy for them to watch a video and follow along. Sometimes the documentation can skip a step or explain something in a confusing way, but there is no confusion when you are watching a video and mimicking the steps on your machine.

I recommend that you use video as your main asynchronous content for a project. Additionally, request that all users watch the videos as a way of introducing them to the system. I believe that you will also find it to be an excellent means for training on the more complex functions in the system.

## Task Recorder

Microsoft Dynamics 365 Finance and Supply Chain Management has a tool called *Task Recorder*, which allows you to capture the clicks and keystrokes that a user made in the system. You can use the output to watch the steps again, play it back in the system, generate a Word document with screenshots outlining the steps taken, use the content in your regression testing with the *regression suite automation tool (RSAT)*, and organize the content by process for process documentation.

Task Recorder, which is shown in Figure 19.4, is a powerful tool that I suggest you take advantage of. It is a great way to generate training content without having to write it all out step by step.

**FIGURE 19.4**
Microsoft Task Recorder

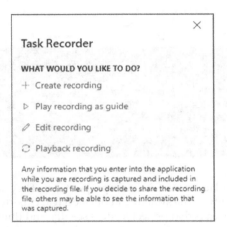

**Task Recorder** ✕

**WHAT WOULD YOU LIKE TO DO?**

+ Create recording

▷ Play recording as guide

✎ Edit recording

⟳ Playback recording

Any information that you enter into the application while you are recording is captured and included in the recording file. If you decide to share the recording file, others may be able to see the information that was captured.

### How Much to Document

In the end, you want your asynchronous content to complement your overall training strategy. If you try to create training documentation, help files, videos, and Task Recorder files for every single process in the system, you will undoubtedly be overdoing it. Also consider that the content is static, so when you upgrade to a future release, your screens may change, and the previous content is now outdated. This is why I suggest that you focus on the content that is easiest to produce so you can reproduce it if it needs to change.

You'd love to think that everyone on the project will read all of the documentation that you put together, but oftentimes end users read only a fraction of the training content produced for their project. It certainly can be more than that, but you should first determine how they are going to find and consume the content and then figure out how much content to produce. Do not create a lot of static documentation that no one can find.

## How to Manage and Distribute Your Content

To pick up from the previous sentence, you first need to focus on how people can find the content that you will produce. Certainly, you can control the content presented in your synchronous training sessions, but a good training plan incorporates far more than synchronous training sessions. It can be boiled down into two initiatives:

1. Setting a learning plan for each role on the project.

2. Providing the content to them in an easy way for them to consume.

## Learning Management Systems

In today's cloud storage world, you have many places to put content. Unfortunately, it is so easy to store the content that people put it everywhere.

*Learning Management Systems (LMS)* (also known as an LMS tool or system) include the ability to store content. Some of them store just videos (some only store videos that are native to that platform), but some also store documentation. It is rare to find one that stores both videos and documentation, so you often must find two places for this content. For the purposes of your implementation project, you want to find an LMS that allows you to upload new videos so that you can share customized videos for your implementation. If it combines a home for documentation, all the better.

An LMS will often allow you to create learning paths for your end users. *Learning paths* outline a set of training and documentation that should be followed for a given user or role. You absolutely want to utilize a learning path concept whether you manage it in an LMS or not.

# Building Your End User Training Schedule

Let's put together some training plans for our team members now that we know what to consider during the process. Table 19.2 shows a sample training plan for customer service representatives who will be working in one of the ERP products.

**TABLE 19.2:**   Training Matrix

| TYPE OF TRAINING | WELL BEFORE | JUST AHEAD OF | DURING | AFTER |
|---|---|---|---|---|
| Navigation Overview | Asynchronous | Synchronous | In-Person | |
| Core Job Functions (Sales Order) | | | In-Person | Synchronous |
| Advanced Job Functions (Returns) | | | In-Person | Synchronous |
| Periodic Activities (Month End) | | | | Asynchronous Reinforced by Synchronous |

In this example, we should consider the type of training that this role needs. In this case, it is the navigation overview, sales order training, returns, and month-end processes. The column headings translate as follows:

**Well Before**: Indicates an asynchronous training "well before" the end user training period, meaning that the user should be tasked with watching a video showing the navigation early in the implementation.

**Just Ahead Of**: "Just ahead of" the end user training so that there would be an online, synchronous version of the navigation training shortly before the official end user training period.

**During**: Indicates that there will be an in-person refresher training session of the navigation overview during end user training.

**After**: Indicates the training that will occur after the end user training period and either shortly before or shortly after go-live.

This model also shows how the user would receive in-person training on sales orders during the end user training period, and then there would be an online training session after the end user training period to sharpen skills in that area before go-live. For the returns functionality, which I consider an advanced class, there would be some review of it during the end user training period but further training after that in conjunction with go-live. For the month-end procedures, there is no training during the end user training period; instead, the user would watch a video on the process shortly after go-live and then receive online training on the topic in week 4 after go-live, shortly before the first month end is set to occur.

I started the chapter by talking about how people like the systems they know. We know the best way for someone to learn something is through repetition. I believe that the best way for someone to learn new software is to give them a base of information, then build on it, and then build on it again. You can put advanced users in a sandbox environment where failure and trying new things is encouraged. That just gets them more comfortable with the software.

One of my pet peeves when it comes to training plans is to see end users being asked to learn everything in one session. They have a lot to learn, and the best way that they can learn is to understand the basics before they learn the advanced concepts. If you are going to teach someone sales orders (of which they must create 100 per day) and a return (of which they do 1 per day), you do not want them to forget how to do sales orders while you teach them returns. I suggest that you break up the training so that you have them complete many sales orders, and thus the process becomes second nature. Then follow up with another session on returns once they really understand the sales order process.

Similarly, you do not want to train people on month-end procedures prior to go-live when they will not have to use them for 5–6 more weeks. Train users on the software shortly before they have to use it, and make sure that they repeat the training so that it really sticks.

## Pre-Training Learning

In the beginning of the chapter, we talked about how the project team and select subject matter experts can learn a lot about the system during the interactive sessions as you are building and testing the software. It is a good idea to build some asynchronous or eLearning content during those early stages of the project, and you can use those recordings as a test to see if the training is effective for a limited number of users before you ask every end user to take it.

As you get further into the project, you should record some of the common training that you will use throughout the project like navigation training, a training session on how to personalize the system, a training session on how to export content to Excel, and training on how to save key functions. All of these are good videos for you to create and to encourage users to watch before they come to training.

## Train the Trainer

*Train the trainer* is the model most implementation partners use for training end users. At Stoneridge Software, we insist on having the end user training led by a member of the customer organization. The main reason is that we want the end users to view an internal person as the expert on the software. If they see the implementation partner as the only one who knows a part of the software, it does not promote internal ownership of the software and end users think of this as "the partner's system" and not their own.

Train the trainer is an activity that occurs before the end user training sessions where the implementation partner provides any final training for the core team leads and subject matter experts who will be leading the end user training. You can also use this time to train other users who might be in training classes in different regions. The goal is to make sure you have enough trainers to cover all of the end user training that you need to do. I suggest that you build your preferred end user training plan, identify your trainers, and then work backwards to figure out how much time you need during the train-the-trainer period.

## Synchronous Sessions

Now we have reached the actual end user training period. Before this checkpoint, you will have scheduled all of the training that needs to occur, identified your trainers and helpers, determined what training material is needed for each session, and prepared the environments so that users can access the system with no issues.

End user training should occur with the precise security access that the users will have once they are live with the system. You should be doing this during UAT as well, but if any changes occur, they should be finalized before end user training so that the users know what they will and will not have access to during training.

Like the CRP or UAT sessions, we recommend a maximum of three-hour sessions in the morning and afternoon. Users have a tough time digesting new information after sitting in the same room in front of a computer for an extended period of time. Make sure to take a break in the middle of the session as well so that people can get up and step away from the computer. Ask everyone to put down their phones and avoid distractions so that the sessions can be focused and productive.

## Advanced Concepts

I consider *advanced concepts* to be those activities that users rarely do in the system. They are activities like returns, refunds, or whatever it might be that you need to do but which you rarely do. These are not good topics to include in the end user training session. I like to suggest that you do a synchronous training session after end user training and back it up with a video that users can use for reference. If I am an average user, I might not have to do a return until Day 5 after go-live, and I may have forgotten how to do it. If I have access to a video about it, I can quickly go watch it and follow the correct steps in the system.

## Testing Users' Knowledge

I rarely ever see any structured way for a company to test how well their users know the system before they go live. I think this is an opportunity that should be embraced. It is quite easy for a user to sit through class, half-pay attention, and go back to their day job without digesting anything from the training. Once you go live, they get into the system, and they are lost because there was no real incentive or test forcing them to learn the material.

You see the idea of *gamification* in sales today to use contests to get more out of your team. You could try an idea like that with your users if you think it might work for them.

**TIP**  People do not learn at the same pace.

Figure 19.5 shows some of the different ways to test the users to make sure that they are learning the content. You can ask them to complete a quiz after training to make sure that they understand the concepts and how the system should be used. You can also ask power users to check in with the end users to make sure that the end users can show them how they understand the system. One of the easiest ways to get confirmation is to have the helper walk around during training and ask anyone who has completed a step to show it again to make sure that they have it down.

**FIGURE 19.5**
Learning valida-
tion options

Learning Validation

Quizzes        One-On-One Reviews        Show Your Work During
                                         Training Sessions

No matter which method works best for you, you will feel a lot better if there is some way of confirming that the users really know the core material and what they will need to do on Day 1 of the new system.

## Office Hours

As outlined in Figure 19.6, one concept that we have used effectively over the years is to set up what we call "office hours" to answer questions for the project team. The concept is that you set up a conference call for 1–2 hours where there is no agenda. It is just a time for users to call in and ask questions. The core team lead and the functional consultant would join the meeting and answer any questions that come up. It is important for the session leaders to remain on the call even if no one immediately joins. Any available time between supporting users may be diverted to completing tasks that are suited for starts and stops.

**FIGURE 19.6**
Office hours outline

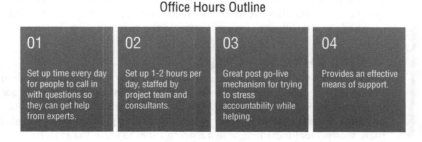

Office Hours Outline

| 01 | 02 | 03 | 04 |
|---|---|---|---|
| Set up time every day for people to call in with questions so they can get help from experts. | Set up 1-2 hours per day, staffed by project team and consultants. | Great post go-live mechanism for trying to stress accountability while helping. | Provides an effective means of support. |

The reason you set it up for 1–2 hours is to give people a window of time to call in. You might be sitting on the call for the first 90 minutes and then someone jumps in with a call at the end because it was the first time during that period when they were free.

This can be done remotely or in person. When it's done in person, there is typically a "war room" set up where all project team members gather, and you invite people to come visit the war room during a period of time. For remote scenarios, you set up a conference call line and then you are ready to help and screen share with the user whenever there is a problem that requires seeing the issue. The remote session is easier in that way because you can very quickly see the user's issue and the functional consultant can use their own machine to look for answers during the session.

We will talk about this concept again when it comes to hypercare as well because it is a great way to open up a line to help users get their questions answered.

## The Bottom Line

**Interactive Sessions**   During the earlier part of the implementation, you will introduce the system to many users during the interactive sessions.

**Master It**   Which of the following is an interactive training session that occurs before formal training begins?

**1.** Discovery

**2.** Conference Room Pilot

**3.** Cutover Plan

**4.** Risk Register

**Training Modalities**   You can deliver training content in three primary ways, and each of the different models has pros and cons.

**Master It**   Which of the following is an example of an asynchronous learning model?

**1.** A Microsoft Teams call with the project team

**2.** In-person training

**3.** Hands-on lab

**4.** Watching recorded eLearning

**Training Time**   As a rule, you should try to hold end user training close to when your users would be using that training. If you train them too far in advance, they may forget how to do the steps by the time they come to use it.

**Master It**   When should users learn the steps to perform periodic activities like month-end close processes?

**1.** Well before training

**2.** Just before training

3. During core training

4. After core training

**Training Validation** It is important to validate that your end users have digested the content from the training. Make sure that you have a mechanism to test what they have learned.

**Master It** Which of the following is not a way that you can validate that someone learned the material about the new system?

1. Asking them to complete a quiz

2. Sending them to a training event

3. One-on-one review session

4. Reviewing output from the system

**Learning Management System** A Learning Management System (LMS) can be a huge help on any implementation project, and I recommend that you investigate and find the right tool for your project.

**Master It** Which of the following is not a benefit of a Learning Management System?

1. Records a Teams meeting

2. Tracks attendance at class

3. Tracks quiz completion after classes

4. Builds learning plans for users or roles

# Chapter 20

# Going Live

Noted philosopher Mike Tyson once said, "Everyone has a plan till they get punched in the face." I think that's a great way of thinking about the process of going live on ERP or CRM software. You spend all of this time planning, and then you have to be ready to bob and weave at the last moment to avoid some unforeseen pitfalls.

   The goal of this chapter is to help you prepare for all of the potential pitfalls and to put you in good position to avoid that punch to the face.

**AFTER YOU COMPLETE THIS CHAPTER, YOU WILL BE ABLE TO DO THE FOLLOWING:**

- ◆ Validate your go-live criteria
- ◆ Develop your cutover checklist
- ◆ Run a mock cutover
- ◆ Test disaster recovery
- ◆ Conduct a go/no-go meeting
- ◆ Execute a successful production or go-live cutover

   This chapter covers the last few weeks of the Deploy stage through the cutover activity or "going live." We will cover how to handle support issues that might arise after you go live in the next chapter—this chapter is all about how to make the cutover process go as smoothly as possible.

## Go-Live Criteria

Long before you get to this stage of the project, you should have established your go-live criteria. Your *go-live criteria* typically combine project readiness with an updated status on outstanding bugs. Figure 20.1 outlines the elements of the go-live criteria.

**FIGURE 20.1**
Elements of the
go-live criteria

Go-Live Criteria

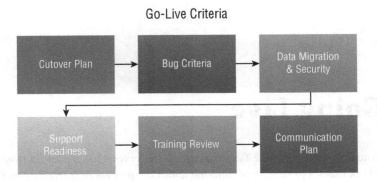

## Cutover Plan

You should have a well-documented and fully vetted *cutover plan* before you are ready to go live. It is the first criterion on your overall go-live criteria, and it should be shared with the project leadership team at the beginning of the Deploy stage. It will often be edited as you go through the Deploy stage, but it should be ready to go at the beginning. The cutover plan is often referred to as the *go-live checklist*. The key deliverables for a successful cutover plan are as follows:

**Cutover Plan**

◆ Documented and agreed upon

◆ Able to be executed in the allotted time (usually a weekend)

◆ Rollback plan documented and staged

◆ Testing complete

The cutover plan should be very granular. I once saw a cutover plan that spanned eight pages in portrait mode with a 14-pt. font—the entire height of a conference door. It is typically an Excel spreadsheet, and it should contain all of the activities that can be done prior to the cutover weekend plus all of the data migration and cutover weekend activities. The data migration activities may be a duplicate of what you're tracking on the data team, but that's okay; I would rather that everyone have visibility into all of the activities that need to occur.

On the plan, make sure to assign each of the activities on the list to the responsible party. Everyone with a task should receive an email with the list of their activities so that they know exactly what they are expected to do and when. Each task would also show any dependent task, so oftentimes you can't complete a task until a prior task has been completed.

The cutover plan should also include a rollback plan. This would indicate all of the steps necessary to revive the old system if you have to switch back to the old system during the cutover weekend.

## Bug Criteria

The bug criteria discussed here are often the most contentious part of the decision to go live. Let's talk through each of these criteria, because the first one is where the gray area may reside.

**All Priority 1 bugs have been resolved.**   Any "showstopper" bugs or bugs that will keep you from completing core functions in the system must be resolved, meaning that the fix has been coded, and it's been successfully tested in the Test environment. This is the one area where you may have to make a call that is not completely based on data. If you have one or a small number of outstanding bugs at the time of the meeting, you will have to make a projection of whether or not they will be resolved in time for you to go live safely. I will typically recommend moving forward if the bugs are code complete at this time. This does not mean that they are ready, but at least it means that they are close, and you can deploy more resources to test and make adjustments between now and go-live.

**All Priority 2 bugs have a plan and agreed-upon timeline for resolution.**   This means those annoying issues that are not preventing you from using the system but slow you down or force you to use workarounds have been evaluated and prioritized in the current or upcoming sprint backlogs. You should know when these issues will be resolved so that you can communicate to the team the length of time where they will have to deal with the error or workaround.

**All process scenarios without open bugs have been signed off by the business process owner.**   This indicates that the business process owner has reviewed and signed off that each of the processes in their purview work as designed. If any open P1 or P2 bugs are there, they will note that they work, with the exception of the bug or bugs.

**All Priority 3 bugs have a post go-live priority ranking.**   This means that those P3 bugs have been logged, and you have sorted them into upcoming sprints based on the priority of those bugs getting completed. Priority 3 bugs are typically bugs that you want to fix (unlike Priority 4 bugs, which is why they are not included in the criteria here), so you should outline the order in which they get fixed. If a Priority 4 doesn't get fixed for 6 months, that's okay— it's not a hindrance to the users, so it shouldn't stop you from going live.

Nearly every implementation has contention around the definition of go-live criteria, and the worst situation occurs when no one looks at the criteria until the *go/no-go meeting* and they want to change the rules. It's important to make sure that the leadership team knows how they will be making their decision. The other problem that frequently arises is the priority definition of the bugs. It's critical that you get alignment from the entire project team on the definitions, and then you also have to establish an arbitrator of the system. If there is a gray area, the project owner and solution architect from the implementer should agree on the status of the bug. Ultimately, the project owner should decide if it is a Priority 1 or Priority 2 bug, but that decision can have a big impact on the project and shouldn't be taken lightly.

## Data Migration and Security Criteria

The list that follows outlines the key *data migration* and security criteria steps. You first want to make sure that all of the steps have been documented and reviewed by the project leadership team, and they should have run through all of these steps in previous iterations to validate that all of the data comes over properly.

**Data Migration and Security Criteria**

◆   Technically validated

◆   Functionally validated

◆ Business validated

◆ Security roles in place and tested

Next, you want to articulate the processes needed to validate the data. The data should be technically and functionally validated and then validated by the business. In the go-live criteria, you would indicate who is responsible for signing off on each of the validation steps, and you should outline the steps that they would take to validate the data.

## Support Readiness

The list that follows identifies the leading three support readiness steps to be mindful of. In Chapter 21, "Hypercare," we talk a lot about the HelpDesk and how the HelpDesk should be ready to take support requests on Day 1 after the cutover. Since they have to be ready by Day 1, you need to go through the steps to get ready for that transition prior to the cutover.

### Support Readiness

◆ HelpDesk ready and trained to handle Tier 1 issues

◆ Project team available for assisting on issues

◆ Users trained on how to access support

You can address this issue in a couple of different ways:

1. You can simply have the project team take the issues that come to the HelpDesk in the first few days after go-live.

2. You can work to educate the HelpDesk team so that they are ready to serve as the first line of defense on support requests on Day 1. Either way, you have work to do to make sure both teams are ready.

As part of the end user training, direct your users to submit tickets to the HelpDesk for any issues they experience in the solution. This will not be their default behavior. They will want to reach out to the people who trained them, and you have to ask those people to actively push those requests to the HelpDesk. You may not think it's a big deal to answer a question or two, but it's really hard to change someone's behavior once they are used to asking the trainer for help.

## Training Review

The list that follows identifies the two trainings for users. You will be managing the go-live criteria at the same time as you go through training, so the training review will be your way of representing progress on the training activities on the go-live scorecard. You should be tracking all of the training for all of the end users on the project and reporting on progress on the training.

### Training Review

◆ Core training completed for all system users

◆ Advanced training schedule for power users

I wouldn't assume that all training activities will go off as planned. You would think that they would, but sometimes a trainer gets sick and is unable to complete the assigned training. At other times, the system isn't ready for training on the scheduled class date. These situations will force you to reschedule training on the fly, which can be difficult to do when you have so much other activity going on.

Make sure that you have a good mechanism to track all of the training and that you are updating it with the results from every class.

## Communication Plan

You should be following the communication plan that you have used throughout the project, but when you get to the Deploy stage, communication becomes even more important. The list that follows states the items to have ready to go. First, you need to communicate with everyone in the company about the go-live date. You should be preparing them for the date and then adjusting if you need to throughout the Deploy stage. You should make sure that all users think through any potential customer impacts of the cutover weekend activities. If you are normally open on a Saturday, you probably have to close on cutover weekend to give yourself more time to complete the cutover activities. That kind of communication is critical to how you serve your customers.

**Communication Plan**

◆   Draft email to the entire company informing them of the cutover

◆   Draft email to project team members outlining project tasks and dependencies

◆   Draft status template to be updated throughout the cutover weekend

You should also be communicating and tracking the activities that your project team members need to complete during these final weeks. Plan to use DevOps, email, or shared spreadsheets to send reminders to the project team on what needs to be done by when. It is helpful to let them know what other tasks are dependent on their tasks, so they know that there is a cascading impact if they don't complete their work on time.

Additionally, the project manager should be in communication with the company leadership team every day throughout the final weeks to let them know if any potential issues could postpone the go-live date. At this point, the whole company is vested in the go-live date, so you need to be ready to communicate any changes as quickly as they are agreed upon.

## Go-Live Scorecard

One great way to keep everyone up-to-speed on the progress toward the go-live is to share a *go-live scorecard* every day during the final weeks before go-live, as shown in Table 20.1. The go-live scorecard would show progress on the key go-live criteria.

**TABLE 20.1:**   Go-Live Scorecard Example

| ACTIVITY | STATUS | NOTES |
|---|---|---|
| Cutover Plan | Green | Done and test |
| P1 bugs | Green | 0 P1 bugs |

**TABLE 20.1:** Go-Live Scorecard Example *(CONTINUED)*

| ACTIVITY | STATUS | NOTES |
|---|---|---|
| P2 bugs | Red | 27 outstanding P2 bugs |
| P3 bugs | Green | |
| Data Migration | Green | |
| Security | Yellow | Bob out of office until Wednesday |
| HelpDesk Readiness | Blue | Plan in place, not yet tested |
| Core Training | Green | |
| Communication | Green | |

The scorecard would show four different colors instead of the three you are used to on the weekly project status report:

**Green**: The work is done and signed-off.

**Yellow**: The work is not yet done, and it's veering offtrack.

**Red**: The work is not yet done, and there is an issue that must be managed.

**Blue**: (The new color) means the work is ready but has not yet been done. The project team should feel comfortable if the color blue shows on the scorecard, but it's important to distinguish between work that is done and work that is yet to be done, so that's why you have the additional color.

Send out this scorecard every day between the end of UAT and the go/no-go meeting, and the team will be well informed about the status of the project and any issues that require immediate attention.

## Mock Cutover and Final Week Activities

The *mock cutover* is a simulated cutover that occurs the week before, or a few weeks before, your official go-live weekend. In the mock cutover, you go through all of the steps that you would go through during the real cutover, but you clear everything out when you're done so that the Production environment remains clean and ready for the production cutover.

The mock cutover is run in your Production environment. Make sure to follow your cutover checklist so that you can validate if you have everything properly documented. This is the best way to test that you will be ready for the production cutover by running through everything. Don't be alarmed if you find issues in the mock cutover; it's designed to find these issues.

During the cutover process, you want to track the time that it takes you to run each activity within the cutover. You track this so you have an estimate of how long each activity will take during your production cutover. You want to have the cutover checklist pulled up, and you want to be ready to edit it as you move along. Anytime you find something out of order or confusing in the cutover checklist, change it so that it can be in very good shape when you are ready for the real thing.

At the end of the mock cutover, test in the new system so that you can validate the data, beginning balances, and processes in the system. The more testing and validation that you can do now will help you find issues that would've been a bigger problem when you do your production cutover.

At the end of the process, conduct a meeting with all parties involved to collect feedback from the mock cutover and update the schedule and any documentation that you need for the production cutover. Your intent is to walk out of that meeting with everyone feeling confident about go-live weekend. If any major issues occurred during the mock cutover, you either have to scramble to resolve them quickly or you need to tell the project team that you won't be able to go live because of them. The latter really shouldn't happen, but if it does, you have to be honest with everyone and do the best thing for the business.

## Disaster Recovery

You don't necessarily have to save this step for the last week, but I think it's a great idea to test forms of disaster recovery before you go live. In the on-premise world, you would have to test restoring from a backup that is located onsite or offsite, depending on your process. This process is typically very time-consuming, depending on the amount of data in your system.

For cloud systems like Microsoft Dynamics, the way that you would test this is to restore a backup of the previous system. You would create a backup (or better yet, use one of the backups auto-generated by the system) and restore that backup over your production instance. Each product will vary slightly in how that works, but if you can do that, you will know it can work if you have to do it in production some day in the future. Let's hope that you never have to use this skill, but it's important to be comfortable restoring from a backup.

## System Setup Before Cutover

The team may not realize it, but there is a lot that you can do in your Production environment before you go live. Take the week between your last mock cutover and your production cutover to get as much of this work done as possible. Here are several things that you can have done ahead of cutover weekend, so you don't have to take the time to do them when you are under pressure for time:

- Set up all of your users in Dynamics
- Install and configure any ISV solutions
- Enter any manual configurations
- Set up all of your companies
- Create your connections to any integrated systems to make sure that you can pass data back and forth

If you are not planning any code changes in the last week, you can pre-set a lot of the code in the empty, new system as well, like the following:

- Apply security roles
- Bring in the production code
- Import, restore, or enter reference data
- Import, restore, or enter master data

You can make it so that you don't have much to do besides migrate data and validate the system during the production cutover weekend.

# Go/No-Go Meetings

I like to say that you should either have a "go" meeting or shouldn't have a "go/no-go meeting." It is pretty defeating for the project team to receive a sentence of no-go, and the project managers and leaders should be able to recognize if they are not ready for the production cutover. If the project leaders can see that several criteria that are required to go live have not been met, you should postpone your go/no-go meeting and schedule one for when you are going to be ready.

## When to Have It

This is tricky—you want to have the go/no-go meeting as close as possible to the actual cutover because you want to give your project team time to resolve the issues that came up during UAT and end user training. If you schedule your go/no-go meeting right after UAT, you will likely have several P1 bugs that are not resolved and then you put the decision makers in a difficult position of guessing whether those bugs will be resolved before go-live. On the other hand, if you schedule the go/no-go meeting the day before cutover, the entire company is expecting to go live the next day, and if you put the brakes on then, that has a huge impact on the confidence in the project team, and it makes everyone scramble to change dates to the new timeline.

The best way to approach this is to be talking about the go-live criteria all throughout the project, especially toward the end. When you go into the Deploy stage, you should take a hard look at how you are progressing toward go-live, and if you don't believe that you can make the date, you should push it back to a later date. You should be looking at your project backlog versus your resource allocation throughout the project and adjusting dates whenever you see that you won't make it. It always looks bad to move back a go-live date, but if you do it early in the project, the broader company will not be as fixated on the fact that you had to move it back in the eleventh hour.

When you get to the Deploy stage, look at the calendar of events and try to set your go/no-go meeting about 10 days before the release. I like to have it on the Thursday ahead of the last mock cutover weekend, which is one week before the go-live cutover. That gives you enough time to fix the key issues that arose during UAT and end user training, and this gives you enough time to inform the team and change the game plan if the answer is "no." As I said in the header of this section, if the project leaders know that they are going to get a "no" answer from leadership, they should communicate that this is no longer a go/no-go meeting, but a replanning meeting to figure out when you can go live.

## Voting Criteria

A few days in advance of the go/no-go meeting, send out a summary of the current project status as well as a guide on how to vote in the upcoming meeting. Highlight the purpose of the go/no-go meeting, which is "To determine if the go-live criteria have been completed and a clear schedule is established that assures a successful go-live for the project." Then you should lay out the three options from which the voters can choose at the meeting:

**Go** By voting this way, the voter is saying "I believe it's in our best interest to move forward with the project timeline as reviewed with me understanding that there are risks."

**Go with caveats**   The voter is saying "I believe it's in our best interest to move forward, but there are one or more items that must be completed to my satisfaction by a given deadline before I would agree to give an unconditional go."

**No go**   The voter is saying "I do not believe that the success criteria have been met, or there is significant risk that could lead to the current launch timing potentially harming the business."

If people choose "go with caveats," the caveats must be objective and provable. The voter must be satisfied that the item is completed to agree to move forward. The number of caveats to go live must be few (like 2–3 at most). If there are more than three caveats, the voter should vote "no go."

If the meeting is held 10 days before the cutover date, you should challenge the "go with caveats" vote, because there is not a lot of time before the system must be fully ready. The "go with caveats" option is mostly intended when you have two or more weeks before the cutover date.

## Meeting Agenda

At the go/no-go meeting, the agenda should be simple and straight-forward. You want to review the criteria, give an update on the project status and outstanding bugs, and ask for the leadership team to vote. Table 20.2 is a go/no-go meeting agenda outline.

You should invite the core team leads to the meeting as well, as often the leadership team will ask them for their opinion on the state of the project. They don't get a vote, but they can very heavily influence the decisions of their leaders with their opinions.

**TABLE 20.2:**   Go/No-Go Meeting Agenda

| TOPIC | TIME ALLOTMENT |
|---|---|
| Review the Go-Live Criteria | 5 minutes |
| Review the Current Status of the Project Against the Go-Live Criteria | 10 minutes |
| Discuss Outstanding Bugs | 20 minutes |
| Vote | 20 minutes |
| Next Steps | 5 minutes |

During the meeting, you don't go through every possible bug on the project, but you highlight any P1s and then summarize the state of the P2 issues. If you know that there is an issue the users will see, even if it's just an annoyance, I find it helpful to bring it up in the meeting so that leadership knows that the project team understands it and is tracking it to resolution.

## Order and Outcome of the Votes

I typically organize the voting so that the business process owner or VP of the most affected area of the business votes first. This should be the operational leader like the COO, VP of

Manufacturing, VP of Sales, and so forth. Then you go in order with the next affected operational leaders. Once the affected operational leaders have voted, you go to the CFO or leading administrative resource. After that, the IT leader votes and then any of the unaffected leadership team members. You put them last because you don't want their less-informed position to impact the decision to go live on the system.

The final vote is the CEO or equivalent. This is the only vote that really matters, as they can decide whatever they want based on the feedback and don't have to follow the voters who came before. I don't like to see a CEO overturn the vote of the other leaders, so they should generally go along with the consensus. If there is one "no" voter along the way, the CEO should vote "yes," unless the case made by that voter is compelling enough to know it will harm the business.

Whatever decision is made by the CEO (or equivalent), everyone must fall in line and support that decision even if they don't like it.

### Next Steps

Immediately after the go/no-go meeting, the project manager should send out a broad communication with the decision and the next steps. If the decision is a "go," the mock cutover should move forward, and all of the final-week activities should go on as scheduled. If the decision is a "no," you send out a communication that the go-live date has been postponed so that specific activity related to the cutover should stop but all other bug-fixing activity should continue.

## Live Cutover

No one will say it at the time, but the project team typically enjoys cutover weekend. It is a lot of work and it can often mean late nights, but the result is that all of your effort is about to pay off.

The events of the live cutover should be scheduled with estimated time for each task. (Most cutovers happen over a weekend, so for my examples, I will explain the timing as if it's happening over a weekend. If you have a shorter window, you will have to adjust accordingly.) You start by identifying the time at which you start the cutover, and then you schedule blocks of time for the next steps to run throughout the weekend. You should focus on kicking off long-running processes on Friday night so that they can run throughout the evening, and you should set a time on Sunday when you would make the call to roll the system back if you won't be ready for Monday morning.

### Go-Live Weekend Criteria

- Turn off previous system at the designated time on Friday.

- Run through all of the steps of the go-live checklist and move to production.

- Work through issues as they arise.

- If any process takes too long, be prepared to revert to the old system.

- Bring core team leads and subject matter experts in to test on Sunday before the normal start of business.

## Impact of the Cutover Start Timing

As soon as you start the cutover, this means that you can no longer use your current system. If you are importing open transactions into the new system, you shouldn't be entering new data into the old system after you chose to start the migration effort. You will also want to run any final routines needed in your old system, like posting inventory, accounts receivable, and accounts payable. Plan to run reports across the business so that you can validate your opening balances after the migration is complete.

You should set the timing of the cutover to begin at the end of the business day on Friday. Whenever the majority of the activity should be done, that should be your start time. You *must* communicate this timing to the company as a whole, because the users will not be able to access the old system after that time. From a system standpoint, disable access to the old system at that time and then initiate your data migration activities from there.

## Completing Cutover Activities

Once the old system is shut down, the real work begins. You start with getting a backup of the old system and the clean, empty Dynamics system, and then you get busy with the remainder of your cutover activities. You will need to import, restore, or enter your configurations into the new system, connect any integrations that need to be done, and start migrating data. The data migration process typically takes the longest during the weekend, so you want to make sure that's been kicked off before the team goes to bed on Friday night. Remember, you have to extract, transform, and load that data, and each of those processes may take a considerable amount of time.

Once the data is in Dynamics, you may have to run a series of routines in your Production environment to make sure that your beginning balances are accurate and you're ready to validate the data between the system. Depending on what modules of the product you are using, you may have to run aged trial balances, run MRP, run fixed asset depreciation, or any number of common ERP periodic activities so that the system is ready for Monday.

At the end of all of those activities, it's time to test. You start by running your automated regression tests wherever possible. Next, you validate all of your beginning balances to make sure that the data in your new system matches your previous system. Then you run through the core functions in the system and make sure that you can perform all of the critical activities. You'll want to invite many of the subject matter experts to test the system so that you can get as much feedback as possible, and also so that your users feel good about how the system will work when all of the end users log in on Monday.

You may discover new bugs or data issues during the process. If you have data issues, you want to work with the data team and the subject matter experts to clean up those issues in real time. If you have bugs, you need to classify them by priority so that you know what impact that will have on the continuation of the go live. If you find any P2, P3, or P4 bugs, you will log them, and the project team will triage them and assign remediation activities on Monday or during the next week. If you find a P1 bug, you have a difficult decision to make. You can see if you can get someone to hotfix the issue right then and there, but if you do, it has to pass through the Build, Test, and UAT environment before it can be moved to production, and you may not have enough time to complete all of those steps. Your other two options are as follows:

◆ Live with it in production until you can run a proper hotfix release.

◆ Roll back the system and go live at another time.

Postponing go-live this late in the game is a really tough decision, and you only want to take that step if you fear the problem may damage data in the system. If it's a case where someone can't do a return or a frequent process doesn't work, you can probably live without doing it for a day or two. If the system is incorrectly tracking data, you may have a major data cleanup mess on your hands or you could be presenting your customers with incorrect data. You don't want either of those situations, so at that point, you'd have to postpone the go-live.

### Rollback Plan

Going into the go-live weekend, have a time in the schedule where you would have to roll back the release if you are not getting the work needed in time to be ready in the new system on Monday morning. I typically recommend setting a time like Sunday at 4 p.m.—if you aren't done with your cutover activities by then, you should really evaluate if you will be done in time for the curtains to come up Monday morning.

If you are in the unenviable position of having to roll back to your previous system, you end up treating this cutover similarly to the mock cutover that you ran before. You restore the backup that you took right before you started the cutover activity, and you turn your old system back on. If you have to run any activities in your old system to get it working again, you should have that documented so that you can use that system.

You will need to communicate to the company that the cutover was unsuccessful and indicate when you plan to attempt it again.

### Acknowledge the Team

At the end of all the testing and cutover activities, have a communication ready to go out (preferably from the CEO or the executive sponsor) highlighting all of the great work the team has done and sharing that the system is live and ready for production use on Monday morning.

The company leadership should take time to acknowledge and appreciate the work that was done by the project team. It's not over yet because you still have to fight through the hypercare period that's coming next, but this was a huge project, and the team should be rewarded for their persistence to make it to a successful go-live.

## The Bottom Line

**Go-Live Checklist**   Your go-live or cutover checklist shows all of the activity that must be completed during the weekend when you go live.

**Master It**   Which of the following is not on your go-live checklist?

1. Configuration work

2. Security work

3. Data migration activities

4. A project plan

**Go-Live Scorecard**   A go-live scorecard is a report that goes out every day during the final stages of the project indicating the status of the go-live criteria items.

   **Master It**   What does the color blue mean on a go-live scorecard?

   **1.** Something that is on track but hasn't been done yet

   **2.** Something that is offtrack

   **3.** Something that is done, but you want to highlight or talk further

   **4.** Something that is at risk of going offtrack

**Mock Cutover**   The mock cutover is a simulated cutover that happens a week or so before you do the production cutover.

   **Master It**   When doing a mock cutover, you should deploy everything to which environment?

   **1.** UAT

   **2.** Production

   **3.** Development

   **4.** Test

**Go/No-Go Meeting**   The go/no-go meeting is the official decision-making forum where the company's leadership team decides if you will be going live on schedule.

   **Master It**   Which of the following is not an option that you can vote on in a go/no-go meeting?

   **1.** Go

   **2.** Decide later

   **3.** Go with caveats

   **4.** No-go

**Go-Live Criteria**   The go-live criteria includes several elements, but the bug count is typically the most contentious. You should agree about the criteria in advance of the Deploy stage to reduce concerns during the final days before go-live.

   **Master It**   When going live, which priority-level bugs must be zero?

   **1.** Priority 1

   **2.** Priority 2

   **3.** Priority 3

   **4.** Priority 1 and Priority 2

# Chapter 21

# Hypercare

If you Google *hypercare*, the top results tell you it's an antiperspirant that works by affecting the cells that produce sweat. This chapter is not about an antiperspirant.

Hypercare is a term that is not universally adopted in the business application implementations world, but I am seeing it more and more. Some partners just call it post-go-live support, and some don't call it anything other than regular support. You should not transition to regular support on Day 1 after go-live.

I define *hypercare* as the period of time (4–8 weeks) immediately following a system go-live where an elevated level of support is available to ensure the seamless adoption of a new system. That's what we'll talk about in this chapter—that period of time shortly after go-live where the project team really needs to work together to make sure that you have a smooth landing to the project.

## AFTER YOU COMPLETE THIS CHAPTER, YOU WILL BE ABLE TO DO THE FOLLOWING:

- ◆ Address issues resulting from the go-live activities

- ◆ Work through the top issues after your first few weeks live on the system

- ◆ Conduct an emergency hotfix release

- ◆ Support the team on the first month-end close

- ◆ Ensure a smooth transition to support and future enhancements

Hypercare is a time of change—the way the project team acts during Day 1 after go-live is very different than how they will act at the end of hypercare. You should set up a plan that outlines expected project team activity for each week of the defined hypercare period.

## Go-Live Support

The goal of hypercare is to provide a great go-live support experience for your end users and to transition the project into the long-term support stage we call the *Empower stage*. Your users will be very nervous on Day 1 of the new system, so you want to give them the best experience possible to help them adapt to this big change.

## Day 1

The first day after go-live can be the most important. You want to have all hands on deck ready to support the team as they use the new system for the first time in production. This means that you want to have your project team and key subject matter experts spread out among your locations and ready to assist with questions and issues as they arise. Your team will have to do a lot of coaching and remind the users of the training during that first day. I'm sure that you will experience some unforeseen user questions, so you'll have to huddle up with other project team members to know how best to handle that situation. It's generally chaos on Day 1, and your goal is to make it through it with your users comfortable in the new system.

---

### WAR ROOM

I mentioned it briefly earlier in the book, but one logistical practice that you can do to help your project is to dedicate a room to your ERP or CRM implementation team. This is often called a *war room*. This would be a room with seating for eight or more, which has conference call capabilities and some whiteboards to allow you to keep key items on the board.

The key to the success of the room is that it is dedicated full time to the implementation team, so that includes the partner and your project team. The room cannot be scheduled for any other purpose, and the room isn't intended to hold meetings—it's intended to be a workspace for people who need to work either by themselves or collaboratively with another project team member.

The reason I bring this up now is that a war room becomes even more important during the first few weeks after go-live. This is where the project team sits and awaits any issues that come their way. By sitting together, the team can quickly agree on the priority of an issue and work collaboratively to solve it. Any core team member or subject matter expert knows where to go if they have an issue that needs immediate attention.

---

Common issues on Day 1 include security problems. You frequently see users try to access part of the system unsuccessfully because they weren't provided with the right authorization. Those issues should be easy to fix, and you should have your technical team on the ready to resolve those issues quickly. You will get many how-to questions, and that's normal and expected behavior. Try to contain your frustration with users who ask a question that was covered in training; you are asking them to learn a lot, and they won't be able to digest everything they learned in training.

## Week 1

For the remainder of Week 1, the plan of attack is similar to Day 1—you want your project team members spread out and supporting the users as quickly as possible. You want to direct issues to the HelpDesk so that you can test out the HelpDesk processes to make sure that they are working well.

Another thing that you should do during Week 1 is to set up advanced training sessions. After the chaos of Day 1, the users should start to get comfortable doing the standard activities in the system. Once they have a good grasp of those processes, you want to teach them advanced concepts, as discussed in Chapter 19, "Training for All." This is when you teach the return process or advanced inventory transfers, bank reconciliation, and other processes that not every user does every day. Users will digest this information much more easily once they have a chance to repeat the standard process a few times.

## Project Change Champions

In Chapter 7, "Change Management Throughout Your Project," we talked about change management and how important it is to the success of your project. The first week is a critical time for the long-term success of the project. If users struggle and don't get support, or they don't understand why they are doing different things in the system, they will lose faith in the system and it will be incredibly hard to convert them back into system advocates.

I recommend that the project team members identify certain subject matter experts to serve as project change champions. These are people who know the system well, understand the process changes, and have a positive attitude toward the impact Week 1 will have on your business. You should identify a champion in each process area and ask them to address their team and be visible to them when questions arise. They can help reinforce the message from leadership and greatly increase the chance of system adoption.

Users will have as many "why" questions as they have "what" questions when it comes to the new system. They will have been through training about the new processes and how they work, but they won't really understand the system until they have to use it. It becomes very real when they have a customer in front of them and they now have to navigate this new system quickly and efficiently so that they don't disappoint their customer. That's when the stress is high, and users can turn against the system if that experience doesn't go well. Help them understand the reason for the process change so that they can internalize how the new system works and provide their customer with a great experience. *If* they can do that, they will become an advocate of the new system.

## Prioritizing Issues

In Chapter 18, "Testing," we outlined the priority levels and provided sample priority definitions. That same need exists after go-live; you will need to prioritize each bug or work effort that is required. Use the same definition that you used before go-live so that the user community knows what to expect.

Typically, P1 issues indicate that the system is down or that a major function cannot be performed in the system and therefore it requires immediate action to remedy the problem. This often leads to a hotfix release, which we'll discuss later in the chapter. Just know that any P1 issues will require all relevant resources to help get the issue resolved quickly.

P2 issues are typically resolved with the next scheduled release, so you would try to schedule releases on a 2- or 4-week basis in the beginning to make sure that you are attacking these annoying issues quickly. Once the system has stabilized, you can move out your regular release cycle. When you do, you won't have your P2 issues fixed as quickly, but hopefully there are very few of them.

P3 and P4 issues may linger for a while after go-live, as they will be prioritized for scheduled releases once the team has completed P1 and P2 issues. It has been my experience that P3 issues are unlikely to get into production during the first 6–12 weeks after go-live. Once you have stability in the system, you will start to see the P3s get resolved. P4 issues are rarely resolved; they typically rot in your product backlog unless something changes that improves their priority rating.

What happens when you can't agree on a prioritization? You want to make sure that your definition is as black and white as possible to avoid any potential conflicts on prioritization, but even with perfect definitions, there will still be conflicts. Ultimately, it's the project owner's job to rule on the priority, but you should know that if the partner doesn't agree, they may respond with a less than full-time effort if they don't think it's a P1 issue. If your partner doesn't agree on your priority level, you will have to escalate to their engagement manager or executive sponsor to gain agreement. Hopefully, everyone will be able to see and understand the intent of the prioritization language so that you can spend time fixing the issues and not arguing over definitions.

## Weeks 2–4

The issues and questions certainly don't go away after Week 1, but they should slowly start to decrease, and you need to take that time to start moving toward a sustainable support process. I don't recommend that you send the project team to all of the different sites on Week 2, as it's a good time to see how users do working on their own. If any sites didn't have a project team member onsite in Week 1, you can send someone there for Week 2. In Week 2, you want users submitting support incidents to the HelpDesk and receiving strong responses quickly. That gives users a better chance to get comfortable handling issues on their own.

Week 3 and Week 4 are a continuation of the trend that you tried to establish in Week 2. You should continue to decrease your onsite presence as you continue to focus on strong responses from your HelpDesk. You may now be encountering more complex issues, so you may need to send resources out to help with advanced issues that didn't come up during Week 1.

By Week 3 or Week 4, you will start to identify those users who are really catching on to the new system and those who are struggling. At that point, you want to reward those people who adapted well, and you want to figure out a support plan for those who are struggling. If users are struggling, you should look to pair them up with a peer who is doing well. Alternatively, you may ask a project team member to spend extra time with those users to get them comfortable. If you ignore problems with users during this time, you risk leaving them behind or creating a wave of negativity in your user base and neither of those is a good outcome.

## First Month End

The first month end after an ERP implementation can be one of the most chaotic times. You may feel like the implementation is going well, but when month end comes around, you have to make sure that your numbers tie out, so you are typically looking for every transaction to be entered accurately. Unfortunately, that is unlikely to occur. It is common that you catch transactional errors at month end, which can be quite time-consuming to fix. You want to fix them now because you want to prevent them from ever happening again.

The other challenge with month end is that it will be the first time you will be tying out the books in the new system. Most accountants have common reports that they use to tie out their books, and they often can adjust transactions in the system quickly because they know the system well. In the new system, the reconciliation process can take a lot longer due to lack of familiarity with the system. From a training perspective, it is common that either there was no training on month-end processes, or it happened before you went live, so you don't remember it now.

If not handled correctly, the first month end can shake confidence in the system. You should certainly expect that the first month end will take a lot longer than your typical close time frame.

If you usually close the books five business days after month end, you should expect it to take 10 days on the first month end. It will gradually improve from there, but you don't want to set too aggressive a timeline on an unfamiliar process.

Let's look at some ways to prepare for month end so that it goes as smoothly as possible:

♦ Set expectations that month-end close will not be complete in the typical amount of time. Give yourself another week beyond the typical time period for the first month-end close.

♦ Train the team on the month-end close process the week before it happens. You want to make sure that the accounting team is trained on month-end procedures, but you want to conduct that training close to when they use the system so that they have had some time in the system, and they remember what's been taught.

♦ Do weekly bank reconciliations during hypercare to get used to tying out discrepancies. You can use these bank reconciliations as a test run of the month-end close. Use this as a way to get familiar with cleaning up errors in the system; this also helps you to have fewer issues to deal with in the end.

♦ Ask the partner to have a financial resource available with month-end close experience. This would be a good time to make sure that you have someone who's been through this process multiple times at the ready to help through the unfamiliar processes.

♦ Plan for your partner's resources to be onsite with your accounting team and any other subledger teams that need to close their books. It is a good time to hand-hold through the month-end close process and then to get ready for the hand-off to support.

♦ Getting through that first month end in the new system can raise the confidence of the entire team, so plan ahead and make it successful. With the capability of the Microsoft Dynamics system, you will likely have an easier time doing your month-end close processes once you get the hang of it.

### Duration of Hypercare

The length of hypercare corresponds to the type of project and the complexity of the new system. Any ERP project is going to require hypercare to last through the first month end because that is your time to test tying out all of the activity from the first month. A small ERP project could have a two-week hypercare with a bonus week of coverage for the first month end. An enterprise ERP project will necessitate a six-week hypercare period to cover the initial change and the first month end. If this is the first company that goes live with many others to go on the same system, you may want to extend your hypercare to 12 weeks. If you are a public company, you don't want to go live on a quarterly reporting date, so you might run a 12-week hypercare to get through your first quarterly reporting date.

# Role of HelpDesk

As with everything on the project, the more that you can plan ahead, the better off you will be. Just imagine if you are six months after go-live and your users are all still going to your project team members with every little question and problem they have related to Microsoft Dynamics. This is not a reality that you want as this is not a process—it's what happens in the absence of a process.

Most every company has a HelpDesk process by which their users submit support incidents on any and all issues that they encounter with any of the software or hardware used in the business. If you don't have a HelpDesk process, you should have one before you go live with Microsoft Dynamics. When incidents flow to the HelpDesk, you can build a process and set expectations with your users on how to submit incidents, when to expect a response, and how best to resolve those incidents. If issues flow to the project team, there will be different preferences on how the team wants to receive incidents, different response times depending on who you ask, and no process for how to escalate issues if the person contacted can't resolve the issue. You want to have a clear and consistent process so that your users know what to expect.

To accomplish this, direct users to the HelpDesk on Day 1 after go-live. By doing so, you establish the habit that you want to see continue in the long run. Most companies don't dictate this process right after go-live, which leaves all of their users scrambling to find a power user who can help them. Once you decide to make the official transition to the HelpDesk, they now have to change yet again. Use your HelpDesk right away and make it a great experience from Day 1; you will be far better off in the future.

## Sample SLA

A *service level agreement (SLA)* is a contractual term that has become synonymous with the expected response time for an incident logged with a support team. This is how you set expectations with your team on how quickly they should receive a response from the HelpDesk. The longer the expected response, the less your users will want to use the process. If you tell them that their incident will receive a response within one week, users will reach out to your project team and circumvent the process that you tried to establish.

The reason why it's called a service level agreement is that there is typically a penalty of some sort for missing the response-time target. If you say the SLA is two hours but you only respond to 25 percent of incidents in that time frame, users will be frustrated and circumvent the process. On one side, you can't make the SLA too long, but on the other side, you can't make it so short that it's not achievable. You have to find the happy medium that will keep the users satisfied and set your team up to be successful.

I strongly recommend that you set up two or more SLAs based on the priority of the issue. If the issue is critical in the eyes of the user, they would like to get an answer right away. Perhaps you set a one-hour response time for critical issues, and you suggest that users call a staffed phone line to get help if they believe the issue to be critical. You may set an important level where the issue is time-sensitive, but not a system-down-level issue. For that, you should set a four-hour SLA. For all other issues, you could set an eight-hour SLA. With each of these SLAs in place, you can be responsive to the most important issues without over-burdening your HelpDesk and escalation team.

This is just an example SLA—you need to determine the right timelines for your user base. If you have users in the system 24/7, you will need to make sure that you either staff the HelpDesk all of the time, or you set different response-time expectations if the issue is submitted in the middle of the night.

## Project Team Support

Many companies ask their core team leads and key subject matter experts to be the front-line support after go-live. You should dedicate their time to support just after go-live until the issues stabilize. The problem comes when you skip the HelpDesk process and users seek out the project team member they know the best and ask them for support. I'll discuss how to break that cycle shortly.

I said that you should dedicate your project team's time to support but you shouldn't have users contact them directly, so how should you use these well-trained resources? You should have them take incidents from the HelpDesk. Train them on HelpDesk procedures and give them access to your HelpDesk tool so that they can help you tackle the issues that arise. This benefits you in two ways:

◆ It reinforces the behavior you want where users submit incidents to the HelpDesk.

◆ It allows you to provide fast and good responses because your experts are dedicated to the HelpDesk so that they can jump on incidents right away and resolve them quickly.

---

### SHOULD YOU SEND YOUR USERS OUT TO YOUR LOCATIONS JUST AFTER GO-LIVE?

Yes. Absolutely. Your project team should be in one of two places the week after go-live—either onsite at one of your locations where your users are using the system for the first time or in the war room with the rest of the project team. You want your project team members to be close to your users so that they can help answer questions in real time. Even if your training plan is perfect, your users will have questions, and they'll make mistakes when they first use the system in production. Invariably, some customer will ask for something that no one considered during the implementation, and you will have to figure out on the fly the best way to do that in the system. It won't be easy, but it will happen. If your users can ask a resource sitting behind them how to handle that request, they will feel supported and be much more open to the change.

If your project team is spread out all over the place, won't that invite users to circumvent the HelpDesk and ask them questions directly? Yes, it certainly encourages users to ask the project team member sitting behind them rather than submitting an incident to the HelpDesk. Here's how you handle that. If it's a how-to question that the project team member can answer, they should answer that question and not log the incident. There's no sense in creating unnecessary administrative overhead there. If the incident is beyond the knowledge of the project team member or it's a bug, the project team member should tell the user to log a ticket with the HelpDesk. Even if it's something that project team member can ultimately tackle, you now have a record of the incident, and you get the user used to the process that you want them to follow long-term.

---

## Support Levels

Not all incidents that come to the HelpDesk are the same. You will get some very basic how-to questions, and you will get some really challenging bugs that your front-line HelpDesk team will not be able to resolve. One of the keys to success for a HelpDesk is to build an escalation path where you can pass incidents from Level 1 all the way up to Level 4 to get the help you need to resolve the issue. Many incidents will be beyond the scope and training of the front-line team, so you need to have a process for escalating those issues to the best resource to resolve it.

The support process typically has four levels. Incidents always start at Level or Tier 1 and then they only progress to the next tier if they can't be resolved at the current tier.

Figure 21.1 shows the progression between the tiers for HelpDesk issues.

**FIGURE 21.1**
HelpDesk ticket
progression

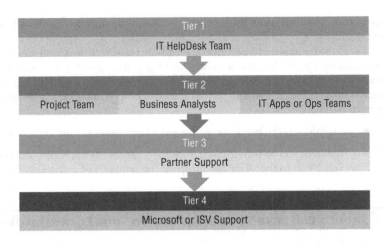

Let's talk through each of these levels in greater detail:

**Tier 1**: This is your front-line HelpDesk team that should be staffed at all times. This team will handle any incident that comes up for any IT product or any computer-related problem. This is typically staffed by members of your IT team, but if you don't have an IT team, you may use a managed service provider (an outside vendor) as your front-line HelpDesk. You may not want to pay a vendor to help with your ERP or CRM issues in a front-line support capacity, but you should use them if that's the practice you use for the rest of your business. The front-line team should have a knowledge base and sufficient system access to handle basic and routine issues. If you have a team who can handle more than that, that's great, but it would be out of the ordinary.

**Tier 2**: This is where your project team members jump in to help take on support incidents. The front-line team will use the tools at their disposal to try to resolve the incident, but if they can't, they will reach out to the project team members—typically the core team leads—to ask them to help resolve the incident. If the problem is due to security or performance, they may escalate it to the IT Operations team. In the first few weeks after go-live, most incidents will need to be escalated past Tier 1; in fact, you may want to have your project team look at the issues first because it's unlikely that the front-line team will be able to provide value. You still want to make sure that the front-line team is trained, though, so you want to share any resolutions that you think may be common so that they can take them the next time. The project team member will diagnose the incident and work on it until they reach a point where they have an answer, or they know they won't be able to resolve it.

**Tier 3**: Once the Tier 2 team has agreed that they cannot resolve the incident, they will reach out to their implementation partner for assistance. Again, during the first week or two after go-live, the partner may have resources watching the queue for any incidents that come in just to help provide a quick resolution to any issue. That is a speed versus cost decision you will need to make. The partner's project team or support team will look at the incident, trouble-shoot it, and see if they can resolve it. If they can, they will communicate the resolution back through the core team and the HelpDesk, so you understand what needed to occur to resolve the incident. They have two paths if they cannot resolve the incident:

◆ If it is a bug with a customization, it is something that the partner can resolve. In this case, it goes on the bug list and is prioritized appropriately. If it's a P1 bug, it is a candidate for a hotfix release. If it's a P2 bug, it would likely be scheduled for the next enhancement release. If it's a P3 or P4 bug, it may not be scheduled at all. Nonetheless, the partner should respond with the priority level and the estimated time to resolution.

◆ If it isn't something that they can fix, it is likely a bug with Microsoft or ISV code, and it moves to Tier 4.

**Tier 4**: If you've reached the end of the escalation path, at this point the partner will submit an incident to Microsoft or the ISV, and you will have to work with them on the expected resolution time frame. You may be in for a long wait in this case depending on the priority assigned by the software provider and their next release. If it's truly a P1 issue, you will likely have to tap your executive sponsor to call Microsoft or the ISV to relay the urgency to the software vendor.

The process of escalating issues all the way up to Tier 4 can take longer than you would like. It's important for everyone on the project team to understand the escalation path and for you to make a decision on how much time you want the project team to dedicate to support incidents during hypercare, and if you are willing to pay for your partner's team to be on call for any incidents that arise just after go-live.

I recommend that you overstaff your HelpDesk during the first week to three weeks after go-live. You want to be sure that your users have a good impression of the new system, and if they can't get an answer quickly, they will be frustrated. You will get a lot of incidents right away and if you establish a good track record of response time and quality, the user base will feel better about the system because they know that support is a priority.

As you think about your HelpDesk strategy, make sure that you build metrics into your HelpDesk tracking system, which keeps track of how many incidents move between the levels. You want to try to limit the amount of incidents that flow to Tier 3 and Tier 4 (due to cost and time constraints), so make sure that your team is well educated on the system to reduce the number of incidents that have to be escalated beyond your walls.

## Refer Users to Training

The goal is for your users to be as self-sufficient as possible. The better they know the system, the more they will like it and the fewer support incidents they will raise. It is a great idea for the HelpDesk team to put the onus back on the users to learn the system. When the HelpDesk sees an opportunity, they should ask users to review the training content in the area where the incident occurred. If you users who struggle with concepts repeatedly, reach out to their manager to recommend that the user take the training again. The best systems are ones where users take ownership of their area of the system, so you want to encourage that as much as you can.

## Making the Transition to HelpDesk Later

Eventually, you need to point your users to reach out to the HelpDesk with any issue they encounter in the new system. If you don't listen to my earlier advice and you have everyone go to the project team directly, you will have to make the transition to HelpDesk later. If you do it later, you will need to break the habit that people have developed of going to their friend or colleague to get their questions answered. This is a difficult habit to break, so let's talk about some ways that you can help make the transition.

**Send the project team members away on vacation.**   First, you should be doing this anyway because they have worked extremely hard for a long, long time. They need a break, and this break can serve as an opportunity to retrain the team. There's no better way to force change than to take away the people the users are relying on.

**Push the project team members to point users to the HelpDesk.**   No one likes to say "Sorry, I can't help you." The only way to break this habit is to ask the project team to tell the users that they can't help them without a HelpDesk ticket. You can also provide project team members with a canned email to send back anytime they get an email request for help. This way, they don't have to worry about the messaging to the users each time they receive a request for help.

**Refuse to answer questions submitted to the project team.**   If option 1 and option 2 don't work, you will need to get to the point where the project team refuses to answer questions posed to them directly. It's hard, but you have to have structure with any incidents that come in. Your project team members will never be free to get back to their day jobs if they always have an obligation to tackle any system-related questions.

I won't go into all of the best practices around how to run an efficient HelpDesk, as that is beyond the scope of this book. If you have an efficient HelpDesk in place today, you should plug your new Microsoft Dynamics system into that process and supplement it in the early days to make sure that your responses are fast and accurate. If you don't have an efficient HelpDesk in place today, you should reach out to an expert to help you establish one before you get to hypercare.

## Post Go-Live Releases

In Chapter 17, "Environment Management and Deployments," I introduced Table 17.1, outlining the four different types of releases that you will do on a Microsoft Dynamics implementation. I've cross referenced this information in Table 21.1. The first two (lower environment and production go-live) have been done now, so it's time to focus on the post go-live releases, the hotfix release, and the enhancement release.

**TABLE 21.1:**   Implementation Releases

| RELEASE TYPES | RELEASE FREQUENCY |
| --- | --- |
| **Lower Environment** | **Definition**: Moving code to Test or UAT, or a production move before you're ready to go live<br>**Considerations**: Make sure configurations and code can easily move between environments |
| **Go-Live** | **Definition**: Go-live move when all of the code is ready and tested for production use<br>**New Environment**: Code can be moved ahead of time, but data migration needs to be done at one point<br>**Existing Environment**: Code can be moved ahead of time if tested—be careful on backups and restores |

**TABLE 21.1:**    Implementation Releases  *(CONTINUED)*

| RELEASE TYPES | RELEASE FREQUENCY |
|---|---|
| Hotfix | **Definition**: Post go-live patch that solves a small number of issues<br>**Considerations**: Not typically thoroughly tested; should be used to resolve Priority 1 issues only; introduces risk and requires unplanned downtime |
| Enhancement | **Definition**: Post go-live production release including new features and bug fixes<br>**Considerations**: This should be planned for regular intervals post-release—everything should be well tested |

## Planning for Future Releases

Before you release any code, you need to use your Agile/Scrum methodology tools to plan when you should have releases and what to release. You typically start by planning how often you want to do scheduled releases. In early hypercare, you may choose to run a scheduled release two weeks after you go live. If you expect many problems to arise after go-live, this is likely the best course of action. Alternatively, you may plan to do a release four weeks after your initial go-live. In either case, you need to have a plan for deciding what should be included in each release. You use the same backlog management techniques that we discussed in Chapter 6, "Sprints and Tools Needed to Run Your Project," and you rank what goes into the releases by priority. The first release or two after go-live will likely only be for bug fixes. As you get further from go-live, you should schedule some enhancements into your releases.

One big challenge that comes up during the implementation is when you have to tell a user that their feature or requirement will not make it into the major release. One way to cushion the blow a bit is to advocate for that requirement to be included in a follow-up release after you go live. If a new request comes up in the mid-to-late stages of UAT, you are very unlikely to have the capacity in your schedule to complete the code change in time for go-live. Your best course of action is to research it and estimate the work effort so that you can see when you can include it in a scheduled release. That user needs to understand that P1 and P2 bug fixes will take priority for the first few releases after go-live, but once those are under control, their request can be part of next release backlog.

As you look to schedule out future releases, make sure that you were tracking all of those features and requirements that came up during the major implementation so that you can prioritize them appropriately for these post go-live releases.

## Hotfix Release

You need to consider hotfix release planning similar to a tornado drill. You hope that you never have to do it for real, but you had better be prepared to do it when the need arises. A hotfix or emergency release is an unscheduled release to production that would occur due to the need to resolve one or more Priority 1 issues in production. It should only be used to address P1 issues, and it only should be done if you don't have a scheduled release in the near term where you can release this code.

I mentioned this type of release in Chapter 17, and you should absolutely plan for them as part of your overall release plan.

Table 21.2 highlights the key facts about a hotfix release.

**TABLE 21.2:**  Hotfix Releases Key Facts

| | |
|---|---|
| **What is it?** | ◆  Post go-live patch that solves a small number of Priority 1 issues. |
| **How often do you do one?** | ◆  Hotfix releases should only occur to resolve Priority 1 issues.<br>◆  You hope not to ever have to do one, but you need to plan for it. |
| **How does it work?** | ◆  Issue is identified and worked on immediately.<br>◆  Code fix is tested.<br>◆  If possible, run automated regression tests. |
| **What are the risks?** | ◆  Because you're introducing new code, but you haven't thoroughly tested everything, there's a possibility that something else might break.<br>◆  You may also not have tested it thoroughly enough and it might not fix the real problem.<br>◆  There is typically a bigger risk of allowing this issue to remain in production. |

When you need to complete a hotfix release, you will ask your developer to prioritize this work, and they will work on it on their development machine. From there, it will go through the build process and get promoted to the Test environment. The project team members will run through thorough tests in the Test environment to make sure that the problem is resolved. I also recommend that they test any high-priority processes adjacent to this fix. If all that passes successfully, the code is promoted to UAT and the same round of testing occurs. If it works well there, it is scheduled for a production code promotion, usually during off hours.

Even with everyone making this issue a top priority, it can take up to a few days to get a hotfix release into production. You want to prioritize any P1 issue with the developer, the testers, and the technical team to make sure that it can be accomplished as quickly as possible. With that said, you need to set proper expectations with the business about how quickly you can turn around the fix.

Hotfix releases carry with them considerable risk that should not be ignored. Because they are rushed out the door, there is minimal testing for any adjacent processes during a hotfix release. There is a greater likelihood that another bug might result from the fix for the original issue. This is why you want to be conservative with the number of hotfix releases you do. You are in a much better state if you can wait for a scheduled release so that you can run automated regression testing and bring in more core team members to test the system thoroughly before the release occurs.

## Scheduled Releases

As mentioned earlier, schedule your post go-live releases before you go live. You should decide how frequently you want to do them, but I suggest that you run the first couple of scheduled releases shortly after go-live so that you can address any high-priority bugs that inevitably come up.

After those initial bug-focused releases, I recommend that you schedule regular releases in perpetuity. The majority of clients do not do this—after the major release, they are ready to move on to other projects. This is a missed opportunity; your new ERP or CRM system is a living organism that should continually be enhanced to bring even more value back to the business.

You should continue to receive enhancement requests from your users after go-live. In nearly every project, I've seen great suggestions come out after go-live that help enhance the user experience and gain efficiencies not foreseen in the original implementation. You certainly want to take advantage of these suggestions.

Given Microsoft's release schedule, you will need to take at least two new releases each year of the latest Microsoft code. I recommend that you schedule your releases to include the latest Microsoft code so that you can take advantage of that innovation while you continue to enhance your system. The on-premise days where you can stay on the same build for multiple years are gone. I believe that's a good thing—you should always be enhancing your business application platform.

---

**MAJOR VS. MINOR RELEASES**

When planning a future release, you may need to decide if you want to consider a major versus a minor release. A *major release* (which is typically called version 2.0) is a release that should be treated like your original main release with additional resources and a hypercare period. This would also be considered a "Phase 2" or named release, so you can identify that it's a major release. When I talk about scheduled releases, I'm typically referring to a minor release (mostly unnamed but sometimes called version 1.1). The *minor release* contains a combination of bug fixes with minor functionality enhancements.

---

# Project Team Transition

As I've reiterated a few times throughout this chapter, it is critical to send your users to the HelpDesk right after your system goes live so that they can get into the habit of using it. If that experience is good, they will continue to submit support incidents to the HelpDesk and then you can staff the HelpDesk as you see fit. Once the front-line team is educated and/or the incident volume is slowing down, you can start to transition your project team back to their day jobs. Similarly, your implementation partner will be looking to transition their team off to another project. You should plan ahead for this so that you are ready to make the transition as seamless as possible.

## Rolling Off the Project Team

At the end of the hypercare period, you will be able to transition your project team back to their day jobs and the partner will be sending their project team members on to a different project. It has been expensive to keep your team away from their day jobs and to pay the hourly rates associated with the partner's resources, so this change will significantly reduce your project cost run rate.

Depending on the size of the project, hypercare may last from two to twelve weeks. As you get close to the end, you need to make sure that you have plans in place to reduce the workload on the project team and to transition any remaining work to your IT team and/or your partner's support team.

First, certainly look to reduce their workloads. This means reducing the number of new enhancement requests. When you have new enhancement requests, direct them to your IT team so that they learn how to prioritize and complete them. You have two ways to limit the project team's work on bugs and support incidents:

◆   Train the HelpDesk.

◆   Send any incidents the HelpDesk team can't resolve to the partner's support team instead of their implementation team.

The training content should all be done at this time, so you shouldn't have any more work for the project team in that area.

If you can't reduce their workload to zero, determine your plan for allocating work to ongoing resources with capacity. This usually means members of your IT team and/or the partner's support team. Try to determine how much work will be needed for ongoing support, and make sure that you allocate time to your internal team and budget to any support that you need from your partner.

Once all of those plans are in place, you can schedule the official transition for the project team. Your partner's resources may no longer be available to you once this date happens, so you don't want to take this transition lightly. You need to be prepared and work with your partner to make sure that their support team is as qualified as the project team to handle new issues that arise.

## Documentation

Once you identify your target roll-off date, ask the project team to create any documentation or training content needed to help educate those who will be taking the work forward. It's a good time to review process documentation and training content to make sure that they are up to date. Any issue that you don't tackle during this time could come back to haunt you in the future if your documentation is not correct and someone relies on it.

Typically, you should establish the set of documentation required to be complete and up to date earlier in the implementation, so the project team knows what needs to be done by the end of hypercare.

## Expectations of Support

Once this transition has occurred, all incidents would be submitted to the HelpDesk. The HelpDesk would follow its documented processes and escalate incidents as needed. You may ask the project team members to be available for Tier 2 incidents, or you may choose to send those incidents to your other IT members first. I suggest that you escalate to the other IT team members to try to take pressure off your project team members and make it so that they are no longer needed as cogs in the support process over time.

During hypercare, work closely with your partner to transition support requests from the project team to their support team. This will require their teams to talk and conduct knowledge transfer sessions, so the support team knows what was implemented, how it was implemented, and where documentation exists on the project. Make sure to check in with your partner to assure that the transition is happening. It is good to have the partner's support team start serving as the Tier 3 HelpDesk resource early in the hypercare period so that they can see how those incidents are resolved and that they can be ready to resolve them on their own. I recommend that you ask your partner to identify how their support team can escalate incidents to the project team members even after hypercare. You want to make sure that there is a path to reach out to those resources after hypercare in case the documentation is lacking in a certain area.

### After the Transition

Once hypercare is complete, the project team should have transitioned, and you are now in the Empower stage of the project. Any issues or enhancement requests should follow the process that we will discuss in the next chapter.

## The Bottom Line

**Hypercare Duration**   The post go-live period where you transition from the project team to ongoing maintenance of the solution is a critical time in the project. You will want to work with your partner to schedule the appropriate duration of hypercare in advance so that you know how long you have to make this transition.

   **Master It**   How long does hypercare typically last?

   **1.** Go-live weekend

   **2.** 1 week after go-live

   **3.** 4 to 8 weeks after go-live

   **4.** The first year after go-live

**Where to Send Issues**   You want to establish a process for each issue that arises after you go live. This process should be consistent and widely communicated, so it can achieve adoption by the user base. A key part of the process is determining who will field user issues as they arise.

   **Master It**   Post go-live support issues should be sent to which of the following?

   **1.** Your internal HelpDesk

   **2.** Partner support team

   **3.** Directly to project team

   **4.** Microsoft

**Month-End Procedures**   After you go live, you will use the first month end as a means of validating all of the activity for the first month on the new system to make sure that all of the numbers tie out as expected. To prepare your team for month end, you will need to train them on the specific processes that need to be followed, as they won't be the same as using the system normally.

   **Master It**   When should you train users on month-end procedures?

   **1.** Prior to the pre-go-live training period

   **2.** During pre-go-live training

**3.** A week or two before the first month end

**4.** During the first month end

**HelpDesk Levels**   All support incidents should be submitted to the HelpDesk, and the front-line resources dedicated to the HelpDesk should review those incidents. They should resolve whatever incidents they can, but they may need to escalate to higher tiers of support.

**Master It**   Which of these represents the Tier 4 resource for a HelpDesk request?

**1.** Partner support

**2.** Microsoft support

**3.** Project team

**4.** HelpDesk itself

**Prioritizing Bugs**   Many bugs will be found after you go live on the new system. Hopefully, the majority of the bugs have a low priority, but those that are not low priority should be tracked and assigned to a post go-live release.

**Master It**   Post-go-live Priority 2 bug fixes should be released in which type of a release?

**1.** Go-live release

**2.** Internal release

**3.** Hotfix release

**4.** Scheduled post-go-live release

# Chapter 22

# Support and Enhance Your Project

Congratulations! You have completed the project and have successfully made it through hypercare. It's time to move on to the next project, right? Many people do, but when you do, you miss an opportunity to enhance the project and get more value out of what you've done.

The first 6–12 months after go-live can be rocky, as you deal with adapting to the new system, learning it at a deep level, and handling potential system issues. Most project and leadership teams are quick to say "mission accomplished" when you get through the first month end. The project cost a lot of money and many sacrifices have been made to get here, so they are ready to turn the page. And these ongoing challenges can wear on already-thin patience.

After that first month end, you are not done with the project, as much as you'd like to be. To use a sports analogy, you may have been playing defense, but now you have the opportunity to go on offense to make the solution even better.

Let's examine how you can maximize the value of your project as you work through the first year after go-live. You are at the end of the Client Journey: the Empower stage, where you have the opportunity to drive even more value out of your system.

### AFTER YOU COMPLETE THIS CHAPTER, YOU WILL BE ABLE TO DO THE FOLLOWING:

◆ Normalize your support processes

◆ Conduct sessions to learn from the project successes and mistakes

◆ Develop an ongoing release plan to continue to enhance the solution

◆ Plan out future initiatives on top of the Microsoft Dynamics platform

## Support After Hypercare

In Chapter 21, "Hypercare," I indicated that hypercare can last anywhere from 2–12 weeks depending on the scope of the implementation and the agreement between the company and the partner when you started the project. At the end of hypercare, you want to transition to a sustainable support model utilizing your HelpDesk and the partner's support team. If everything goes according to plan, that's what will happen. However, I have seen many cases where companies get to the end of hypercare, and the volume of support incidents is quite high—too high to transition into a sustainable support mode. Let's talk about how to handle the typical hypercare period and the exception case where hypercare has to continue beyond its agreed upon deadline.

## Extending the Transition from Consulting to Support

In cases where you have to do many hotfix releases and you're still experiencing some P1 issues at the end of hypercare, you will have to look to extend resources beyond the normal hypercare period. You really can't let go of the resources that you need on the project if you are still fighting fires every day.

If you find yourself at the second-to-last week of hypercare and you can't see a smooth transition to support, you will need to engage your partner to extend their resources on the project. You will also have to be ready to tell your team, who was expecting to go back to their day jobs, to extend their tour of duty on the project until you can safely make the transition to support.

You can't continue to hold on to the full project team forever, so you should set exit criteria for hypercare. You can still get a Priority 1 (P1) issue after hypercare is over, so a reasonable exit criterion should include a small number of P1 and Priority 2 (P2) issues happening on a weekly basis and the ability for the HelpDesk and partner support team to take on the majority of questions.

### Engaging Your Partner for Support

In the support hierarchy model introduced in Chapter 21, I showed Figure 21.2 (cross-referenced here in Figure 22.1), which outlined the four tiers of support.

**FIGURE 22.1**
HelpDesk ticket
progression

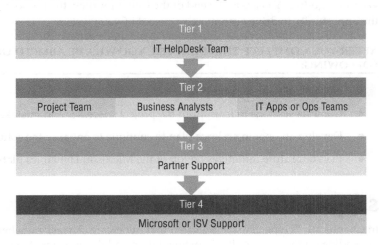

Incidents start with the HelpDesk, then they can be escalated to the project team or the core IT team, and incidents that can't be resolved at that level move to Tier 3, which typically means your partner.

Each partner is different, and you will want to talk to your partner as early as the sales cycle to understand what support plans they offer and what the response time expectations are. Partners typically offer three types of plans:

◆ **Pay as you go**: This is a model where you pay for their time as you need it at their currently published support rate. This is the most flexible plan, but it can be difficult to budget for this as it is highly dependent on the amount of support hours you need. Your partner may offer a discounted rate if you are willing to prepay for a set number of hours on this type of plan.

◆ **Unlimited subscription support**: This is a model where you pay an additional amount for support each month or year based on the number of users on the system. You may pay $5 per user per month for support, and your partner would then provide unlimited support for any incidents that you submit to them. Partners will still require that you have triaged the issue before sending it over, so you won't be able to have them serve as your HelpDesk under this model. This is a good option if you want to be able to budget a certain amount for support and know what you will spend each month. The fact that you get unlimited support with this plan gives you insurance in case you have a significant number of issues arising from a post go-live release.

◆ **Premier support**: This is a model where you pay more for an enhanced level of support. You may receive a named account manager who will advocate for you and review your support incidents to see if training can help you reduce the number of incidents that you need to submit. You will receive an improved SLA with this plan so that you can get responses back on your incidents more quickly. You may also receive additional services for your environment under this type of plan.

Review the different support plan options and talk to your partner about which plan may be right for you. If you are just exiting hypercare, you will likely need more support than you will three years after you go live. I encourage you to side toward having too much as opposed to too little support in the first year after go-live. Once you have stabilized your system after year one, you can potentially downgrade your plan and save some money.

You should make sure to ask your partner to explain their SLA and what their hours of operation are for support. Generally, everyone is looking for a 24×7 support option nowadays in case you have employees working late—they would be able to submit a critical incident no matter the time of day. You will want to seek out a plan that provides you with a better response time for any critical issue. If you are experiencing a P1 issue, you want a 1-hour or less response time at any hour of the day and the ability to pick up the phone and call someone to help you through the issue.

You should also understand your partner's stance on issues with ISVs. Partners will escalate ISV-specific issues to that company, but they may also be able to introduce workarounds to keep you up and running if the ISV can't create the fix as quickly as you need it. That's an important value a partner can provide, so talk to them about how they handle ISV-related issues to make sure that you can get service on them quickly and a temporary fix if need be if your ISV only provides regular releases.

## Microsoft and ISV Support Plans

Microsoft can provide direct support for your application if you so choose, so instead of Tier 3 of your HelpDesk going to your partner, it could go to Microsoft instead. Before you choose that option, remember that Microsoft support won't be able to provide assistance for issues with any ISVs you own, so if you go this route, you will need to make sure that you have direct access to your ISVs as well.

As of this writing, Microsoft offers three support options that you can find on this site: `dynamics.microsoft.com/en-us/support/plans`. Subscription support is included with the price of your Microsoft Dynamics subscriptions, so it is essentially free considering that you require the subscription to use your product. Response times are based on the severity of the incident, and Microsoft will try to provide you with an answer through its knowledge base to minimize its expenses in supporting clients. It is a good solution for critical issues, as Microsoft will provide a response time of under one hour for those issues. If there is a system outage affecting your ability to access your Microsoft Dynamics product, you should go directly to Microsoft with those incidents, as your partner will not be able to help directly in that case.

Figure 22.2 shows the benefits of Microsoft's Subscription support plan.

**Figure 22.2**
Microsoft Subscription support plan

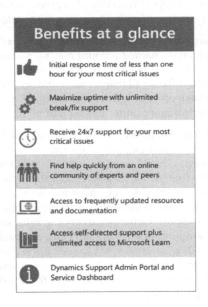

Microsoft also offers *Professional Direct Support*, and this is the best option if you don't want to engage with your partner for Tier 3 support. As of this writing, the cost of Professional Direct Support is $9 per month for each system user, with a minimum of $180 per month. With this plan, you will get faster access to senior support resources who can help you solve your incidents more quickly. The Subscription plan only offers online incident submissions, but you can call directly with the Professional plan.

Microsoft also offers *Unified Support*, which is a comprehensive plan that covers all of your Microsoft products. The cost of Unified Support depends on the level of access you seek (Core,

Advanced, and Performance) and the number of cloud subscribers across Microsoft 365 and your other Microsoft subscriptions. With Unified Support, you get access to an account manager or an account management team who will represent you and work with the support team to deliver the results you're seeking. It offers unlimited support plans and the ability to participate in proactive support directly from Microsoft engineers.

All of the Microsoft plans offer 24×7 support, so you can submit incidents at any time. For production down issues, it offers good peace of mind knowing that your incident will receive attention no matter what hour of the day it is.

If you opt for a Microsoft Direct Support plan, you will need to work directly with your ISVs on a support plan for that product. Microsoft may troubleshoot an issue related to an ISV, but once it determines the root cause comes from the ISV code, it will point you to the ISV for a resolution. If you have a limited number of ISVs in scope and several Microsoft products, you may want to choose the Microsoft Direct Support option for your Tier 3 support needs.

# After Action Review

An *after action review (AAR)* is a meeting that you can run after any type of project (or milestone) has been completed to gather feedback from everyone on the team about how the project went, what went well, and what could have gone better. It is frequently called a post-mortem, but I personally don't like that term. The term "retrospective" sounds like it would apply here as well, but it's commonly used in projects to look back at the previous sprint instead of the larger project.

The goal of the AAR session is to solicit open and honest feedback and rate areas of the project, so that you know what went well and what improvement areas exist. It is not uncommon for a participant to state that something another member of the team did wasn't good. All participants should provide feedback on the "what" could have gone better and not attack any particular user. The AAR is intended to be future-looking—not specifically judging the events of the past, but looking to learn from what you did well or what you could have done better.

## Who to Invite

An AAR session should be led by a facilitator who did not have an active role on the project so they can be impartial and ask for candid feedback. It's important to give members of the team time to provide insight into each of the areas, and you don't want a leader to show biases by avoiding feedback in areas that they participated in or giving someone more time to level criticism against someone they don't like. You often want to invite a scribe to the session as well who can write down the feedback given by the members as the session goes along.

We've found the most success resulted from doing two AAR meetings at the end of the project. One AAR would be attended by the project leadership team—the executive sponsors, project owner, project manager, engagement manager, architects, and core team leads. In this group, the facilitator asks the team to focus on the makeup of the team, role definitions, project schedule, project management plan, and the ongoing management of activities on the project. You would also ask about each of the ISVs or outside vendors on the project to rate their effectiveness in helping you to meet your goals.

The second group, led by the same facilitator, would include the individual contributors on the project like the consultants, subject matter experts, and IT specialists. This session largely focuses on the tactical activities and what could have been better there. You also seek feedback from that team on how well the project was led to see if any inefficiencies should be noted for future reference.

It is best if you can do an AAR session that includes members of the customer and implementer team together in one meeting, but you may get more candid feedback if you separate the groups. However, you may also see the groups trying to blame all of the mistakes on the other party instead of taking a holistic approach to what each group could have done better. Having both parties on one call can result in the healthier feedback that you want to solicit.

## How to Run the Meeting

The meeting begins with four ground rules for the session:

**The feedback should be professional** The comments should not include personal attacks, and everything said in the meeting should be something that you'd be willing to say to someone's face.

**The feedback should be objective** It's okay for each party to admit that they could have done better as well. Ask the participants to step back and look at the big picture as they give their feedback.

**The feedback should inform future projects** There's no future value in complaining about something that happened on the project unless you specifically cite how you should do it differently in the future. Tell the participants not to complain for the sake of complaining; the feedback should be actionable.

**Remind participants that feedback is a gift** You can learn from constructive feedback and get better next time. You should have an open mind to understand how another team member might have seen something differently than you saw it. It is the responsibility of each member to do something productive with that feedback.

Next you ask everyone to introduce themselves and their role as it related to the project. From there, you get into the heart of the session, which includes asking questions to each of the participants and writing down their feedback. You ask them each five questions in the session:

1. What were the project objectives? You ask them this to see if there is consensus on the objectives or to find out if one of the problems was that no one really knew what the goal of the project was.

2. How would you rate any vendors or ISVs on a scale of 1–10 (10 being the highest) and any comments that they have to justify the rating? Here you are asking for perspective on those people who contributed to the project to see if they contributed in a positive or negative way.

3. What went well on the project? Ask each participant to cite 2–5 things that went well on the project from their perspective.

4. What could have gone better on the project? Ask each participant to cite 2–5 things that they feel could have gone better on the project and how it could be done better next time.

5. What is your overall rating, from 1–10, of the project as a whole? Here you attempt to balance the positive and critical feedback and get a good perspective on the teams' view of the project as a whole.

The review session ends once everyone has had a chance to answer each question and provide their rating of the project. Most of the conversation is between the facilitator and the individual participant; there is some interaction between the participants, but you don't want one person cutting off another person if they provide critical feedback in a particular area.

## What to Do with the Feedback

Now that you have had the meeting, you want to collect that feedback and benefit from the lessons learned. The facilitator and scribe will review the notes from the session and share that feedback with the group.

It's best if the facilitator can highlight certain themes that came from the feedback, so the summary includes elements like the following:

◆ Average rating for the project based on the team's feedback.

◆ Vendors who excelled that you should use again and those who should be avoided in the future.

◆ The top 5–10 things that went well.

◆ 5–10 lessons that can be learned from the project based on critical feedback.

A summary that includes those elements will be very useful as you plan on future projects.

# Ongoing Releases

In Chapter 21, we talked about the need to do post go-live releases and how there will be hotfix and enhancement releases. I will assume that you have the *hotfix release process* figured out and you shouldn't have to do any hotfix releases after hypercare. Let's focus on enhancement releases—when to do them, how to plan them, and how to use them to increase the value of your project.

## Microsoft Dynamics 365 Release Cadence

You will never have to do a major upgrade to your cloud-based Microsoft Dynamics 365 solution. That's a major benefit of a cloud-based solution. The trade-off is that you will get enhancements to your system through regular updates that Microsoft releases at least twice per year.

To incorporate the new features from Microsoft, you will want to schedule your releases in a window that allows you to test the new Microsoft releases before you push them to production. Look at the latest scheduled release dates from Microsoft and be sure to track the first date where you can receive the update and the date by which you have to take that update. You should be able to schedule the update into your environment, and you want to make sure that you have ample time between the "sandbox" or Test/UAT deployment and the production deployment.

## Release Testing

Before you plan your release schedule, you should determine what level of testing you want to do before each release. The spectrum of potential approaches is quite broad here. You could choose to test everything in the entire system through manual testing (way too much time and effort) or test nothing and hope for the best (way to risky).

As I discussed in Chapter 18, "Testing," you want to develop a broad set of test cases for your system so that you know what all should be tested. From there, you should prioritize the test cases in the most critical areas of your business, such as creating customers and sales orders. You should make sure to test each of those critical areas before each release. Those critical test cases would make up your *regression testing* components, because you are testing these scenarios even though they weren't changed in the latest release.

For any new functionality that you are introducing with the release, you should build new test cases that go through all of the different ways that you can use that new functionality. These test cases should become part of your overall end-to-end testing to make sure that you have all of the functionality covered. You would combine your regression and your new functionality testing to make up the suite of tests that you need to run before each enhancement release.

You want to try to automate as many tests as you can. This was discussed in more detail in Chapter 18, but you should specifically try to invest in automation for your critical regression tests. If you have to run tests on these components every single time you do a release, that means you'll be running those tests a minimum of twice a year and probably four or more times. You should do the math on the cost of automating the tests, but if you want 3–5 people to run each regression test case every time you do a release, you can see how much time and cost would be associated with this effort. It is likely that it is cheaper to invest in automation than to spend all that human capital each time you do a release. Also, you want to try to make your releases as automated as possible to encourage more releases. The more releases you do, the more you will be able to extend your solution and take advantage of Microsoft's enhancements.

Once you build your list of tests, you divide them up into those that can be run through automated testing and those that need to be run manually. You then find people who can start the automated testing and people who can run through all of the manual tests. Once you have them in place and scheduled, you can build your release schedule.

## When to Schedule Your Releases

After the hypercare period and the first six months after go-live, you want to settle into a long-term release cadence that balances the need to introduce new functionality without over-burdening the team. I typically suggest a monthly or quarterly release cycle, depending on how many resources you have allocated to help with the release process. The more resources you have, the more releases you can do. Most companies tend to settle on quarterly releases, so we'll use that in our upcoming examples.

Once you have your frequency set, three major factors typically affect when you do your releases:

**Month or quarter end**: In all ERP deployments and most CRM deployments, you want to try to target a month end for your releases so that you can tie out your previous month's numbers before you introduce new functionality. This becomes less important over time because the changes are not as massive, but generally they are targeted for month end. If you are a public company, you may want to avoid doing a release at the same time as your 10-Q reporting period end date, just because there is more work to the month ends that correspond to your reporting quarter end.

**Microsoft's release schedule**: As mentioned earlier, you want to schedule your release between the initial release of the new software and the last date you can take the software so that you have sufficient time to test.

**Seasonality of your business**: Many businesses have particularly busy times of year when they want to avoid system changes that could impact the team. If you are a retail business, for example, your busiest time of the year is typically between November and the end of December. Thus, you would want to avoid running a release on Black Friday for obvious reasons.

## What to Include in Releases

When it comes to planning the contents of your future releases, your imagination is your only limit. Let's classify the types of release contents into three groups:

**Bug fixes**: You certainly want to include any P1 and P2 bugs in your releases. Those are high-priority issues that should be resolved as quickly as possible. You may need to do a hotfix release for any P1 bugs, but if you they are happening near a scheduled release, it's always better to release them as part of your scheduled release. P2 bugs should be scheduled for release during the regular releases. P3 and P4 bugs can be included in these releases as well, but you should weigh their priority against enhancements that may provide more value to the business. Sometimes, companies will have one enhancement release that is solely focused on bug fixes just to reduce the number of bugs in the system, even if they aren't top priority.

**Postponed or de-scoped items**: This is correlated with the future enhancements category, but I call it out separately because these were priority items at one point and just didn't quite make the release. Throughout the implementation, you will run into constraints that might affect your ability to get everything you originally had in scope done. When that happens, you have to make the difficult decision to postpone release components. You won't win a popularity contest when you do that, but sometimes it must be done. If you postpone items, you should put them at the top of the list of future enhancements to complete and even target them for planned releases after go-live. It can serve to calm the person whose item is being postponed if you can identify when that item will be released.

**Future enhancements**: I'll address several different enhancements that you could make in the next section.

# Future Enhancements

One of the best things about Microsoft Dynamics is the platform that Microsoft has created around the ERP and CRM functionality. With the Power Platform, Azure, and Microsoft 365, you can easily extend the solution to add whatever capability can impact your business in the most positive way. I'll cover the different types of enhancements that you can make to the system and why you may want to invest there.

## New Functionality

New functionality could include postponed or de-scoped items from the main release, but this can also include extending the functionality in an area or taking on a whole new module in the system. At Stoneridge Software, we are constantly adding to our Dynamics 365 ERP and CRM systems with additional functionality like an Industry lookup in our Customer Engagement platform so that we can change industry from an option set to a lookup data type. We also add to our Dynamics 365 Finance and Supply Chain Management system by adding new features in the project management module to give commissions for billable hours worked or to simplify the time entry approval process.

If you choose to implement a new module (such as Project Management in Business Central or Customer Service in CRM), you may want to consider a "Phase 2"–style release where you would bring more resources to the table and treat it as a major release. You'll have to decide based on the estimated hours whether to consider a new module a major or minor release. When you deploy a major release, it typically requires you to pull together the full team used on the original project or something similar.

Figure 22.3 shows the main modules in Microsoft Dynamics 365 Business Central.

**FIGURE 22.3**
Microsoft Dynamics 365
Business Central
main modules

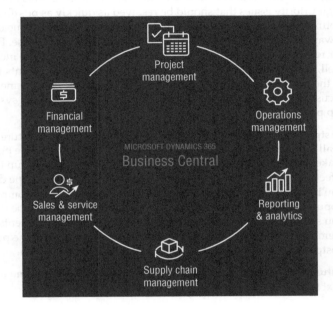

## Usability

Everyone tries to think about *usability* during the main release, but you often don't know how you want to get around in the software until you've had time to use it. Users often struggle with the usability of the software in the beginning because the functions may not be in the order they were expecting, or they want to jump to another function from a certain screen, but that connection is not there.

It's a great idea to poll the users at the end of hypercare to learn what they like about the new system and where they see opportunities for improvement. You'll end up discovering several usability enhancements from that feedback that could really make the users like the system more. Take advantage of that feedback, and budget hours of time to help make the system easier to use.

## Guardrails

This may be an uncommon term, but *guardrails* generally refers to anything that you can do to prevent the user from doing something that they shouldn't. This could be security related, or it could be a system change. It's difficult to develop guardrails before you have gone live with the system because you can't anticipate what users might do wrong. You can ask users to do *negative testing*—where you purposely do something you shouldn't do in the system to see if it generates the proper error message or response. Negative testing is usually very low on the priority list of your original implementation, so what ends up happening is that you do negative testing in production after you're live on the software.

When you find these areas where users are performing actions that lead to problems in the software, you want to document the exact steps they are taking. From there, you want to consider what options you have for preventing them from performing that action. One of the easiest ways to stop this activity is to remove their access to the problematic action. You can do that without a release, so that's a change you can make quickly.

If you find a problem where it's too easy to do the wrong thing in the software, or you present the user with an option that they shouldn't use, you will need to customize the software to keep them from performing the problematic action. This will require an *enhancement release*, so any changes would need to be scheduled for the release that best fits the priority of the fix.

## Business Intelligence

One of the main reasons you decided to implement Microsoft Dynamics 365 is to take advantage of the reporting capability in the system. You can now get more insights out of the system than you could have before, but you need to know what you want to measure so that you can build the right business intelligence into your system. It often occurs that the implementation team doesn't define the key metrics that you want to measure, so you get to the end of the implementation and can't see the insights that you were expecting. Microsoft is world-renowned for its ability to create software, but it can't tell every business what the most important metrics are for them. You will generally find common reports provided by the software out of the box, but if you made customizations to those areas of the product, they won't show up on the report. Depending on your level of customization in the product, you may end up having to update many, many reports as part of your deployment. Many times, these customizations are not considered or not prioritized for the original release.

That pushes a lot of work to the enhancement release, and it can take a year to get all of the reporting that you are seeking out of the system. That's certainly a trend we'd all like to see move faster, and it can come faster if more implementations can limit the number of customizations needed.

When companies do a great job of developing reporting requirements, it often leads to new functional requirements. Sometimes, the data you're seeking to report on is not something that you're currently tracking. To get to the reporting you need, take the following steps:

1. Define the metrics that you want to see.

2. Outline a process for inputting the data necessary for the report.

3. Assign a process owner with the responsibility for the data so that there is accountability for the data being accurate.

4. Connect to the data source and do any transformation necessary so that the data can easily be visualized.

5. Develop the report visualization in a tool like Power BI or Excel.

6. Validate that security is properly set for the right users to access the report.

7. Train the users on how to use the report and what ways they can slice and dice the data.

Many people feel like reports should just be there, but several steps are necessary to make reports into true business intelligence. Don't short-change the process if you really want to get value from your new solution.

## Incorporating Dynamics Data into Your Daily Business

Another way to extend your solution is to connect your data to the Power Platform. Microsoft's Power Platform includes Power BI, Power Automate, Power Apps, and Power Virtual Agents. Power BI is a business intelligence tool, and we covered that in the previous section, but Power Automate, Apps, and Virtual Agents all provide you with the ability to extend the power of your Microsoft Dynamics system. We recently used Power Apps to build an app for a customer to manage their inventory. In this app, they have mobile access to purchase requisitions, inventory counts, on-hand inventory, and transfer orders. The availability of the app allows our client to move from a monthly to a daily reconciliation of inventory, which will save significant shrinkage over time.

Power Automate allows you to perform an action once a triggering action fires. You could use that to send an email to one of your customers whenever an invoice has been posted, for example. Power Virtual Agents allows you to provide chat responses to your customers when they visit one of your web properties. You can use this tool to look up data in your Microsoft Dynamics system to provide interaction with a customer without having to pull in a customer service representative.

Your imagination is the limit when it comes to extending your Microsoft Dynamics system. You can learn more about Microsoft's Power Platform at `powerplatform.microsoft.com`.

## Integrations

Microsoft Dynamics 365 products have open *application programming interfaces (APIs)*, so you can easily connect your system to another open solution. You may want to take the opportunity to connect another key business to your ERP or CRM system. It's always great to have Dynamics as the master data, as you want to keep your ERP and CRM systems as your source of truth for other systems.

## Machine Learning and Artificial Intelligence

Microsoft Dynamics 365 is starting to incorporate more advanced computing concepts like *machine learning (ML)* and *artificial intelligence (AI)*. Machine learning is when the system learns and adapts to new data without human interference. It is commonly used for use cases where the system can improve forecasts over time as more data passes through it. Artificial intelligence is a more general term that incorporates machine learning. It's any computing capability that allows the system to learn and reason like humans.

Microsoft has introduced several different "Insights" solutions like *Customer Insights*, *Sales Insights*, and *Customer Service Insights*, which are AI solutions that learn from the data and provide dashboards to the user indicating which customer may be more willing to buy your products or whatever you configure it to show.

Figure 22.4 displays the *Business Central Intelligent Cloud Insights* capability where it shows relevant KPIs to the user, along with interesting information like how many customers are late with their payments.

**FIGURE 22.4**
Business Central
Intelligent Cloud
Insights capabilities

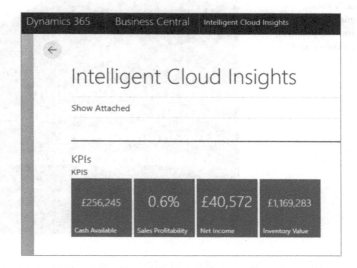

These Insights solutions only get better with more time and more data, so I encourage you to consider implementing these solutions as part of your enhancement releases.

## Calculating Return on Investment

In Chapter 2, "What to Do Before You Begin a Project," we talked about the importance of building a *return on investment (ROI)* calculation to show how much value you would achieve from the project. You have spent a lot of money on the project, and you should have a good handle of the expense side of that calculation. Now it's time to look at the value you've received.

After hypercare, you transition from the high-cost period, where you have many resources on the project, to a smaller, consistent level of resources. You should calculate your costs through the end of hypercare and consider those your implementation costs. This includes the software subscriptions and license purchases, your partner's labor costs, any hardware investments you needed to make, and your internal costs. This represents the full cost of the implementation of the solution, and it serves as a key data point in your ROI calculation.

You will not achieve a full payback on your implementation costs by the time hypercare is over, so you should consider at what point and what measurements you want to use to determine the value gained by the implementation.

In September 2018, Forrester produced a Total Economic Impact study on the cost savings and business benefits enabled by Dynamics 365 Finance and Supply Chain (cover page previewed in Figure 22.5):

info.microsoft.com/rs/157-GQE-382/images/EN-CNTNT-eBook-Forrester-TEI-Microsoft--Dynamics-365-For-Finance-Operations.pdf

**FIGURE 22.5**
Forrester's Total Economic Impact study of Microsoft Dynamics 365 for Finance and Operations

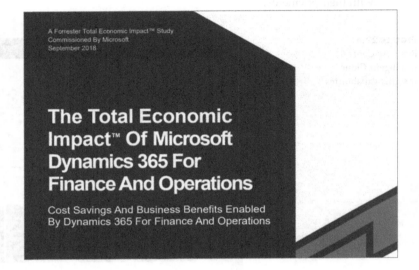

This case study provides you with examples of benefits that can come from the new system. In that study, they referenced quantifiable benefits like operational efficiency, wholesale and retail profit, and legacy cost avoidance. It also makes an estimate on the number of unquantifiable benefits, like cloud simplicity, improved user experience, enhanced security, and governance. You will have to make educated guesses at the value of those unquantifiable items, but it is a key part of the value equation of the new system.

## ROI Checkpoints

I suggest that you do your first analysis of the benefits after one year on the new system. If your benefits exceed your costs after one year, you are well above average, and you stand to gain a tremendous amount of value over the life of the new system. An 18-month timeline for the return on investment is generally considered quite good. You will want to do an analysis every six months after the initial one-year analysis to see how the benefits are adding up.

Why would you spend time calculating ROI on a project you already completed? You go through this exercise for two reasons:

◆ It is important for future system implementation to have an accurate depiction of the value of the system.

◆ It may help you identify another system adjustment that could increase profit or decrease costs.

If your company makes $100M in revenue and has $90M in costs and you can increase revenue or decrease expenses by 1 percent, you just added 10 percent to your overall profit. I think everyone would agree that's a worthwhile use of time.

## The Bottom Line

**Post Hypercare Support**   After hypercare, support volume should start to normalize, and you want to focus on building consistency in your support processes. You will still be seeing a fair number of incidents after hypercare, particularly in certain areas.

> **Master It**   What is an example of something that may require additional support after the hypercare period?
>
> **1.** Project plans
>
> **2.** Month-end support
>
> **3.** Go-live support
>
> **4.** Change requests

**Partner Support**   Your HelpDesk will tackle all of the incidents that are raised from your users, but you will find that you'll need to escalate some incidents to your partner and potentially to Microsoft or an ISV. Partner support plans vary, but some general components are offered in each area.

> **Master It**   Which of the following is not a common partner support model offered?
>
> **1.** Unlimited support through monthly fee
>
> **2.** Pay as you go plans
>
> **3.** Premier support
>
> **4.** Phone support only

**After Action Review**   Once you have completed hypercare, you should run an after action review.

> **Master It**   What is the goal of an after action review?
>
> **1.** To collect broad feedback from the project team on what went well and what could have gone better on the project
>
> **2.** To review each action done on the project
>
> **3.** For leadership to share their thoughts on what the team should have done better
>
> **4.** To have the customer share their criticism of the partner and the partner to share their criticism of the customer

**Testing for Future Releases**    After hypercare, you will want to run regular releases to fix outstanding bugs and enhance your solution. To prevent introducing new issues, you want to have a good testing plan for your releases.

   **Master It**    What is regression testing?

   1. Developing tests for new code that was just developed

   2. End-to-end testing of processes

   3. Testing functionality already in place in the system

   4. Training for users of existing functionality

**Post Go-live Enhancements**    As you plan for future enhancement releases, you can add any number of new capabilities to your system.

   **Master It**    Which is not an example of common enhancements to make to your system post go-live?

   1. Reporting

   2. Usability

   3. Guardrails

   4. Status reports

# Chapter 23

# Bringing It All Together

Let's finish the book by bringing all of the content together and organizing it in chronological order. As I was putting this book together, I wanted it to be grouped in logical order so that you could learn all about data migration in one chapter rather than in eight different chapters. Now that you know all about data migration, let's identify the data migration steps that should happen in their chronological order. We won't be covering any new ground in this chapter; rather, we'll be putting all of the concepts into a timeline that I hope you find useful.

Let's go back to the original steps in the Client Journey and put each component of the project into the right stage of the project. As a refresher, here are the five stages of the project and a brief summary of each:

- **Align**: The stage where you prepare for the project and identify what's important for your success on the project.

- **Define**: The stage where you select the solution and the implementer, and you put all of the pieces into place to run the project successfully.

- **Create**: The stage where you build the solution to meet your needs.

- **Deploy**: The stage where you test the solution, train your users, and launch the system to production.

- **Empower**: The stage where you look for new opportunities to enhance the system after the successful deployment.

## Align Stage

The *Align stage* corresponds with the start of the project, and it includes the steps that you take before you fully commit to a project. The purpose of the Align stage is to make sure that you are ready for a project and you know what kind of solution you want and who you would want to implement it (see Figure 23.1).

From a chronological perspective, Chapter 2, "What to Do Before You Begin a Project," and Chapter 3, "Four Keys to Consider When Buying an ERP or CRM Solution," represent the activity that should be happening during the Align stage. Figure 23.2 depicts the key activities that would occur during this time frame.

**FIGURE 23.1**
Align stage

**FIGURE 23.2**
Key activities during the
Align stage

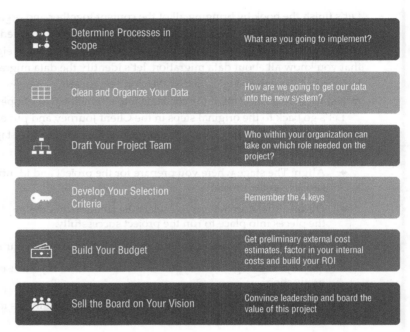

## Define Stage

The *Define stage* corresponds with the beginning of the buying cycle and ends with the kickoff meeting. The purpose of the Define stage is to select the right ERP or CRM system, choose the right implementation partner, and prepare the team to build the solution. Once you've signed contracts to buy your solution and pay your implementer, you spend the new few weeks working to put the right game plan in place for how you will run the implementation. This is the most important time on the project to integrate your team with the implementer's team, to define the rules for how you'll run the project, and to settle on a scope that will achieve your success criteria without blowing your budget, as outlined in Figure 23.3.

The Define stage activities are mostly aligned to the content in Chapters 4–10, but a few things happen out of order and several activities from later chapters should occur during the Define stage. Figure 23.4 lays out the step-by-step activities, and you'll see a lot of activities in the "develop your project management plan and schedule" step, which are defined in Chapters 14–18.

**FIGURE 23.3**
Define stage

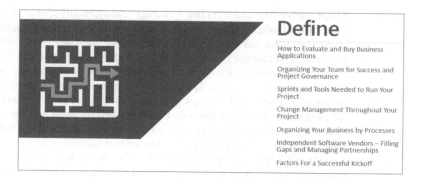

**FIGURE 23.4**
Key activities during the
Define stage

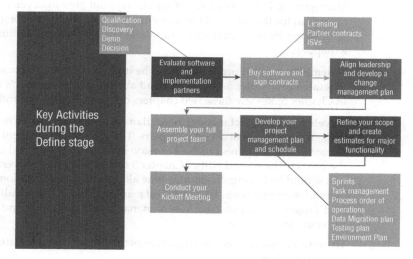

Figure 23.4 sets out the activities in chronological order. Let's walk through each step and point you to the relevant chapter for these activities.

**Evaluate software and implementation partners.** The criteria you use for your selection is laid out in Chapter 3, and that activity happens in the Align stage. The majority of the activities in the evaluation process are detailed in Chapter 4, "How to Evaluate and Buy Business Application Software," but you should also review Chapter 9, "Independent Software Vendors—Filling Gaps and Managing Partnerships," before conducting your evaluation. It may be that you don't require an ISV as part of your core solution, in which case it is not relevant at that time, but you should know what to look for before you go through that process.

**Buy software and sign contracts.** The steps involved with completing the acquisition of the subscription for the software and signing contracts with your implementer is primarily laid out in Chapter 4. Like the preceding activity, if you are incorporating an ISV into your core solution, you should read ahead through Chapter 9, to make sure that you know what you're getting into with that ISV.

**Align leadership and develop a change management plan.** To have your leadership team fully aligned to support the project, you should read through Chapters 5–7, so your leadership team has a better understanding of the roles and events of the project and the importance of change management. In Chapter 5, "Organizing Your Team for Success and Project Governance," we cover the roles that exist on the project, so the leadership team should name the executive sponsor, project owner, and project manager for the project before taking any further steps. The leadership team should understand all of the roles on the project including the roles that will be filled by your implementer. They should also read the project management plan so that they understand the rules under which the project will be run. From there, the leadership team should receive a briefing on the content of Chapter 6, "Sprints and Tools Needed to Run Your Project," so they understand how sprints work and how progress will be measured on the project. Chapter 7, "Change Management Throughout Your Project," lays out how to develop your change management plan for the project. This is essential reading for the leadership team, so they understand their importance in the success of the dramatic amount of change that's about to happen.

**Assemble your full project team.** The internal roles are discussed in Chapter 2 and then reiterated in Chapter 5. You'll also read about the implementer's team during the project in Chapter 5. Review these two chapters before building your full project team.

**Develop your project management plan and schedule.** This is the activity that pulls in content from the most diverse chapters. The project management plan is an encompassing document that requires much discussion before it's fully agreed upon and ready to govern the project. The second half of Chapter 5 covers the project governance conversations that you should be having during this time along with an explanation of the project management plan components. I also suggest reading Chapter 14, "Dealing with Challenges Mid-Project," to understand how to manage risks and issues and to develop a good plan for your status reports.

To build a strong project management plan, you will need to gather learnings from several chapters:

◆ Sprints and task management are covered in Chapter 6.

◆ The process hierarchy and what should be included in scope are covered primarily in Chapter 8, "Organizing Your Business by Processes," with the deeper detail added in Chapter 11, "Designing the Software Collaboratively."

◆ The data migration plan is covered in Chapter 16, "Data Migration—Early and Often." As stated in that chapter, you want to start early on data migration so you should develop your data migration plan as part of the project management plan and get to work right after that.

◆ The testing plan is covered in Chapter 18, "Testing," and you should take the time to determine your testing plan and your entrance and exit criteria for the different milestones during the Define stage time frame.

◆ The environment plan is covered in Chapter 17, "Environment Management and Deployments." You will need to start the setup of your Development, Build, and Test environments as soon as you settle on your plan.

**Refine your scope and create estimates for major functionality.** This is an extension of the work needed for the project management plan. This is the activity of refining scope down to the process level, where you are typically at the process group level when you sign the implementation contract. Read Chapter 8 to understand the process hierarchy at a deeper level and Chapter 11 to understand how the process refinement will occur. I also suggest that you read Chapter 12, "Requirements Gathering and Staying 'In the Box'," so that you understand what a fit/gap analysis is, as you often want to refine your original fit/gap level during the Define stage.

**Conduct your kickoff meeting.** The final step of the Define stage is the kickoff meeting. All of the preceding activities should be completed in advance of the kickoff meeting, and the contents of the meeting are covered in Chapter 10, "Factors for a Successful Project Kickoff."

As noted in the specific activity areas, you should really read through all of the chapters up to Chapter 18 to prepare for the Define stage.

## Create Stage

The *Create stage* corresponds to the time from the kickoff meeting until the code is complete and ready to be tested. The purpose of the Create stage is to build the solution to your needs. To achieve your goals, you will need to determine what you require by taking the processes in scope and defining your requirements. You will use the JPD iterations to make sure that you have all of your requirements defined, and then you'll configure the system and build the customizations to make your solution complete. Figure 23.5 lays out the activities in chronological order with three activities going on through the Create stage.

**FIGURE 23.5**
Key activities during the Create stage

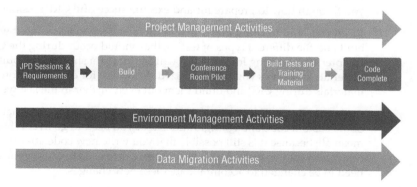

Let's walk through each step and point you to the relevant chapter for these activities.

**Project management** Throughout the Create stage you will perform your regular project management activities including your sprint-related meetings, updating your status reports and budget spreadsheets, and managing risks and issues. There is little change in the progression through the Create stage, but you have to be prepared to adapt to risks and issues and potential timeline adjustments. Review Chapters 5, 6, 7, and especially Chapter 14 to understand how project management should occur during the Create stage.

**Joint process design sessions and requirements**   You will run anywhere between two and four JPD sessions for each process group and during that time that you will go through the out-of-the-box functionality and identify any new requirements, as you determine how to build the solution. This process will make up more than half of the elapsed time in the Create phase, and some of the next activity, building the solution, will occur during that time. Review Chapter 11 and Chapter 12 to see how you should proceed through these activities.

**Building the solution**   You will start building the solution as you start your JPD sessions with some amount of configuration. Once you understand what you are going to build (which can happen after JPD1, but more of it becomes clear after JPD2 and JPD3), you start configuring the system, writing design documents, and developing custom code. These activities become more prevalent from the middle to the end of the Create stage. After the CRP sessions, you will have a little time left to finalize any code before achieving the code complete milestone at the end of the stage. Review Chapter 15, "Customizations vs. Configurations and How You Manage Them," for the details around the elements necessary to build your solution.

**Environment management**   You will start the Create stage focused on the Development, Build, and Test environments. You will be moving data back and forth between these environments throughout the early and middle part of the stage, and then you'll start preparing for your CRP session. After the CRP session, you will need to have your UAT and Production environments ready to go before you start the Deploy stage. Chapter 17 takes you through the activities that happen throughout the Create stage.

**Conference room pilots**   The CRP sessions happen at the end of the Create stage, and they serve as the opportunity for subject matter experts to use the system and provide feedback before you run out of time to make changes. Chapter 13, "Conference Room Pilots," walks you through how to prepare for and execute successful CRP sessions.

**Build tests and training material**   In Chapter 18, you learn about what test cases need to be built and the different types of testing that should occur during the Create stage. In Chapter 19, "Training for All," you will see that you should start building your training materials as soon as you have finalized the design for each area. You can pilot your training materials during CRP and build them out even further in the last weeks of the Create stage.

**Code complete**   The final step in the Create stage is to validate that you have completed all of the custom code and configurations that you need to go live. When I say all, I don't literally mean all, because it is still possible that you write new code after the end of the Create stage, but you should be very judicious about any new code because your testing and training plans need to be changed to accommodate these new changes.

As noted, you will have testing and training activities that need to be done within the Create stage. It certainly wouldn't hurt to read ahead through the final chapters while you are working on all of the tasks necessary to get through the Create stage.

# Deploy Stage

The *Deploy stage* corresponds to the time from code complete until the end of hypercare. The purpose of the Deploy stage is to test the system, train your users, go live, and work through any post go-live issues before transitioning to the long-term support model outlined in Figure 23.6.

**FIGURE 23.6**

Deploy stage

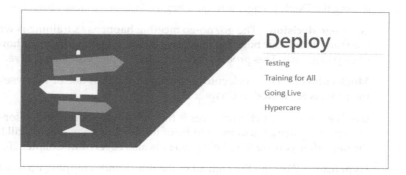

The Deploy stage activities are mostly addressed in Chapters 16–21, but it still incorporates ongoing concepts from earlier chapters like those concerning project and change management. Figure 23.7 lays out the activities in their chronological order.

**FIGURE 23.7**

Key activities during the Deploy stage

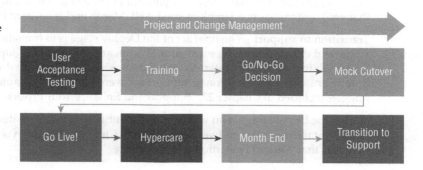

Let's walk through each step to point you to the relevant chapter for these activities while understanding project and change management happen throughout the Deploy stage.

**Project and change management**   Similar to the Create stage, the regular project management activities continue to occur in the Deploy stage. Change management is a constant throughout the project, but this is where the new process meets the user population and where you often have the most pushback. For project management, read through Chapters 5, 6, and 14, and for change management, review Chapter 7.

**User acceptance testing** The opening ceremony in the Deploy stage is UAT, and that will continue for the first few weeks of the Deploy stage. You will do testing in the Create stage, but you will have designated sessions during the Deploy stage as outlined in Chapter 18.

**Training** Like testing, training starts in the Create stage with the development of training materials. After UAT, train the trainer and end user training sessions are the prime activity during the Deploy stage. Review Chapter 19 to read more about the process.

**Go/no-go decision** The go/no-go meeting happens as training is wrapping up and you have the majority of your bugs resolved, so you have a good picture of how the system will work once you go live. This process is covered in Chapter 20, "Going Live."

**Mock cutover** The mock cutover typically happens one or two weeks before you go live and the process is covered in Chapter 20.

**Go-live** The production cutover is the step you've been waiting for—this is when you go live on the system. It's in the middle of the Deploy stage, as you still have hypercare to get through after you are live. This process is also covered in Chapter 20.

**Hypercare** Working through all of the issues and wrapping up any final training make up the first few weeks of hypercare. You want to activate your HelpDesk process right away, and the number of incidents will go down as you get further from the go-live date. The hypercare activities are covered in Chapter 21, "Hypercare."

**Month end** The first month end after going live is nearly the end of the hypercare period. This is your chance to make sure that your numbers tie out—that's the best way to validate that your system has been implemented well. Month end is covered in Chapter 21.

**Transition to support** The final act of the Deploy stage is to transition out your project team. At the end of hypercare, you want your IT team and the partner's support team to take over the remaining work as you start to think about what more you can do with the system in the Empower stage. The transition to support is covered mostly in Chapter 21 with a few more nuggets included in Chapter 22, "Support and Enhance Your Project."

During the Deploy stage, you will certainly identify future release items that will go into enhancement releases after go-live. Read ahead to Chapter 22 so that you know how to handle the requests that you can't get into the main release.

## Empower Stage

The *Empower stage* starts right after the final transition to support, and it goes as long as you'd like it to continue. The goal of the Empower stage is to provide ongoing support and enhance your solution to create even more value from the project, as shown in Figure 23.8.

The timeline of events in the Empower stage is up to your current needs so that you can decide on your enhancement plan shortly after go-live and adjust as you go along.

Since we just covered this in Chapter 22, I will direct you back there for what you can do during the post-hypercare period.

FIGURE 23.8
Empower stage

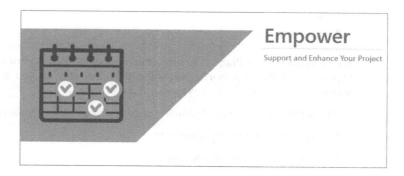

## Additional Resources

The goal of this book is to provide you with a thorough understanding of each of the steps required to implement Microsoft Dynamics successfully. A book covering everything at the most detailed level would be 2,000-plus pages, so that wouldn't be much fun to read. If you are a core team lead or IT team member, you may want to find the 400-level content for your particular area. Fortunately, there is a good amount of information online that can help you get to that extra level of depth:

**Microsoft's Dynamics 365 home page**: dynamics.microsoft.com

**Microsoft Dynamics 365 pricing**: dynamics.microsoft.com/en-us/pricing

**Microsoft Dynamics 365 documentation**: docs.microsoft.com/en-us/dynamics365

**Microsoft Dynamics 365 Learn site**: docs.microsoft.com/en-us/learn/dynamics365

**AppSource**: appsource.microsoft.com

**Lifecycle Services**: lcs.dynamics.com

**Microsoft Dynamics 365 videos on YouTube**: youtube.com/channel/UCJGCg4rB3QSs8y_1FquelBQ

**Stoneridge Software blog and events page**: stoneridgesoftware.com/resources

You can find all sorts of content on Microsoft Dynamics 365 by searching the Internet, but these links will help you start at the most common places people go for help.

## The Bottom Line

**Selection Criteria**   You should evaluate four key criteria as part of your software selection process as outlined in Chapter 3.

> **Master It**   Which of the following is not one of the four keys to consider when buying an ERP or CRM solution?
>
> **1.** Fit
>
> **2.** Cost

   **3.** ISV

   **4.** Platform

**Project Management Plan**   The project management plan is your rulebook for how to run the project. It is defined shortly before the kickoff meeting as you and your partner come together to determine the best way to run the project.

   **Master It**   Which of the following is not a component of your project management plan?

   **1.** Environment management plan

   **2.** Budget management process

   **3.** Risk and issue management

   **4.** Month-end procedures

**Define Stage**   The purpose of the Define stage is to select the right ERP or CRM system, choose the right implementation partner, and prepare the team to build the solution.

   **Master It**   Which of these activities would not happen during the Define stage?

   **1.** Selecting the software

   **2.** Writing FDDs

   **3.** The kickoff meeting

   **4.** The development of the change management plan

**Create Stage**   The purpose of the Create stage is to build the solution according to your in-scope processes and requirements.

   **Master It**   Which of these activities would not happen during the Create stage?

   **1.** Go/no-go meeting

   **2.** JPDs

   **3.** CRP

   **4.** Configurations and customizations

**Deploy Stage**   The purpose of the Deploy stage is to test the system, train your users, go live, and work through any post go-live issues before transitioning to the long-term support model.

   **Master It**   Which of these activities would not happen during the Deploy stage?

   **1.** UAT

   **2.** Go/no-go meeting

   **3.** Cutover

   **4.** CRP

# The Bottom Line

Each of "The Bottom Line" sections in the chapters suggest exercises to deepen skills and understanding. Sometimes there is only one possible solution, but often you are encouraged to use your skills and creativity to create something that builds on what you know and lets you explore one of many possible solutions.

## Chapter 1: Stages of an Implementation Overview

**Organizing your project in sprints**   One of the key elements of the Agile and Scrum implementation methodologies is the concept of using a sprint to create interim deadlines within a project to make sure that you can deliver the full project on time.

**Master It**   What is the first thing you do during a new sprint?

1. Run a retrospective

2. Do a planning session

3. Do a review session

4. Outline the following sprints

**Solution**   2. Do a planning session

**Waterfall methodology**   The Waterfall methodology is the classic way to execute on an ERP or CRM implementation, but I recommend that you use a hybrid of the Waterfall and Agile methodologies for your project.

**Master It**   What is a part of the Waterfall methodology?

1. The implementation is done in a step-by-step process

2. Sprints are used

3. New requirements are placed in the backlog

4. The Create phase

**Solution**   1. The implementation is done in a step-by-step process

**Sure step** Microsoft put together a methodology in the early 2000s called "Sure Step," which was widely adopted for Dynamics implementations during the 2000–2015 period.

**Master It** Microsoft Sure Step follows which methodology?

**1.** Agile

**2.** Scrum

**3.** Client Journey

**4.** Waterfall

**Solution** 4. Waterfall

**Challenging projects** ERP and CRM implementations are challenging projects that often go over time and over budget. The goal of this book is to prepare you better for a project so that you can complete it on time and within the budget.

**Master It** What percentage of implementation projects go over budget?

**1.** 100 percent

**2.** 60 percent

**3.** 40 percent

**4.** 20 percent

**Solution** 2. 60 percent

**Triple constraints** The triple constraints diagram is a triangle that represents a common concept in project management which shows how a change in one of the sides of the triangle affects the other two sides.

**Master It** Which of the following is not part of the triple constraints of project management?

**1.** Cost

**2.** Scope

**3.** Sprint

**4.** Time

**Solution** 3. Sprint

# Chapter 2: What to Do Before You Begin a Project

**Project roles** Your project team has a number of different roles that play a critical part of the success on the project. It's important to understand and assign people to each of these roles.

**Master It** Which of the following is not a required role for your implementation project?

**1.** Selection consultant

**2.** Project owner

**3.** Project manager

**4.** Subject matter expert

**Solution**   1. Selection consultant

**Project schedule**   When you are preparing for your project, it's important to understand any seasonality that might impact your schedule.

**Master It**   Which of the following is not something that should impact your proposed go-live date?

**1.** Year-end close of financials

**2.** Seasonality of business

**3.** Everyone is busy all the time

**4.** Expiration of support for existing product

**Solution**   3. Everyone is busy all the time

**Process categories**   All businesses have common processes, and when determining your scope, it's helpful to associate your business activities to these common processes.

**Master It**   Which of the following is not one of the core process categories?

**1.** Procure to pay

**2.** Hire to retire

**3.** Quote to cash

**4.** Dollars to cents

**Solution**   4. Dollars to cents

**Client journey**   There is a common set of stages that occur on a business application implementation project that we call the Client Journey. This journey has stages that need to go in order, and it's important to understand the order of operation to complete a project successfully.

**Master It**   Determining your project success criteria and ROI should occur in which stage of the ERP/CRM journey?

**1.** Align

**2.** Define

**3.** Create

**4.** Deploy

**Solution**   1. Align

**Project budget** Implementation projects are expensive, and it's important to set aside adequate budget to make sure that the project is successful. The budget should include internal and external costs.

**Master It** An ERP project should cost between which percent of your annual revenues?

1. 0 and 0.5 percent

2. 1 and 2 percent

3. 3 and 7 percent

4. 10 and 20 percent

Solution 3. 3 and 7 percent

# Chapter 3: Four Keys to Consider When Buying an ERP or CRM Solution

**Selection criteria** In this chapter, we reviewed the four keys to make the right software selection. Review the summary to understand which is the most important—if there is one that is most important.

**Master It** Which of the following is the most important factor to consider when buying an ERP or CRM system?

1. Product fit

2. Cost

3. Implementation partner

4. You need all the above plus the platform

Solution 4. You need all the above plus the platform

**Degree of fit** The degree of fit is the percentage of features in the software that meet your particular requirements. You are very unlikely to have a 100 percent degree of fit, so you should compare the results from the different products you reviewed and rate the products based on the one closest to 100 percent.

**Master It** How do you best determine the degree of fit?

1. Run a fit/gap analysis

2. Ask your ERP evaluator to determine

3. Look at industry benchmarks

4. Estimate it based on your team's gut reaction

Solution 1. Run a fit/gap analysis

**Platform criteria**   Several elements go into the decision about the right platform for your ERP or CRM solution. Review the section of the chapter that covers this to familiarize yourself with the various elements.

> **Master It**   Which is a reason why the platform matters when choosing an ERP or CRM system?
>
> **1.** It keeps costs down
>
> **2.** Your upgrade costs could be minimal for your industry
>
> **3.** It makes sure that your product is a good fit for your industry
>
> **4.** You can keep track of your project plan on that platform
>
> **Solution**   2. Your upgrade costs could be minimal for your industry

**Implementation partner experience**   Your implementation partner will help guide you to a successful project with experience from similar projects in the past. You should rate this criterion based on your perception of their ability to lead you to a successful project.

> **Master It**   Your implementation partner should have experience with all of the following except:
>
> **1.** The specific version of the product
>
> **2.** Active Directory and Exchange
>
> **3.** Yours or a similar industry
>
> **4.** Your agreed-upon implementation methodology
>
> **Solution**   2. Active Directory and Exchange

**Project costs**   One of the four keys to consider when deciding on the right software and partner is the cost of the project. Business application implementations are expensive, and it's important to understand all of the costs so that you are not surprised in the end.

> **Master It**   Which of the following is not one of the costs to consider during an implementation?
>
> **1.** The implementation partner's consulting fees
>
> **2.** The cost of subscription fees of the software
>
> **3.** Board member compensation
>
> **4.** Internal resources and contractors
>
> **Solution**   3. Board member compensation

## Chapter 4: How to Evaluate and Buy Business Application Software

**Steps in the Sales Process**   It's important to understand each of the steps in the sales process so that you know what to expect as you go on this journey and so that you can set proper expectations on the amount of time it will take to make the selection.

**Master It**   Which of the following is not a step in the purchase of enterprise software?

**1.** Discovery

**2.** Demo

**3.** Deployment

**4.** Contract negotiations

**Solution**   3. Deployment

**Matching the Software to Your Key Requirements**   As you review software solutions for your business, you should first understand and prioritize the requirements that you have for this software. The more time you take to define your requirements upfront, the better fit you'll be able to achieve for your needs.

**Master It**   What is the purpose of a request for proposal (RFP)?

**1.** Compile a list of vendors

**2.** Assess the vendor's degree of fit based on your requirements

**3.** Gather high-level information about the vendor

**4.** Overload the vendor with work to see how badly they want the business

**Solution**   2. Assess the vendor's degree of fit based on your requirements

**Steps in the Sales Process**   Each step in the sales process accomplishes a particular goal that's important to the overall decision to purchase the right software for your business.

**Master It**

What is the purpose of a discovery session?

**1.** To demonstrate the product

**2.** To determine the implementation timeline

**3.** To finalize contracts

**4.** To provide the vendors with your requirements and pain points

**Solution**   4. To provide the vendors with your requirements and pain points

**Four Key Criteria**   There are four key criteria to use to make the best decision on which software to buy and which implementation partner will help guide you through the process.

> **Master It**   What are the four key criteria for evaluating a vendor for a business application implementation?
>
> 1. Fit, platform, implementer, cost
>
> 2. Budget, authority, need, timeline
>
> 3. Cost, cost, cost, cost
>
> 4. Industry fit, industry experience of implementer, degree of fit, industry references
>
> **Solution**   1. Fit, platform, implementer, cost

**Understanding Contracts**   As you get ready to move forward on the project, you will need to sign several contracts that govern software and consulting terms.

> **Master It**   Which of the following is not a contract you'll need to sign before starting the project?
>
> 1. Master Services Agreement
>
> 2. Statement of Work
>
> 3. Software subscription or End User License Agreement
>
> 4. Change Request
>
> **Solution**   4. Change Request

# Chapter 5: Organizing Your Team for Success and Project Governance

**Project Governance**   Before you formally kick off the project, you should prepare several documents that outline how you want to run the project. There is one central document that captures the key elements of how the project should be run.

> **Master It**   What is the document that encompasses all areas of project preparation, which is required in advance of the kickoff meeting?
>
> 1. Plan of record
>
> 2. Project management plan
>
> 3. Budget file
>
> 4. Success criteria
>
> **Solution**   2. Project management plan

**Project Roles**   In this chapter, we reviewed the roles on the project, looking at both your team and the partner's implementation team. Review these roles to make sure that you have people in the most important roles.

**Master It**   Which of these internal roles is optional on a project?

**1.** Executive sponsor

**2.** Project manager

**3.** Subject matter expert

**4.** Business intelligence designer

**Solution**   4. Business intelligence designer

**Responsibilities for Project Roles**   Each different role on the project brings with it a certain set of responsibilities. Reporting on the budget activity is a key responsibility fulfilled by one of the project team members.

**Master It**   Who updates and manages the budget file weekly on the project?

**1.** Executive sponsor

**2.** Project owner

**3.** Project manager

**4.** Core team

**Solution**   3. Project manager

**Project Estimates**   To complete your project on time, you will need to estimate how much time it takes to complete the full project. Once you get into the project, you'll need to update the estimates continuously in order to know if you're still able to complete the project within the original timelines.

**Master It**   What is T-shirt sizing?

**1.** Estimating the project work at a high level

**2.** Getting swag for the project team

**3.** Creating a project schedule

**4.** Another name for the daily stand-up meeting

**Solution**   1. Estimating the project work at a high level

**Project Meetings**   As explained in this chapter, key meetings should be held on projects with different purposes. Review the list of meetings and make sure that your project team is following them.

**Master It**   At which meeting do you report progress to the executive team?

**1.** Weekly internal team meeting

**2.** Daily stand-up

**3.** Sprint planning

**4.** Steering committee

**Solution**   4. Steering committee

# Chapter 6: Sprints and Tools Needed to Run Your Project

**Setting up the Appropriate Sprint Duration**   Sprints allow you to deliver value in short amounts of time, so everyone has visibility to progress but also as an opportunity to adjust if needed. When choosing your sprint length, you want to find a happy medium between a sprint that is short enough to course-correct if needed, but not so short that you are spending all of your time in planning meetings. It's important that once you set your sprint duration, you stick with it.

**Master It**   All sprints must be the following length:

**1.** 2 weeks

**2.** 4 weeks

**3.** 30 days

**4.** Whatever the project team agrees to

**Solution**   4. Whatever the project team agrees to

**Coordinating the Necessary Sprint Meetings**   Sprints have defined meetings used for planning and checkpoints during each sprint cycle. These meetings are critical to the overall success of the project. You need to have these checkpoints and planning sessions to hold people accountable and to adjust during a project.

**Master It**   Which is not one of the core sprint meetings?

**1.** Sprint retrospective

**2.** Sprint planning

**3.** Steering Committee meeting

**4.** Stand-up meeting

**Solution**   3. Steering Committee meeting

**Organizing the Stand-up Meeting**   Stand-up meetings are among the most valuable meetings that you can have on a project. They are often meetings where they start out being run correctly but ultimately devolve into mini status reports. It's important to run these meetings correctly and stick to the formula that has proven effective here.

**Master It**   How long is a stand-up meeting?

**1.** 2 minutes

**2.** 15 minutes

**3.** 30 minutes

**4.** 1 hour

**Solution**  2. 15 minutes

**Tracking Work with Azure DevOps**  DevOps is a set of practices that combines software development (Dev) and IT Operations (Ops). The Azure DevOps product from Microsoft is designed as a database that you can use to track all activity on a project, including development and how you release the code or configurations to production IT systems.

**Master It**  What field on a DevOps item do you use to show how much work is ahead of you?

**1.** State

**2.** Remaining Work

**3.** Original Estimate

**4.** Completed Hours

**Solution**  2. Remaining Work

**Reporting on Progress**  An issue is something that has occurred that requires some kind of mitigation plan. An issue is not the same as a bug—it's bigger than a bug. An example of an issue may be a resource leaving the project. You now have to develop a plan to bring in a replacement resource, which may affect multiple tasks and delay the project. These then become Priority issues.

**Master It**  Which of the following definitions is considered Priority 1?

**1.** The issue does not affect core functionality or data—it is an inconvenience.

**2.** A non-critical business function is not performing correctly, or an individual or small group of people is unable to perform something that's not an everyday occurrence.

**3.** A high-priority business function is not working correctly, or functionality is limited but still achievable with a workaround.

**4.** A critical business function is not working or is unavailable to the majority of users.

**Solution**  4. A critical business function is not working or is unavailable to the majority of users.

# Chapter 7: Change Management Throughout Your Project

**Understanding Change Management**  Many project stakeholders don't understand the definition of change management and therefore aren't in a good position to implement it on the project.

**Master It**  What is change management?

1. A series of sessions that talk about how change impacts a project

2. The approaches that you need to prepare your team for and support them through the process or organizational change

3. Trainings before go-live

4. A leadership seminar to prepare the leadership team to be aligned

**Solution**   2. The approaches that you need to prepare your team for and support them through the process or organizational change

**Components of Change Management**   Implementing change management successfully requires nine steps. It's important to understand each of these steps and make sure that you have a game plan for each one.

**Master It**   Which one of these is not a step in the change management process?

1. Leadership alignment

2. Organization evaluation

3. Communicate effectively

4. Hypercare

**Solution**   4. Hypercare

**Organization Assessment**   One of the steps in change management is to assess your organization to understand how willing and able they are to accept the change that is about to come.

**Master It**   Your organizational assessment should include which step?

1. Attitude toward advancement

2. Joint process design

3. Enterprise process review

4. Training plan

**Solution**   1. Attitude toward advancement

**Project Motivation**   When the leadership team agrees to go forward with a business application implementation project, it's important for all team members to understand the success criteria and the motivation for the project.

**Master It**   Which benefit is most commonly sought by the leadership team on a project?

1. Limited clicks

2. Ease of use

3. Reporting and analytics

4. Uncluttered screens

**Solution**   3. Reporting and analytics

**Setting Expectations**   A core component of change management is setting proper expectations for the end users. If they expect the system to be perfect and easy, they will be disappointed when they discover reality.

**Master It**   Just after go-live, which of the following situations is most likely to occur?

**1.** The system is bug free.

**2.** Users can find all of the reports they need.

**3.** Security is set up perfectly.

**4.** It will take longer to get through processes.

**Solution**   4. It will take longer to get through processes.

# Chapter 8: Organizing Your Business by Processes

**Associating Activities to Process Categories**   It's important to identify the common activities you do in your system today and associate them back to the top-level categories so that you can start to see all of the activities across your different departments that are really the same.

**Master It**   In what process category would creating a vendor belong?

**1.** Quote to Cash

**2.** Procure to Pay

**3.** Acquire to Retire

**4.** Financial Record to Report

**Solution**   2. Procure to Pay

**Understanding the Process Hierarchy**   You will want to understand the process hierarchy so that you can quickly classify activities into the correct level on the hierarchy.

**Master It**   Which of these process levels is the top level (broadest)?

**1.** Process Category

**2.** Process Group

**3.** Process

**4.** Sub-Process

**Solution**   1. Process Category

**Setting Up the Proper Hierarchy in Azure DevOps**   Azure DevOps is a valuable tool to use on your project. You want to set up a hierarchy in that system that maps to the hierarchy of Process Categories, Process Groups, and Processes.

**Master It**   A process category most closely aligns to what type of record in DevOps or Agile methodology?

**1.** Requirement

**2.** User story

**3.** Feature

**4.** Epic

**Solution**   4. Epic

**Adding Work Impacts Your Timeline**   Anytime a new process becomes part of the project scope, this adds work to the project. That work will need to be managed, and resources will need to be assigned to complete it. You will need to notify the project stakeholders about this change.

**Master It**   If you add a major requirement or scope item after the beginning of the project, you will need to complete which of the following?

**1.** A Master Services Agreement

**2.** A Process Category

**3.** An Earned Value Curve

**4.** A Change Request

**Solution**   4. A Change Request

**Understanding Terms**   It's important to create a common language on your project—some team members may not be familiar with implementation project terms, so you will need to educate the team involved on the project.

**Master It**   Which of these constitutes a software requirement on a project?

**1.** A user story

**2.** A function or piece of information needed to run your business

**3.** Everything you do in the business

**4.** Showing up to work

**Solution**   2. A function or piece of information needed to run your business

# Chapter 9: Independent Software Vendors—Filling Gaps and Managing Partnerships

**Common Terminology**   It's important for project stakeholders to understand commonly used terms in the industry.

**Master It**   What does the abbreviation ISV stand for as it relates to Microsoft Dynamics?

1. Integrated Solution Vendors

2. Independent Software Vendors

3. Isolated Solution Vehicles

4. Third Parties

**Solution**  2. Independent Software Vendors

**Different Focuses of ISVs**  There are three types of ISVs, and each focuses on providing different functionality to augment Microsoft Dynamics.

**Master It**  Functional ISVs are used to provide which of the following?

1. An add-on solution specific to an industry

2. A solution for gaps in one functional area

3. Core Microsoft Dynamics capability

4. Hosting for the software

**Solution**  2. A solution for gaps in one functional area

**ISV Examples**  Many different ISVs could be useful in your project. It's important to understand if the ISV is focused on an industry or a functional gap.

**Master It**  A sales tax filing software extension would be an example of what type of ISV?

1. Industry ISV

2. Functional ISV

3. Integrated ISV

4. Hosting ISV

**Solution**  2. Functional ISV

**Role of Industry ISV**  Industry ISVs can be a mandatory part of the solution depending on the industry you are in.

**Master It**  An Industry ISV provides which of the following?

1. Core Microsoft Dynamics capability

2. An add-on solution specific to an industry

3. Hosting for the software

4. A solution for gaps in one functional area

**Solution**  2. An add-on solution specific to an industry

**AppSource Marketplace**  Microsoft introduced a marketplace for customers or prospects to look for approved products and services.

**Master It**  What is AppSource?

1. Microsoft's app store where you can download apps for your Microsoft Surface computer

2. Microsoft's business application marketplace for extensions and consulting services

3. An independent site with community information about ISVs

4. Microsoft's partner portal

**Solution**   2. Microsoft's business application marketplace for extensions and consulting services

# Chapter 10: Factors for a Successful Project Kickoff

**Kickoff Meeting Timing**   It is often assumed that the kickoff meeting starts while the ink is still wet on the contract. It's important to set expectations about when it occurs and what needs to be done to be ready for it.

**Master It**   When should the kickoff meeting happen?

1. As soon as the contracts are signed and the software is purchased

2. At the end of the Define phase before the Create phase begins

3. As you are ready to begin testing the software

4. Before you start evaluating vendors

**Solution**   2. At the end of the Define phase before the Create phase begins

**Order of Operation**   Throughout a project, it's critical to understand the order in which events need to occur. The kickoff meeting ends up being the culmination of a lot of preliminary work.

**Master It**   Which of the following does not have to be done before your kickoff meeting?

1. Define your success criteria

2. Outline your project schedule

3. Define your change management plan

4. Develop your go-live checklist

**Solution**   4. Develop your go-live checklist

**Kickoff Meeting Agenda**   In this chapter, I outline the suggested agenda for the kickoff meeting. Many people start with introductions, but I suggest a different approach that has proven to be more successful.

**Master It**   Who should speak first at the kickoff meeting?

1. The project manager

2. The project owner

**3.** The executive sponsor

**4.** The implementation partner

**Solution**   3. The executive sponsor

**Success Criteria**   We defined success criteria in Chapter 2 and talked about them again in Chapter 5. They are a critical part of the kickoff meeting, as it's your executive's chance to explain them and get everyone on the same page with the direction the company is heading and why this project is important.

**Master It**   What are the success criteria?

**1.** Top, measurable goals of the project

**2.** Top reports that need to be created

**3.** The process categories in scope

**4.** The project manager's communication plan

**Solution**   1. Top, measurable goals of the project

**Project Artifacts**   A project manager should be knowledgeable about the core artifacts or deliverables needed on the project. The project manager also needs to communicate the definition of these terms to the rest of the participants on the project team.

**Master It**   What is a project schedule?

**1.** Your DevOps sprint cycles

**2.** Your Microsoft Project plan, which lays out the events on the project

**3.** The plan for the first two weeks of the project

**4.** The change management plan activities

**Solution**   2. Your Microsoft Project plan, which lays out the events on the project

# Chapter 11: Designing the Software Collaboratively

**JPD Definition**   This chapter is focused on how to design software collaboratively using a concept called a Joint Process Design. To design the software, you end up going through several JPD sessions.

**Master It**   Which of these features is part of a Joint Application Design or Joint Process Design approach?

**1.** Identifying requirements in a spreadsheet

**2.** Iterative workshops to develop the approach and software together

**3.** Questionnaires that need to be returned with answers to requirements questions

**4.** Tracking system for all requirements

**Solution**   2. Iterative workshops to develop the approach and software together

**JPD Elements**   The cycle of going through each iteration of JPD sessions leads to a variety of outputs that are needed to move forward on the project.

**Master It**   Which one of these steps is not a part of the Joint Process Design flow?

**1.** Analyze

**2.** Design

**3.** Construct

**4.** Hypercare

**Solution**   4. Hypercare

**Incorporating Data into the JPDs**   We'll discuss this in greater depth in Chapter 16, "Data Migration—Early and Often," but you want to coordinate your data migration efforts with your JPD sessions. The more relevant data that you have while you go through examples, the easier it is for the team to understand the processes.

**Master It**   In which JPD session would you start using a subset of your actual data in the system?

**1.** JPD1

**2.** JPD2

**3.** JPD3

**4.** None

**Solution**   3. JPD3

**Order of Operations**   Throughout an implementation, it's important to understand the logical order of operations throughout the project. As you go through iterative design sessions, there is an order of operation to be followed to get the best output.

**Master It**   Which comes last in the iterative sequence of events through a project?

**1.** JPD1

**2.** JPD2

**3.** JPD3

**4.** CRP

**Solution**   4. CRP

**JPD Goals**   The ultimate goal of the Joint Process Design iterative design session is to develop the best software to meet the company's needs. Within that flow are other benefits as well, like the one in the question that follows.

**Master It**   Which of the following is one of the goals of a JPD session?

**1.** Demonstrate Dynamics functionality for selected processes

**2.** Design the entire application

**3.** Training the end users

**4.** Teach change management concepts

**Solution**   1. Demonstrate Dynamics functionality for selected processes

# Chapter 12: Requirements Gathering and Staying "In the Box"

**Definition of Out-of-the-Box**   In the beginning of the chapter, we talk about what out-of-the-box means using the software as it was designed by Microsoft.

**Master It**   Which of the following is not considered "out-of-the-box" functionality?

**1.** Configuration

**2.** Settings

**3.** Core system screens

**4.** Customizations

**Solution**   4. Customizations

**Definition of Requirement**   A requirement is a fundamental concept in software design—something you will see a lot of on your implementation project.

**Master It**   Which of these constitutes a software requirement on a project?

**1.** A process category

**2.** A function or piece of information needed to run your business

**3.** Everything you do in the business

**4.** Showing up to work

**Solution**   2. A function or piece of information needed to run your business

**Fit/Gap Analysis**   The fit/gap analysis exercise is where you look at all of your requirements to determine which of them can be met by the software and which require customizations to be built.

**Master It**   Which of the following is not a choice for classification on a fit/gap spreadsheet?

1. Fit

2. Fit w/Configuration

3. Fit w/Customization

4. Gap

**Solution**   3. Fit w/Customization

**Verifying a Requirement**   When you have completed the configuration and customization of the system, you need a means to identify if the requirement has been satisfied by the new system.

**Master It**   What does it mean when we say a requirement needs to be verifiable?

1. It needs to have a verified priority

2. It needs to have a verified owner

3. It needs to be able to be tested

4. It needs to be verified by another core team member

**Solution**   3. It needs to be able to be tested

**Cost of Customization**   Each customization you make to the system increases your short-term and long-term costs of owning the software, so you want to try to use the system out of the box as much as possible.

**Master It**   Which of the following is *not* considered a cost related to a customization?

1. Designing the customization

2. Testing the customization

3. Deploying the customization

4. Training the team on the customization

**Solution**   3. Deploying the customization

# Chapter 13: Conference Room Pilots

**Order of Operations**   CRPs occur after the JPD sessions in the implementation and before you start UAT sessions. It's important to do each step in the right order.

**Master It**   During which stage of the implementation journey do you find the conference room pilots?

1. Define

2. Create

3. Deploy

4. Empower

**Solution**  2. Create

**Content of CRP Sessions**  The goal of a CRP session is to walk through a part of the overall process from end to end to make sure that the hand-offs between processes work as designed.

**Master It**  CRP sessions should be organized by which of the following?

1. Process groups

2. Departments

3. Lines of business

4. Team schedules

**Solution**  1. Process groups

**Data Migration**  We discuss data migration further in Chapter 16, "Data Migration—Early and Often," but in this chapter we talk about what iteration of data migration you should use during the CRP cycle.

**Master It**  What data should be used for testing in a CRP?

1. Demo data

2. Hand-entered data

3. A sample of the migrated data

4. The latest migrated data from your previous system

**Solution**  4. The latest migrated data from your previous system

**Understanding Acronyms**  We try not to use too many acronyms on projects, but we do use a few standard acronyms and it's important to understand the order of these events.

**Master It**  Put these acronyms in their proper order during an implementation:

1. CRP-EPR-JPD-UAT

2. EPR-CRP-UAT-JPD

3. EPR-JPD-CRP-UAT

4. UAT-JPD-EPR-CRP

**Solution**  3. EPR-JPD-CRP-UAT

**Benefits of CRP**  In this chapter, we discussed several of the benefits of running through the end-to-end processes before you finish off the Create stage.

**Master It**  Which of these is not one of the benefits of a CRP?

1. Gives you the chance to practice the end-to-end process before code is complete

2. Helps with usability by identifying ways to streamline the processes

**3.** Raises the confidence of the team that the solution is getting ready for deployment

**4.** Practices the go-live cutover

**Solution**   4. Practices the go-live cutover

# Chapter 14: Dealing with Challenges Mid-Project

**Issues vs. Bugs**   I discussed the difference between issues and bugs in this chapter. Issues can be bugs, or they could be problems with scope, resources, or budget.

**Master It**   What best explains bugs in a project?

**1.** They are technical issues with the expectation that there will be many in a project.

**2.** They are personnel/non-technical issues.

**3.** They are the same thing as an issue.

**4.** They are microscopic mites that infect one's hardware.

**Solution**   1. They are technical issues with the expectation that there will be many in a project.

**Color of Your Status Report**   For each of the core elements of the project, you should report the status weekly as either Green (on track), Yellow (at risk), or Red (offtrack).

**Master It**   Status Report Situation: The project has just begun, and everything is off to a good start, but you don't have your project measurements and milestones in place yet. Which status color should the overall project be tracked as?

**1.** Green

**2.** Yellow

**3.** Red

**4.** Orange

**Solution**   2. Yellow

**Risks and Issues**   For each of the core elements of the project, you should report the status weekly as either Green (on track), Yellow (at risk), or Red (offtrack).

**Master It**   Status Report Situation: Several components of the project are at risk, and one of the eight parts of the project is offtrack. Which status color should the overall project be tracked as?

**1.** Green

**2.** Yellow

**3.** Red

**4.** Orange

**Solution**   3. Red

**Project Challenges**  An infinite number of challenges could occur on your project. Project managers should identify possible challenges and put them on the risk register so that you can start to build mitigation plans.

**Master It**  Which of the following are mid-project challenges?

**1.** Key person is leaving the project

**2.** Project team members are not making decisions

**3.** The project is trending behind

**4.** All of the above

**Solution**  4. All of the above

**Psychological Safety**  No one likes to hear bad news, nor does anyone like to share bad news. Unfortunately, bad things will happen on implementation projects, and it's important to create an environment where you can effectively deal with the bad news quickly.

**Master It**  Psychological safety is a key component to keep a project moving forward successfully. Which of the following are ways to support safety within a project?

**1.** Establish a pattern of always trying to find solutions, not of placing blame

**2.** Take a moment between hearing something and reacting to it to choose the right decision

**3.** All problems are team problems, not problems for individuals

**4.** All of the above

**Solution**  4. All of the above

# Chapter 15: Customizations vs. Configurations and How You Manage Them

**Commonly Used Definitions**  In implementation projects, participants should know commonly used terms so that they understand exactly what's being discussed.

**Master It**  Which of these is a definition of configuration?

**1.** Code change of any variety within the application

**2.** Individual user changing columns on a grid

**3.** Data that provides information about other data

**4.** A setting made in the user interface of the software that affects how the application works

**Solution**  4. A setting made in the user interface of the software that affects how the application works

**Customization vs. Configuration**   One of the big decisions you will face on projects is whether to use configurations or customizations to achieve what you want in the system.

**Master It**   When should you choose to customize the system?

**1.** An ISV exists that provides all of the necessary functionality

**2.** The system lacks functionality that you need in a particular area

**3.** Users want to modify a standard process because that's what has always been done

**4.** To automate entering configurations

**Solution**   2. The system lacks functionality that you need in a particular area

**Configuration Tracker**   Three common ways exist to track configurations, so make sure that you know what has been changed and in which environment.

**Master It**   Which of the following is not one of the ways to track configurations?

**1.** Configuration tracking spreadsheet

**2.** Lifecycle services

**3.** Personal notebook

**4.** Gold environment

**Solution**   3. Personal notebook

**Customization Lifecycle**   The lifecycle of a customization consists of eight common steps that take the idea from a requirement to a live, working customization.

**Master It**   Which of these is not a step in the lifecycle of customization?

**1.** Functional design document

**2.** Development completed

**3.** Code review

**4.** Joint process design

**Solution**   4. Joint process design

**Project Activity Tracking**   When developing customizations, you want to log three different tasks in your Azure DevOps system to manage the effort related to the customization.

**Master It**   Which three DevOps tasks are tracked related to the lifecycle of the customization?

**1.** Design, development, test

**2.** Requirements, design, approval

**3.** Development, code review, deployment

**4.** Unit test, regression test, end-to-end test

**Solution**   1. Design, development, test

# Chapter 16: Data Migration—Early and Often

**Core Concepts**   The acronym ETL actually describes the important steps in the data migration process, so it's a key term to know.

**Master It**   What does the abbreviation ETL stand for?

**1.** Extract, transition, logistics

**2.** Enter transactional lines

**3.** Extract, transform, load

**4.** Export, troubleshoot, load

**Solution**   3. Extract, transform, load

**Data Cleaning**   "Garbage In, Garbage Out" is a phrase that you will hear a lot on projects. You want to put a good amount of effort into making sure that there's no garbage when you are migrating data.

**Master It**   When should you start data cleaning on a project?

**1.** As soon as possible

**2.** After JPD1

**3.** Before CRP

**4.** Before UAT

**Solution**   1. As soon as possible

**What Should You Migrate?**   One of the most difficult decisions to make in the data migration process is how much data to migrate. The more data you migrate, the more history you have in the new system, but that effort takes time and money.

**Master It**   In which of the following cases would it be a good idea to migrate all transactional history?

**1.** You have 4 TB of data

**2.** Your previous system will soon no longer be accessible to you

**3.** You can query your previous data

**4.** You have significant data issues with your previous transactional data

**Solution**   2. Your previous system will soon no longer be accessible to you

**Understanding Transformation**   After you extract the data, the most challenging part of data migration is to transform the data so that it's ready to be loaded into Microsoft Dynamics 365.

> **Master It**   What happens in the transform step of data migration?
>
> **1.** You clean your data
>
> **2.** You load the data into the new system
>
> **3.** You run Iteration 3 of the data migration effort
>
> **4.** You map your source data to your target system
>
> **Solution**   4. You map your source data to your target system

**Iteration Timing**   During the project, you want to do several runs or iterations of data migration so that you can keep refining your process and making it better. You want to associate these iterations with major events on the functional side of the project.

> **Master It**   Which data migration iteration typically lines up with UAT?
>
> **1.** Iteration 0
>
> **2.** Iteration 1
>
> **3.** Iteration 2
>
> **4.** Iteration 3
>
> **Solution**   4. Iteration 3

# Chapter 17: Environment Management and Deployments

**Understanding Environments**   Four core environments are recommended for most implementations so that you can move your code from development to production while providing adequate means for testing.

> **Master It**   Which of these is the lowest-level environment?
>
> **1.** Build
>
> **2.** Test
>
> **3.** UAT
>
> **4.** Production
>
> **Solution**   1. Build

**Environment Usage**   In this chapter, we explain how each environment is used and when it is used. Each environment has a certain function that project team members need to understand.

> **Master It**   Which of these is the closest environment to production?

1. Build

2. Test

3. UAT

4. Sandbox

**Solution**   3. UAT

**Code Moves**   During code moves, it's as important to know what moves between environments as what doesn't, so you can plan for how to handle that information.

**Master It**   Which of the following does not typically move between environments through packaged solutions?

1. Custom development

2. Custom reports

3. Security

4. Data

**Solution**   4. Data

**Types of Releases**   Four different types of releases happen during the implementation project and after you go live. Each has a different process from the release, including different environments that would be used.

**Master It**   What would you call the type of release used when you move code from your build server to UAT?

1. Lower environment

2. Production

3. Hotfix

4. Enhancement

**Solution**   1. Lower environment

**Environment Plan**   We discuss many elements of the environment plan in this chapter. The environment plan is your guide to what environments are needed and how you use them.

**Master It**   Which of the following elements shows up on an environment plan?

1. Project schedule

2. Change request deployment plan

3. Functional design document

4. Planned environment outline

**Solution**   4. Planned environment outline

# Chapter 18: Testing

**Understanding Definitions**   Many different types of tests exist, as discussed in the early part of the chapter. Make sure that your team knows the common types of testing so that they can distinguish what type of testing is needed.

**Master It**   What is the term for code written to test the functionality just developed?

1. Load testing

2. Unit test code

3. Use case testing

4. Security testing

**Solution**   2. Unit test code

**Key Terminology**   Educating the team on the terms used during the implementation and the UAT sessions is key to keeping everyone on the same page throughout testing. You should introduce key terms in the UAT kickoff meeting.

**Master It**   Which of the following is a sequence of transactions in a scenario a user follows in the system.

1. Use case

2. Test plan

3. Test case

4. Pass

**Solution**   1. Use case

**Functional and Non-functional Tests**   It's easy to remember to run the functional tests, as that is what the users will see in the new system. It's equally as important to remember to run non-functional tests, as that will affect the quality of the new system.

**Master It**   What is an example of non-functional testing?

1. Unit test

2. Regression test

3. Performance test

4. End-to-end testing

**Solution**   3. Performance test

**Roles and Responsibilities**   It takes a concerted effort by the project team to make it through UAT successfully. The end goal is to get sign-off on the processes that you ran through during the testing sessions.

**Master It**   Which project role is responsible for signing off on the process at the end of UAT?

1. Core team lead

2. Business process owner

3. Executive sponsor

4. Project manager

**Solution**   2. Business process owner

**Exit Criteria**   At the end of UAT, it's important to look back on the goals that you had for the UAT sessions and to review the exit criteria that you set going into it. You can consider UAT complete only when those criteria have been met.

**Master It**   To exit UAT, which of the following conditions must be met?

1. All Priority 3 issues must be resolved.

2. All test cases must have been run.

3. All Priority 4 issues must be prioritized.

4. All Priority 1 issues must be resolved.

**Solution**   2. All test cases must have been run.

# Chapter 19: Training for All

**Interactive Sessions**   During the earlier part of the implementation, you will introduce the system to many users during the interactive sessions.

**Master It**   Which of the following is an interactive training session that occurs before formal training begins?

1. Discovery

2. Conference Room Pilot

3. Cutover Plan

4. Risk Register

**Solution**   2. Conference Room Pilot

**Training Modalities**   You can deliver training content in three primary ways, and each of the different models has pros and cons.

**Master It**   Which of the following is an example of an asynchronous learning model?

1. A Microsoft Teams call with the project team

2. In-person training

3. Hands-on lab

4. Watching recorded eLearning

**Solution**   4. Watching recorded eLearning

**Training Time**   As a rule, you should try to hold end user training close to when your users would be using that training. If you train them too far in advance, they may forget how to do the steps by the time they come to use it.

**Master It**   When should users learn the steps to perform periodic activities like month-end close processes?

1. Well before training

2. Just before training

3. During core training

4. After core training

**Solution**   4. After core training

**Training Validation**   It is important to validate that your end users have digested the content from the training. Make sure that you have a mechanism to test what they have learned.

**Master It**   Which of the following is not a way that you can validate that someone learned the material about the new system?

1. Asking them to complete a quiz

2. Sending them to a training event

3. One-on-one review session

4. Reviewing output from the system

**Solution**   2. Sending them to a training event

**Learning Management System**   A Learning Management System (LMS) can be a huge help on any implementation project, and I recommend that you investigate and find the right tool for your project.

**Master It**   Which of the following is not a benefit of a Learning Management System?

1. Records a Teams meeting

2. Tracks attendance at class

3. Tracks quiz completion after classes

4. Builds learning plans for users or roles

**Solution**   1. Records a Teams meeting

## Chapter 20: Going Live

**Go-Live Checklist**  Your go-live or cutover checklist shows all of the activity that must be completed during the weekend when you go live.

**Master It**  Which of the following is not on your go-live checklist?

1. Configuration work

2. Security work

3. Data migration activities

4. A project plan

**Solution**  4. A project plan

**Go-Live Scorecard**  A go-live scorecard is a report that goes out every day during the final stages of the project indicating the status of the go-live criteria items.

**Master It**

What does the color blue mean on a go-live scorecard?

1. Something that is on track but hasn't been done yet

2. Something that is offtrack

3. Something that is done, but you want to highlight or talk further

4. Something that is at risk of going offtrack

**Solution**  1. Something that is on track but hasn't been done yet

**Mock Cutover**  The mock cutover is a simulated cutover that happens a week or so before you do the production cutover.

**Master It**  When doing a mock cutover, you should deploy everything to which environment?

1. UAT

2. Production

3. Development

4. Test

**Solution**  2. Production

**Go/No-Go Meeting**  The go/no-go meeting is the official decision-making forum where the company's leadership team decides if you will be going live on schedule.

**Master It**  Which of the following is not an option that you can vote on in a go/no-go meeting?

1. Go

2. Decide later

3. Go with caveats

4. No-go

**Solution**   2. Decide later

**Go-Live Criteria**   The go-live criteria includes several elements, but the bug count is typically the most contentious. You should agree about the criteria in advance of the Deploy stage to reduce concerns during the final days before go-live.

**Master It**   When going live, which priority-level bugs must be zero?

1. Priority 1

2. Priority 2

3. Priority 3

4. Priority 1 and Priority 2

**Solution**   1. Priority 1

# Chapter 21: Hypercare

**Hypercare Duration**   The post go-live period where you transition from the project team to ongoing maintenance of the solution is a critical time in the project. You will want to work with your partner to schedule the appropriate duration of hypercare in advance so that you know how long you have to make this transition.

**Master It**   How long does hypercare typically last?

1. Go-live weekend

2. 1 week after go-live

3. 4 to 8 weeks after go-live

4. The first year after go-live

**Solution**   3. 4 to 8 weeks after go-live

**Where to Send Issues**   You want to establish a process for each issue that arises after you go live. This process should be consistent and widely communicated, so it can achieve adoption by the user base. A key part of the process is determining who will field user issues as they arise.

**Master It**   Post go-live support issues should be sent to which of the following?

1. Your internal HelpDesk

2. Partner support team

**3.** Directly to project team

**4.** Microsoft

**Solution**    1. Your internal HelpDesk

**Month-End Procedures**    After you go live, you will use the first month end as a means of validating all of the activity for the first month on the new system to make sure that all of the numbers tie out as expected. To prepare your team for month end, you will need to train them on the specific processes that need to be followed, as they won't be the same as using the system normally.

**Master It**    When should you train users on month-end procedures?

**1.** Prior to the pre-go-live training period

**2.** During pre-go-live training

**3.** A week or two before the first month end

**4.** During the first month end

**Solution**    3. A week or two before the first month end

**HelpDesk Levels**    All support incidents should be submitted to the HelpDesk, and the front-line resources dedicated to the HelpDesk should review those incidents. They should resolve whatever incidents they can, but they may need to escalate to higher tiers of support.

**Master It**    Which of these represents the Tier 4 resource for a HelpDesk request?

**1.** Partner support

**2.** Microsoft support

**3.** Project team

**4.** HelpDesk itself

**Solution**    2. Microsoft support

**Prioritizing Bugs**    Many bugs will be found after you go live on the new system. Hopefully, the majority of the bugs have a low priority, but those that are not low priority should be tracked and assigned to a post go-live release.

**Master It**    Post-go-live Priority 2 bug fixes should be released in which type of a release?

**1.** Go-live release

**2.** Internal release

**3.** Hotfix release

**4.** Scheduled post-go-live release

**Solution**    4. Scheduled post-go-live release

# Chapter 22: Support and Enhance Your Project

**Post Hypercare Support**  After hypercare, support volume should start to normalize, and you want to focus on building consistency in your support processes. You will still be seeing a fair number of incidents after hypercare, particularly in certain areas.

> **Master It**  What is an example of something that may require additional support after the hypercare period?

1. Project plans

2. Month-end support

3. Go-live support

4. Change requests

> **Solution**  2. Month-end support

**Partner Support**  Your HelpDesk will tackle all of the incidents that are raised from your users, but you will find that you'll need to escalate some incidents to your partner and potentially to Microsoft or an ISV. Partner support plans vary, but some general components are offered in each area.

> **Master It**  Which of the following is not a common partner support model offered?

1. Unlimited support through monthly fee

2. Pay as you go plans

3. Premier support

4. Phone support only

> **Solution**  4. Phone support only

**After Action Review**  Once you have completed hypercare, you should run an after action review.

> **Master It**  What is the goal of an after action review?

1. To collect broad feedback from the project team on what went well and what could have gone better on the project

2. To review each action done on the project

3. For leadership to share their thoughts on what the team should have done better

4. To have the customer share their criticism of the partner and the partner to share their criticism of the customer

> **Solution**  1. To collect broad feedback from the project team on what went well and what could have gone better on the project

**Testing for Future Releases**  After hypercare, you will want to run regular releases to fix outstanding bugs and enhance your solution. To prevent introducing new issues, you want to have a good testing plan for your releases.

> **Master It**
>
> What is regression testing?
>
> **1.** Developing tests for new code that was just developed
>
> **2.** End-to-end testing of processes
>
> **3.** Testing functionality already in place in the system
>
> **4.** Training for users of existing functionality
>
> **Solution**  3. Testing functionality already in place in the system

**Post Go-live Enhancements**  As you plan for future enhancement releases, you can add any number of new capabilities to your system.

> **Master It**  Which is not an example of common enhancements to make to your system post go-live?
>
> **1.** Reporting
>
> **2.** Usability
>
> **3.** Guardrails
>
> **4.** Status reports
>
> **Solution**  4. Status reports

# Chapter 23: Bringing It All Together

**Selection Criteria**  You should evaluate four key criteria as part of your software selection process as outlined in Chapter 3.

> **Master It**  Which of the following is not one of the four keys to consider when buying an ERP or CRM solution?
>
> **1.** Fit
>
> **2.** Cost
>
> **3.** ISV
>
> **4.** Platform
>
> **Solution**  3. ISV

**Project Management Plan**   The project management plan is your rulebook for how to run the project. It is defined shortly before the kickoff meeting as you and your partner come together to determine the best way to run the project.

**Master It**   Which of the following is not a component of your project management plan?

1. Environment management plan

2. Budget management process

3. Risk and issue management

4. Month-end procedures

**Solution**   4. Month-end procedures

**Define Stage**   The purpose of the Define stage is to select the right ERP or CRM system, choose the right implementation partner, and prepare the team to build the solution.

**Master It**   Which of these activities would not happen during the Define stage?

1. Selecting the software

2. Writing FDDs

3. The kickoff meeting

4. The development of the change management plan

**Solution**   2. Writing FDDs

**Create Stage**   The purpose of the Create stage is to build the solution according to your in-scope processes and requirements.

**Master It**   Which of these activities would not happen during the Create stage?

1. Go/no-go meeting

2. JPDs

3. CRP

4. Configurations and customizations

**Solution**   1. Go/no-go meeting

**Deploy Stage**   The purpose of the Deploy stage is to test the system, train your users, go live, and work through any post go-live issues before transitioning to the long-term support model.

**Master It**   Which of these activities would not happen during the Deploy stage?

1. UAT

2. Go/no-go meeting

3. Cutover

4. CRP

**Solution**   4. CRP

# Glossary

## A

### Acquire to Retire

One of the 12 process categories that covers Asset Management or Fixed Assets end-to-end from acquisition to disposal.

### Advanced concepts

For the purposes of this book, it refers to activities in the system such as returns or refunds that are completed on a limited basis.

### After Action Review (AAR)

A meeting one runs after any type of project (or milestone) has been completed to gather feedback from everyone on the team about how the project went, what went well, and what could have gone better.

### Agile Manifesto

Four values and 12 principles for developing software efficiently and effectively born in 2001 from a meeting of 17 IT professionals.

### Agile methodology

A software implementation that follows the Agile manifesto and is focused on creating a more flexible and adaptive system for implementing software. It was built out of the thinking that there was a better way than the stagnant Waterfall methodology.

### Align stage

The first stage in the Client Journey to get your team internally aligned and provide an idea of what to be looking for in the best product for your company.

### Application lifecycle management (ALM)

The management of applications including governance, development, and maintenance.

### Application Programming Interfaces (APIs)

Open standards used for connecting data and objects between systems.

### AppSource

Microsoft's specific search engine serving as a one-stop shop to find approved Microsoft independent software vendors and their products.

### Artificial Intelligence (AI)

Intelligence demonstrated by machines or any computing capability that allows a system to learn and reason like humans.

### Asynchronous training

Self-paced training by which students access learning content, take assessments, and communicate at their own pace.

### Authentication

The process of confirming one's identity when logging in to a system.

### Authorization

The act of granting permissions or privileges to take action in a system.

### Azure DevOps (ADO)

A Software as a Service (SaaS) platform from Microsoft that provides an end-to-end DevOps toolchain for developing and deploying software. It is designed as a database that you can use to track all activity on a project, including development and how you release the code or configurations to production IT systems.

# B

### BANT

An acronym that stands for budget, authority, need, and timeline, which represents a sales qualification methodology that lets salespeople determine whether the prospect is a good fit for the product or service they are selling.

### Blocker

A bug that is blocking the ability to complete a test or another task.

### Budget

An estimate of income and expenditure for a set period of time. For the purposes of this book, it is the expected amount that the project will cost, and it is typically tied to the implementation partner's statement of work.

### Bug

A flaw or defect in the system that causes a function not to perform as intended.

### Build environment

One of the core system environments where all development activity converges.

### Business analyst (BA)

A resource whose job it is to translate business requirements into system requirements.

### Business Central Intelligent Cloud Insights

AI solutions that learn from the data and provide dashboards to the user indicating which customer may be more willing to buy your products or whatever you configure it to show.

### Business intelligence (BI)

Often synonymous with reporting or analytics, it is the strategies and technologies for collecting and processing data from internal and external systems and presenting it in a way that makes it easy for leaders to make business decisions.

### Business intelligence lead

Responsible for gathering requirements for and delivering on the key business intelligence (reports) that you need to run a business.

### Business process owner

One of the key roles on the project, the business process owner is a leader in the business who is accountable for one of the main business functions. Their primary responsibility on the project is to approve the end-to-end process for their area of accountability.

### Business scenario

A process that occurs in your business today, typically made up of several steps.

### Business validation

The act of verifying that a set of end-to-end business processes function as intended, and it is performed by the core team.

# C

### Change management

A collective term for the strategies that help the management of change within a business or similar organization, also known as *change leadership*.

### Change management plan

The agreed-upon plan for implementing approaches in the organization that help the team adapt to the business change.

### Change request

A formal document that should be signed by both parties anytime there is a change in the project that impacts scope, schedule, or budget.

### Change request process

A process to approve any changes to scope or resources that might affect the project budget or timeline.

**Changeset**

A deployment package containing the most recent collection of code that has changed.

**Client Journey**

High-level stages developed by Stoneridge Software outlining the path to complete the implementation of Microsoft Dynamics.

**Cloud**

Software that is hosted directly by the vendor and accessible via a browser. This could be a Software-as-Service (SaaS) solution like Business Central or Customer Engagement or Infrastructure-as-a-Service (IaaS) like Finance and Operations.

**Code coverage**

A means of validating what percentage of your code has a unit test running against it.

**Code review**

A software quality assurance activity in which one or more developers review the source code, also known as a *peer review*.

**Conference Room Pilot (CRP)**

A session or set of sessions that test business scenarios in a proposed new system to uncover potential system issues and to generate suggested changes to the software.

**Configuration**

The data or fields in the software that provide flexibility on how the application is used.

**Configuration tracker**

A spreadsheet used to track the parameters and basic configurations in a system.

**Consumers**

In the SIPOC model, the users or companies who consume the output generated by the process.

**Contingency**

The amount of project budget not specifically allocated to a task.

**Core processes**

Those processes and business scenarios that are most the important to the business.

**Core team**

A set of people assigned to the implementation project from the business areas affected by the project.

**Core team lead**

The resource responsible to represent the business interests in one area of the business, generally equivalent to one process category, also called workstream lead.

**Cost**

The total amount of expenses associated with the implementation project.

**Create stage**

The third stage in the Client Journey with the purpose to build a solution to one's business goals by determining and defining the requirements by taking the processes in scope.

**Critical**

Any task, bug, or activity that the system has to have for the system to be viable.

**Customer Insights**

Artificial intelligence (AI) solutions that learn from data and provide dashboards to the user indicating which customer may be more willing to buy products or whatever one configures it to show.

**Customer Service Insights**

Artificial intelligence (AI) solution that helps both agents and customer service managers make better decisions and proactively improve customer satisfaction.

## Customization

An extension or modification of a software feature that requires custom coding and or some form of implementation.

## Cutover plan

The plan that articulates the activities that need to occur to go live with the system.

# D

## Data migration

The process of selecting, preparing, extracting, and transforming data and transferring it from one computer source system to a destination system.

## Data migration iteration

An attempt to extract the data from the source system, transform it into the format needed by the destination system, and then to load it into the destination system and validate the data.

## Data migration plan

A game plan for moving one's data from a source system to a destination system and all the steps required to make that migration successful.

## Defect management

The process of managing bugs and system defects.

## Define stage

The second stage in the Client Journey where the client selects the right ERP or CRM system and implementation partner, and then prepares the team to build the solution.

## Deliverables

Artifacts such as documentation, plans, budgets, code, and configurations that need to be completed for the project to meet its planned timelines.

## Deploy stage

The fourth stage in the Client Journey focused on system testing, training users, go-live, and working through any post-go-live issues before transitioning to the long-term support model.

## Design task

A task assigned to a functional consultant to create a functional design document or another form of a design for a customization.

## Developer environments

Specific environments developers use to develop and test their code.

## Development lead

Resource tasked with understanding the customizations, estimating them, and updating the project team on progress. This resource typically attends the meetings with the project manager to represent all development activity.

## Development task

Specific task assigned to a developer once a design is approved where developers review the design, develop the game plan, write the custom code, develop a unit test, write up how it was done, and show the customization to the functional consultant.

## DevOps

A set of practices that combines software development (Dev) and IT Operations (Ops).

## Discovery Session

The initial meeting with a vendor to review your key system needs.

## Document repository

A centralized site to store all of the documents and artifacts from a project.

# E

## Earned value

The process to put a value on the amount of work that has been completed.

## Empower stage

The final stage in the Client Journey which provides ongoing support to enhance a solution to create even more value from the project.

**End user training content**

Training designed to be consumed by end users of the system.

**End-to-end testing**

Testing that walks through an entire process to test multiple use cases or processes.

**Engagement manager**

The resource responsible for the delivery of the project from the partner side.

**Enhancement release**

Post go-live production release including new features and bug fixes.

**Entity definitions**

The definition of a table showing the available fields and their data types. Once constructed, you can use these definitions to connect to them in Power BI and build the visuals there that you want to see.

**Environment plan or environment management plan**

A list of all of the environments needed to run a project (test and production) and how to manage deployments.

**Environments**

A hosted instance of the software where you can deploy the customized and configured solution.

**Epic**

A large user story that incorporates many user stories, features, and requirements.

**Estimate at Completion (EAC)**

The forecasted cost of the project at its end based on the actual costs to this point and the forecasted future expenses.

**Estimate to Complete (ETC)**

The expected remaining cost to complete the project from the current point of the project.

**ETL process**

A type of data integration process referring to three distinct but interrelated steps (Extract, Transform, and Load).

**Executive sponsor**

The resource who takes overall accountability for the project. Their job is to put the right team in place, manage the key relationships, and remove blockers for the team.

**Executive Summary**

A brief introduction and summary found in the front of documents.

**Extract**

The process of pulling data out of a source system or systems.

# F

**Fail**

A test that does not complete all criteria.

**Feature**

A business function or an attribute of a system. In DevOps it refers to a set of components that allow the software to perform this business function.

**Financial Plan to Report**

One of the 12 process categories that covers the posting and management of all financial transactions and reporting.

**Fit**

When the software contains the functionality necessary to accomplish the desired business process.

**Fit/gap analysis**

A high-level analysis to review the functionality of the solution compared to the desired business processes and requirements.

**Functional consultant**

An implementation partner resource who is an expert in functionality in a certain area of the product.

**Functional design document (FDD)**

A document that is a part of a set of software specifications. It outlines how a feature or requirement should be designed in the software via a customization.

**Functional requirement**

A system need that you have identified which provides information needed to perform tasks.

**Functional testing**

A quality assurance process based on analysis of the specification of the functionality of a component or system.

**Functional validation**

The process of running through transactions in the system to validate if the imported data works as designed in the system.

# G

**Gamification**

A set of activities and processes to solve problems by using or applying the characteristics of game elements.

**Go/no-go Meeting**

A critical meeting in which key project stakeholders agree whether the project moves into implementation and go-live with three potential outcomes: go, no go, or go with caveats.

**Gold Environment**

A specific environment used in addition to the configuration tracker. It is a separate instance of Microsoft Dynamics only used to track configurations.

**Go-live criteria**

Specific criteria required in order to move the system into the production environment.

**Go-live iteration**

The final data migration iteration occurring the weekend of go-live, also known as the *cutover iteration*.

**Go-live scorecard**

A report that shows progress on the key go-live criteria.

**Guardrails**

Specific code or configurations designed to prevent users from doing something in the system outside of the intended path.

# H

**Happy Path**

The typical path a process should take that most users follow.

**Helper or expert**

A name for the resource in a CRP or training session who walks around the room to answer questions and help users.

**Hire to Retire**

One of the 12 end-to-end process categories that covers Human Resources, starting with recruitment and ending when an employee is no longer working for the organization.

**Hosted**

On-premise or Windows client software hosted by the provider or a third party.

**Hotfix release process**

Post go-live push of code that solves a small number of issues.

**Hypercare**

The period of time (typically 4–8 weeks) immediately following a system go-live where an elevated level of support is available to ensure the seamless adoption of a new system.

# I

**Idea to Product**

One of the 12 core process categories that covers defining a product starting with an idea and ending with the product being released to a company.

**Implementation**

The process of installing a new software system, moving financial data over to the new system, configuring users and processes, and training users on the software.

**Implementation Partner or Implementer**

The organization with whom you partner to help you complete the implementation of the software.

**Implementation Review**

An opportunity during the implementation discussion to understand the implementation partner's approach to the project.

**Important**

A priority rating lower than critical, but it indicates a necessary software requirement or a system defect.

**Independent Software Vendors (ISVs)**

Software companies that provide extensions to the Microsoft Dynamics platform to fill a particular gap in the software.

**Industry ISV**

An Independent Software Vendor focused on extending the functionality of the product for a particular industry.

**Infrastructure-as-a-Service (IaaS)**

A form of cloud computing that delivers fundamental compute, network, and storage resources to consumers on-demand, over the Internet, and on a pay-as-you-go basis. The software would be installed on the provided infrastructure.

**Inputs**

Materials, services, or information from a supplier that go into the process as outlined in the SIPOC model.

**Installation**

The steps needed to set up the software.

**Integration**

Connection to another system that does not run in the same database.

**Integration architect**

A resource who understands the data structure and application programming interfaces (APIs) of each of the systems involved so that a solution can be modeled to connect the data between the systems.

**Integration testing**

Testing that assures the connection works and that data is passing as it should between systems.

**Issue**

A problem with the project that requires a mitigation plan, not the same as a system defect or bug.

**Issue to Resolution**

One of the 12 core process categories outlining the customer service process of identifying an issue to the point where you resolve it to the customer's satisfaction.

**Iteration**

The repetition of a process to gain further practice with the system and feedback from the users.

### Iteration 0

Known as the first data migration iteration and considered to be the technical preview to validate that the technical connections work.

### Iteration 1

Typically, the second data migration iteration and first public data migration activity to pull data over to consider using in the new system.

### Iteration 2

Typically, the third data migration iteration factoring in what was learned from Iteration 0, Iteration 1, and JPD3 to put representative data into the new system.

### Iteration 3

Typically, the last test data migration happening during the Deploy stage.

# J

### Joint Application Design (JAD)

The process of involving a client in the design of an application through a succession of collaborative workshops known as *JAD sessions*.

### Joint Process Design (JPD)

A working session during an implementation where consultants work jointly with clients to design how the new solution will handle a specific process.

### JPD1

The first iteration of a JPD with the goal of showing the standard process flow in the out-of-the-box functionality.

### JPD2

The second iteration of a JPD in designing a solution focused on refining the process in the software.

### JPD3

The third iteration of a JPD in designing a solution focused on complex scenarios in the software.

### JPD4

The fourth iteration of a JPD in designing a solution which should wrap up any design issues collaboratively.

# K

### Kickoff Meeting

The introduction of the implementation project goals, plans, and schedule to the team.

# L

### Learning Management System (LMS)

A software solution that tracks learning content, learning plans, and what content has been viewed by users.

### Learning paths

A set of training and documentation that should be followed for a given user or role.

### Lifecycle Services

A cloud-based service platform from Microsoft that provides tools to help drive predictable implementations.

### Low-code, no-code strategy

A strategy to use software that can be fully customized with a minimal amount of programming, or the ability to tailor an application to a user's needs with no programming knowledge.

# M

### Machine learning (ML)

The use and development of computer systems that learn and adapt to new data without human interference.

**Major release**

A release that should be treated like an original main release with additional resources and a hypercare period.

**Mapping the data**

The process of taking a field in a user's source system and mapping it to the destination system.

**Market to Opportunity**

One of the 12 core process categories that starts with marketing campaigns and leads to acquisition and ends with closing an opportunity.

**Master data**

Non-transactional data stored in the system such as customers, vendors, employees, and products.

**Master Services Agreement (MSA)**

An overarching contract that stipulates who owns the intellectual property to the works created, the limits on liability for each party, the billing terms, and the process for any potential conflict.

**Metadata**

Data that provides information about other data.

**Microsoft Dynamics 365**

A set of business application software built by Microsoft and focused on Enterprise Resource Planning (ERP) and Customer Relationship Management (CRM).

**Microsoft Project**

A project planning tool developed and sold by Microsoft designed to assist a project manager in developing a schedule, assigning resources to tasks, tracking progress, managing the budget, and analyzing workloads.

**Microsoft Teams**

A business communication platform developed by Microsoft that includes instant messaging, file storage, conversations, and voice communications.

**Minor release**

A release containing a combination of bug fixes with minor functionality enhancements.

**Mock cutover**

A simulated cutover that occurs the week before, or a few weeks before, your official go-live weekend where you go through all of the steps that you would go through during the production cutover.

# N

**Negative testing**

Testing focused on trying out functions that should not work in the system to see if it generates the proper error message or response.

**Non-functional requirements**

A requirement that specifies criteria that can be used to judge the operation of a system rather than specific behaviors.

**Non-functional testing**

Testing that does not specifically cover functionality in the system; instead, it covers how the system operates.

# O

**On-premise**

Software that runs on dedicated servers in a local or customer-hosted environment.

**Output**

Materials, services, or information generated by the process and given to a consumer as outlined in the SIPOC model.

# P

**Parameter**

A type of configuration where the setting can be turned on and off or adjusted.

**Parking lot**

A list of ideas that are worth remembering but not relevant to the matter at hand.

**Pass**

A test that fully meets its expected result.

**Peer review** (*see* **Code review**)

**Performance**

The speed at which the system executes functions.

**Performance testing**

Testing where you simulate multiple resources hitting the system at the same time to measure the speed of the system.

**Personalizations**

Configurations that are saved to a user's profile and specific to the user.

**Plan to Inventory**

One of the 12 core process categories outlining the forecasting, production, and distribution planning of demand and supply, or the management of your site, warehouses, and bins for inventory.

**Platform**

The technical foundation of the software including all integrated functionality.

**Point-of-sale (PoS) systems**

A place where a customer executes the payment for goods or services and where sales taxes may become payable.

**Power Apps**

A Microsoft software solution that allows users to create apps, services, connectors, and a data platform for a variety of business needs.

**Power Automate**

A Microsoft software solution that allows users to create automated workflows between apps and services to synchronize files, get notifications, collect data, and more.

**Power BI**

A Microsoft software solution that allows users to build business intelligence and analytics using interactive visualizations.

**Power Platform**

Microsoft's combined term for low-code, no-code solutions including Power BI, Power Apps, Power Automate, and Power Virtual Agents.

**Principal or senior project manager**

*See* project manager for the base definition. A principal or senior project manager typically has significant experience and may have achieved certification, such as the Project Management Professional (PMP) certification

**Priority**

The level of importance associated to an issue, risk, defect, or a task.

**Privilege**

Security that dictates whether you can access an object, and if you can, what you can do with that object or a record.

**Process**

A set of one or more activities that will accomplish a specific business function.

**Process and Sub-processes**

A set of one or more activities that will accomplish a specific business function and that includes other sub-processes and activities.

**Process Catalog**

A list of business processes that are organized by process category, then process group, and finally processes. Processes may also be made up of other sub-processes and/or activities and tasks.

**Process categories**

End-to-end scenarios made up of a set of business processes. Each category has a clear starting point in the overall flow of business processes with defined preconditions and a clear end point with post conditions.

### Process classification framework (PCF)

A cross-industry framework developed by the American Productivity & Quality Center (APQC) laying out a hierarchy of processes that can be applied to businesses across different industries.

### Process groups

The second level of the process catalog, which is made up of more detailed processes

### Processes in scope

The identification of the processes included in the implementation project.

### Procure to Pay

One of the 12 end-to-end process categories that starts with vendor management and ends with payment of a vendor invoice.

### Production environment

The final environment your users use when the system is live.

### Professional Direct Support

A subscription plan providing direct access to Microsoft resources for support.

### Project backlog

A prioritized list of tasks that teams need to work on within the scope of a project.

### Project charter

A formal document that describes a project in its entirety, also referred to as a *project management plan*.

### Project collaboration site

A centralized location, such as a SharePoint site, Teams site, or Slack channel used to share documents and updates on a project.

### Project communication plan

The outline of the regular meetings and messages that will be sent to project stakeholders.

### Project coordinator

A resource who assists the project manager by scheduling meetings, taking notes, and sending out status reports.

### Project governance

The management framework in which project decisions are made.

### Project management plan

The summary document that pulls together all of the decisions that have been made about how to plan and run a project.

### Project Management Professional (PMP)

A certified resource who has received a professional project management designation offered by the Project Management Institute.

### Project manager

A resource responsible and accountable for the project plan who coordinates the activities of people and other resources as necessary to write and execute the plan. Ensures that information related to project progress is complete, accurate, and accessible.

### Project owner

A resource in charge of defining the scope of the project and making day-to-day decisions on the project.

### Project roles and responsibilities

A roster of project roles and accountabilities for a project.

### Project schedule

The artifact laying out the key activities and timelines for the project, commonly referred to as the *project plan*.

**Project to Profit**

One of the 12 core end-to-end process categories that starts with the creation of project estimates and/or forecasts and ends with the completion and analysis of a project.

# Q

**Qualification meeting**

An initial meeting to identify if both parties feel that the other is a potential partner for the project.

**Quality assurance (QA)**

A resource responsible for testing the solution and guaranteeing a level of quality for the project.

**Quote to Cash**

One of the 12 core process categories covering everything from generating a quote or selling something with shipments to the point where you collect the cash for the product or service.

# R

**RACI**

A responsibility-assigned matrix that describes the participation by various roles in completing tasks for a project process. It stands for Responsible, Accountable, Consulted, and Informed.

**Recorded video**

The ability to record steps within a training session and utilize them for learning content.

**Reference data**

Data held in a system used to classify or categorize other data.

**Reference data configuration**

The setup of reference data in the system.

**Regression suite automation tool (RSAT)**

A Microsoft tool used to run recorded software steps through automated tests.

**Regression testing**

Testing that is done on a previously tested component once changes were introduced elsewhere in the system.

**Remote, synchronous training**

Instructor-led training done virtually where the participants are listening to the instructor in real time.

**Reporting**

For testing, the reports shared with the project team on the progress of testing.

**Request for information (RFI)**

A process where companies request specific information from vendors which is intended to better inform buying decisions.

**Request for proposal (RFP)**

A process where companies request a proposal from vendors based on information provided.

**Requirement**

A condition or capability needed by a user to solve a problem or achieve an objective.

**Research task**

A set of hours allocated to a resource to research a potential solution.

**Resource load**

The total assigned hours of work divided by the number of hours required to do the work.

**Resource plan**

A document that summarizes the level of resources needed to complete a project.

### Return on investment (ROI)

The estimated or actual cost savings or revenue increase associated with the investment into the project.

### Rework

Work redone when a customization didn't meet the mark, the requirement changed, was not sufficiently documented, or the code had a bug in it.

### Risk

An activity or event that may compromise the success of a project.

### Risk and issues management

The process of managing the actual and potential problems that you can face on a project and your game plan for how to address them.

### Risk Register or Risk and Issues Register

A document used to track risks, the likelihood of a risk or risks occurring, the severity if it does occur, who owns the risk, and a mitigation plan.

### Rollback

The process of rolling back a release to a previous version because of a problem with the latest release package.

### Rule book

The standards for how data should look in the system.

### Rule of 7

A marketing technique that states it takes an average of seven interactions with a brand before a purchase will take place.

## S

### Sales Insights

AI solutions that learn from the data and provide dashboards to the user indicating which customer may be more willing to buy your products.

### Sandbox environments

Environments that have multiple, different purposes in supporting the product environment.

### Sarbanes-Oxley controls

Rules and audit trails in the system that promote segregation of duties required for all U.S. public companies.

### Schedule to Produce

One of the 12 core process categories that starts with a planned production order and ends with the receipt of a finished good.

### Scope

A well-defined boundary, which encompasses all of the activities that are done to develop and deliver the product.

### Scrum methodology

A form of agile methodology with defined roles and activities including planning meetings and project backlogs.

### Security testing

Testing intended to reveal flaws in the security mechanisms of an information system that protects data and maintains functionality as intended.

### Selection process

The process of selecting the software and implementation partner for your project.

### Service Call to Profit

One of the 12 core categories focused on field service processes like dispatching, service contracts, and collections.

### Service Level Agreement (SLA)

A contractual term that has become synonymous with the expected response time for an incident logged with a support team.

**Session leader**

The person leading a CRP or training session, walking through the software and explaining the processes.

**SharePoint**

A web-based collaborative platform that integrates with Microsoft 365 and used to store, organize, share, and access information.

**SIPOC**

A high-level process map method to improve processes and summarizes the inputs and outputs of one or more processes. The acronym stands for Supplies, Inputs, Processes, Output, and Consumers.

**Software-as-Service (SaaS)**

A software licensing and delivery model in which software is licensed on a subscription basis and is centrally hosted.

**Solution architect**

A resource responsible for the design of one or more applications or services within a project.

**Sprint**

A defined period of time (typically two or four weeks) used to plan out work.

**Sprint backlog**

The amount of work to be done within a sprint cycle.

**Sprint planning meeting**

A meeting led by the project manager (or scrum master) to allocate work for an upcoming sprint cycle. Held either right before the start of the sprint or on the morning of the start of the new sprint.

**Sprint review meeting**

A meeting led by the project manager (or scrum master) to review activity from the current sprint. Held either the day of or after the last day in the sprint.

**Stand-up meetings**

A brief (15 minutes or less) meeting where project team members huddle to provide brief updates on what they accomplished, what they are committed to accomplishing, and what they need help with, also known as a *daily scrum* or *huddle*.

**Statement of Work (SoW)**

A legal document that defines project-specific activities, deliverables, and timelines for services, signed by both parties.

**Status report**

A report sent to the leadership team and stakeholders (typically weekly) that provides an update on the progress, an outline of what's coming up, statuses on the key elements of the project, and the budget summary.

**Subject matter expert (SME)**

A resource who performs a function in the business and knows that function well.

**Success criteria**

The key objectives for the project that can be used to measure achievement against them.

**Suppliers**

The vendors or others who provide inputs as part of the SIPOC model.

**Sure Step Methodology**

Microsoft's full customer lifecycle methodology which can be applied to all Dynamics solutions.

**Synchronous learning**

In-person, classroom-style training.

**System defect**

A bug or system defect is a flaw in the system that causes a failure.

# T

### Task management system

A tool used to keep track of all of the tasks on the project and your progress on each of them, such as SharePoint list or Azure DevOps.

### Task recorder

A tool used to record your activities in the system, which allows you to capture the clicks and keystrokes that a user made in the system.

### Technical consultant

A resource responsible for environments, security, performance, and releases that are part of the implementation process.

### Technical validation

A process in the data migration effort to confirm that the data came over properly by visualizing the data, testing the record counts, and assuring that the data adheres to standards.

### Test

A task of detecting defects or bugs in order to guarantee the quality of the software.

### Test case

The outline of the steps required to accomplish a scenario in the software which should be tested to validate that the software meets the intended purpose.

### Test environment

An environment used in the implementation process where the functional consultants and core team members are testing all different types of activities in the system.

### Test execution

The process of executing code and comparing the expected and actual results.

### Test plan or testing plan

A document describing the scope, approach, resources, and schedule of test activities.

### Test task

The time required to write up a test case and do the initial testing of a customization.

### Testing schedule

The plan for how tests will be reviewed, tracked, and approved and when they will be executed.

### Total cost of ownership (TCO)

A financial estimate intended to help buyers and owners determine the direct and indirect costs of a product or service.

### Train the trainer

The process of training the resources who will provide training to the end users of the system.

### Triple constraints

A theory in project management that states every project operates within the boundaries of scope, time, and cost.

### T-shirt sizing

A technique used to estimate how much work is needed for each task.

# U

### UAT or user acceptance testing environment

A type of testing environment used to verify the application before moving the software to the production environment.

### Unified Support

A Microsoft support plan providing comprehensive support across all Microsoft solutions owned by the client.

**Unit test**

A test to determine if the entire code or elements of the code work correctly.

**Usability**

Refers to the quality of a user's experience when interacting with products or systems, including websites, software, devices, or applications.

**Usability testing**

A technique used in user-centered interaction design to evaluate a product by testing it on users.

**Usage plan**

The process of defining how frequently you plan to use an environment.

**Use case**

A sequence of transactions in a dialog between an actor (user) and a system.

**Use case testing**

Testing that walks through all of the components of particular use cases.

**User acceptance testing (UAT)**

A type of testing performed by the end user or the client to verify/accept the software system before moving the software application to the production environment.

**User acceptance testing (UAT) sessions**

Specific sessions where UAT testing is performed.

**User interface**

The features of a computer system that allows the user to interact with it.

**User story**

An informal, natural-language description of one of more features of a software system.

**Users or students**

Individuals who are using the system in some way, but it also means participants in CRP or training sessions.

## V

**Valuable**

A priority definition that indicates the field or function is useful but not critical or important.

**Variance at Completion (VAC)**

The difference between the Estimate to Complete (ETC) and the budget. The formula is as follows:

$$VAC = EAC - Budget$$

## W

**War room**

A dedicated room for the implementation team intended as a workspace for people who need to work either by themselves or collaboratively with another project team member.

**Waterfall methodology**

The oldest and most common practice used in business application implementations which is a step-by-step methodology that tries to keep all of the activities in linear order from start to finish.

**Wish List**

A priority definition that indicates the field or function would be nice-to-have, but it could be implemented at a later date.

# Index

## A

accountability, culture of, 90
Accountable, in RACI acronym, 57–59
achievable, as a success metric, 21, 89
Acquire to Retire category, 102, 353
activities, 104
actual, 175
add-on license costs, 24
adoption, importance of, 96
advanced concepts, 353
after action review (AAR), 295–297, 353
agenda, for go/no-go meetings, 269
Agile Manifesto, 7, 353
Agile methodology, 7, 285, 353
Align stage, 2, 307–308, 353
aligned with organizational goals, as a
    success metric, 21, 89
American Process & Quality Center, 18
American Productivity & Quality Center
    (APQC), 100–101
analytical views, 83
application lifecycle management
    (ALM), 223, 353
Application Programming Interfaces
    (APIs), 302, 353
application software, 45, 47–54, 322–323
approval, gaining, 28
AppSource Marketplace (Microsoft),
    117–119, 315, 353
artificial intelligence (AI), 302–303, 353
"As-Is," 136–137
asynchronous training, 251, 353
authentication
    authorization vs., 226
    defined, 353
authorization
    authentication vs., 226
    defined, 353

automation, 114
Avalara, 113
Azure DevOps (ADO)
    about, 66, 82
    analytical views, 83
    defined, 353
    DevOps field, 82–83
    progress reporting, 83

## B

backlogs
    about, 75
    allocating work to team members, 76
    project backlog, 75
    sprint backlog, 76
    success rate of sprints, 76
BANT acronym, 49, 354
blocker, 231, 354
budget
    defined, 175, 354
    for ISV solutions, 115
    managing, 175–177
    tracking, 68
Budget file, 60
bug (defect)
    criteria for, 262–263
    defined, 81, 231, 354
    fixes, 299
    issues vs., 179
Build environment, 217, 354
business analyst (BA), 15, 17, 354
business case, building, 23–28
Business Central Intelligence Cloud
    Insights, 354
business intelligence (BI), 301–302, 354
business intelligence (BI) lead, 16, 17, 354
business process
    common language, 99–101

discovering, 104–106
hierarchy, 102–104
organizing by, 99–106, 328–329
steps to change, 95–96
business process owner
about, 13, 17, 59
as CRP role, 162
defined, 354
business scenarios, 19, 354
business validation, 211, 354

**C**
calculating return on investment
(ROI), 303–304
capitalized costs, 25–27
CEO, visibility of, 90–91
change management
about, 87–88, 326–328
defined, 354
reasons for, 87–88
satisfaction surveys, 89
steps to, 90–96
success criteria, 88–89
change management plan
defined, 354
for pre-kickoff meeting activities
checklist, 123
change request, 68, 82, 354
change request process
defined, 354
for pre-kickoff meeting activities
checklist, 123
changeset, 82, 355
checklist, for pre-kickoff meeting
activities, 121–124
cleaning data, 200–201
Client Journey, 2–4, 355
cloud platform, 35–36, 355
cloud software, on-premise software
compared with, 155
code
defined, 82
deploying, 194, 223–225

frequency of moves, 222
for mapping data, 209
code coverage, 217, 355
code review
defined, 355
in development process, 193
colors, on status reports, 173–175
communicate effectively, as a step to change
management, 92–93
Communication Management, in project
management plan, 69
communication plan, go-live
criteria and, 265
Conference Room Pilots (CRPs)
about, 157, 335–337
agenda, 159–160
common elements of, 159
defined, 355
end of Create stage and, 167
goals for, 168
issues and questions, 160–161
logistics, 160
organizing, 158–159
place in schedule for, 163–166
preparing for, 195
purpose of, 157–161
roles and responsibilities, 161–163
training during, 246–247
User Acceptance Testing (UAT)
*vs.*, 166–167
configuration
about, 186
defined, 355
deploying code, 194
development process, 192–194
functional design document
(FDD), 190–191
functional testing, 194
populating, 222–223
preparing for CRP, 195
preparing for UAT, 195
tracking, 188–189
configuration tracker, 189, 355

Conflict Management, in project
  management plan, 69
Consultant Playgrounds environment, 218
Consulted, in RACI acronym, 57–59
consumers
    defined, 355
    in SIPOC tool, 105
content, distributing and managing, 254–255
contingency, 27, 355
contracts, 53
core processes, 355
core team members, 106
core team/core team lead, 14, 17, 355
costs
    about, 24
    capitalizing, 25–27
    of customizations, 154–155
    defined, 355
    to include in calculations, 24–25
    as a key buying consideration, 41–44, 45
    travel, 43–44
COVID-19, impact on remote training of, 249
Crawford, Tony, 133–134
Create stage
    about, 3, 307, 311–312
    between CRP and, 167
    defined, 355
critical, 355
CRM, buying considerations for
    about, 31, 320–321
    building scorecard, 44–45
    keys to, 33–44
    selection process, 31–33
Customer Insights, 355
customer managed ISVs, 115
Customer Service Insights, 355
customization
    about, 145, 185
    configuration *vs.*, 185–188, 338–340
    cost of, 154–155
    defined, 356
    fit-gap analysis, 151–154
    lifecycle of, 195–196

no-code, 186
requirements, 147–151
staying in the box, 145–147
writing requirements, 150–151
cutover plans, 60, 262, 356

**D**

daily scrum. *See* stand-up meetings
dashboards, 83
data
    cleaning up, 19–21
    finding, 206
    incorporating into daily business, 302
    mapping, 208
    master, 187, 222–223
    normalizing, 207
    quantity of, 202
    reference, 187–188
    validating, 210–211
data migration
    about, 199–200, 340–341
    data migration plan, 200–205
    defined, 356
    Extract, in ETL process, 206–207
    go-live iteration, 212
    Load, in ETL process, 210
    security criteria and, 263–264
    technical validation, 211–212
    Transform, in ETL process, 208–209
    validating data, 210–211
Data Migration environment, 218
data migration iteration, 203–205, 356
data migration plan
    about, 200
    Data Migration tool, 202–203
    defined, 356
    pre-kickoff meeting, 201–202
    for pre-kickoff meeting activities
      checklist, 123
    proactive cleaning, 200–201
    quantity of data, 202
data migration specialist, 62
Data Migration tool, 202–203

decision making, 33
decision-making, 52–53, 129
defect (bug). *See* bug (defect)
defect management, 356
Define stage, 3, 307, 308–311, 356
Demiliani, Stefano
    *Mastering Microsoft Dynamics 365 Business
       Central,* 223
demonstration, 50–51
Deploy stage, 4, 307, 313–314, 356
deploying code, 194, 223–225
Deployment phase environment, 219
design, customization and costs of, 154
design complete section, in functional
    design documents (FDDs), 191
design task, 80, 356
develop a system vision that provides
    benefits to all stakeholders, as a step to
    change management, 92
developer, 15–16, 17
Developer environment, 216–217
Developer environments, 356
developers, 61
development, customization and
    costs of, 154
Development lead, 61, 356
development process, 192–194
development quotation section, in functional
    design documents (FDDs), 191
development task, 81, 356
DevOps
    defined, 356
    environment flow using, 224
    field, 82–83
disaster recovery, 267
Discovery and Demonstration stage, in
    buying application software, 49–51
Discovery session, 356
discovery system, 47
document repository, 67–68, 356
duplicates, finding and resolving in data,
    20

**E**
earned value, 68, 176, 356
earned value curve, 75
eCommerce, 114
Empower stage, 4, 275, 307, 314–315, 356
end, of sprints, 74
end user training content, 251, 357
end user training schedule, 255–259
end-to-end testing
    about, 230
    customization and costs of, 154
    defined, 357
engagement manager, 60, 357
engagement release, 357
entity definitions, 83, 357
Entrance and Exit Criteria, in project
    management plan, 69
entrance criteria
    for conference room pilot (CRP), 164
    for pre-kickoff meeting activities
       checklist, 124
    User Acceptance Testing (UAT), 235–236
environment flow, using DevOps, 224
environment management
    about, 215, 341–342
    environment plan, 220–223
    types of environments, 216–220
environment management plan
    defined, 357
    for pre-kickoff meeting activities
       checklist, 123
environmental plan
    about, 220
    defined, 357
    types of releases, 220–222
environments
    Build, 217
    creating, 182
    defined, 357
    developer, 216–217
    Production, 219–220
    Sandbox, 218–219

Test, 217–218
epic, 79, 357
ERP, buying considerations for
    about, 31, 320–321
    building scorecard, 44–45
    keys to, 33–44
    selecting based on platform, 38–39
    selection process, 31–33
Estimate at Completion (EAC), 176, 357
Estimate to Complete (ETC), 176, 357
Excel, 208
executive overview, in kickoff meeting,
    125, 127–128
Executive Sponsor, 12, 17, 59, 60, 357
executive summary, 172, 357
exit criteria
    for conference room pilot (CRP), 164
    for pre-kickoff meeting activities
        checklist, 124
    User Acceptance Testing (UAT), 236
expectations, for kickoff meeting, 124,
    126, 128–129
expense costs, 25
extensions, reporting, 114
Extract, in ETL plan, 206–207, 357
Extract, Transform, and Load (ETL) plan
    about, 62
    defined, 357
    Extract, 206–207
    Load, 210
    Transform, 208–209
extraction tools, 206–207

**F**
fail, 231, 357
feature, 79–80, 357
final week activities, 266–268
finance and administration, 100
Financial Plan to Report category,
    102, 357
fit
    analyzing, 51
    defined, 357
    as a key buying consideration, 33–35, 44
fit/gap analysis
    about, 33–34, 112, 151–152
    defined, 357
    spreadsheet, 152–153
    trade-offs, 153–154
forecast, 175
forms, customization to, 146
functional consultant, 61, 357
functional design document (FDD), 150,
    190–191, 358
functional ISVs, 113–114
functional requirements, 149–150, 358
functional testing
    about, 230
    customization and costs of, 154
    defined, 358
    in development process, 193–194
functional validation, 212, 358
funding, securing, 23–28

**G**
gamification, 358
general data migration tool, 209
goals, conference room pilot (CRP), 168
Gold environment, 189, 358
go-live
    about, 261, 346–347
    criteria for, 261–266, 358
    final week activities, 266–268
    go/no-go meetings, 268–270
    live cutover, 270–272
    mock cutover, 266–268
go-live iteration, 205, 212, 358
go-live scorecard, 358
go-live support, 275–279
go/no-go meetings, 60
    about, 268
    defined, 358
    meeting agenda, 269
    order and outcome of votes, 269–270

voting criteria, 268–269
when to have, 268
guardrails, 301, 358
*A Guide to the Business Analysis Body of Knowledge, 3rd Edition*, 147

# H

Happy Path, 136, 358
hardware costs, 24
Help content, 252
HelpDesk, role of, 279–284
helper/expert
as CRP role, 162
defined, 358
hierarchy, process, 102–104
Hire to Retire category, 102, 358
hosted platform, 35–36, 358
hosting providers, 110–114
Hotfix release process, 285–286, 358
huddle. *See* stand-up meetings
hypercare
about, 275, 347–348
defined, 359
go-live support, 275–279
post go-live releases, 284–287
project team transition, 287–289
role of HelpDesk, 279–284
support after, 291–295

# I

Idea to Product category, 102, 359, 360
impact rating, 178
Implementation Partner, 359
implementation partner ISVs, 115
Implementation Review, 51–52, 359
implementations
compared with installation, 88
consulting costs for, 24–25
core roles, 12, 58
defined, 359
of ISVs, 116
methodologies for, 5–7
stages for, 1, 2–4
stages of, 317–318

traps in, 41–42
triple constraints, 8–9
implementer
defined, 359
as a key buying consideration, 39–41, 45
*Implementing Microsoft Dynamics 365 for Finance and Operations Apps: Learn best practices, architecture, tools, techniques and more* (Yadav and Shukla), 223
important, 359
incorrect data, finding and resolving, 20
Independent Software Vendors (ISVs)
about, 109, 329–331
buying licenses/subscriptions, 115–116
defined, 359
functional, 113–114
hosting providers, 110–114
implementation of, 116
industry, 111–112
license costs, 24
Microsoft and support plans, 294–295
Microsoft's AppSource Marketplace, 117–119
for pre-kickoff meeting activities checklist, 123
purpose of, 109–110
working with, 114–117
industry ISVs, 111–112, 359
Informed, IN RACI acronym, 57–59
Infrastructure-as-a-Service (IaaS), 35, 359
in-person, classroom-style training, 248–249
INPUT, in SIPOC tool, 104
inputs, 359
installation
compared with implementation, 88
defined, 359
integration architect, 61–62, 359
Integration environment, 218
integration testing, 230, 359
integrations
about, 186–187, 302
customization of, 147
defined, 359
interactive sessions, learning during, 246–247

internal team costs, 25
in-the-box examples, 146–147
introductions, in kickoff meeting, 125
issue, 82, 359
Issue Management, in project
  management plan, 69
Issue to Resolution category, 102, 359
issues list, 241, 277–278
IT Applications, 15, 17
IT Operations, 15, 17
IT resources, 15–16
iterations
  data migration, 203–205
  defined, 359–360
  go-live, 205, 212
  Joint Process Design (JPD), 137–142

**J**

Joint Application Design (JAD), 133–134, 360
Joint Process Design (JPD)
  about, 134
  conference room pilot (CRP) and, 164
  defined, 360
  iterations, 137–142
  keys to successful, 140–141
  output, 141–142
  sessions, 134–136
  training during, 246

**K**

Kanban Boards, 83
kickoff meeting
  about, 121, 331–332
  activities for pre-, 121–124
  content for, 124–127
  defined, 360
  executive message, 127–128
  expectations for project team, 128–129

**L**

leadership alignment, as a step to change
  management, 90–91
Leadership or Board Approval stage, in
  buying application software, 54

learning
  during interactive sessions,
    246–247
  modalities for, 247–254
Learning Management System (LMS)
  about, 255
  costs, 25
  defined, 360
  missing functionality and, 113
learning paths, 360
length, of sprints, 74
Levridge, 111–112
lifecycle, of customization, 195–196
Lifecycle Services, 189, 315, 360
likelihood rating, 178
live cutover
  about, 270
  completing activities, 271–272
  impact of start timing, 271
  rollback plan, 272
Load, in ETL plan, 210
load testing, 230
load time, 210
logic, customization of, 146
low-code, no-code strategy, 360

**M**

machine learning (ML), 302–303, 360
Magento, 114
major releases, 287, 361
mapping the data, 208, 361
mapping tools, 208–209
Market to Opportunity category,
  102, 361
master data
  about, 187
  defined, 361
  identifying, 19–20
  populating, 222–223
Master Service Agreement (MSA),
  53, 361
*Mastering Microsoft Dynamics 365 Business
  Central* (Demiliani and Tacconi), 223
*Mastering Microsoft Dynamics 365 Customer
  Engagement* (Somani), 223

maximize the team's time in the new system, as a step to change management, 94
measurable, as a success metric, 21, 89
meetings, running, 296–297
metadata, 187, 361
methodologies, for implementations, 5–7
Microsoft
    AppSource Marketplace, 117–119
    ISV support plans and, 294–295
Microsoft Dynamics, 1
Microsoft Dynamics 365, 223, 297, 315, 361
Microsoft Learn, 253
Microsoft Project file, 66, 361
Microsoft Teams, 67, 361
minor releases, 287, 361
missing connector, 113–114
missing functionality, 113
mock cutover, 266–268, 361
modalities, learning, 247–254
modification section, in functional design documents (FDDs), 190
Morris, Chuck, 133–134

**N**

naming conventions, developing, 20
navigation overview, in kickoff meeting, 127
negative testing, 361
no-code customizations, 186
non-disclosure agreement (NDA), 148
non-functional requirements, 149–150, 361
non-functional testing, 230, 361
normalizing data, 207

**O**

office hours, 258–259
OfficeVibe, 177
ongoing releases, 297–299
on-premise platform, 35–36, 361
on-premise software, cloud software compared with, 155
operations
    about, 100
    order of, 210

order of operation, 210
organization evaluation, as a step to change management, 91
outing, before kickoff meeting, 124
outline your business process change steps, as a step to change management, 92
output
    defined, 361
    Joint Process Design (JPD), 141–142
    in SIPOC tool, 105
overview section, in functional design documents (FDDs), 190
owner rating, 179

**P**

paid discovery, 52
parameter, 186, 361
parking lot, 160, 362
partners
    engaging for support, 292–293
    implementation team, 59–62
pass, 231, 362
pay-as-you-go model, 293
peer review. *See* code review
performance
    defined, 362
    as a non-functional requirement, 149
    at scale, for platforms, 37–38
    testing, 230, 362
personalization, 187, 362
Plan to Inventory category, 103, 362
platform
    defined, 362
    as a key buying consideration, 35–39, 44–45
point-of-sale (PoS) systems, 37, 362
populating configurations and master data, 222–223
Post go-live environment, 219
post go-live releases, 284–287
post-User Acceptance Testing (UAT), 240–242
Power Apps, 362
Power Automate, 362

Power BI, 362
power of positivity, as an expectation for
 team members, 129
Power Platform, 113–114, 186, 362
pre-deploy stage
 developing test cases, 234–235
 regression test, 233–234
 testing strategy, 232–233
 UAT entrance criteria, 235–236
 UAT exit criteria, 236
 unit test, 233–234
premier support, 293
principal project manager, 13, 362
prioritizing issues list, 277–278
priority, 362
private hosting, 111
privilege, 362
proactive cleaning, 200–201
Process Catalog, 18, 362
Process Categories, 18, 102–103, 362–363
Process Classification Framework
 (PCF), 100, 363
Process Groups, 18, 103, 363
process sign-offs, 241
process-based testing, 230
processes
 about, 103–104
 defined, 362
 discovering, 104–106
 hierarchy of, 102–104
 requirements link to, 148
 in SIPOC tool, 104
 sub-processes and, 18
processes in scope
 defined, 363
 for pre-kickoff meeting activities
  checklist, 123
Procure to Pay category, 103, 363
product listing, on Microsoft's AppSource
 Marketplace, 118
Production Copy environment, 218
Production environment, 219–220, 363
Professional Direct Support, 294, 363
Professional Services Agreement (PSA), 53

progress reporting, 83
project backlog, 75, 363
project budget maintenance, for pre-kickoff
 meeting activities checklist, 123
project challenges
 about, 171–172, 337–338
 common, 179–183
 managing project status, 172–177
 risks and issues, 177–179
project change champions, 277
project charter. *See* project management plan
Project Closure, in project
 management plan, 69
project collaboration site
 defined, 363
 for pre-kickoff meeting activities
  checklist, 123
project communication, 62–65
project communication plan
 defined, 363
 in kickoff meeting, 126
 for pre-kickoff meeting activities
  checklist, 123
project coordinator, 13, 363
project enthusiasm curve, 171–172
project estimate, 52
project governance
 about, 57, 323–325
 budget tracking, 68
 change requests, 68
 defined, 363
 document repository, 67–68
 partner's implementation team, 59–62
 project communication, 62
 project management plan, 68–69
 project schedule, 66–67
 RACI acronym, 57–59
 resource loading, 62–66
Project Management Plan
 about, 60, 68–69
 defined, 363
 in kickoff meeting, 126
 for pre-kickoff meeting activities
  checklist, 122

Project Management Professional
 (PMP), 13, 363
Project Management Scope, in project
 management plan, 68
project manager, 13–14, 17, 59, 60, 363
project owner, 12–13, 17, 59, 363
project plan. *See* project schedule
project preparation
 about, 11, 318–320
 building business case, 23–28
 cleaning up data, 19–21
 defining success metrics, 21–22
 identifying possible benefits, 22–23
 identifying processes in scope, 18–19
 identifying project team and
  stakeholders, 11–17
 securing funding, 23–28
project pulse, 177
project resources, setting expectations
 with, 16–17
project schedule
 about, 60, 66–67
 defined, 363
 in kickoff meeting, 126
 for pre-kickoff meeting activities
  checklist, 122
project status, managing, 172–177
project teams
 about, 58–59
 identifying, 11–17
 support for, 280–281
 transition to, 287–289
Project to Profit category, 103, 364
pr-training learning, 256
psychological safety, 182

**Q**

qualification meeting, 49, 364
Qualification stage, in buying application
 software, 48–49
quality assurance (QA)/tester, 16, 17, 364
Quality Management, in project
 management plan, 69

queries, 83
Quote to Cash category, 102, 103, 364

**R**

RACI acronym, 57–59, 364
recorded video, 364
recording sessions, 253
reference data, 187–188, 364
reference data configuration, 186, 364
regression suite automation tool (RSAT),
 234, 253–254, 364
regression testing
 about, 230
 customization and costs of, 154
 defined, 364
 in pre-deploy stage, 233–234
Release Management, in project
 management plan, 69
releases
 Hotfix, 285–286
 major, 287
 Microsoft Dynamics 365 release
  cadence, 297
 minor, 287
 ongoing, 297–299
 planning for future, 285
 post go-live, 284–287
 scheduled, 286–287
 scheduling, 298–299
 testing, 297–298
 types of, 220–222
 what to include in, 299
remote, synchronous training, 249–250, 364
reporting
 customizing, 146
 defined, 364
 extensions, 114
request for information (RFI), 48, 364
request for proposal (RFP), 48, 364
requirements
 about, 104, 147, 334–335
 defined, 80, 364
 functional, 149–150

link to processes, 148
non-functional, 149–150
out-of-the-box fields as, 147–148
tips for, 150–151
verifying, 150
Research task, 80, 364
resource level, 364
resource loading, 62
resource plan, 364
resources, in kickoff meeting, 126
response rating, 179
Responsible, in RACI acronym, 57–59
return on investment (ROI)
about, 27–28
calculating, 303–304
checkpoints for, 304–305
defined, 365
revision and sign-off section, in functional
design documents (FDDs), 191
rework
customization and costs of, 154
defined, 365
Risk Management, in project
management plan, 69
risks
about, 177–178
bugs *vs.* issues, 179
defined, 81, 365
for pre-kickoff meeting activities
checklist, 123
risk register, 178–179
Risks/Issues Register, 60, 178–179, 365
role review, in kickoff meeting, 125
roles and responsibilities
conference room pilot (CRP), 161–163
defined, 363
of HelpDesk, 279–284
for pre-kickoff meeting activities
checklist, 122
User Acceptance Testing (UAT), 237–238
rollback, 224–225, 365
rule book, 365
Rule of 7, 93, 365

**S**
SaaS-style hosting, 111
sales, 100
Sales Insights, 365
Sandbox environment, 218–219, 365
Sarbanes-Oxley controls, 365
satisfaction surveys, 89
Schedule to Produce category, 103, 365
scheduled releases, 286–287
scope
about, 106
defined, 365
identifying processes in, 18–19
Scope Control and Change Management, in
project management plan, 68
score rating, 178
Scrum methodology, 7, 285, 365
security
criteria and data migration, 263–264
customization to, 146
managing, 225–226
testing, 230, 365
selection consultant
about, 32
costs, 25
selection process
as a buying consideration, 31–33
defined, 365
senior project manager, 13, 362
Service Call to Profit category, 103, 365
service level agreement (SLA), 280, 365
services listing, on Microsoft's AppSource
Marketplace, 118–119
session leader
as CRP role, 161–162
defined, 366
sessions
Joint Process Design (JPD), 134–136
recording, 253
synchronous, 257
User Acceptance Testing (UAT),
236–240

set realistic expectations for the system just after go-live, as a step to change management, 94
SharePoint, 67, 366
Shukla, Sandeep
 *Implementing Microsoft Dynamics 365 for Finance and Operations Apps: Learn best practices, architecture, tools, techniques and more*, 223
SIPOC tool, 104–106, 142–143, 366
software design
 about, 133, 332–334
 iterations for JPD, 137–142
 Joint Application Design (JAD), 133–134
 Joint Process Design (JPD), 134–142
 SIPOC tool, 142–143
 terms for, 136–137
software evaluation team, 21
software subscription costs, 24
Software-as-a-Service (SaaS), 35, 366
solution architect, 60–61, 366
solution delivery manager, 60–61
Somani, Deepesh
 *Mastering Microsoft Dynamics 365 Customer Engagement*, 223
spreadsheet, fit/gap, 152–153
sprint backlog, 76, 366
sprint meetings
 sprint planning, 77
 sprint retrospective, 78
 sprint review, 77
 stand-up, 78–79
sprint planning meeting, 77, 366
sprint retrospective, 78
sprint review meeting, 77, 366
sprints
 about, 73–74, 325–326
 backlogs, 75–76
 defined, 7, 366
 delivering value in, 74–75
 end of, 74
 length of, 74

start of, 74
success rate of, 76
stakeholders, identifying, 11–17
standard processes, 100–101
stand-up meetings, 78–79, 366
starts, of sprints, 74
Statement of Work (SOW), 53, 366
status report, 172–175, 366
staying in the box, 145–147
Stoneridge Software (website), 315
subcontractor costs, 25
subject matter experts (SMEs), 14, 17, 366
subprocesses, 104, 362
success criteria
 change management and, 88–89
 defined, 366
 for pre-kickoff meeting activities checklist, 122
success metrics, defining, 21–22
success rate, of sprints, 76
suppliers
 defined, 366
 in SIPOC tool, 104
support
 about, 291, 349–350
 after action review (AAR), 295–297
 after hypercare, 291–295
 calculating return on investment, 303–305
 expectations of, 288–289
 future enhancements, 299–303
 levels of, 281–283
 ongoing releases, 297–299
 for project team, 280–281
support readiness, 264, 275–279
support your team members after go-live, as a step to change management, 95
supportability, of platforms, 37
Sure Step Methodology, 5, 138, 366
synchronous learning, 248–250, 366
synchronous sessions, 257
system defect, 231, 366
system owners, identifying, 20
system setup, before cutover, 267–268

# T

tables, customization of, 147
Tacconi, Duilio
    *Mastering Microsoft Dynamics 365 Business Central*, 223
task management system
    defined, 367
    for pre-kickoff meeting activities checklist, 123
Task Recorder, 234, 253–254, 367
tasks
    about, 104
    managing, 195–196
team members, allocating work to, 76
technical consultant, 61, 367
technical validation, 211, 367
technology platform, 36–37
test automation, 231
test cases
    customization and costs of, 154
    defined, 81, 231, 367
    developing, 234–235
Test environment, 217–218, 367
test plans
    defined, 231, 367
    executing, 238–239
test task, 81, 367
testing
    about, 229, 343–344
    customization and costs of, 154
    defined, 81, 367
    definitions, 229–231
    post UAT, 240–242
    pre-deploy stage activities, 222–236
    release, 297–298
    section in functional design documents (FDDs), 190–191
    types of, 230–231
    UAT sessions, 236–240
    users' knowledge, 257–258
testing plan, for pre-kickoff meeting activities checklist, 123

testing schedule, 367
testing strategy, 232–233
text execution, 367
time commitment
    as an expectation for team members, 128–129
    by role, 17
"To Be," 136–137
tools
    extraction, 206–207
    mapping, 208–209
total cost of ownership (TCO), 367
trade-offs, 153–154
train effectively, as a step to change management, 94
train the trainer, 256–257, 367
training
    about, 245–246, 344–345
    building end user schedule for, 255–259
    learning during interactive sessions, 246–247
    learning modalities, 247–254
    managing and distributing content, 254–255
    referring users to, 283
training review, 264–265
Transform, in ETL plan, 208–209
transitioning
    extending from consulting to support, 292
    to HelpDesk, 283–284
    project teams, 287–289
travel costs, 25, 43–44
triple constraints, 8–9, 367
T-shirt sizing, 367

# U

UAT environment, 218–219
Unified Support, 294–295, 367
unit testing
    about, 230
    defined, 368

in development process, 192–193
in pre-deploy stage, 233–234
unlimited subscription support, 293
updates section, in functional design
   documents (FDDs), 191
upgrading platforms, 37
usability
   defined, 368
   releases and, 300
usability testing, 231, 368
usage plan, 368
use case, 231, 368
use case testing, 231, 368
User Acceptance Testing (UAT)
   conference room pilot (CRP) *vs.*, 166–167
   defined, 367, 368
   entrance criteria, 235–236
   exit criteria, 236
   post-, 240–242
   preparing for, 195
   sessions, 236–240, 368
   training during, 247
user interface, 186, 368
user story, 80, 368
users/students
   as CRP role, 162–163
   defined, 368
   referring to training, 283
   testing knowledge of, 257–258

**V**

validation
   business, 211
   of data, 210–211
   functional, 212
   technical, 211
Validation of Core Functionality
   environment, 218
valuable, 368
value, delivering in sprints, 74–75
Variance at Completion (VAC), 176, 368
Vendor Selection stage, in buying
   application software, 51–54
vendors, quantity of, 48
verbal commitment, 53–54
verifying requirements, 150
Vertex, 113
virtual machine (VM), 216
visibility, of CEO, 90–91
voting criteria, for go/no-go
   meetings, 268–269

**W**

war room, 276, 368
Waterfall methodology, 5–6, 138, 368
wish list, 368
Wolters Kluwer, 113
work definitions, 79–82
writing requirements, 150–151

**Y**

Yadav, JJ
   *Implementing Microsoft Dynamics 365 for
   Finance and Operations Apps: Learn best
   practices, architecture, tools, techniques
   and more*, 223